Multimedia Creations

HANDS-ON WORKSHOP FOR EXPLORING ANIMATION AND SOUND

Philip Shaddock

WAITE
GROUP
PRESS™
Corte Madera, CA

Editorial Director · *Scott Calamar*
Acquisitions · *Mitchell Waite*
Content Editor · *Harry Henderson*
Technical Reviewer · *Max Templeton*
Design and Production · *Cecile Kaufman*
Illustrations · *Pat Rogondino*
Part opener illustrations · *Marlyn Amann*
Cover Design · *Michael Rogondino*
Production Manager · *Julianne Ososke*

Published by Waite Group Press,™ 200 Tamal Plaza, Corte Madera, CA 94925.
© 1992 by The Waite Group? Inc.

Waite Group Press™ is distributed to bookstores and book wholesalers by Publishers Group West, Box 8843, Emeryville, CA 94662, 1-800-788-3123 (in California 1-510-658-3453).

All terms mentioned in this book that are known to be registered trademarks, trademarks, or service marks are listed below. All other product names are trademarks and registered trademarks of their respective owners. In addition, terms suspected of being trademarks or service marks have been appropriately capitalized. Waite Group Press™ cannot attest to the accuracy of this information. Use of a term in this book should not be regarded as affecting the validity of any registered trademark, trademark, or service mark.

The Waite Group® is a registered trademark , and Waite Group Press™ and The Waite Group Logo are trademarks, of The Waite Group? Inc.
Adlib is a registered trademark of Adlib Inc.
Atari is a registered trademark of Atari Corporation
Autodesk, Animator, Animator Pro, and 3D Studio are trademarks or registered trademarks of Autodesk, Inc.
Band-in-a-Box is a trademark of PG Music, Inc.
Betacam is a registered trademark of Sony Corporation
Cakewalk is a trademark of Twelve Tone Systems, Inc.
CompuServe Information Service is a registered trademark of CompuServe Incorporated
Genus Microprogramming is a trademark of Genus Microprogramming, Inc.
IBM, XT, and AT are registered trademarks of International Business Machines Corp.
Media Vision, Pro AudioSpectrum, Pro AudioSpectrum 15, Stereo Studio F/X are trademarks of Media Vision, Inc.
Microsoft, MS-DOS, and Windows are registered trademarks of Microsoft Corporation
Voyetra and Sequencer Plus Junior are trademarks of Voyetra Technologies

Printed in the United States of America
92 93 94 95 • 10 9 8 7 6 5 4 3 2 1

Library of Congress Cataloging-in-Publication Data
Shaddock, Philip
        Multimedia creations: hands-on workshop for exploring animation
and sound / Philip Shaddock.
        p.   cm.
        Includes bibliographical references and index.
        ISBN: 1-878739-26-3 : $44.95 ($56.95 CAN.)
        1. Multimedia systems. 2. GRASP (Computer file)   I. Title.
QA76.575.S53   1992
006.6--dc 20
                                                                    92-3 1058
                                                                    CIP

Dedication

For Scott Calamar
Patience, Kindness, Humor, Honesty

Acknowledgments

This new book author is permanently spoiled by the Waite Group Press style: care, enthusiasm, professional pride, and the genuine warmth of its people. My sincere thanks to Mitch Waite. Your high standards and personal warmth permeate this book. Scott Calamar said, "I'm keeping this book for myself." All that's best about this book belongs to him. The author's only redeeming grace is that he learned to recant and follow Scott's advice. You lead an extraordinary team: Julianne and Cecile in Production, Lise in Marketing. Thanks to all.

Harry Henderson's content edit gives this book its feeling of mastery. The sure touch is his. Max Templeton (GRASP technical support) solved all the really tough technical challenges. His tech edit saved the author from the much dreaded gaffe. Steve Belsky, GRASP Product Manager, helped make this book possible and generously supported its development. Thanks for taking it personally. Thank you Paul Mace for your kind words.

Music is a big part of multimedia and this book. Kevin Weiner not only wrote the MIDI TSR that comes with the book, he tech edited the MIDI sections as well. His contribution was enormous. Thanks also to John Mitchell for Mitch's Brew, and the Roland Corporation for Leya's Song. Doug Smith at Roland Canada was particularly helpful. Roy Smith from Turtle Beach and Ken Nicholson from Media Vision were helpful on digitized sound technical matters.

Don Magnusson contributed an appendix and was helpful at sticky points in the progress of the book. The author of GRASP, John Bridges, generously contributed time and code to the project. Gary Yost, the wizard behind 3D Studio and Animator Pro, was highly supportive and quick to respond to the author's questions.

Mabyn Martin and Murry Christensen helped extend the scope of the book through contributions of program examples. Bob Buford, Charles Jameson, Paul Unterweiser, and Tom Hudock contributed programs that did not make it into the final cut. Thanks.

Thanks to Sylvia Bak for making 6.5 equal 10 and making readers feel "welcome." Gary Dickens shared the vision and has spent years listening to the author pontificating about the new media. Thanks for being a believer.

Louise Quinn provided much needed perspective and was a silent partner in the book's creation.

Greg Lang beta tested the book and distracted the author with philosophical ruminations. Brian Fawcett coached the author on the business of writing. Marianne Van de Leygraaf was a creative partner. Harold Berner from the Software Alley in Vancouver was a reality tester. Joe Powell from John Fluke Manufacturing read the book and provided intelligent, incisive commentary.

There were many more helping hands that made this book possible. Only the danger of making the acknowledgements longer in length than the book prevents the author from naming the other people who were so generous with their time and support. I am grateful.

Foreword

It is not just the annual buzzword—Multimedia is something new! So new that the word itself probably won't survive, but what it describes will. Multimedia—it conjures images of lasers, fireworks, and big screen TV at a rock concert. What you see on your computer monitor may seem, at first, modest. It is not; it is something revolutionary. What multimedia describes is the marriage of television, digital sound, and the desktop computer.

If the whole were simply the sum of the parts, Multimedia would still be interesting. Television has begged for a computer for a decade. The advent of hundred-channel cable made the problem obvious: who was going to manage this bounty of information and entertainment? With what tools? A hundred button remote? Why not the PC? I know, the manufacturers have been promising smarter television sets for decades, but they are a stodgy industry whose last innovation, color, came thirty years ago. It proved easier to bring TV to the computer monitor, and in the last year the hardware for accomplishing this has proliferated and the prices have dropped to a few hundred dollars—close to the cost of an equivalent color TV set.

Similarly, our desktop computers now sport music compact disks doing double duty as storage devices. They have digital sound boards with the same MIDI interfaces our favorite recording stars use to create best-selling albums, and all of it under the control of our mouse and keyboard.

Programming, in the old-fashioned sense, has begun to return. I don't mean what computer experts do with arcane bits of code, I mean selecting what information you want, when you want it, and what form the display will take. Personalized programming, with each of us his own DJ, newscaster, and TV station manager, becomes possible. And the personal computer is the ideal instrument for each of us to exert control over a modern world of electronic devices.

Multimedia software, such as GRASP, lets us rein in all this horsepower and make it pull in one direction. What started six years ago as a simple animation package for the PC has grown to take advantage of the promise of the electronic environment. Sound control, animation, and video hardware control are built-in. More importantly, GRASP adds human control, the power to make audiovisual material interactive. Placing human beings in control is what Multimedia is all about. It's what distinguishes it from its constituent elements, what makes it revolutionary, and GRASP excels in letting you do just that.

    Phil Shaddock has been a part of the Multimedia revolution since long before it had a name. When we first met there were only a handful of people who understood the potential of what was happening with personal computers to put together sound and images from a wide variety of sources. So, Phil is ideally placed to explain the components of Multimedia presentations and how you go about integrating them. I was gratified when he asked to include GRASP as part of Multimedia Creations. His explanations of its use are lucid and his advice invaluable. It is my pleasure to invite you to the revolution. *Multimedia Creations* is a lesson in how to shake the world.

Paul Mace
Paul Mace Software
August 1992

About the Author:

Philip Shaddock has multimedia in his background. After doing graduate studies in English at Simon Fraser University, he studied media design at Capilano College. He then worked for 12 years in Toronto as a writer and producer of corporate print, multi-image, and video productions for such clients as Coca-Cola, Procter & Gamble, Colgate Palmolive, Apple, and IBM. His multi-image and video work has won international awards. Four years ago he fell down the rabbit's hole of multimedia and has never scrambled out. He now devotes himself exclusively to programming and producing multimedia productions for business communications. His consulting company, Philip Shaddock Associates, assists clients in the design and production of multimedia communications. He can be contacted on CompuServe, 70274,2146.

Dear Reader:

I have always been inspired by "multimedia." In fact the first book I ever wrote was called Projects in Sight, Sound, and Sensation. It included such avant garde topics (for those days) as Kirilian photography and Alpha Brainwaves and focused on the use of electronics to record or generate audio or visual information based on sensory stimuli. I've always tried to push the state of the art to approach sensory reality—hence our recent emphasis on graphics and virtual reality books.

Multimedia is the next wave of personal computing. We've seen the IBM PC mature from a silent, monochrome, character-mode machine to a full-color, high-resolution, mouse and menu-driven powerhouse that talks, sings, and makes music. The capabilities of computers for reflecting and altering reality now totally exceed what humans can do by hand.

Therefore it was obvious to us that publishing a multimedia book was the way to go, and indeed it was the subject of no end of our editorial discussions. We thought of, and discarded, many different approaches. We had a basic problem: all books on multimedia survey the tools but do little to help you make a presentation. In keeping with our "How to Wow" approach we wanted to do a hands-on book that would get you creating animated audio-visual projects without buying anything extra. Further we didn't want to require an outrageously expensive high-end machine. Yet at the time we wrote this book there were only a few good programs that let you create multimedia, and they were pretty pricey: too much so for the reader who is new to multimedia and simply curious.

WAITE
GROUP
PRESS™

Everything came together when I met Phil Shaddock. Phil has been a specialist in multimedia for years and had been using a program called GRASP to make beautiful demos. GRASP, it turns out, is basically the standard amoung professionals for making DOS-based presentations. It works with a standard VGA and does not need gobs of memory. We decided to see if Paul Mace Software would license us a version to write a book around and sure enough it happened. The book you hold in your hand gives you aeverything that you need to make multimedia kiosks, interactive audiovisual games, gorgeous demos, and more. I think you will find that this book goes way beyond the titles on the market. If you have any suggestions or opinions about this book please fill out the Reader Satisfaction Card, or send me email on Compuserve: 75146,3515.

Mitchell Waite

Mitchell Waite
Publisher

200 Tamal Plaza   Corte Madera   California   94925   415-924-2575   FAX   415-924-2576

Introduction

This book teaches you how to craft dazzling and effective multimedia applications in the comfort of your chair. No need to go across the room, or across town, to gather the elements of your sight and sound spectacle; we'll transform the computer on the desk in front of you into a hands-on workshop. You'll learn tricks and techniques for converting pedestrian computer presentations into flights of fancy. Sound, animation, interaction with the user; games, demos, and a graphical interactive menu system—it's all here. We supply the software tools, including a powerful multimedia programming language. With the software tools we supply, your PC will fly. Feel the need for speed? It's at your fingertips.

How fast? The special version of the program bundled with this book, GRASP, is a graphics programming language used by many professional developers. With GRASP we place you at the controls of one of the industry's fastest and most nimble multimedia authoring environments. When you run the demo program bundled with this book, you will see what we mean. No other program on the market, other than a high-level programming language like C, can pack so much into so little.

What is *multimedia?* It may be little more than a buzzword for you. You've heard that it has something to do with bringing graphics, animation, and sound to the PC, but what is really involved in doing this? Chapter 1 gets you started by giving you an overview of the elements in multimedia, and the steps involved in developing a multimedia production.

Chapter 2 moves from theory to practice. It takes you on a tour of GRASP's digital studio and quickly puts you at the control board.

Need some examples of what you can do with GRASP? In Chapter 3 we'll teach you how to create a software slide projector that is just as capable at sequencing images as the slide-show programs that come with many graphics packages. But here's the difference: Because the program is written in clear, understandable GRASP code, by the end of the book you'll be able to extend the projector to include the playback of digital or synthesized sound and Autodesk Animator 2D and Autodesk Studio 3D animations. You'll be able to add text and graphics to the screen on the fly, minutes before you present to your audience. With the knowledge you gain in this book, you'll be able to grow the slide projector into a highly interactive and flexible presentation system that harnesses the computer's data processing muscle. Because you create the blueprints to the projector, you become the architect of your own idiosyncratic presentation system. No waiting for the next upgrade. You add capability as you need it. And yes, it will also impress friends and wow clients.

Multimedia Creations teaches you how to fashion useful programs you can use over and over again in your own work. You learn by doing, with little time spent in the lecture hall. An example is the software magazine you "write" in GRASP's script language in Chapter 4. We show you how to build an animated sight and sound front end to an interactive information system. You then build a menuing system that includes a link to the slide projector created in the previous chapter. The example we use is a "Treasure Tour of Rome." (We toss in the lion's roar free!) Press a button and up pops an interactive map of ancient Rome that you can tour in grand style using GRASP's program flow tools.

Chapter 5 lays bare the inner workings of a complete 3-minute demo, including animation and music. Have you been wondering how game and multimedia wizards pack so much action into so little disk space? This chapter shows you how. GRASP becomes the *edit suite* that brings together the visuals and animations created in packages such as Paintshop Pro, Aldus Photostyler, Autodesk Animator Pro, and Autodesk 3D Studio. Here's where you'll learn professional animation tips and techniques.

The balance of *Multimedia Creations* treats selected topics in greater depth. Sound is the focus of Chapter 6. We show you how to add music and voice to interactive programs using the Sound Blaster or MIDI cards. In Chapter 7, we show you how to build a music cueing application in GRASP that you can use to create your own music videos.

Chapter 8 returns the focus to programming. Because GRASP has many of the features of a high-level programming language, it can create quite sophisticated applications. We include the plans for a product knowledge computer game. Chapter 9 includes a complete menuing system that you can shape into a complex interactive information system.

READY TO ROLL

By now you've undoubtedly noticed that this book comes with two high-density disks. These disks contain everything you need to create the multimedia projects covered in this book. You get a custom version of GRASP; each project, ready to run; custom graphics and sounds; and utility programs which help create the graphics you'll need. You'll even find a demo MIDI song and other goodies! The contents of these disks are described more fully in Appendix B. Installation instructions are provided in the Installation Note.

By the end of *Multimedia Creations,* you'll have learned multimedia programming the way a moonshiner learns driving—very fast, with a total disregard for the speed limits and obstacles imposed by the PC's architecture. CD-ROM? Don't need it with this book. The MPC (Multimedia PC) standard? Don't have to conform to it.

If you want to know the lay of the land before embarking on this journey, we suggest you check out the primer on multimedia in the first chapter. If you're a speed demon, go right to Chapter 2. It gets you up and running in GRASP fast.

So, put on the coffee, clear the desk, and prepare to ascend into the exciting animation and sound possibilities waiting for you in the multimedia workshop on your desktop.

Installation Note

Two high-density (HD) 5 1/4" disks are included with this book. They contain the GRASP program files, utilities, and example programs. These files are archived and compressed so they cannot be run from the floppy drive. Appendix A (*Multimedia Creations* Disk) provides a complete listing of the files as they will appear when they have been uncompressed and installed on your hard drive. The automatic Install program is detailed below. You'll find instructions on running the demo at the end of this note.

REQUIREMENTS

Hardware and MS-DOS Version Requirements

All of the programs in this book will run on an 80286 PC with a standard (256K) VGA adapter, DOS 3.3 or higher, a hard drive, a mouse, and 470K of random access memory free. You will not need a sound board throughout most of the book, since GRASP will output digitized sound to your system speaker. However, the examples in chapters six and seven do require a sound board.

GRASP will run on machines with DOS 2 or higher, but we recommend DOS 3.3 for the example scripts. GRASP will run on an XT, but we do not recommend this for the examples in the book, especially when playing digital sound with the animations.

Random Access Memory Requirements

The special version of GRASP bundled with this book does not support expanded, extended, or virtual (disk-based) memory. It runs entirely in the conventional memory space below 640K. (The commercial version does run in extended memory.) The example programs in this book require a minimum of 470K of conventional memory free, as reported by DOS's CHKDSK or MEM programs. Consult an MS-DOS reference text that shows you how to maximize conventional memory. See Appendix F, GRASP Error Messages for other types of errors that may be generated when you try to run GRASP.

Hard Disk Space

You must have 3.5 megabytes free on your hard drive. During the course of the exercises you will require an additonal 1.5 megabytes free for a total of 5 megabytes. Before installing the disks bundled with the book, use DOS's CHKDSK program to determine free drive space:

```
chkdsk
```

where (drive) is the hard drive directory where you want to install the files. For example, type this to check c: drive for available disk space.

```
c:
chkdsk
```

The program listing should show at least 5,000,000 bytes free. Free up hard disk space if you have less than the minimum bytes free.

RUNNING GRASP

Running GRASP Under Windows

Because of the way GRASP directly accesses hardware, it is not possible to play the sound and animation examples under Windows. If you do, your computer system may lock up. Paul Mace Graphics Software, which distributes GRASP, sells a utility program called WINGRASP that allows you to run GRASP under the Windows environment.

Running GRASP on Networks

GRASP will run on most networks if there is enough memory free to meet the example programs' minimum requirements (470K). GRASP doesn't open files with the share attributes set to "on," so it's not ultimately a good network citizen. However, for the most part, we've successfully distributed GRASP programs to users with networks.

USING INSTALL.EXE

We've written an Install program in GRASP called INSTALL.EXE (elements of it were kindly provided by GRASP tech support). You must have a VGA adapter installed to run the Install program. If you don't, INSTALL.EXE will generate an error message. You'll find INSTALL.EXE on the first of two disks supplied with this book. Place the disk in your computer's floppy drive, change to that drive, and type install. Assuming a: is your floppy drive, type this:

```
a:
install
```

Substitute b: if your 5 1/4"-floppy drive is the second drive. Then sit back and let the 5 megabytes decompress on your hard disk. This will take a few minutes. You'll hear the disk activity and see a reassuring screen. The Install program automatically sets up a directory called \GRASP on the root directory of your hard drive, along with a number of subdirectories. It will also ask permission to alter your AUTOEX-EC.BAT file. You may want to rename your original AUTOEXEC.BAT file (for example, AUTOEXEC.OLD) before installing GRASP.

It's important that the AUTOEXEC.BAT file set the GRASP and Pictor paint program environment variables. These DOS environment variables tell GRASP where to find its overlay files when you are not in the main GRASP directory. You will see the following appended to your AUTOEXEC.BAT file:

```
set GRASP = (drive):\GRASP
set PICTOR = (drive):\GRASP
```

where (drive) is the hard drive directory in which \GRASP is installed.

e.g.

```
set GRASP = c:\GRASP
set PICTOR = c:\GRASP
```

GRASP must be installed in a directory off the root directory (\GRASP) for the environment settings to work. Also, example scripts look for support files in \GRASP. The GRASP subdirectory should be added to your DOS Path statement.

```
path=(drive):\GRASP
```

Here (drive) is the name of the hard drive where GRASP is installed.

e.g.

```
path=c:\dos;c:\bin;c:\GRASP
```

This tells the computer where to find the main GRASP program file (GRASPC.EXE) when you are not in the GRASP subdirectory.

Remember, after using the automatic install program, if you run GRASPC.EXE and PICTOR.EXE and DOS reports "Bad command or file name," then your AU-TOEXEC.BAT file has been changed or was corrupted. Either install the program again or add \GRASP to your DOS path. If either GRASP or Pictor report that they cannot find their "overlay" files, then you have not set the environment settings for GRASP or Pictor.

See the installation note called README.TXT in the GRASP directory for additional sound installation information.

RUNNING THE DEMO

After installing GRASP, run the demo. You must change into the new GRASP directory. Assuming GRASP was installed on C:, type:

```
c:
cd \GRASP
demo
```

The demo for *Multimedia Creations* will run. You will be asked to install the sound configuration for the book. If you do not have a sound card, choose that option. If you choose to install a sound card later, run the sound installation routine again.

```
c:
cd \GRASP
install
```

If you do not have GRASP installed on c:, change c: to the appropriate drive letter.

The Multimedia Creations demo brings together everything you'll learn in this book. It showcases more than three minutes of animated graphics, slide projector techniques, video transformations, digital sound effects, and synchronizedd music. Those of you

Figure I-1 Sylvia bids you "Welcome" to *Multimedia Creations*

with sound boards and external speakers will hear three channels of sound that include the PC's internal speaker. Figure I-1 gives you a preview of one of the welcoming screens from the demo.

Don't forget to restart your computer, so the changes to your AUTOEXEC.BAT can take effect, after watching the demo and before running GRASP. Then you'll be on your way to becoming a multimedia producer!

Table of Contents

Contents

Part 2: Multimedia Cookbook

PART ONE

Opening the Show

1

What Is Multimedia?

S OMEDAY ETYMOLOGISTS will dig into the roots of the word *multimedia* and shake their collective heads. To begin with, using *multi* in conjunction with *media* is redundant, since the word *media* implies a mix of disparate "mediums." The word multimedia has long described mixed-media art, and has a slightly more specialized meaning for business presentations. Multimedia business presentations may include everything from video, slides, and audio to a live circus act!

Within the computing industry, the term multimedia was originally applied to describe the integration of sound and motion graphics on Macs, Amigas, and PCs. Now that multimedia has become a media buzz word, it currently describes any audiovisual device that incorporates digital technology. For example, the transmission of motion video over telephone systems or Local Area Networks (sometimes called video mail) is termed a "multimedia development." The PC trade news media calls new digital signal processing chips (DSPs), which convert such analog information as voice into digital data, "multimedia chips."

Digital technology has brought motion graphics and sound to an incredibly wide range of products and services, from talking cars with animated street maps to consumer-interactive television in the living room. This is not, however, the subject of our book.

Multimedia Creations presents the subject of multimedia in the context of the common, garden-variety PC. We do not provide a survey of the entire field or of the specialized hardware used in specific applications of multimedia technology, such as audiovisual kiosks that provide direction in malls. Our interest is in general tools and general applications, especially those that can be distributed on high-density diskettes.

GRASP, the program bundled with this book, supports such multimedia peripherals as video disks and touch screens, but we do not cover these. Instead, we provide practical hands-on knowledge for those who want to use the computer on the desktop exclusively as an audiovisual production and playback platform. We explore the kinds of programs that can be created on an average PC—that is, a 286 or 386 with 640K of RAM and a 256K VGA card. This entry-level class of computers is the mass market for multimedia content distributed on floppy disk. We leave aside consideration of specialized hardware, such as CD-ROM, the IBM/INTEL DVI (Digital Video Interactive) technology, the Philip's CD-I (Compact Disk-Interactive) technology or the boards that incorporate JPEG and audio and video compression hardware. We assume you, like most computer users, do not own these peripherals (yet) and are interested in sharing your work with friends and clients who don't have them either. Besides, there are books devoted to these spe-

---

DEMOS

Attend a computer show and look at the floppy-disk-based animated demos companies are producing to market their products and services. Order demos from services that supply them (see the GRASP library on CompuServe or in ads at the back of PC magazines). Many of them have been created in GRASP! So-called multisensory, interactive multimedia is not the sole province of specialized hardware and fixed installations; it's playing on small screens everywhere. Just as videotape helped define video as a distribution medium (the video movie), the floppy disk has helped to define an enduring form of multimedia, the *demo*.

COMPUTER GAMES AND MULTIMEDIA

If you want to see what kinds of multimedia effects are possible on entry-level computers, take a look at computer games. Games like Spectrum Holobyte's flight simulator series push the envelope on interactive entertainment on 286 or 386 desktop computers equipped with nothing more than a VGA card and a Sound Blaster sound card. CD-ROM games take gaming to a high level of cinematic realism. Music, voice, animation, and graphics are fully integrated into a cinematic experience. The major difference between what you'll see on game screens and the kinds of visuals you'll see on screens created by programs in this book is in screen detail. We've chosen to use sharper, more finely detailed video modes than the low-pixel resolution modes used by games. The mode we emphasize, VGA 640x480 16-color, is a standard mode for electronic business presentations. VGA's 320x200 256-color mode is a standard mode for video games. You trade more colors and more animation for better detailed screens and better looking type. You'll be amazed at the 2-minute demo we've provided with this book. It's in 16 colors and features animation.

cialized technologies, such as Arch Luther's Digital Video in the PC Environment (McGraw-Hill), which features DVI Technology.

Many photography courses begin by teaching students how to build and shoot pictures with a simple pinhole camera. The exercise is intended to show that good photography is an acquired skill, not necessarily the product of a high-tech camera and a bag full of camera gadgets. This is a good analogy for the approach we take in *Multimedia Creations,* but it is not a perfect analogy. The difference is that even a plain vanilla computer is a much more complex and powerful machine than the most complex and most sophisticated 35mm camera. Also, instead of learning how to produce simple and ultimately useless programs, you will learn to create professional multimedia productions. You can use most of the applications in this book commercially in your own work. We ask only that you purchase the professional version of GRASP if you intend to distribute the programs commercially.

This book presents multimedia from a producer's point of view. We answer the questions, "What do you have to know to produce a multimedia application on the PC? What skills are required? What equipment?" The information you learn in *Multimedia Creations* will give you a solid base from which to judge the ever-changing tools of multimedia. For advice on specific hardware, check magazines or CompuServe.

CREATING MULTIMEDIA CONTENT

Multimedia bridges a chasm between two separate and relatively isolated cultures. The culture of film, television, and professional video lies on one side, and the culture of data processing, computers, and programming lies on the other. The professional video producer and the professional programmer both sit in chairs and stare at screens, but that's about all that they have in common. The former talks of color, movement, rhythm, dialogue, and plot, and defers mysteriously to *audiences*. The latter talks of interface design, heuristics, and event-driven programming, and defers (well, sometimes) to *users*.

This cultural isolation cannot last. The desktop revolution that shook the mainframe world, and then the print world, is spreading into film, television, and industrial video. Meanwhile, the new visual and sound possibilities of computers are changing the way professional programmers think about computing. They are learning new ways to use sound, color, motion, and drama to interact with users.

From the perspective of computing, what is occurring is a shift away from a strict definition of the computer as a "data processing engine" to include the computer as a delivery platform for *content*. In the new paradigm, users do more than crunch numbers and retrieve data; they acquire *knowledge* from desktop computers, using all of their senses. The benefit is increased depth of understanding of the data computers helped create and disseminate in the first place.

From the point of view of the video producer, multimedia is a set of technologies for creating video rather than a definition of new content. The shift is away from the linear, step-by-step manufacturing of video sequences to a digital production process that is interactive, nonlinear, and information rich. Instead of shuttling videotape, the video producer is storing, arranging, and accessing video clips in the same discrete, flexible way as any other computer data: randomly. So far, multimedia technology has had little impact on how professional video programs are structured, mainly because the distribution system for video has not changed. The VHS video playback deck and broadcast television encourage linear, noninteractive programming.

HOW MULTIMEDIA IS PRODUCED

For video producers who have drifted into multimedia, there is a long learning curve. At first they will dream up three impossible things to do with video on computers before breakfast. Soon, however, they find it necessary to become knowledgeable about computer hardware. The most successful acquire programming literacy, if not thorough competence in a high-level programming language.

ANALOG VIDEO VERSUS DIGITAL VIDEO

When analog video (the kind of video your camcorder records on videotape) is converted into a stream of digital data, stored on a mass medium such as CD-ROM or a hard drive, and eventually played back on a computer monitor, it is called *digital video*. Right now, digital video is said to be close to the level of VHS quality. What does this mean? After all, we rarely talk about the *technology* of television as being high, medium, or low. "Professional" video maintains high production values throughout the creation of the video program. The result is an end product that has few visual artifacts, faithfully reproduces the original scene's colors and details, has a stable picture, and conforms to specifications laid down by the National Television Systems Committee (NTSC)—that is, it looks like the programs we see on prime time broadcast television. Broadcast TV really has only one quality level: high. (The program content is another matter.)

The term quality means something quite different in discussions about consumer video or digital video. Marketing brochures often describe quality as VHS quality (low), industrial quality (medium), or broadcast quality (high). These terms are misleading, since they are subjective ratings of image quality that are not easily measured. Perhaps "looks bad," "looks better," and "all things considered, looks great" are more appropriate terms. Let your own eyes be the final judge of acceptable quality.

Digital video in the computing environment is a desirable addition precisely because people think it is "television." Audiences are conditioned by the conventions of broadcast television, and multimedia producers can rely on television's program structures (for example, the game show) and visual techniques (such as rolling credits) to entertain and inform computer users. However, digital video as a standard feature of the desktop computer is several years away. The hardware is expensive, and universal standards are slow to emerge.

Multimedia producers with a computing background are often faced with the equally daunting task of learning the communication arts (art, humor, drama, visual design) in order to use the PC's high-resolution motion graphics and sound equipment to communicate thought and emotion. (A thorough discussion of this topic can be found in Brenda Laurel's *Computers as Theater.*)

At first glance multimedia production can appear to be enormously complex because it requires so much knowledge of the hardware and software environment of the PC. However, let us compare professional multimedia production to professional film and television programming.

Video Production

Production practices in video have largely grown out of the linear nature of this medium. Video is shot on magnetic tape and assembled at a video edit suite. Putting a professional video program on a final distribution tape is no easy feat. Since professional video producers rely on outside services or in-house video department specialists, they are insulated from the complex knowledge and skills necessary to meet professional standards. They still require a good secondhand knowledge of the characteristics of video equipment and video production methods.

There are so many people and so many steps between inception and screening that the final production generates more paperwork than film or tape. Video production requires a large support team of skilled specialists. Scripts are written by writers, storyboards created by artists, scenes shot on videotape by camera "shooters," art prepared by artists, animations created by animators, sound recorded by sound technicians, and the master tape is finally edited by an editor. One false step along the way can create disaster at a later stage. The process is so

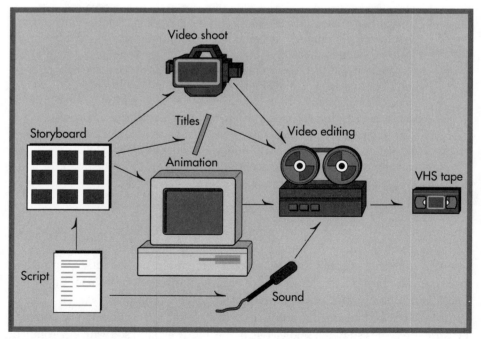

Figure 1-1 The video production process

complicated it has to be "storyboarded" beforehand. This consists of creating a series of cartoon pictures (the board) depicting the main action scenes (the story line) and graphics of the video. This allows everybody involved in the production to "preview" the video on paper. Figure 1-1 shows the process of producing a television program or a video.

This is a linear path that does not leave much room for mistakes. Much of the television production process consists in preserving the integrity of the video signal that was originally so carefully recorded on tape at the location shoot. Each time a videotape is copied, it degrades the video information stored on it. If you've copied videotapes at home, you've probably noticed that with each copy colors smear, detail is lost, and sound is muffled. Producers avoid copying videotape at all costs. Once the production is copied to the distribution tape, going back to change the video is difficult and costly. The master elements must be pulled from storage and used in the alteration of the master videotape.

Multimedia Production

In an all-digital medium like multimedia, the producer enjoys the benefit of collapsing the production process into fewer steps. And most of the work can be performed at one location by a much smaller group of people. Compare the video production process to the multimedia production process, illustrated in Figure 1-2.

Once the material for a multimedia presentation is converted into digital data by a scanner, a video frame capture board, or a sound digitizing board, the computer can manipulate it and it becomes a lot easier to work with. All the hardware and software tools required to create a multimedia presentation can be centrally located. In many cases a single PC can become a complete production environment.

Multimedia is a business communications tool that will see explosive growth as a desktop tool. Business users will eventually use stock video clips, stock music, and elements copied from past presentations to create quick, short-term programs that are distributed on networks.

Fewer production steps means less paperwork, fewer people to organize and brief, better creative control over the elements of the production, and better security (no outside services). Best of all, in a world where digital information makes a marketing presentation obsolete almost as soon as it is done, digital production tools make the process of updating and distributing digital presentations much easier and quicker.

Centralizing the image and sound assembly stage at the desktop also encourages new production methods for producers used to working in linear media. Multimedia production encourages a much less rigorous and linear approach to assembling the final production, giving the producer the ability to respond more

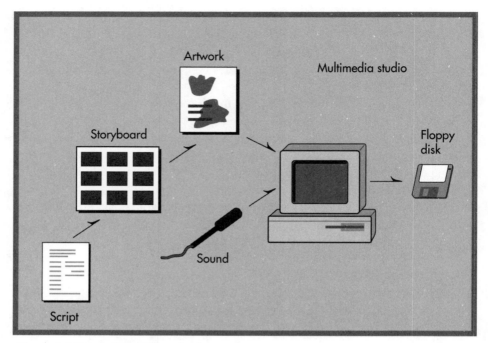

Figure 1-2 The multimedia production process

dynamically to the client's needs. Once the elements of the production are brought into the computer environment, they are relatively easy to edit. The results of decisions are apparent immediately, and the producer can test different approaches quickly. Clients' requests for changes are more easily accommodated. Digital information does not degrade when it is copied, so preserving the quality of the image is much easier throughout the editing process.

In *Multimedia Creations* we'll show you how to turn the PC into a complete production studio. We'll introduce you to all the tools that we use to create professional multimedia productions, and to the methods used in a professional multimedia production. You may not own a color scanner that digitizes flat artwork, or a frame capture board that digitizes and saves to disk single frames of video from a tape or a camera; but that won't prevent you from producing high-quality multimedia shows. The service bureaus in your area that provide scanning for desktop publishers can convert your pictures into the computer files that you'll need for sequencing in GRASP (CompuServe GIF or Zoft PCX format). If your project requires the inclusion of selected frames of video from an existing video, and you do not have a video frame grabber, contact a local video edit suite for this service or buy one of the many inexpensive "frame grabber" video boards on the market.

Some of the software tools we use in our work, such as Autodesk Animator Pro, Autodesk 3D Studio, and Corel Draw are expensive and require many hours to master. You will not need to use these programs to work with the applications we present in this book. Our purpose in introducing them to you is to give you a complete picture of the professional multimedia production process. We've provided GRASP's companion paint program for image processing, and several utility programs, so you can get started without buying expensive software.

Multimedia Programming

The video producer rarely carries around much more than a rather battered briefcase and a cellular phone—the tools of the trade. A special chair is reserved for the producer in the sound studio and video edit suite. From that vantage point, the video producer can direct the action using a special language for communicating instructions to technicians and editors.

The multimedia producer, on the other hand, spends a great deal of time staring into a computer screen in solitude, mumbling. Most of the multimedia producers we know are also programmers. Do not let this frighten you. Multimedia programming using tools like GRASP or Microsoft's Visual Basic is considered to be simple by most professional programmers. By the end of this book you will have the skills of an entry-level BASIC programmer and you'll be able to do amazing things.

Learning programming is important because what distinguishes multimedia programs from video programs is *interaction*. The user enters information into the com-

VIDEO FRAME CAPTURE HARDWARE

You can capture a single frame of video from a camera or a VCR using specialized video boards variously called frame grabbers, video overlay cards, and sometimes frame buffers. Many video window boards, such as Truevision's Bravado, the Creative Labs Video Blaster, or the New Media Graphics Super VideoWindows boards, include the ability to capture and save to disk a single frame from a video sequence. Attach a video camera to these boards to digitize artwork or three-dimensional objects. This is not a good solution for finely detailed artwork, however, since the quality of the video signal is poor. Use a scanning service or purchase a color scanner for flat, detailed artwork. The picture files created by frame grabbers or scanners can be imported into image processing programs such as Corel Draw or Paint Shop Pro for further processing or refinement.

puter program, the program processes that information and returns something different. A computer program that alters data uses algorithms, or instructions for transforming data and creating input. Whether you're dragging an icon around on a screen to alter program flow in a multimedia authoring environment, or entering lines of computer code, you are ultimately creating the same thing: an algorithm. Television programs can only be started, stopped, rewound, or fast-forwarded. Multimedia programs put the content under user control, making the user an active participant in the creation. Up until now the producer has played God in a universe where the viewer has no free will. Multimedia frees the viewer to explore the universe you have created at will, even to change it and adapt it to his or her own needs. This is a very powerful motivational and learning environment indeed.

The custom version of GRASP bundled with this book will help you come to terms with the PC's complex architecture and the logic behind interactive programming. The following sections provide you with just enough knowledge of the hardware to get you started.

CREATING MOVING VISUALS FOR MULTIMEDIA PRESENTATIONS

The video producer uses motion video to hold viewer interest, provide story continuity, and illustrate concepts that develop over time. A training video that teaches employees how to respond to customers with complaints is much more effective in video than in print. This is because video can "set the scene" and show realistic situations with visual impact. The video producer is free to devote most of his or her attention to the production and artistic issues motion video raises, leaving the technical details of equipment to the technicians. The multimedia producer does not have this luxury.

Displaying motion graphics or video on a computer is a major challenge. PCs may excel at providing instant access to text-based information, but they become sluggish when high-resolution images become part of the data stream. To understand why, let's compare television and computer display systems.

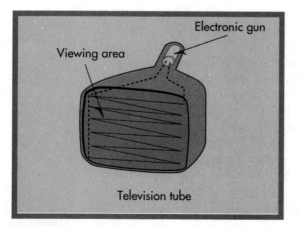

Figure 1-3 Display of an interlaced television signal

Electronic gun

Viewing area

Television tube

NTSC VIDEO IN A WINDOW ON A COMPUTER DISPLAY

Some specialized video display cards convert NTSC video into a signal that can be displayed on the computer monitor. These cards, such as the New Media Graphics Super VideoWindows or the Creative Labs Video Blaster, display full-motion digital video in a window on the screen. However, without some form of control over the source VCR, it's difficult to use this type of full motion video in a multimedia environment. Although videodisk is a popular storage and playback system, and does provide control over the source video, it is expensive to produce videodisk masters. Video window cards and videodisk players are best suited to highly dedicated multimedia applications, where the information doesn't change rapidly over time.

A video windowing card can be coupled with a video compression board that stores segments of video on the hard drive in a compressed form. This is a technology that promises to be the preferred method of creating and displaying full motion video in the PC environment. Rewritable CD-ROM will be the ultimate fulfillment for multimedia.

Television versus Computer Display

Television displays and computer displays are fundamentally different, but they do share some similarities. For example, they both cause tiny illuminated dots to be displayed on the screen. These tiny dots are called *pixels,* a contraction of "picture elements." Figure 1-3 illustrates what goes on behind the scenes in a television or computer picture tube, the cathode ray tube (CRT).

The television gun that sits at the back of the picture tube is methodically spraying the inside of the television screen with electrons, which make the phosphor that coats the inside of the picture tube glow. The electrons are fired at the screen in alternating lines. The gun begins at the top left, spraying electrons in a row, proceeds to the right, and skips down two rows to the beginning of the next line. When it reaches the bottom of the screen, it jumps back to the top and begins with a row below the first row of pixels. While it is doing the second scan, the phosphors excited by the first scan are decaying. The process is repeated. The scanning of the screen happens so fast (60 times a second) that your eye is fooled into seeing a continuous image.

Interlacing allows television systems to broadcast half the amount of information at any given time and yet display a full picture. This reduces both the cost of transmitting video signals and the cost of building television sets. The basic way video images are generated hasn't changed since the 1940s.

You'll often hear broadcast television or industrial video referred to as "NTSC video." NTSC is an acronym for the organization that established the technical standards for video broadcast signals, the National Television Systems Committee. It's the standard for U.S., Japanese, and Canadian broadcast television, and for other countries as well.

Unfortunately, the characteristics of the NTSC video signal make television signals incompatible with computer display systems. NTSC uses a 15.734-KHz horizontal scanning frequency (RS170A). The 15.734-KHz scanning frequency determines the density of each horizontal line of pixels (dots) on the screen. A typical VGA computer display system has a horizontal scanning frequency double that of television, 31.47 KHz. This means that more pixels can be displayed on a computer display.

Images with much higher spatial resolution can be displayed on computer screens than television screens. This means that the images have finer detail because they are composed of more pixels. Better yet, many computer display systems do not use interlacing. If you look at a television screen from one or two feet away, you will see the individual lines that make up a television picture. Because television screens are seen from across the room, television can get away with interlacing.

Another major difference between television and computer display systems is how the display information is stored. Television signals are analog. (An analog signal continuously varies in amplitude over time. It's usually represented as a wave pattern.) This signal can be recorded on videotape or videodisk as analog information. The information displayed by a computer display system is stored as computer data. (Computer data is a stream of binary numbers, usually represented as 0 and 1.) Computer display systems must convert digital data into an analog signal for display. Specialized circuitry on the video adapter does this.

The video signal that is broadcast to your television set or comes from your VCR cannot be edited as easily as computer data. Once you have assembled the video program in the editing suite, the user has little control over the order of the presentation. Computers, however, maintain a highly dynamic relationship with data. In the next section we'll explore some of the implications this has for the multimedia producer.

Creating Multimedia Content as Computer Data

Computers provide random access to data. *Random access* means the ability to arbitrarily select particular items of data without having to "wind through the tape." How do they do this in a multimedia environment? Let's look at the way images are displayed by computer systems. (Figure 1-4 illustrates a computer display system.)

Computers actually build each frame of video that they display. They use *frame buffers,* which are areas in RAM (random access) memory, to store the results of computer processing for display. Another type of buffer, usually located on the video adapter rather than RAM, is used by the video system to update the screen.

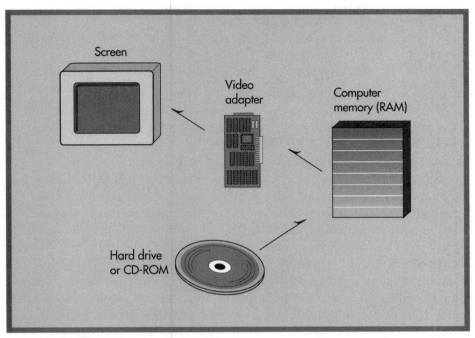

Figure 1-4 The computer display system

This is called a *refresh buffer* because the display is "refreshed" from this special buffer located on the video card. In this simple system, the picture data is retrieved from a storage medium, such as a hard drive, and placed in a temporary holding area, called a frame buffer. There it can be altered under program control. It is then moved into a refresh buffer and converted by the circuitry in the video card to analog information used to create the video signal. The result is then displayed on the screen. When you load an image into a buffer in programs such as GRASP, you are using RAM to create a temporary buffer. When you use a command such as Line to draw a line between two points on the screen, however, you manipulate the refresh buffer directly. As you will see later in this book, these commands are much faster when only simple drawing is needed.

Since the entire process is under CPU control, you can easily alter the order in which the video information is displayed, or the way in which it is displayed. You can tell the computer what order to use to display images, or you can ask the user to determine the order. Ultimately, you can put the information under the user's control. Television only lets the user switch channels or make simple adjustments to the contrast and color balance of the screen image. Videodisks, which store analog video, used in combination with computers, provide some of the advantages of both media. When used with the appropriate software, computers allow users to take full control over the flow, quality, and order of multimedia information. They allow users to alter the information, temporarily or permanently. Multimedia makes the audience a partner in program production, personalizing the user's interaction with the program material. This helps explain why users find multimedia programs especially interesting.

Multimedia's Lack of Standards

Random access to information is an advantage of multimedia over television. The advantage is offset to a large extent by the lack of standards in multimedia computing. Standards are important if users are to be given access to the widest range of audiovisual material. Television uses a standard display system that is many decades old. It's a mature, predictable, and fairly well-behaved standard. An NTSC signal can be displayed on any television set in the countries where the standard is officially sanctioned.

Unfortunately, there is no single standard in computer display systems. Computer displays are at their "terrible twos" stage—hardly predictable and rarely under control. The multimedia producer must sort through a rat's nest of video modes, from text, CGA, EGA, and VGA to Super VGA, and specialized "standards" such as Targa boards. Throw in Hicolor DAC replacements and S3 chips for good measure, and you've got a lot to consider.

The plethora of video modes has often been cited as a stumbling block on the road to a universal multimedia standard. It is a challenge that is unlikely to go away, but we can cope with it by focusing on the features available in common desktop computer configurations.

The Problem of Distribution

The lack of a universal video standard is only one consideration in planning distribution of your multimedia product. The lack of universal standards in other peripherals in computer systems can also hamper distribution of multimedia programs. You may not be able to assume your user has something as simple as a mouse. High-speed animations must be adjusted to the speed of the lowest common denominator among your users. Will it play on a 286 class machine with a hard drive with a 40-millisecond access time?

Fortunately, this lack of standards is being addressed. Microsoft has promoted the MPC (Multimedia PC) minimum standard for playback of multimedia programs. The Windows environment (particularly with the multimedia support added with version 3.1) is also making the creation and distribution of multimedia programs easier.

Multimedia's Processing Overhead

Multimedia programs exact a considerable toll on system resources because of their use of large digitized sound files and high-resolution graphics. High-resolution images are slow to load, and the loading speed varies with the size of the file. The more files you include with the program, the slower the hard drive becomes as it searches for the file specified by the user. Slow video subsystems affect the speed of visual transitions, or refuse to load images at all because of limited memory resources. Because of the way computers manage internal resources, the responsiveness of the computer to user requests slows as the number of competing demands within the system increase. Let's look more closely at the problem of managing computer resources for multimedia.

The demand placed on computer resources in loading and displaying images can be calculated. In a 640x480 16-color VGA mode, a computer displays 480 horizontal scan lines for every frame of video. The horizontal resolution, 640, refers to the number of pixels the video mode is capable of displaying on each scan line. If you think about the electronic gun at the back of the CRT as a paint gun hooked up to a compressor, 640 would be the number of spray particles painted from left to right on each of the lines applied to the surface of the screen. When you multiply the horizontal resolution by the vertical resolution (640 times 480), the computer will need to address 307,200 pixels on the screen. This happens to be the resolution of a frame of television, although the television only has to address half that number at any moment in time because of interlacing.

Continuing with our paint analogy, if you now increase vertical resolution to 1280 scan lines and horizontal resolution to 1024 pixels for display of detailed images, then you will have to draw a lot more paint from the bucket at a higher rate to paint your screen. There are now 1,310,720 pixels on the screen, more than four times as many as the VGA mode. Your compressor would have to run four times as fast. Your bucket would have to be four times as big. Your paint hose would have to be twice as large in diameter.

As we said earlier, each pixel on the screen is coded. If you increase the color depth of the image to 256 colors from 16 colors at this pixel resolution, the demand placed on a computer system is doubled. That's because in 16-color modes each pixel on the screen can be represented by 4 bits, or half a byte; while in 256-color mode, each pixel is represented by 8 bits or 1 byte. Increase color resolution to 16 bits or 2 bytes for display of more than 32,768 simultaneous colors, and the demands on the system double again.

The higher color and spatial resolution of today's VGA display systems mean that computers can display more colorful images with more detail than ever before. Unfortunately, the increase in data rates necessary to sustain high-resolution images on computer monitors has not kept pace. In order to display a full-color (24-bit or

16 million colors) 640x480 pixel resolution image, at the television rate of 30 frames per second, today's computers would need to feed 27.65 megabytes of information into the refresh buffer every second to maintain the display. Today's computers do not have a sufficiently high data rate to display full-color, high-resolution full motion video. And 27.65 megabytes per second would quickly exhaust hard disk space! Even at Hicolor resolution (640x480 32,768 colors) the requirement is for 18.43 megabytes of data per second.

The television screen is viewed from across the room, so spatial resolution is not as important as it is on the computer display where data is presented in fine detail. Television uses color and movement to attract our attention and hold it. Now that the cost of displaying high color resolution on computer monitors has dropped to a mass market level, what can be done to overcome the PC's limited data rate? What about the storage requirements demanded by multimedia? This leads us to a discussion of data compression.

Using Data Compression in Multimedia

We know that the internal data rate of computers will be a limiting factor in multimedia production for years to come. The need in the short term is for a way to compress motion video so that it fits within the limits of the PC's data rate. This is a very active area of multimedia research.

All data compression schemes rely on the fact that a frame of video contains much redundant information. Let's look at how data compression schemes work in a general way. Rather than encoding every pixel on the screen, the data compression algorithms store the instructions for the first frame in a series. The instruction might be, "Make all the pixels in this frame black." If the second frame had a white circle at the center of it, the instruction might be, "Make all the pixels in this frame black, except for the center region, which has a white circle 50 pixels in radius." We can improve the compression rate further by accounting only for the differences between frames. If a third frame adds a red dot at the center of the white circle, the instruction would be, "This frame adds a red dot at the center." The instruction for a fourth frame might be: "Add a green line at the top."

Data compression is a lot more complicated than this because the real world rarely contains huge areas of flat color. A blue sky has clouds and thousands of shades of blue in it. The underlying idea is that the video frame archived at the storage device such as a CD-ROM or hard drive is a much reduced version of the frame ultimately displayed on screen. The redundant information has been removed.

Not all compression schemes preserve the original image faithfully. *Lossy* data compression does more than remove redundant information. It removes (loses) information from the original image. Much of the information lost is not detectable by the human eye. JPEG, an acronym for the Joint Photographics Expert's Group, is an established standard for lossy compression of still images. It is also being used by hardware manufacturers for digital video. MPEG, an acronym for Motion Picture Expert Group, is the emerging standard for frame-to-frame compression, rather than still images. MPEG compression algorithms look for differences between successive images and only record the changes. Because it doesn't record redundant information between frames, it can potentially offer a much higher compression ratio than JPEG still-frame compression. But, as always, there is a penalty. MPEG systems make access to individual still frames in a series difficult, since only the first frame of a series is recorded in its entirety.

You will learn about data compression as you work through *Multimedia Creations*. The trio of products that form the backbone of our multimedia environment—GRASP, Animator Pro, and 3D Studio—use data compression. These programs support the type of compression that we have just described. Autodesk's FLI and FLC formats and GRASP's DFF format allow for the rapid display of images on computers and they don't require the addition of compression hardware to your computer. We'll be exploring this topic in depth in the chapters ahead.

There is another form of data *reduction* that helps lighten the data burden on the computer's system. In *Multimedia Creations* we use color image reduction extensively. When a program (such as JASC Inc.'s Paint Shop Pro or Handmade Software's Image Alchemy) reduces a full-color image from 32,768 colors to 16 colors, there is a significant reduction in file size. In the chapters ahead we teach you how to artfully dodge the PC speed barrier. The lessons learned will last you a lifetime.

So far, our emphasis has been on the visual display of information. Multimedia also integrates sound into the computing environment. Let's turn to that now.

USING SOUND IN MULTIMEDIA PROGRAMS

It's a common rule of thumb in professional video that the soundtrack accounts for 50 percent of the impact of the program. Try watching a music video with the sound turned down. Without the sound, you do not know what to think or feel about the visuals. Sound is an important channel of communication.

The video producer normally creates a soundtrack in a sound studio. Since this is a book that turns the computer into a teaching machine, we will show you how to add sound to your production without the trip to the sound studio. We'll be turning your computer into a sound studio. Let's first consider a simpler way of integrating sound with visuals. Since the CD-ROM is becoming a common multimedia peripheral, we should consider the option of creating a CD-ROM soundtrack.

CD-ROM Soundtracks

You can create a soundtrack in a sound studio and send it to a service that will master it on CD audio. Some services will press one CD disk, or thousands. (Check the back pages of music magazines for a CD mastering service in your area.) The audio disk that comes back from the service can be placed in a CD-ROM drive and controlled by the computer through software. GRASP allows you to control CD audio disks using the track position information encoded on the CD audio disk.

This approach is problematic, however, because animation sequences run at different speeds on different computers due to variations in processor speed and device response time. There's no guarantee that the sound will stay in synch with the visuals on another computer. Creating a soundtrack and mastering it on CD is very expensive. Expect to spend at least several thousand dollars for a professionally produced track and for CD mastering. Besides, by committing the soundtrack to CD-ROM, you give up one of the main advantages of digital multimedia: the ability to continuously update elements of the production. That's an important benefit in the fast-paced nineties. We should consider a more flexible alternative.

Sound Cards

Sound cards are relatively inexpensive and have gained wide distribution because of the popularity of computer games. Most so-called multimedia sound boards, such as the Sound Blaster boards, support two types of sounds: synthesized and digitized.

Synthesized Sound

Synthesizers generate music electronically. If you reduce them to a couple of chips and place them on a sound card, you've got part of a multimedia sound card. The synthesizer chips can then be placed under computer control for synchronization with visuals. The synthesizer chips generate music by taking simple sound waveforms (sine waves) and manipulating them until a buzz is shaped into a guitar twang. Over the years, synthesizers have improved in imitating natural sounds through digital synthesis.

You can also attach external synthesizers to many sound cards. Again, the synthesizers can be placed under program control for synchronization with visuals.

Digitized Sound

Most multimedia sound cards have special circuits that convert natural sound (voice, sound effects, and music from a source like a compact disc player) to computer data. This data can be stored on a hard drive and played back in synchronization with visuals. When the digital sound file is played back, it is converted back to analog signals by the sound card and output to speakers.

Sampling Synthesizers

A hybrid type of sound generation uses both sampled sound and synthesis. Some cards, like the Turtle Beach Multisound, have sampled sounds stored right on the card in ROM. The baby grand piano sound you hear is composed of samples of individual notes produced by an actual piano. The card's hardware algorithms combine and manipulate these tiny samples, producing the dynamics of musical instruments artificially. Other cards, such as the Roland SCC1, use specialized DSPs (digital signal processors) to resynthesize sound samples.

Using the PC Speaker

We'll show you how to use the system speaker for creating simple sounds. Most multimedia programs have commands that directly manipulate the system speaker. Some allow you to output digitized sound files to the system speaker. The sound is often muffled and tinny, but it does allow you to distribute multimedia programs to users without sound cards.

Parallel Port Audio Devices

The chip that converts digital audio to an analog signal that can be amplified and played back on speakers can be built into devices that attach to the computer's parallel port. These devices make it possible to play digitized sound on laptops.

MULTIMEDIA SOUND PRODUCTION ISSUES

Producing soundtracks for multimedia presentations offers some important technical challenges. In order to retain compatibility with the widest possible installed base of sound cards, the recording should be made in mono at 12 KHz or less. That's because the majority of the installed base of cards are older generation monophonic cards that have a top-end sampling rate of 12 KHz. Although more recent cards have stereo sampling rates equal to those of CD audio decks, 44.1 KHz, playback of sampled sound at this rate requires a fast hard drive and a 486 computer. What do these sample rates signify?

Sampling Frequency versus Sound Frequency

Sound travels in analog waves. Your ear vibrates to these frequencies, interpreting high-frequency sound waves as high-pitched sounds and low-frequency waves as low-pitched sounds. The limits of human sensitivity to sound are in the range of 20 Hz to 20 KHz (1 KHz is 1000 vibrations per second). For perspective, the sound you hear from the speaker of a handheld AM radio is about 9 KHz.

Sampling frequency and sound frequency are not directly related. This has led to confusion among buyers of digital audio cards. The 12-KHz sampling rate limit of first-generation sound cards translates to a sound frequency of 6 KHz. For technical reasons, the sampling frequency is always made at twice the sound frequency. That's why the sampling rate used by consumer CD audio (44.1 KHz) is roughly twice that of the upper limit of human hearing (20 KHz).

You can also see that 12 KHz, the sampling limit of the first generation of sound cards, translates to about 6 KHz in sound frequency. That's close to the frequency limit for telephone sound reproduction. For perspective, the frequency that is dominant in a male voice is close to 3 KHz. So first-generation sound cards are adequate for sampling voice but inadequate for sampling music, which has a much greater frequency range.

Recording Resolution

Sound cards are rated as having either 8-bit or 16-bit recording resolution. You are probably familiar with this concept in consumer sound equipment as "dynamic range." Dynamic range is the difference in loudness between the music being recorded and the noise inherent in the recording device. With 8-bit recording, the sound at any particular instant is saved as a value between 0 and 255. With 16-bit recording, the sound is saved as a value between 0 and 65,535. This means 8-bit sound cards can recognize 256 different levels of loudness versus 65,535 different levels for 16-bit sound cards. An analog sound wave is continuously variable in its loudness. The more levels you can capture digitally, the more accurate the digital representation of a continuously varying sound wave. Your ear can hear the difference between 8-bit and 16-bit audio. Eight-bit audio has hiss. A 16-bit stereo 44.1 KHz recording has more detail than an 8-bit 44.1 KHz recording. More of the richness and clarity of the sound are recorded and played back. True "audio" CD quality sound means 16-bit stereo at 44.1 KHz. Only sound cards that match these specifications can really claim to record and play back CD quality music.

Playing back digitized sound on a computer is similar to playing back digitized images in this respect: a burden is placed on the computer's internal resources. Let's turn to that now.

Sound File Size and Sound Quality

Higher-quality sound is achieved at a cost in increased file size. If you record stereo sound (two channels of data) at a 44.1-KHz sampling rate, 16-bit resolution, 88,200 samples are recorded every second. Since each sample is 2 bytes, 1 minute of recording consumes 10.6 megabytes per minute! A 2-minute mono recording at 12 KHz will fill a high-density floppy. Digitized sound consumes enormous computer resources.

Using Audio Compression

Once again, data compression is the sword that will cut through the knotty problem of digitized sound file size. Because of the natural dynamics of sound, sound files are highly resistant to compression—even more resistant than video. However, because of the data compression work that has been done in telecommunications and in synthesizer technology, compression ratios have been steadily improving.

What is the short-term prospect for multimedia production that uses a high-quality soundtrack? The solution lies in using the strengths and weaknesses of the two sound generation facilities of sound cards: digitized and synthesized sound.

Combining Digitized and Synthesized Sound

When used in combination, synthesized sounds and digitized sounds can meet the needs of the multimedia producer who wants to stay within the limits of current desktop technology and yet produce a high-quality product. The strategy is to use synthesizers (or the synthesizer chips on a sound card) for music, and use the digital sound section of a sound card for sound effects and voice. Let's look at the two methods.

USING MIDI FOR MULTIMEDIA MUSIC

A special protocol allows computers to communicate with synthesizers. It's called MIDI, the acronym for Musical Instrument Digital Interface. MIDI provides a way for software to manipulate the synthesizer chips on a sound board.

When a MIDI data stream is fed to the synthesizer, or the synthesizer section on a sound card, it is interpreted as instructions for instrument notes and their dynamics over time. Think of the synthesizer as a coprocessor that does most of the work of creating the sound, much as a math coprocessor off-loads floating point math from the CPU. Sending a synthesizer chip 1-, 2-, and 3-byte messages takes a tremendous burden off the CPU and the bus. In addition, the MIDI specification includes rudimentary compression. In the case of digitized sounds, on the other hand, large amounts of digital information are being moved off the hard drive, and this large quantity of data must be translated into analog information. The difference is dramatic. A 2-minute MIDI file can be as small as 14K or smaller! The MIDI file can be up to 100 times smaller than an uncompressed digitized file.

FM Synthesis

MIDI has a prominent role to play in the future of multimedia. It's supported by the MPC multimedia standard. However, at this point in multimedia's evolution, the installed base of PCs with first-generation sound cards (like the original Sound Blaster) limits the sonic possibilities of the method. Most of the first-generation sound cards use an old version of the Yamaha FM synthesis chip, which is not very good at simulating natural sound. Newer cards use newer Yamaha chips, which generate 20 voices versus 11 voices and create more complex, fuller sounds. Look for newer and better synthesizer technologies to be incorporated in multimedia sound cards. In particular, look closely at cards that have sampled sounds built right into them. Your ears will notice a dramatic difference. We use a Roland SCC1 card, which has excellent sampled sounds, in conjunction with the Sound Blaster Pro. The Roland card plays the music, the Sound Blaster Pro plays sound effects and voice. They are installed in the same computer.

In fixed multimedia installations, you can use external synthesizers in conjunction with digital sound cards. This opens up the rich possibilities of advanced synthesizer sound. Let's look at the actual hardware interface between computers and external synthesizers.

The MPU 401 MIDI Interface

You will see "MPU 401" listed as a device option on many games and multimedia programs, and in Microsoft Windows. The reference is to a type of interface between computers and musical instruments that is analogous to the serial port on a computer. The serial port card incorporates the circuitry that makes it possible for computers to talk to modems. The MPU 401 card and its descendants connect computers and synthesizers. The original MPU 401, designed by Roland Corporation, has become a standard that is emulated by a host of other manufacturers. Like most early standards, it has yielded variations that are less compatible with the original.

Using MIDI Channel Assignments

So far, we've talked about MIDI instruments as if they were single instruments played like a grand piano or a trumpet. Most synthesizers can reproduce many different instrument sounds, and they can play these sounds simultaneously. MIDI specifications sometimes refer to the individual instrument sounds as voices. Indeed, a small band lurks inside many synthesizers, and sound cards. For example, Sound Blaster compatibles have 11 voices that operate in two different modes. You can either play 11 melody sounds simultaneously (instrument mode), or six melody sounds and five percussion sounds simultaneously (drum mode). Cards with the newer Yamaha chips can produce 20 different voices, which means they can play more instruments simultaneously.

MIDI File Format

MIDI data is sent as a continuous stream of bytes to the synthesizer, or module. This data is stored as a long sequence of these bytes in files with a .MID or .MFF file extension. The two extensions are two different ways of naming files that conform to the same MIDI specifications.

Adding Voice and Sound Effects with Digitized Sound

While the MIDI protocol allows the producer to add music to multimedia programs, sound effects and voice require a separate treatment. Sound card technology has advanced to the point where high-quality voiceover can be digitized on desktop computers and saved to disk as digital sound files. These digital sound files encode natural sound in a way analogous to how a scanner encodes a photograph. The sound is converted to digital data.

Most multimedia authoring tools support playback of Creative Lab's Sound Blaster VOC sound files, or the WAV sound file format popularized by Windows software. VOC and WAV digitized sound file formats are virtually identical, except VOC files have header information at the beginning of the file. If you rename a WAV file as a VOC file and attempt to read it into the Sound Blaster Pro's digital editor, VEDIT2, the program will tell you the file is in "raw" format. It will prompt you to convert it to VOC format. Other programs will convert between the two different sound formats, including Blaster Master, a Shareware program that edits digitized sound files.

The advantage of using synthesized sound (MIDI) for music and digital sound for voice and sound effects is the reduced burden on computer resources. Another major advantage is the ability to continuously update the sound and music elements of a multimedia presentation.

Updating Multimedia Soundtracks

MIDI music is edited in dedicated programs called sequencers, which help the composer arrange notes and instruments. VOC and WAV digital files are edited in waveform editors, which are like word processors for sound. One of the major drawbacks of a video production is that the final product cannot be edited or changed without major expense. Once CD-ROM disks become easily and inexpensively rewritable, keeping sound and visuals in an "editable" form will finally make computer-based multimedia a preferred production format for business presentations.

MULTIMEDIA: BRINGING IT ALL TOGETHER

It has been said that the best way to reach audiences who grew up in front of television is through audiovisual media, rather than books or lectures. However, television is a one-way, linear mass-communication medium. Now that computers have become a home appliance, we are about to come to terms with a different kind of audience, an audience that loves poking and wandering around in your production, an audience who delights in surprise, an audience who loves to be in control of the flow of images and sound.

Until recently, people have had to stare into small electronic screens and decipher monochromatic symbols, translating them into visual terms. Multimedia allows the viewer to actually experience the message. Information is something we can acquire from text-based terminals or books. It is experience that is the alchemy that transforms information into knowledge. Multimedia provides us with a means to do this.

You can see that multimedia is really an almost inevitable development in the evolution of computer display systems. Human beings use all their senses to gather and process information about the world around them. They lose interest in objects that don't move, they depend on color to figure out what is important, and sound tells them how to feel about what they are looking at. Because we think in three dimensions, 3D animated presentations help people visualize abstract ideas.

Let's now move on to putting the theory we've just learned into practice. It's time to teach the elephant to dance.

Using GRASP's Digital Studio

I N THE WORLD of multimedia programming, GRASP provides instant gratification. No forced labor at the keyboard,
GRASP reduces the intricacies of sound and image programming to a few deft strokes. Want to create a simple
slide show that sequences a series of images? Four or five
commands will do the job. Encoded in those commands are
years of programming craft. With GRASP, you'll never need to know
how to set up registers on a video card to display high-resolution color
images on the screen. A single command (the Video command) does
that for you. GRASP frees your imagination to dance.

GRASP has unjustly acquired the reputation of being difficult—a programmer's tool rather than an artist's tool. While programmers do love and use GRASP because it simplifies animation programming, the program was originally developed for artists. The most interesting GRASP programs are still created by professional artists. You'll meet some of those artists in the last chapters of *Multimedia Creations*.

Over the years GRASP has been extended to include many of the features common to high-level programming languages. That's because GRASP's power users have become much more literate in programming concepts and techniques and demand more features and capability. Today, GRASP is a powerful language indeed for creating highly interactive multimedia programs on the PC.

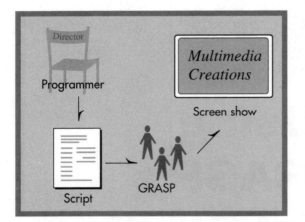

Figure 2-1 GRASP's multimedia production process

Do you have to know programming to produce multimedia? It depends on how multimedia is defined. Simple image sequencing probably works best with a point-and-click interface that places little demand on the multimedia producer. However, highly interactive multimedia productions require literacy in programming concepts and practices. And script-based systems, where the flow of the presentation is controlled by a series of commands and control statements, are easiest for newcomers to learn and understand. Learning GRASP is an excellent way to acquire basic programming knowledge while having fun!

How far can you go with GRASP? GRASP's programming language is completely open-ended. You can extend GRASP well beyond its over 140 commands and functions. You can link it to programming languages like C and Pascal, and you can include code from these languages in GRASP programs. Now that GRASP supports digital video, Autodesk's FLI and FLC animation formats, input and output devices like touchscreens, and facilitates simultaneous playback of digital sounds and MIDI music, the multimedia producer and director really can embark on a new era in interactive learning and entertainment.

In this chapter we're going to familiarize you with GRASP's digital production studio. A dozen pages from now, you'll have mastered the art of sequencing images on the screen. A good start for a future Spielberg of the silicon screen!

LIGHTS, CAMERA, ACTION!

Think of a GRASP program as a movie script. A script contains more than dialogue for actors: Directors use the script to design every image and every action that occurs on the screen. Words are the alchemy of the director's vision, transforming that vision into audio and visual creations; and words are also the medium of exchange for all participants in a movie's creation.

GRASP scripts perform the same function for the computer as a movie script does for a production team. You give detailed instructions to GRASP for sequencing images, adding text and artwork to the screen, and adding sound or driving external devices like a CD-ROM or videodisk player. GRASP translates these instructions into the machine language the computer understands and acts on. Figure 2-1 shows the process of creating a multimedia production using GRASP.

When films are finally edited, copies are shipped in small metal cans to the theaters where they are shown. The props, wardrobe, and script are filed away, forgotten, and eventually lost. GRASP, on the other hand, never lets go of the script. Each time you run a GRASP program, the script is read into the GRASP interpreter and the commands are reenacted.

What's more, GRASP facilitates something no conventional movie script does: interaction with the audience. GRASP scripts make it possible for the viewer to control the flow of the presentation . . . even alter it on the fly. The director's chair is now occupied by the viewer.

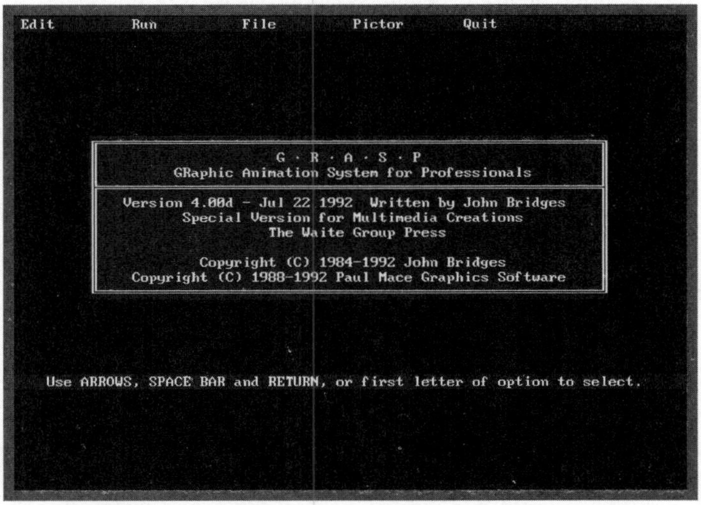

Figure 2-2 GRASP's working environment

Ready to enter the private multimedia production studio hidden in your computer? Lights, camera, action!

WORKING WITH GRASP'S MENU

Change into the GRASP directory where you have installed the two disks that accompany this book. Type `graspc`. GRASPC.EXE is GRASP's main program file. When you run this file, you are first presented with GRASP's menu. Figure 2-2 shows you what it looks like.

Active menu options are highlighted in red. Interaction with the menu is accomplished with the arrow keys, the space bar, or the first letter of the menu option. GRASP's working environment does not support a mouse, although the companion paint program, Pictor, does. Here are the menu options.

- Edit: Edit a GRASP script in GRASP's editor.
- Run: Run a GRASP script.
- File: Load a file into GRASP's editor.
- Pictor: Not active in the version bundled with this book.
- Quit: Exit back to DOS.

THE COMMERCIAL VERSION OF GRASP

The special version of GRASP bundled with this book (GRASPC.EXE) runs programs only in the GRASP editing environment. The complete commercial version of the program includes a utility (GLIB.EXE) that allows you to store GRASP scripts in library files (called GL files) along with support files and pictures or clippings. You can then create a single executable file by compiling the library file with another utility called GLEXE.EXE. The file can then be run from the DOS prompt. This makes GRASP programs easy to transport or distribute, and hides the script and its code from the user. If you intend to distribute applications written in GRASP, purchase the full commercial release of the program. The special version of GRASP bundled with this book is meant to create a learning workshop for multimedia.

In the commercial release of GRASP, the Pictor paint program is accessible from the GRASP menu. It's a feature rarely used by GRASP professionals, because the convenience of accessing the paint program from the GRASP menu is offset by a liability: It adds 128K of overhead to the working environment. We prefer to access Pictor from the DOS prompt.

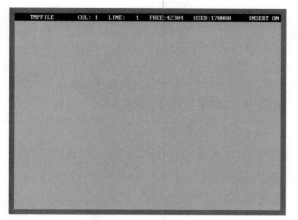

Figure 2-3 GRASP editor menu bar

Think of GRASP's menu choices as rooms in a production studio. The door to the edit suite where images are sequenced, animations composed, and user interaction implemented is the Edit menu. The door to the screening room, where assembled projects are reviewed, is the Run menu option. Scripts for GRASP productions are stored in the File menu. (The Art Department is located at the Pictor menu but the room is empty! It's not used in the special release of GRASP that comes with this book.) Finally, the exit door is found at the Quit menu choice.

Working with GRASP's Editor

GRASP's editor is very much like a simple word processor. The scripts that make up a GRASP program are saved as text files with a .TXT extension. You can edit a GRASP script in MS-DOS's EDLIN.EXE or EDIT.COM text editors, although you cannot run GRASP from these editors. If you do not understand how to use a simple word processor, refer to our short lesson in Appendix B.

GRASP and BASIC

If you've written a BASIC program, then you'll understand how to write a GRASP program right away. Just like BASIC, GRASP programs are written and executed line by line. GRASP reads each line and converts the command to machine language. GRASP is called an interpreted programming language because it sits in RAM memory during both program creation and playback, carefully transcribing your commands into machine language on the fly. Compiled programming languages like C or Pascal also use editors during program creation. However, once the instructions are compiled into machine code, then linked with other modules and specialized libraries into an executable form (an EXE file), that's the final form of the program. Only the final executable code is played back at run time. Programs created by compilers tend to be faster and smaller. However, interpreted programming languages are easier to learn and use. The success of Microsoft's Visual Basic is testimony to that. GRASP is akin to Visual Basic for DOS multimedia programs.

Composing the Script

Let's enter GRASP's edit suite and create our first GRASP program. With Edit high-lighted, press (ENTER). You are now in the editor. Your screen should look like Figure 2-3.

The red highlight on the menu bar disappears, and the name of the current file appears in its place. GRASP defaults to TMPFILE.TXT as the name of the current file. When GRASP first starts up, it looks for the file by that name and loads it as the default file.

Enter the following lines in the editor. If you enter an error, use (BACKSPACE) to erase the mistake.

```
video m

pload cover.pic p1
palette p1
pfade 20 p1 200

waitkey

exit
```

Once you've entered these lines, check to make sure they are correct—GRASP will insist on perfection.

Running the Script within the Editor

When the movie director has positioned the props (such as furniture) and has blocked out the actors' movements (told them where to stand), he or she yells, "Action!" The (F10) key is GRASP's yell for action. Press it now.

If you entered the program correctly, you should see an image sparkle onto the screen. It's a red-tinted version of the cover graphic for *Multimedia Creations,* and it will remain on the screen until you press a key on the keyboard. When you do, you abruptly exit back to the GRASP editor. Congratulations! You've just written your first GRASP program.

If you pressed (F10), and all you see is a blank screen with a white banner at the top, you've made a typing error. One small mistake will elicit a dread error message. GRASP will refuse to process your code. The white banner at the top of the screen will announce:

```
Unknown command at line x
Press Any Key to Continue
```

X is the number of the line where you blundered. Find the line GRASP indicates is faulty, use the arrow keys to move to it, and correct the mistake. Press (F10) again.

If you succeeded in correctly entering the script, try altering one of the lines to force an error. Now run the program again. We want you to become familiar with the error message—you'll be staring at it many times as you toil at the keyboard. See Appendix F for the list of error messages and their meanings.

Learning Safe Programming

Learning programming is only fun if it does not involve an inordinate amount of pain. Programs that are difficult to read or make sense of after a few days spent away from the keyboard are a serious pain for their authors and interested onlookers alike. It's no fun reading a Russian novel in the original if your native tongue is English. The English translation is hard enough to follow, given the Russian propensity for nicknames. Cryptic code really does take the joy out of programming.

In this book we're going to be extensively commenting GRASP code. *Commenting* is the practice of annotating your source code with explanations. Here's what the first program looks like commented:

```
; TMPFILE.TXT An example of a simple GRASP program.

video m                 ; Sets video mode (VGA 640x480 16 colors)

pload cover.pic p1      ; Loads picture into buffer 1.
palette p1              ; Sets palette as buffer 1.
pfade 20 p1 200         ; Two second sparkle fade of picture.

waitkey                 ; Waits for user key press.

exit
```

Notice the use of semicolons. Semicolons tell GRASP to ignore everything that follows on the same line. The semicolon says to GRASP, "Skip the rest of this line, it's here for the convenience of humans."

GRASP'S VIDEO MODES

GRASP supports a wide range of video modes. The special version of GRASP does not support the so-called Super VGA modes (640x480 256 colors or higher) or video cards with the Hicolor DAC. The commercial version of GRASP has a range of resolutions from 40-column text mode to graphics resolutions up to and including 1280x1024 pixels at 8-bit color resolution (256 colors). The commercial release of GRASP includes support for 16-bit color. It also supports the VESA standard, an industry software interface for the extended VGA color modes (above 640x480 pixels and 16 colors).

In this book we'll be working primarily in the standard VGA mode (640x480 16 colors), which is sometimes called an extended EGA mode.

The very first line of the example program begins with a semicolon. This is a conventional message entered at the top of a GRASP script. As you will learn, a program can be composed of many individual scripts, just as a movie script has "acts." Placing a descriptive line like this at the beginning of the script keeps you on track and helps others make sense of your program.

This book will teach you basic programming practices. If you develop a deep love for programming and graduate to a high-level programming language, such as C, you will have developed good habits here. That's it for the lecture. Now let's go back to the studio and walk through the example script in detail.

The First Step: Setting the Video Mode

The first command in the first script of a program is the Video command. The Video command tells GRASP to set up the screen in a specified video resolution. (If you don't

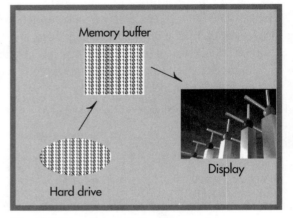

Figure 2-4 Loading and displaying a picture

specify the video mode, GRASP will default to text mode.) Setting up the video mode is like telling your movie production team what film stock to use for the motion picture: Will it be 35mm or 70mm? In this case we specified Video M, or standard VGA (640x480 pixels 16 colors). If you don't understand pixel and color resolutions, don't worry about that now. We'll explain it later.

LOADING PICTURES INTO BUFFERS

The line that begins with the Pload command ("pload cover.pic p1") loads a picture from the hard drive into an area of RAM memory called a buffer. (Pload is a mnemonic for "picture load." The "p," for picture, in front of the buffer number is optional for the version of GRASP bundled with this book and essential for the commercial version of GRASP.) A buffer is a temporary area in memory assigned for a picture. It is assigned a number so that GRASP can seek to that area in memory later.

It may help to visualize the process of loading and displaying pictures. Figure 2-4 illustrates the process. The file is stored on disk in a compressed binary format. That's what the 1 and 0s stand for. When you issue the Pload command, GRASP loads the file into memory, expands the picture to its original size, and stores it in a buffer. When you subsequently issue the Pfade command, the picture is transferred to the video adapter for display. Storing pictures in buffers allows you to load them long before you need to display them.

Learning to Read Commands

If you've ever attended a video edit session, then you know that the language spoken by editor and director can become strangely cryptic. GRASP has its own language and syntax. Commands are rarely one-word expressions. They can be qualified by one or more other words, much as nouns in a spoken language can be qualified or modified by adjectives. In this book, as we introduce each new command, we'll explain its usage and the optional or essential parameters it takes. The command for loading pictures into memory is a case in point.

`pload name [buffer]`

Parameters follow a command on the same line. Optional parameters are enclosed in square brackets. The essential parameter here is the name of the file we want to load into memory. However, we don't have to specify the buffer the picture will be loaded into. If we don't specify the buffer number, GRASP will load the picture into buffer 1 by default. If another picture is already assigned to buffer 1, it will be overwritten (erased).

Displaying Pictures

At the beginning of a film, the movie director can choose among many ways of displaying the first few frames of the picture. A common method is to slowly increase the brightness of the projected image from black to full brightness. This is called a *"fade up* from black." Transitions between scenes in a movie can be instant (a *cut*) or gradual (a *dissolve*). GRASP's command for displaying pictures takes several optional parameters, because GRASP gives the multimedia producer a lot of control over the way images are displayed.

`pfade fade [buffer] [speed] [delay]`

The command above says, "Display the image stored in the specified buffer at the specified speed, using the specified fade." The fade can be any number between 0 to 25 inclusive. GRASP has 26 different ways of displaying an image, from a quick *snap wipe,* where the picture instantly appears, to a *double slant dissolve,* where the picture is slowly revealed along serrated edges from the center outwards. (To see a list of fades, press (F3) while in the editor and use the (ENTER) key to move to the third page, where the list is stored.) Experiment with different fades by changing the fade number. You can vary the length of the fade by changing the speed parameter.

Speed is measured in hundredths of a second. The slowest speed for a fade is 100 seconds (10,000-hundredths of a second). Pressing (ENTER) during a slow fade speeds up the fade to its fastest speed (the fastest speed for a fade is 0). The optional delay parameter is the amount of time the command will wait before executing the next command. If you issue the command without specifying optional parameters, the default buffer is 1 and the default speed is 0.

Setting the Palette

We'll discuss palettes in detail in a later chapter. You can readily see the effect of the command if you place a semicolon in front of the line "palette 1" in our example code. The line should now look like this:

```
; palette 1
```

The command above says, "Display the image stored in the specified buffer at the specified speed, using the specified fade." The fade can be any number between 0 to 25 inclusive. GRASP has 26 different ways of displaying an image, from a quick snap wipe, where the picture instantly appears, to a double slant dissolve, where the picture is slowly revealed along serrated edges from the center outwards. (To see a list of fades, press 3 while in the editor and use the P key to move to the third page, where the list is stored.) Experiment with different fades by changing the fade number. You can vary the length of the fade by changing the speed parameter. Speed is measured in hundredths of a second. The slowest speed for a fade is 100 seconds (10,000-hundredths of a second). Pressing Y during a slow fade speeds up the fade to its fastest speed (the fastest speed for a fade is 0). The optional delay parameter is the amount of time the command will wait before executing the next command. If you issue the command without specifying optional parameters, the default buffer is 1 and the default speed is 0.

Commenting out a command by placing a semicolon in front of it is a *debugging* technique. It's used to isolate troublesome commands in your program (a software *bug* is a fault in your program). When you now run the example code, by pressing (F10), the screen will look pretty exotic! The posts will be pink and yellow, the sky green, red, purple, gray, brown, and several other colors. The word psychedelic comes to mind. What has happened to the picture?

Each picture that we load into a GRASP program has a tiny table of colors attached to it. By issuing the palette command, we tell GRASP to "use the colors attached to the picture to display the picture." Just as painters consult their palettes to decide which color to dab on the canvas, GRASP consults the palette attached to a picture to decide how to "paint" the screen. GRASP, however, has to be told to consult the palette. Otherwise, it will use the default system palette. The default palette is a standard selection of colors, including greens, blues, reds, purples, grays, yellow, black, and white. These will be maliciously applied to your picture without regard to your artistic intent. Mercy has yet to be coded in silicon, so arm yourself. Learn to use the palette command. In our example "buffer p1" instructs GRASP to use the palette stored with the picture in buffer 1. Here's the syntax of the command.

```
palette [buffer]
```

The buffer number is optional for the version of GRASP bundled with this book, but it's always good practice to make references explicit. It makes code easier to read.

Creating User Interaction

The command that transforms this short slide show into an interactive program is very simple. It's the Waitkey command. Waitkey instructs GRASP to pause and wait for the user to press a key. If you're not impressed by this feature, think back to the moment when you first tentatively reached out and touched a computer. Now imagine the new sound and image possibilities that you can put into motion with the touch of a key. Waitkey is the most important command in the entire GRASP command set. It transforms GRASP programs into interactive time-based presentations. The syntax for the command is as follows:

```
waitkey [time] [label]
```

When used without parameters, Waitkey suspends program execution until the user presses a key. You can optionally specify a wait time. Program execution will continue after the wait time has elapsed. Modify the last line of TMPFILE.TXT by adding a 5-second wait time:

```
waitkey 500
```

When you run the program again, by pressing the (F10) function key, the program will pause for 5 seconds before exiting back to the editor. The command says in effect, "Wait for 5 seconds. If the user presses a key before 5 seconds elapses, proceed. After 5 seconds, proceed anyway." The label parameter that is part of Waitkey's syntax causes a jump to a label somewhere else in the script. Ignore that option for now. We'll be treating labels in depth later.

Pausing Program Flow

There is an exception to the Waitkey command's check for keyboard input. By default GRASP uses the space bar as a pause key. You can pause a GRASP script at any time by pressing the space bar. It's like the pause button on your VCR. Pressing (ENTER) causes program execution to continue. Pressing (ESC) exits to the editor. Pressing any other key has no effect.

HELP WITH THE GRASP COMMANDS

To access on-line help for GRASP commands while in the editor press the ⒡ function key. GRASP has over a hundred commands available to the programmer. Many of the commands are specific to the video modes we won't be covering in this book. Also consult the command summaries found in Chapter 10. The summaries cross-reference commands in the book. The introduction to the chapter familiarizes you with GRASP's on-line help.

Exiting from the Script

The last command in the script, (EXIT), terminates execution of TMPFILE.TXT and returns control of the computer to the GRASP editor. (In the commercial version of GRASP, a program compiled with the GLIB and GLEXE utility programs returns control to DOS or a calling program.) The syntax for the command is as follows:

```
exit [value]
```

Exit is comparable to that famous utterance of the movie director: "Cut!" The shot is complete, and the camera stops filming. The optional *value* is used when GRASP has been called from another programming language. It is a number that can be used to set the DOS errorlevel value. We'll use this parameter later in the book

```
════ P I C T O R - The Painter's Easel - by John Bridges ════
       Choose a Video Mode by Pressing a Letter or Press ESC to Quit

        A -> CGA              320x200     4 colors
      * B -> Tandy 1000/PCjr  320x200    16 colors
        C -> CGA              640x200     2 colors
        D -> EGA              640x200    16 colors
        E -> EGA              640x350     2 colors
        F -> EGA              640x350     4 of 64 colors
        G -> EGA              640x350    16 of 64 colors
      * H -> Hercules Mono    720x348     2 colors
        I -> EGA              640x350    16 of 256K colors
        J -> EGA              320x200    16 colors
      * K -> AT&T/Toshiba     640x400     2 colors
        L -> MCGA/VGA         320x200   256 of 256K colors
        M -> EGA/VGA          640x480    16 of 256K colors
      * N -> Hercules InColor 720x348    16 colors
        O -> MCGA/EGA/VGA     640x480     2 colors
        P -> EEGA/VGA         800x600     2 colors
        Q -> EEGA/SVGA        800x600    16 of 64 or 256K colors


    Modes marked with '*' are DEFINITELY not available on this system.
        ════ Copyright(C) 1990 - Paul Mace Graphics Software ════
```

Figure 2-5 Pictor's video modes

In our short program, the Exit command is not always required by GRASP. If you omit it, GRASP returns by default to the editor. It's always useful, however, as a visual clue to the termination point of a GRASP script. When you come to add subroutines to a GRASP script, the Exit command will be essential.

USING THE COMPANION PAINT PROGRAM

Preparing graphics for sequencing in GRASP using the companion program Pictor is like having an art department in your movie production studio. A movie studio art department will do simple artwork in-house. However, the most sophisticated effects and sequences are contracted to outside specialists. Similarly, most of the images you will import into the GRASP working environment will originate in specialized graphics programs. For instance, if you're a user of the Paint Shop Pro program from JASC, Inc., or one of the business presentation programs like Corel Draw, you'll find it convenient to use these programs to generate specialized parts of your presentation. GRASP's Pictor paint program is primitive compared to today's advanced paint or

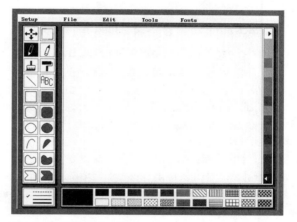

Figure 2-6 Pictor's viewport

draw programs, but it does have some features indispensable to GRASP programs. Let's go on a brief tour of the GRASP art department.

As we mentioned earlier, in the case of the version of GRASP bundled with this book, Pictor cannot be accessed from within the GRASP working environment. Exit GRASP by pressing the (ESC) key. If you are not in the GRASP directory, change into it.

`cd \GRASP`

Make sure your mouse is installed. Run Pictor by typing `pictor`.

Selecting the Video Mode

The first screen you will encounter is the video modes information screen. It will look like Figure 2-5. You are presented with a number of choices for the pixel and

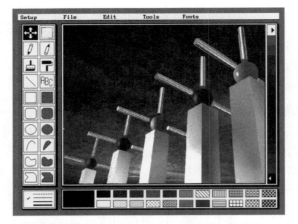

Figure 2-7 The cover graphic loaded into Pictor

color resolutions of the images you create in Pictor. The video mode numbers correspond to those used in the GRASP editor. Note that the version of Pictor bundled with this book does not support the extended VGA modes, such as Video S's 640x480 256-color mode. Select Video M, the principal mode we will be using in this book.

Working in Pictor's Viewport

Figure 2-6 shows Pictor's viewport and paint tools. Pictor has most of the basic tools found in paint programs. The program's author, John Bridges, calls the working environment "the artist's studio." This is a good way of thinking about the program. Just as an artist uses different tools and media on the surface of the canvas, the electronic artist paints over the white area of the screen using a variety of electronic tools. The tools, menus, palette, and patterns you work with are arranged around a central area that acts as a viewport on a larger canvas. If you press the (ESC) key, the tools will disappear, and you'll see the entire canvas. Press (ESC) again to toggle back to the viewport.

Let's begin by loading the book cover image into Pictor and adding text to it.

Select File at the top of the screen by clicking on it. (The mouse behaves exactly like mice in other graphical environments. A *click* is a quick press and release of a mouse button. *Dragging* means pressing a button, moving an object about, or stretching a box to a certain size, and finally releasing the button.) When you click on the word File at the top of the screen, a menu drops down. Now click on the word Load. A window pops up on the screen. Click on the down arrow of the menu until the file name COVER.PIC appears. Click on the file name and then on Load. GRASP loads the file into the viewport. Your screen should look like Figure 2-7.

The cover graphic should now be in the viewport. Toggle between full screen view and partial screen view by pressing the (ESC) key. When you are in full screen view, the paint tool currently selected is active.

Pictor provides keyboard alternatives to point-and-click commands. This is especially useful when you're in the full screen view. For example, while in full screen view, you can pop up the file loading window by pressing the letter (l) (small

IMPORTING FILES

Pictor will import CompuServe's GIF file format, the Zsoft Corporation's PCX file format, and Pictor's native PIC file format. This means you can import graphics from other programs that store images in any of these formats. Pictor will also import tiny picture files with the PAL extension, created by utility programs or in Pictor. These small picture files are useful for loading picture palettes quickly, when you have no need to load the accompanying picture. Pictor creates, saves, and loads special picture files without palettes, called clippings. They have a .CLP extension. We'll be discussing this format shortly.

You can load PCX, GIF, and PIC pictures into GRASP's editor and programs; however, GRASP will load PIC files much faster. That's why it's a good idea to convert these and other files to the PIC format. We often use the Shareware program VPIC.EXE for this purpose. It has the advantage of loading and displaying images from the DOS command line.

See Appendix C: Using GRASP's Utilities, for information on using WHATPIC.EXE, SHOWPIC.EXE, TXTCLP.EXE, and CONVPIC.EXE to process images. These utilities help you analyze, show, or convert images for use in GRASP scripts.

L) for Load. Similarly, you can save pictures to files while in this screen by pressing (s) for Save. A list of keyboard alternatives for Pictor commands can be found in the Appendix D: PICTOR Keyboard Alternatives.

Using the Paint Icons

We think you'll prefer to work with a much more sophisticated paint program than Pictor, so we'll only briefly touch on the program's paint and drawing tools. Most of the paint tool icons running vertically on the left of the screen are pretty simple to use. Here are the important tools.

Picture Mover

Using the left mouse button, click on the Picture Mover tool (the four arrows) at the top left of the paint tools. This tool moves the picture around within the viewport. Try it! Click on the screen and move it about by dragging.

Edit Box

The Edit Box right beside the Picture Mover allows you to select a portion of the screen for moving, copying from one area of the screen to another, or saving an area of the screen to Pictor's clipboard. Click on the Edit Box with the left mouse button. Now click on the screen with the left mouse button, holding the button down to drag a marquee box around an area of the screen. Release the mouse button, and click again inside the marquee to drag the square to another part of the screen. If you do not like the new position, click on the Edit menu and click on Undo. The box pops back into its original position. Repeat the process. Once you are happy with the placement of the clipping on the screen, *release* the button and click on the outside of the marquee box to paste the edited screen clip in its new position. The change to the screen is now permanent. You cannot Undo the change.

Pencil Tool

The Pencil tool, just below the Picture Mover tool, works like a pencil. Choose a color from the palette on the right. Click on your choice with the left mouse button. Draw on the screen. Then Undo your doodle!

Eraser Tool

The tool beside the Pencil tool is the Eraser. It erases portions of the screen, revealing the *background* color. Select the background color by clicking on a color in the palette with the right mouse button. The left mouse button chooses the *foreground* color, color that is laid down by one of the drawing tools.

Line Tool

The Line tool creates straight lines. Click on the tool to select it. Then click on the screen and drag the line to the spot where you want the line to end. When you release the mouse button, the line is drawn on the screen.

Text

Before using the Text tool, select a font from the Fonts menu. (You can also load a font with a .SET extension from the GRASP directory. In order to do so, pop up the files menu by pressing (l) on your keyboard. Select Font. A list of SET files appears in the dialogue box. Click on a font file to use it. PICTOR defaults to using fonts with a .FNT extension. GRASP defaults to using fonts with a .SET extension.) After selecting a font, click on the ABC text icon. Drag a box on the screen. Now type your copy in the box. When you're finished, click with the right mouse button. We'll explore the text tool in detail in the next section.

The Other Paint Icons

The Line, Rectangle, Curve, Freehand Shape, and Polygon tools each have two forms, outline and filled. Outline thickness is set by selecting a line thickness from the box at the bottom left of the screen. The currently selected foreground color will determine the color of the outline. For filled shapes select a color from the palette with the left mouse button to determine which color will fill the shape; or select one of the patterns at the bottom of the screen. The patterns use the foreground and background colors.

Other Tools and Functions

Some of the most common functions you will perform with Pictor include the following.

Undoing Picture Changes

Undo the last change you made to the image by selecting Undo on the Edit menu.

Magnifying Areas of the Image

Drag a box around an area of the screen with the Edit Box. It's located at the top right of the paint icons, at the left side of the screen. Then choose Magnify from the Tools menu. The viewport zooms in on the area you've defined. You can now edit your image pixel by pixel. Choose Magnify again to return to the viewport.

Using the Clipboard

You can store portions of the screen in a temporary buffer called the clipboard. The clipboard will store the screen clipping between images. You can paste part of one picture into another, or you can repeatedly paste the clipping over the entire image. Here's how.

Once again, use the Edit Box to capture an area of the screen. When you've defined the edit area, select Copy from the Edit menu or press ⓒ. This places the area inside the edit box onto the clipboard. Now choose Paste from the Edit menu, or press ⓟ. The clipboard clipping is pasted on the screen. The marquee remains active around the clipping you've just pasted on the screen. Click inside the marquee and drag the clipping to another location on the screen. Clicking on the outside of the box permanently pastes the clipping on the screen.

Editing the Image

Some of the options in the Edit menu are active when you have created an Edit Box on the screen. Some of the commands modify the entire screen image.

In mastering paint programs, our recommendation is to learn by doing. The commercial release of GRASP fully documents Pictor and includes enhancements, such as Hicolor (32,000 and more colors) and extended VGA support. Alternately, purchase a more sophisticated paint package, like Animator Pro, or one of Zsoft's paint programs. Corel Draw is an excellent all-around package to use, because it includes both object-oriented modules and a paint module. Most paint programs will save in GIF or PCX format. The images can then be imported into Pictor for final processing.

CREATING A NEW SLIDE FOR TMPFILE

Let's create a new image that will be added to the slide we created earlier in GRASP. We'll add a title to the screen: Multimedia Creations. Let's start with a fresh picture. Press ⓛ (lowercase L) for Load and click on COVER.PIC and then Load. COVER.PIC loads into the viewport. Use the Picture Mover to position the viewport so that the top left of the cover graphic is in the viewport. Now select the Font menu and choose the following options: Roman, Large, Center. This selects the large Roman font and centers the text in the Text Edit box. Now select the text icon (ABC). Choose an area at the center of the empty sky. Drag the Text Edit box to a width of about 4 inches and a height of about 2 inches. Select white as the text color by clicking on the white square at the top of the palette. Now type the word **Multimedia** and press the (ENTER) key. The text should appear at the top of the Text Edit box. If you make a mistake, use (BACKSPACE) to correct the error. Choosing Undo from the Edit menu erases the entire Text Edit box. Pressing (ENTER) key moves the text entry cursor to the next line. Press it again to open up a larger space between the first word and the second word. Now type the word **Creations.** Press the left mouse key to permanently paste the type into the background. You cannot Undo text once it is pasted on the screen. It's a good idea to save the image often. Press (ESC) to look at the entire image in full screen mode.

Saving TITLE.PIC

Now that you have created the title slide, save it to disk. Select the Save option on the File menu. Make sure the Picture and PIC options are selected in the Save menu that pops up. Now click on the File Name box. It will show the name of the current file, COVER.PIC, in it. When you click on the box it goes black. Enter the name TITLE.PIC in the box. Now click on Save. The picture is saved as TITLE.PIC.

Exiting Pictor

Let's return to GRASP. Select Quit from the File menu or press (ALT)-(Q) to return to the DOS prompt. Run GRASP by typing **graspc.** You are presented with GRASP's menu. Press (ENTER) to enter the editor. When GRASP starts up, the default file is TMPFILE.TXT, so the file is already loaded in the editor.

ADDING IMAGES TO GRASP PROGRAMS

You can easily add the image you have created to TMPFILE.TXT. Move the cursor down to the space between the Pfade and the Waitkey commands. Type the lines:

```
waitkey

pload title.pic p1
```

The entire file should now look like this:

```
; TMPFILE.TXT An example of a simple GRASP program.

video m                  ; Sets video mode (VGA 640x480 16 colors)

pload cover.pic p1       ; Loads picture into buffer 1.
palette p1               ; Sets palette as buffer 1.
pfade 20 p1 200          ; Two second sparkle fade of picture.

waitkey

pload title.pic p1
pfade 1 p1 300           ; left-to-right 3 second wipe

waitkey 500              ; Waits for user key press.

exit
```

Press (F10). When you press (F10), TMPFILE.TXT is automatically saved. The first image sparkle-fades onto the screen. We've entered a Waitkey to cause GRASP to wait for the user to advance to the next image. When the user does, the next image wipes on the screen from the left. This time the program waits for 5 seconds and then exits. You've just modified the TMPFILE script and added a new electronic slide to the series!

Notice that it was unnecessary to include the Palette command after the second Pload command. That's because the second slide has the same palette (uses the same colors) as the first slide.

Remember that every time you press (F10), GRASP automatically saves the text file in the editor.

Alternate Options Pressing (F10) runs the current script from the top of the file. Pressing (F9) runs the script from the current cursor position in the script. Pressing (ALT)-(l) (lowercase L) restores the last saved version of the script.

FADE TO BLACK

The last instruction on the movie script is, "Fade to black," and it encodes a sigh of relief. The production is done!

Writing a slide show in GRASP is incredibly easy, once you've found your way around the program's desktop studio. Our tour of that studio has been brief and hurried, but you will get a much more thorough working knowledge of the environment as you complete the examples in *Multimedia Creations*. In the next chapter, you'll learn to create a much more sophisticated GRASP slide show. GRASP's strength is its programming features, and you'll learn how to use those features to design your own software slide projector.

The programming approach GRASP uses might appear at first to be archaic and awkward at a time when the virtues of GUI (Graphical User Interfaces) have been heralded everywhere. However, in learning to work with GRASP's features and commands, you will absorb a tremendous amount of knowledge about the architecture of the PC, and you'll learn how to turn the reluctant PC into a multimedia machine that can dazzle and amuse audiences. The patient, line-by-line approach results in a design not compromised by the need for simplicity. With GRASP, you really do have the opportunity of scripting your own vision of multimedia.

PART TWO
Multimedia Cookbook

3
Building a Software Slide Projector

T HE HUMBLE overhead projector and time-honored slide projector have long been the dominant tools for getting attention and illustrating concepts in business and educational presentations. Now, however, the reign of these analog audiovisual devices is coming to an end. Converting digital information to analog hard copy, such as slides and overhead transparencies, is expensive, error-prone, and time-consuming. The hard copy produced by analog output is inflexible—you can't easily change slides or transparencies without re-creating them—and they are difficult to transport and set up. Worse, you have to show slides in a darkened room. Today, more and more information is stored in digital form, in databases accessed by local or wide area networks, and over telecommunication lines. It is becoming more convenient and cost effective to display digitized information on a digital output device.

Figure 3-1 Prototype of a software slide projector

The standard device for displaying digital information is none other than the monitor at your desktop. Unfortunately, desktop PCs are difficult to disentangle from networks and too bulky to transport from the desk to the meeting room table. Many companies have installed large monitors in meeting rooms, or use LCD panels in combination with overhead projectors. But truly portable solutions have had a difficult birth. The "luggable" computer gave way to heavy laptops that needed to be plugged into a power source, and portable computers are continuing to shed weight and the power cord. Today battery-operated, notebook computers are the feather-weight champions of computing, and will soon gain the muscle for heavy-duty multimedia work.

Color notebooks are dropping quickly in price, now run on batteries, and sport bright, colorful wide-view screens. They will certainly revolutionize one-to-one and small-group presentations. In combination with LCD panels and portable LCD projectors, electronic slide presentations can show large, movie-sized images and are making audiences applaud everywhere. Figure 3-1 shows a prototypical setup for large audiences: a color notebook attached to an LCD panel on an overhead projector.

Electronic presentations on notebooks are more convenient for presenters who already create slides in desktop presentation packages or capture their presentation data from a central resource. Electronic slides can be changed easily at the last moment or rearranged to suit a particular audience. As sound and motion video compression chips are added to the color notebook, portable electronic presentations will become powerful audiovisual aids indeed.

In this chapter you will build a presentation system in software. The "software projector" we create can be extended to suit your own particular style and your own needs. With GRASP, you're not stuck in someone else's slide show metaphor. You can use programming tools to alter the slide projector for your own needs. Let's begin by building a very simple slide projector.

CREATING THE BLUEPRINT FOR THE PROJECTOR

If you were building a mechanical slide projector, you would want to build a prototype before creating the final product. And before building a test machine, you would test your ideas out on paper, and ask for input from others. Programmers develop programs using an analogous design process.

For example, the elementary GRASP script (TMPFILE.TXT) presented in the last chapter does little more than load and display one picture file after another, using the screen as an "electronic projector." How would we build a model for this simple software projector? It's often useful to develop something called *pseudocode* before actually writing the code using a programming language. Pseudocode is a step-by-step series of statements in plain English describing what a program is supposed to do. It's useful as a way of outlining a program's purpose and structure, much as you might outline a report that you are going to write. The programming logic of TMPFILE.TXT is as follows.

- Load the picture.
- Tell GRASP to use the picture's palette for displaying colors.
- Show the picture on the screen.
- Wait for a keypress.

PEEKING AHEAD

The script PROJECTO.TXT in the CHAPT03 subdirectory contains the code for the exercises in this chapter. You can run it now to see how the program will eventually work. (You first must run MAKESLID.TXT in the GRASP editor to create the slides used by the PROJECTO.TXT software slide projector.) During exercises, if you find your code produces errors, compare your work with the code in this file.

Now that we know what the program is supposed to do and the order in which it is supposed to do it, we can translate our pseudocode statements into actual code. Here it is:

```
pload picture.pic p1      ; loads picture into memory buffer 1
palette p1                ; tells GRASP to use  buffer 1's palette
pfade 0 p1                ; uses a quick snap fade for buffer 1
waitkey                   ; wait for a key press
```

We could then use this code to build a simple slide show. The commands that load and display images can be repeated for each electronic slide we want to project. But writing a program like this would be tedious and not very flexible. If we had seven slides to display, we would need to write 28 lines of code. That's analogous to a slide projector that only accepts one slide at a time, which you have to manually place in the projector gate for viewing. This simple software slide projector would not be able to back up through a list of slides, and the program would become long and difficult to change. Kodak, the maker of the ubiquitous Carousel slide projector, solved a similar problem for mechanical slide projectors. They developed a circular tray that holds 80 slides (larger trays hold 140). The tray spins around on its axis, dropping one slide at a time into a projector gate. Figure 3-2 is an artist's conception of a Kodak Carousel Projector.

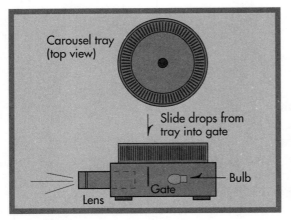

Figure 3-2 Kodak Carousel projector

What would be the equivalent solution for sequencing electronic slides in GRASP? How would we reduce the program listing from 28 lines of code to a more manageable size?

One way of solving the problem is to create a list of file names in memory and use that list to sequence the slides. The pseudocode would look like this:

1. Create a list of slides names in memory.
2. Set a counter equal to the number of slides.
3. Load a slide into the "gate" using a name from the list.
4. Use the color table (palette) stored with the slide.
5. Show the slide.

6. Wait for a key press.

7. Repeat steps 2 to 5 until we've exhausted the list.

The list of slide names is an ordered sequence of slides, just like the slides in the numbered slots of a slide tray. Initially, the first slide from the list is loaded and displayed. Advancing the tray to the next slide is accomplished by *looping* back to step 2, decreasing the counter, and loading the second slide from the list. This continues until the counter tells us that we are out of slides. We've reduced the program from 28 lines to seven lines. Best of all, adding to the slide list does little to increase the program size.

Now let's translate this into actual GRASP code.

Creating the Electronic Slides

First we need to perform a small housekeeping chore. Exit from GRASP if you are currently running the program. Change into the GRASP subdirectory \GRASP\CHAPT03:

```
cd \GRASP\CHAPT03
```

Note: Make sure the environment variable has been set for GRASP so that it can find its program files (set GRASP = *(drive)*:\GRASP). And make sure you've made the GRASP directory part of the DOS path. You should be able to run GRASPC.EXE from the CHAPT03 subdirectory. The install program should have done this for you automatically.

We've written a short GRASP program that will generate the slides you're going to use in this exercise. Manufacturing the slides with GRASP saved a lot of disk space on the distribution disks for this book. You must run this file before doing the other exercises in this chapter.

Highlight the File menu (use the (SPACE BAR), the (↑)(↓)(←)(→) keys, or the (ENTER) key). Select the Load File option. Highlight MAKESLID and press (ENTER). Press (ENTER) again. MAKESLID is now loaded into the GRASP editor. Press (F10) to run the program. You should see a series of images of Rome form against a gray patterned background. Our slide show will feature a small tour of Rome's cultural treasures. The electronic slides that will fill our software carousel are created by GRASP. Figure 3-3 shows a statue, one of the images from the series.

Creating the Software Slide Projector

Now we'll create the software slide projector that will sequence these slides on the monitor. Press (ESC) to exit the editor back to GRASP's menu. Highlight the File menu. Press (ENTER) to choose Create File. Name the file TMPFILE, and press (ENTER). Type in the following lines. (Be careful to add the semicolons where they are called

Figure 3-3 A statue from the Rome tour

for. Remember that a semicolon tells GRASP to ignore everything that follows on the same line. Also, note the way we've indented the code using the (TAB) key. We've also lined up the comments using the (TAB) key. Laying out the code this way makes the program easier to read.)

```
; TMPFILE.TXT Software Slide Projector

video m

; The slide tray.
        data slide001 slide002 black

; The projector and gate.
mark 3                          ; place marker for loop, plus loop count
        pload @ p1              ; this is where items from the list are placed
        palette p1
        pfade 9 p1 100          ; use fade 9 to display picture in buffer 1,
                                ; fade lasts for one second (100/100 secs.)
        pfree p1
        waitkey
loop                            ; loop back to "mark"

exit
```

When you have entered the code, press (F10). The slide show advances through each of the three slides, waiting for a keypress after each slide is displayed. We use a 1-second top-down wipe to display the pictures. The last slide is a blank, black slide. After three loops (corresponding to the three file names in the data list), the script exits back to the editor. This is a small tray! It has only three slots for slides. We'll expand it later.

We've introduced several new commands. Let's look at them in turn.

Using Pfree to Free Memory

The command Pfree is important in GRASP programming. The syntax for the command is:

```
pfree buffer [buffer]  ...
```

Pfree frees the buffer that was previously allocated to a picture. When GRASP allocates an area of RAM memory for a picture, it doesn't release it until told to explicitly, or until you load another picture into that buffer. It's always good practice to free a picture's buffer immediately after using it. Good memory management is an issue we will come back to again and again in *Multimedia Creations*.

Using the Data Command

The software slide tray was implemented using the Data command. Syntax for the command is:

```
data item item item ...
```

Data items can be numeric values, file names, or text strings. Only data item names that fit on one line can be included in the data list. Commas or spaces divide data items. Enclosing quotation marks around a text string creates a single data item. This also preserves capitalization. Data creates a list of file names in memory that GRASP can access sequentially, much as you might access slides in a Carousel tray by advancing the tray one slide at a time with a remote-control switch. (Note that it is not the slides that are stored in memory, it is the names of slides.)

Using @ to Access the Data List

The @ symbol is used by GRASP to access a data list one item after another. Think of a data list in GRASP as a slide tray, and the @ symbol as the gate into which each visual is dropped for viewing. We can then use a programming feature called a *loop* to repeatedly load the slides in the list until the list is exhausted. This is the rotating (Carousel) feature of our slide tray. Figure 3-4 is a conceptual drawing showing the @ symbol pointing to an area of memory holding the name for the second slide in a series.

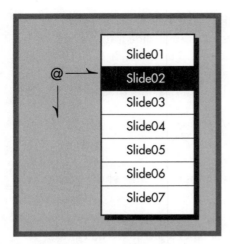

Figure 3-4 The @ symbol accessing names from a list

The Mark/Loop Command

Our example used a program flow method common in most programming languages: the loop. In GRASP a Loop command repeats a portion of code a specified number of times. In the example above, we added a loop that causes GRASP to cycle back to a *mark* and go through the load-and-display sequence again. Each time it does this, it encounters the @ symbol and substitutes a file name from the list. It then moves an internal pointer to the next slide on the list. This is the command sequence that powers our electronic slide projector, rotating the "tray" around the "loop" to each new slide. The syntax for the Mark/Loop command is:

```
mark count
...                             ; body of loop
loop
```

A Mark must be paired with a Loop. *Count* is the number of times to repeat the loop. The value can be 1 to 65,535.

How a Loop Works

When GRASP enters a loop, it decreases the mark count by one. It executes the loop and returns to the mark statement to check to see if it is 0. If it is not 0, GRASP executes the body of the loop again and returns to the mark to check it again. This time, if it is 0, GRASP skips the body of the loop and exits to the line after the body of the loop. Figure 3-5 is a flow diagram of a loop.

Nesting Loops

You can nest Mark/Loop combinations, one within the other, up to 16 times. The inner loop is executed in its entirety first. (Later we'll introduce you to the Break command, which allows program execution to escape from a loop before the count is reached.) Here's what a nested loop looks like:

```
mark 2                  ; the outer loop
    ...                 ; command
        mark 4          ; the inner loop
            ...         ; body of inner loop
        loop
    ...                 ; command
loop
```

Notice the way the code statements (indicated by the ellipsis "...") and inner loop are indented. This indicates that the second loop is controlled by the outer loop.

Let's see how GRASP reads these lines. After the loop is entered, a command (...) is executed and then the inner loop is entered. The inner loop cycles four times and then exits. Another command is encountered (...). GRASP then loops back to the original mark and goes through the whole process again. We'll be using loops extensively in *Multimedia Creations*. It's an economical method of repeating code, or as in the case of our example, reading values from a list.

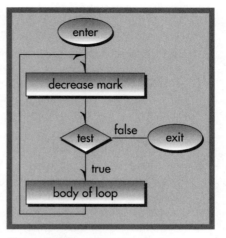

Figure 3-5 Flow diagram of a loop

Expanding the Slide Tray

The Data command is useful for short, single-line lists of file names, text strings, or numeric values. Our slide tray needs to be larger than one line allows. When the item list exceeds a single line, the Databegin and Dataend commands are required to define the boundaries of your list. Databegin and Dataend act like brackets enclosing the data items. GRASP always reads your script one line at a time. When it finds the end of the line, it looks for a new command on the next line. Databegin instructs GRASP to keep reading data until GRASP sees a Dataend demarcation. Here's the electronic slide projector with the "tray" expanded:

```
; TMPFILE.TXT Software Slide Projector

video m

; This is the slide tray expanded.
        databegin
                slide001.pic slide002.pic slide003.pic slide004.pic
                slide005.pic slide006.pic black.pic
        dataend

; The projector and gate.
        mark 7
                pload @ p1
                palette p1
                pfade 9 p1 100
                pfree p1
                waitkey
        loop

exit
```

CREATING SLIDES FOR A GRASP PROGRAM

Let's take a brief side excursion into the area of slide creation. GRASP will load and display a variety of picture formats, including CompuServe GIF files, Zsoft Corporation's PCX files, GRASP's native PIC, or GRASP PAL formats. Use the format's extension when loading the file into GRASP. (For example, pload picture.pcx.) GIF files will take the longest to decode and load into memory. However, GIF files are highly compressed, so use them where space is at a premium, such as on a floppy. GRASP's PIC format loads and displays the fastest. The GRASP PAL format is not really a unique image format. It is a tiny 8x8 image used for setting palettes. We don't actually display the image, we'll just put it up into a buffer to gain access to its palette.

Remember, GRASP scripts begin with a Video command that tells GRASP what video resolution you're working in. When you load an image with a different resolution from what you originally specified, you must precede the display of the new image with an appropriate video command. In the case of the example script, the slides you add to the list must be Video M mode slides (VGA, 640x480 pixels 16 colors). If you try to load a Super VGA picture (for example, 640x480 256 colors), GRASP will generate an out-of-memory error message. If you enter a file name for a file that does not exist, you will get an error message ("Error loading picture") and you will be returned to the point in the script where GRASP ran into trouble. If you try to load a Video L image (320x200 256 colors), it will appear distorted on the screen. You'll find in the \GRASP directory a small utility called WHATPIC.EXE that examines the picture file and reports back its video mode. Run WHATPIC.EXE from the command line for help on using it, or consult Appendix C: Using GRASP's Utilities.

Convert all images that are part of a sequence to the same video resolution. You can load PCX, GIF, IMG, and BSAVE pictures into Pictor and save them as PIC files. Or use the conversion program CONVPIC.EXE in the \GRASP directory. See Appendix C. If you must display slides with mixed video resolutions, you will need to reset the video mode each time you show a new slide with a new video resolution. Changing the video mode causes the screen to blank and the presentation becomes jerky. Fortunately, there are many utility programs that convert pictures from one file format to another and from one video resolution to another. The Waite Group's *Image Lab* treats image processing in depth and comes bundled with a widely used image-processing program. For image reduction or conversion in the Windows en-

(continued from page 58)

vironment, we like the Shareware program Paintshop Pro, from JASC, Inc., which runs under Windows. It will resize an image, alter its color resolution, and perform a variety of other image processing tasks. From the DOS prompt, we use Bob Montgomery's Shareware program VPIC.EXE, available on many bulletin boards, to quickly display and convert a picture from one format to another. Another DOS command line program that is useful for batch processing is Image Alchemy from Handmade Software, Inc. It's an all-purpose image conversion and color reduction program.

CAPTURING SCREENS FROM PROGRAMS

If you can't find your way through the maze of PC picture formats, try capturing the picture with a screen capture utility, such as CAP.COM supplied with this book. It's found in the \GRASP directory. See Appendix C. We've used PCXGRAB.EXE from Genus Microprogramming, Inc. Unfortunately, the utility is not sold separately from their PCX programming tool kit.

We think of GRASP as a slide projector rather than a slide studio. It excels at projecting images, although it does have tools for last minute touch-up of electronic slides.

Note that we have changed "mark 3" to "mark 7" to reflect the addition of more slides to the slide tray. You can experiment with the viewer by entering your own file names in the data entry area.

Storing the Slide List Externally

GRASP reads a script line by line. Putting the data item list or Databegin/Dataend commands at the beginning of a file is convenient, but ultimately impractical. What if we want to use the list of slides over and over again in a long and complex program? What if we want to include several different lists? There is a more convenient place to store the data list in your presentation. We can store the list where GRASP would not encounter it in normal execution. We can place the list after the Exit command. (Remember that Exit causes the script to terminate and return to the editor.) Figure 3-6 diagrams the code flow.

The labeled portion of code that exists externally to the main body of the script can now be modified easily. It can even be stored in another script. We'll show you how to do that in a later chapter. Let's see how we implement this logic in the software slide projector.

```
; TMPFILE.TXT Software Slide Projector

video m

; The slide tray.
        databegin slides                      ;label "slides" is at end of the script

; The slide projector and gate.
        mark 7
                pload @ p1
                palette p1
                pfade 9 p1 100
                pfree p1
                waitkey
        loop

exit

slides:                                        ; list is placed AFTER  the exit command
        slide001.pic slide002.pic slide003.pic slide004.pic
        slide005.pic slide006.pic black.pic
dataend
```

The Databegin command takes on a different form here. The word slides points to a *label* after the Databegin command:

```
databegin slides
```

The word slides: is the label. (A label is defined in GRASP as a word that ends with a colon.) Used without a colon, slides directs GRASP to jump to the word slides: elsewhere in the script, in this case after the Exit command. The data list is stored after

the exit point in the script so that it is not encountered in the normal sequence of commands in the script. Placing it after the exit point means it can be accessed again and again by repeated "Databegin slides" commands throughout the body of the script. Each time "Databegin slides" is issued, GRASP looks for the word slides with a colon (slides:).

```
slides:
```

The colon is important. If you forget, and add the colon when using a label as a parameter in a command (that is, databegin slides:), GRASP won't find the label and will generate an error message. You can have a maximum of 512 labels in a GRASP program.

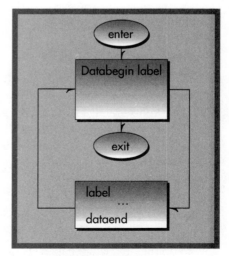

Figure 3-6 Accessing an external slide list

Using Labels for Program Flow

We saw earlier that looping is one way to alter the flow of a script. Labels are another way. When GRASP branches to a label, there is an abrupt change in the order of the execution of commands. Instead of proceeding to the next line, GRASP jumps to the point indicated in the script by the label. It will read the data list until it reaches the Dataend statement. It will then return to the jumping off point, where it will read the next command.

Placing sections of code outside of normal flow of the script is like storing a slide tray on a shelf where you can easily find it. Potentially, you could create several trays of slides and access them with labels. We'll be using labels extensively in *Multimedia Creations*. You'll see that they have a variety of uses.

Using When to Implement User Interaction

Let's explore another method of altering program execution. The user may decide to quit the slide presentation after viewing only one or two slides. It would be useful if GRASP watched for a special key like the (ESC) key, so that when you pressed it, GRASP would terminate the slide show immediately. By default, GRASP makes the (ESC) key a sudden exit to the editor (or the DOS environment, in the case of the commercial program). This is a rather rude way to treat the user. We'll need to implement a way to exit from the program gracefully.

The answer is GRASP's When command. It defines actions that will be performed when specified keys are pressed. This gives the user the ability to interact with the presentation. Let's add a When command to the projector script and then review the commands that allow us to assign actions to the (ESC) key:

```
; TMPFILE.TXT Software Slide Projector

video m

; Sets up special keys.
        set esc off                 ; turns off sudden dump to DOS/Editor
        when esc goto quit          ; jump to quit: label if Esc key  pressed
                                    ; more graceful exit

; The slide tray.
        databegin slides

; The projector and gate.
        mark 7
                pload @ p1
                palette p1
                pfade 9 p1 100
                pfree p1
                waitkey
        loop
```

```
; Turns the projector off.
quit:                                    ; jump to here if Esc key is pressed
        pfree p1                         ; free up buffer one
        when esc                         ; cancel "esc key" assignment
        exit

slides:
        slide001.pic slide002.pic slide003.pic slide004.pic
        slide005.pic slide006.pic black.pic
dataend
```

Press (F10) to save and run the script. Press the (ESC) key while the script is running. You are immediately returned to the editor. Note the "pfree p1" command just before exit. The Pfree command frees up memory (buffer 1) before exiting. This is good programming practice, and it becomes important in programs that link many scripts together. In these cases the return may not be to DOS or the editor, but to another script. Placing a Pfree command at the exit point ensures that picture buffers have been freed.

Changing System Settings

In our example the command "set esc off" turns off the default assignment for the (ESC) key, and the When command reassigns the action attached to the key to a branch to the label quit:.

```
set esc off
when esc goto quit
```

The "when esc goto quit" instruction says, "When the (ESC) key is pressed, jump to the label quit: and execute the commands following it (in this case, "pfree p1," "when esc" and then "exit").

The form of the When command is:

```
when key command (parameters)
```

"Key" is the key GRASP checks for constantly, even while the computer is doing other things. For a list of special keys and key combinations used with the When and Ifkey commands, press (F2) while in the GRASP editor and cycle to the last page. "Key Names" lists the valid keys and key combinations. The table is also included at the back of this book.

The When key assignment stays in effect while the program runs. The key assignment can be canceled at any time by issuing a When command without a key assignment. Here's the syntax:

```
when key command (parameters)       ;sets up key assignment
when key                            ;cancels key assignment
```

After the quit: label, we used a "when Esc" command to cancel (ESC)'s key assignment. This is not really necessary, but it's good programming practice. Explicitly unassigning keys that are no longer needed will save you many hours of debugging when the program becomes complex.

Creating a Remote Control Switch with Dataskip

Our electronic slide projector is missing something most people who use slide projectors cannot do without: the ability to back up to a previous slide with a remote-control switch.

When you press the reverse button on a slide projector or on a remote "pickle" switch three times, it backs up three positions and drops a new slide in the gate. We can implement this function in the projector script with the Dataskip command. The syntax is:

`dataskip number`

where the number can be positive (go forward) or negative (go back). Dataskip moves GRASP's internal pointer forward or back in the data list. One important caveat: You must ensure that Dataskip does not step beyond the boundaries of the list. Doing so will produce an error message. Figure 3-7 shows how the tray modeled in software compares to the Kodak tray.

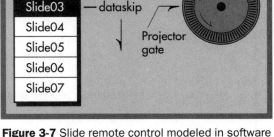

Figure 3-7 Slide remote control modeled in software

Remember that it is the *names* of slides that are stored in memory in GRASP, not the slides themselves. Think of the Dataskip command as a remote-control switch with forward and reverse buttons. Let's implement a backup key in the electronic slide projector using Dataskip.

```
; TMPFILE.TXT Software Slide Projector
video m

; Sets up  keys assignments.
        set esc off
        when esc goto quit

; The slide tray.
        databegin slides
```

```
; The slide projector and gate.
  display:                       ; new label
        pload @ p1
        palette p1
        pfade 9 p1 100
        pfree p1
        waitkey
        ifkey pgup backup1       ; Checks to see if Page Up key
                                 ; was pressed during last wait,
                                 ; jumps to backup1 label if so.

        goto display             ; Forces jump back to display: label.

; Backs the tray up one slide.
 backup1:
        dataskip -2              ; moves tray back
        goto display             ; jumps back to display: label


; Turns the projector off.
quit:
        pfree p1
        when esc
        exit

slides:
        slide001.pic slide002.pic slide003.pic slide004.pic
        slide005.pic slide006.pic black.pic
dataend
```

Remember that when the @ symbol reads an item from the data list, GRASP's internal pointer automatically moves forward to the next item in the list. We need to use "dataskip -2" to move back to the previous slide, because the pointer is presently pointing to the next slide. If we had entered `dataskip -1,` it would have moved the pointer back to the slide now on the screen. The slide now on screen would be displayed again.

How did GRASP know that the user wanted to back up one slide?

Backing Up with Ifkey

The command we used to create the back up key is called Ifkey. The Ifkey command is similar to the When command. The When command continues looking for a keypress until it is turned off, the Ifkey command only looks for the specified key during the last Waitkey. Syntax for the command is as follows.

```
ifkey key [label] [key label] ...
```

"Key" is the key or key combination to check for. If a label is supplied, GRASP will branch to the label specified elsewhere in the program. If a label is not specified, Ifkey works like a conditional If programming statement. We'll be studying conditional Ifs in a moment. The concept can be illustrated by a logic flow diagram. Figure 3-8 shows how an Ifkey command is processed.

When GRASP encounters the Ifkey command just after a Waitkey, it tests the key the user the presses to see if it is the specified key. If the user did press the specified key (true), a branch is made to a label. If the user pressed any other key (false), the branch to the label is not made and execution continues with the command following the Ifkey command.

GRASP will only check for lowercase keys or key combinations. To force GRASP to check for only uppercase letters, use quotation marks around the letter.

`ifkey "L" [label]`

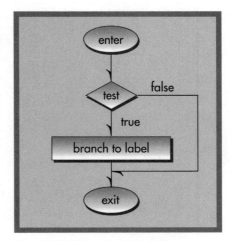

Figure 3-8 Operation of an Ifkey command

When building multimedia applications with user interaction, Ifkey is a much less troublesome implementation of user interaction than the When key. When you are creating the script, you never know at what point during the running of the script the user will press the key assigned to a When action. Once sound, animation, and user interaction are implemented, the parameters of the situation can become highly complex. Use Ifkey in place of When as much as possible.

Ifkey uses the same key assignments as the When command. Use the (F2) key in the GRASP editor to cycle to the table where those keys are listed.

Branching with Goto

Look at the Goto command that follows the Dataskip command in the script. The Goto instruction causes execution to jump back to the display: label. It replaces the original Mark/Loop combination (which cycled seven times) with an endless loop. Without the Goto instruction (goto display:), there would be nothing preventing GRASP from simply resetting the pointer to the previous slide, then abruptly exiting! Test this by temporarily placing a semicolon in front of the Goto instruction.

Implementing a back up key in the electronic slide projector has created some problems that you may have already discovered if you've been playing with the script. In the main body of the script, we used Goto to effect another change. We replaced "mark 7" with the label "display:" and replaced the loop command with a Goto command. This created a loop that endlessly cycles until the (ESC) key is

Figure 3-9 Variables as storage lockers

pressed. The reason? The Dataskip command has created a problem with the original design. Now that we can back up and go forward in our electronic slide tray endlessly, the original loop count (mark 7) no longer applies. That is, GRASP thinks backing up is just another run through the loop. Not only that: If you've tried running the script, you will notice that GRASP generates an error message if you try to back up past the first slide or go past the last slide.

What is happening? The original mark7/loop combination allowed us to read through the seven items on the list and then exit. But the endlessly looping routine we've created in its place doesn't know when to stop and attempts to read beyond the list. The solution to this problem lies in the next section.

Using Variables and Expressions

We need to find a way to prevent the user from backing up past the first slide and from going past the last slide. But when we write the script, we don't know where the user is going to be at any given moment in our slide presentation! Fortunately, GRASP's use of programming conventions bails us out!

GRASP, like most programming languages, allows us to create a *variable*—a temporary storage area in memory in which we can store computational results.

Think of a variable as the locker you were assigned at your sports club. The contents of your locker is variable because you're always removing and replacing items in it. Your locker has a certain numeric address within all the lockers of the club. You put your name on it (Sam) to make it easier to find. Your friend Maria has a storage locker that also has an address permanently assigned to it by the club filing system: x1369. However, it's harder to remember numbers than names, so she too put her name on her locker. *Variable names* give computer memory addresses symbolic names humans can remember. Figure 3-9 will help you visualize this method of storing information.

If we create a variable called gate and use it to keep track of our position in the slide tray, we will solve the problem of determining where we are in the presentation. We can give gate a starting value of 0 (the 0 position on a slide tray when it is first placed on a projector), and then use simple arithmetic to keep track of its position. Whenever we go forward, we just add one to our gate total. The pseudocode would look like this:

- Set the gate position initially at 0.
- Move ahead 1 by adding one to the gate position.

Translated into GRASP coding this becomes:

- `set gate 0`
- `set gate @gate+1`

Just like the gate of a real projector, our variable gate points to the current tray position. We are saying, in effect, let the value stored at memory location gate represent the tray position. There is no space between the @ symbol and variable gate.

WARNING: GOTO NO-NO!

Goto causes execution to jump abruptly to another area of code. The command has earned a bad reputation among programmers because its indiscriminate use can lead to much-dreaded "spaghetti code." This is unreadable code that resembles a bowl of spaghetti with long, entangled strands that start nowhere in particular and end nowhere in particular.

GRASP does use—and to some extent encourages—the use of Goto. Use Goto sparingly. Later we'll introduce you to a command much more acceptable to veteran programmers: gosub. Gosub causes program execution to temporarily continue at another point in the script. Once those commands are processed, execution returns.

On its own, the @ symbol is used in conjunction with the data command to sequentially access a list of data items. Used without a space following it, the symbol notifies GRASP that what follows is the name of a variable. @ is similar to the indirect operator * in C.

The @ sign tells GRASP to give us the value stored at an address in memory, and the address is the name of the variable. If you look at Figure 3-9 again, you will see what we mean. A friend of Maria wants you to bring her something from Maria's locker. She says bring the tennis racket in Maria's locker (@maria). The memory address of Maria's locker is x1369, but it's only used by the club to keep track of all the lockers in the club. The symbolic name that Maria and her friends use is "Maria." And the way of retrieving the contents of the locker is to use the expression @maria. It's a little difficult to think in programming terms, but once you understand it, magic gives way to science.

Once we've created a variable for the gate position, we can manipulate and test it, just as if it really were the tray position number. It keeps score for us, subtracting the tray position when we back up and adding to the tray position when we step forward. Having the ability to store results of computations using variables makes GRASP a powerful tool for multimedia programming.

Defining Variables

GRASP uses a shorthand method for creating variables and using them in expressions. GRASP defines a variable with the following syntax:

```
set name (value)
```

where *name* is the symbolic name of the variable. Value can be a character string, expression, or another variable. (Later we'll explore Local and Global variables, necessary for complex programs. Set can alter an existing local or global variable, but it can only define a local variable.) In the example above, setting the gate at the original tray position is done in the following fashion:

```
set gate 0
```

This defines the variable gate and sets its initial value at 0.

We've defined the variable, now how do we use it?

Using Expressions to Change Variables

GRASP has a special syntax associated with operations performed on variables. Operations performed on variables are called *expressions*. You can perform simple arithmetic:

```
set gate 0
set gate @gate+1
```

This is how we change the value of a variable. As we just noted, we are telling the computer to add 1 to the value that is currently stored in memory location @gate. How does GRASP analyze the second line and make sense of it?

First of all, GRASP reads the line from left to right. It sees the word "set" and knows that it is a command because it finds the word Set in its list of words reserved for commands. GRASP looks at the word following set and knows that you are defining (or in this case, re-defining) a variable. That's because the Set command, like all GRASP commands, has a strict syntax you must follow religiously. GRASP then looks at the last series of letters (@gate+1) and "knows" how to process the expression it finds there into a new value for @gate. Figure 3-10 shows the different elements of the expression.

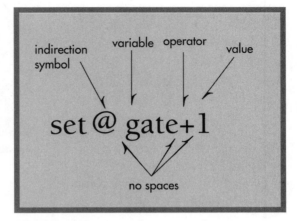

Figure 3-10 Elements of an expression

GRASP sees the @ symbol and the + symbol and knows they are special symbols, called operators. GRASP sees the word gate and knows that it is the name of a variable because you have previously defined it as such. It looks at the memory location @gate, takes the value there, 0, and adds it to 1. It uses the operator + to do this. Note the spacing of characters in an expression. Spaces are very important. There is no space between a variable name, the operator, and the value.

A thorough discussion of variables and expressions is outside the scope of this book. GRASP's implementation of programming conventions is fairly standard, so any good introductory programming book will help you become a GRASP power user. The Waite Group's *Master C++* is an excellent interactive learning environment for the novice.

A list of valid operators can be found while in GRASP's editor by cycling through the (F2) help screens to the page titled "Operators Listing." They include arithmetic operations like multiplication, division, addition, and subtraction.

Using Relational Operators for Evaluation

Now that we have a way to keep track of our tray position, how can we use this knowledge to prevent our user from advancing beyond tray position 80 or backing up past tray position 0?

We can test the variable @gate to see if it is out of bounds. In a presentation that uses 80 slides, the 81st click on the remote-control switch would send us out of bounds. The expression @gate>80 compares the value of gate to 80. It can be used in a expression like this:

```
if @gate>80 error
```

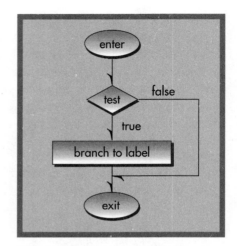

This statement says, "If the current value of @gate is greater than 80 (i.e., exceeds tray position 80), then the expression is true, and script execution will jump to a label called error: below. If the current value of @gate is 80 or less, than the expression is false, the expression will be ignored, and execution will continue at the following command.

Figure 3-11 If command logic flow

Implementing User Interaction with If

Remember the logic flow diagram we created earlier for the Ifkey command? The logic flow diagram for If commands is similar. Figure 3-11 presents the logic flow of If commands.

Instead of testing for a key, an expression is evaluated by GRASP. GRASP branches according to whether the expression evaluates to true or false. The syntax for the If command is:

```
if expression label
```

The If command is an important way to implement user interaction and change the flow of the script.

These kinds of comparisons, where a statement is evaluated to true or false, are standard in most programming languages. A list of GRASP's relational operators can be found in the same place as the arithmetic operators (press (F2) and (PGDN) to the listings).

Let's see how variables and expressions work in practice by using them to solve the problem we encountered earlier. Here's the entire script.

```
; TMPFILE.TXT Software Slide Projector

video m

; Sets up variables.
```

```
        set gate 0                    ; tray position counter set initially at  0
        set total 7                   ; set the maximum number of slides at 7

; Sets up key assignments.
        set esc off
        when esc goto quit

; The slide tray.
        databegin slides

; The slide projector and gate.
display:
        pload @ p1                    ;loads first slide
        palette p1
        pfade 9  p1 100               ;displays first slide
        pfree p1
        set gate @gate+1              ;increments tray position counter
        if @gate>=@total recycle      ;recycle: if last tray position reached
        text 1,1 @gate                ;displays tray position on screen
        waitkey
        ifkey pgup backup1
goto display

; Cycles tray back to position 0.
    recycle:
        text 20 1 "Last slide of "$@total     ;Message to user on screen
        waitkey 200
        ifkey pgup backup1
        set gate 0                    ;resets tray position
        databegin slides              ;read from beginning of slide list
        goto display

; Backs up one slide.
backup1:
        dataskip -2
        set gate @gate-2              ;resets tray position to previous slide
        if @gate<=-1 error1           ;goto error1 you back up past slide one
        goto display

; User tried to back up past one (error sub-routine).
    error1:
        text 15,1 "First Slide"       ;on-screen message to user
        waitkey 200                   ;wait 2 secs to see if pgup pressed
        ifkey pgup lastslid           ;jump to lastslid: if pgup pressed
        set gate @gate+1              ;resets tray position to first slide
        dataskip 1                    ;points to first slide
        goto display                  ;jump back and display first slide again

; Backs up tray past 0 to last slide in presentation.
lastslid:
        dataskip @total               ;skips to last slide
        set gate @total-1             ;sets tray position to last slide
        goto display                  ;jump back and display this slide

quit:
        pfree p1
```

```
        when esc
        exit

slides:
        slide001.pic slide002.pic slide003.pic slide004.pic
        slide005.pic slide006.pic black.pic
dataend
```

In the first section of the script, we define two variables: one that sets our tray position at 0 (set gate 0), and another that defines the total number of slides in our presentation, in other words, the limit for tray positions (set total 7).

The tray position is not updated (set gate @gate+1) until after we load and display our first slide, that's why it is initially set at 0. That makes sense, because when you advance a slide projector tray from 0 to the first tray position, that counts as "one." And the "one" corresponds to the first tray position.

Setting up the @total variable ("set total 7") is a good use of GRASP's programming resources. Wherever GRASP sees the "@total" symbol in the script, it will replace the symbol with the number 7. This makes changing the size of our slide tray, to exactly match the number of slides in our presentation, very easy. Otherwise we would have to manually go through the presentation, changing the total number each time it is used. Also, we can perform arithmetic operations on @total. For example, the expression @total-1 is a way of referring to the second to last tray position.

We use both variables in the main body of the slide projector. The expression

```
if @gate>=@total recycle
```

says, "If the present value of @gate exceeds or is equal to the value of @total, then jump to the label called recycle:, if not, ignore this line." The variable @gate allows us to keep track of where we are in the presentation as we go through the loop in the labeled display: section. The expression gives us a way of preventing the user from going beyond the last tray position in the presentation.

Using Databegin to Reset the Slide Tray

When the user reaches the last slide, we put a message on the screen announcing this fact. Here's the segment of code again.

```
; User tried to back up past one (error sub-routine).
   error1:
        text 15,1 "First Slide"        ;on-screen message to user
        waitkey 200                    ;wait 2 secs to see if pgup pressed
        ifkey pgup lastslid            ;jump to lastslid: if pgup pressed
        set gate @gate+1               ;resets tray position to first slide
        dataskip 1                     ;points to first slide
        goto display                   ;jump back and display first slide again
```

Figure 3-12 Screen coordinates on a VGA screen

We wait to see if the user still wants to back up or go forward. If the user goes forward, we reset the entire presentation back to its original starting position by issuing the Databegin command once again. We reset GRASP's Dataskip pointer to the first slide in the "tray." We also reset the tray position to its original value of 0.

Displaying Text on the Screen

The message "Last Slide of 7" is displayed using GRASP's text command. (We will explore this command in detail in the next chapter.) The text command's syntax is:

```
text [x,y] string [delay]
```

Text puts a string (series of characters) on the screen at the specified screen location. If you do not specify an x,y (horizontal, vertical) position for text to appear on the screen, the default position is in the top left corner of the screen or a window. (The Window command will be introduced later.) Figure 3-12 shows a computer monitor, with the dimensions of the screen indicated. The coordinates describe VGA's 640x480 pixel resolution.

The command "text 1,1" places text at the bottom left of the screen, one pixel to the right (x = 1) and one pixel up (y = 1). (Because computers count 0 as the first number in a series, text 0,0 places the text at the origin point, the left bottom corner of the screen.) The command "text 639,479" would place text at the absolute top right corner of the screen. You will get an error message if you try to place text at the 640,480 coordinates, because 640 is actually the six hundred and forty-first pixel and 480 is the four hundred and eighty-first pixel.

If you have previously issued a Text command, text will begin where the last text left off. The optional delay parameter specifies how fast text will "write" on the screen. (The default is instant display.) Specifying where you want the text to appear on the screen is also optional.

The text that will be displayed on the screen is enclosed in quotation marks. If you leave out either of the quotation marks, GRASP will become confused. The quotation marks define the boundaries where text is contained, much as the Databegin and Dataend commands bracketed the slide list in our earlier example.

Using Concatenation

The dollar sign ($) that immediately follows the second quotation mark and immediately precedes the @total variable is useful for stringing text together for display:

```
text 1,1 "Last slide of "$@total
```

The $ symbol also helps display non-text information, such as the value assigned to a variable. If you placed the @total variable within the quotation marks, GRASP would not print the value of @total on the screen. Rather, GRASP would treat @total as a text string. Move the quotation mark to the end of the line to test this.

```
text 1,1 "Last slide of $@total"
```

This will write on the screen:

```
Last slide of @total
```

The text command gives us a valuable way of communicating information to the user. We use it to show the viewer a running total of the slides. In the display section of the script the line

```
text 20 1 "Last slide of "$@total
```

displays the current tray position (and indirectly, slide number) on the screen. GRASP displays the value of the variable on the screen.

BUILDING A DELUXE MODEL SLIDE PROJECTOR

The computer has been called a "universal machine" because it is endlessly malleable and it uses "software" to model and implement an increasing array of mechanical functions. In this chapter we've shown how to build a slide projector in software that has most of the functions a generation of presenters have come to expect using the venerable Kodak Carousel slide projector.

We didn't want to bury you in code in your first GRASP programming lesson, so we kept the software slide projector relatively simple. However, if you are feeling confident and adventurous, load the file PROJECTO.TXT into the GRASP editor and run it. We've built a more sophisticated software projector in this script. It has features such as:

- an adjustable dissolve rate, using the up and down arrow keys
- a selection of fades assigned to the numeric key pads

Using the commercial version of GRASP, you will be able to compile this file into a single executable program called PROJECTO.EXE. This hides the mechanical innards of our software projector. You need to create a file external to PROJECTO.EXE called SLIDES.TXT that contains the list of slides included in the presentation, and other information, such as the size of the tray (total number of slides in the presentation) and the types of GRASP fades you want to use. (We show you one way to do this in SLIDES.TXT.) You can edit this file with DOS 5's editor, or any word processor that saves in DOS "text" or ASCII format. This makes the software slide projector more "portable" and less confusing to use for the non-GRASP user.

By the time you finish working through *Multimedia Creations,* you will have gained enough knowledge and experience to build an even more elaborate electronic presentation system, with animation, sound, and built-in control over external devices.

Flexibility. Sophisticated control over the audiovisual elements of your presentation. That's the power of building your own multimedia creations.

4
Creating a Software Magazine

THE METAPHOR of a magazine is an ideal way to present audiovisual information in a form users will recognize and intuitively understand. When you read a book, you've settled in for a long, slow read. But a magazine is a different animal.

When you pick up a new magazine, you're in a hurry. You look at the title and examine the cover. You make some judgments about the magazine's content from the colors, layout, and visual messages you find there. You open the magazine and flip through it (usually from the back!), then you turn to the table of contents. You browse. You flip to an article that interests you, and you read the

---

PEEKING AHEAD

The scripts MAGAZINE.TXT and ROMEMENU.TXT in the CHAPT04 subdirectory contain the code for the exercises in this chapter. Run MAGAZINE.TXT from the GRASP editor. ROMEMENU.TXT is linked to MAGAZINE.TXT. Both scripts use font and sound files that are located in the \GRASP subdirectory, so make sure you have made GRASP a subdirectory of the root directory. During exercises, if you find your code produces errors, compare your work with the code in these two files.

---

opening paragraph. This is where a good magazine will attempt to catch your attention with a great "teaser" or a striking visual image. Now you're hooked—you're really reading the magazine.

The essence of the design for the software magazine is that it should make information quickly and easily available for harried users. Ideally, it should use motion footage as well as stills. (GRASP supports interfaces to boards that put video on the screen.)

This chapter will show you how to build a software magazine with a mouse-driven graphical interface using the tools GRASP provides. The interface, with minor modifications, can be used in your own work. It's a travel magazine. We're going to use scans from photographs the author shot in Rome to illustrate a quick tour through Rome. Got your passport? Let's go on the Rome Treasure Tour!

CREATING THE COVER

The cover for our software magazine is the first image seen by the viewer. Let's give the cover a rich look, with a textured background for titles and pictures. We've already manufactured the background for you. Make sure you have GRASP's DOS environment variable set so that GRASP can find its program files. Change into the CHAPT04 subdirectory in the main GRASP directory.

```
cd \GRASP\CHAPT04
```

Now type `graspc`. Once the GRASP menu appears, type `Enter`. You are automatically placed in the editor with the default TMPFILE.TXT file active. Now type in the following lines:

```
; TMPFILE.TXT Software Magazine

video m

; background image
        pload romeback.pic p1
```

```
palette p1
pfade 13 p1 200
pfree p1
```

```
waitkey
```

Check your typing! Then press (F10). The cover background wipes on the screen from the top and bottom simultaneously. This will be the background for the cover and the subsequent menu page. The image originated from a photograph of a granite rock face. The scan of the photograph was imported into Aldus's image processing program, Photostyler, and the *contour trace tool* was used to give it the blocky, pixelated look that is vaguely reminiscent of an aerial shot of a city. The image was then texture-mapped onto a surface in Autodesk's 3D Studio. A light was shone on the top left corner to give the "surface" a dimensional feel.

The textured feel of the image is accomplished by using a variety of grays. The glossy magazine we want to produce is going to use only 16 colors! Designing a palette for a program that uses only 16 colors is quite a challenge. Let's see what tools GRASP and its companion paint program, Pictor, provide to the artist interested in image magic.

Examining the Palette in Pictor

Let's load the background image into Pictor, GRASP's paint program, to learn how to manipulate the palette. Exit from the editor by pressing (ESC) twice. Change into the

WORKING WITH THE HIGHEST RESOLUTION

The cover photograph was scanned in 16 million colors and the resulting scan was processed in Photostyler using 16 million colors. The general rule in any kind of production, whether video, slides, or multimedia, is to capture the original images in the highest resolution possible. The Mode M image you see on the screen retains much of the visual richness of the original image. This would not have been true if the image was captured and processed with 16 colors instead of 16 million. You can easily remove "information" from a picture, but once it's gone, it cannot be re-created.

You don't need to invest in a color scanner and 3D software to create interesting backgrounds for images. Look in the back of Integrated Media's *Publish* magazine, available in computer stores and bookstores that have a large computer book section. You'll see ads from companies that sell scanned images or backgrounds, such as Artbeats in San Bernadino, California. Or create your own images with any of the paint packages that include tools like airbrushes and fills.

GRASP subdirectory (cd \GRASP). Type pictor at the DOS prompt. Select Mode M. Your screen should look like Figure 4-1.

When you first enter Pictor, you'll see a blank white screen and a default palette arranged in a vertical row of colored boxes on the right side of the screen. A *palette* is a table of colors used by the computer system to paint the screen, much as artists use a palette to hold the colors they need to paint a scene on a canvas. Since there is no picture currently loaded into Pictor, the program uses a default palette composed of greens, blues, reds, white, and black. Each colored square is called a *palette slot*. In the case of Video M (standard VGA), there are 16 palette slots. Because computers begin counting at 0, the palette slots are numbered from 0 to 15. As you can see in Figure 4-1, palette slot 0 (black) is the color at the bottom of the row of colors. Palette slot 15 (white) is at the top.

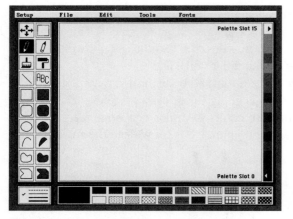

Figure 4-1 Pictor's viewport and palette

Now load ROMEBACK.PIC into Pictor. Since you ran Pictor from the GRASP main directory, you'll have to change into the subdirectory where ROMEBACK.PIC is located. Begin by pressing the letter (l) (small l for load). A dialogue box pops up on screen. Click on CHAPT04, the subdirectory where ROME-BACK.PIC is located. Notice that the line at the top of the dialogue box changes to indicate that we are now in the CHAPT04 subdirectory. Click on ROMEBACK.PIC in the File dialogue box. Then click on Load.

The background image loads into the viewport. Notice that the palette has changed: The default palette has been replaced by the palette stored with ROME-BACK.PIC. Again there are 16 colors, the limit for this VGA video mode. This palette has a graduated series of grays, ranging from the black background color in the bottom palette slot to a light gray in the tenth palette slot. Above that there are six more pastel colors.

Only 16 Colors

In this book we focus on the VGA standard color mode, 640x480, 16 colors, because it is the lowest common denominator for the target audience we identified for this book, and for demos that are distributed widely to business computer users. If

COMMON VIDEO MODES

The most common video modes you will use in a GRASP program include the following.

Video Mode	Resolution
0	40-column text
1	80-column color text
2	80-column mono text
A	320x200 4-color CGA
G	640x350 16-color EGA (16 displayed from 64)
I	640x350 16-color VGA (16 displayed from 256,000)
L	320x200 256-color VGA (256 from 256,000)
M	640x480 16-color VGA (16 from 256,000)
S	640x480 256-color VGA (256 from 256,000)

Note that some modes display a limited amount of color from a much
larger palette. These are the *analog* VGA video modes. The basic architecture of VGA cards potentially supports unlimited colors. It's the
specific manufacturer's card and the amount of video memory installed on it that limits displayable colors. For example, a VGA card
with only 256K video ram installed on it can only display 16 colors
from a palette of 256,000 at 640x480 resolution. If the same card is
upgraded to 512K video ram, 256 colors at the same pixel resolution
can then be displayed. VGA video adapters produce analog output.
That is, the screen pixels are produced by electronic pulses that vary
in intensity. EGA adapters, on the other hand, produce electronic pulses that are either off or on. That's why VGA systems can potentially
display an unlimited amount of colors, while EGA video display systems produce a maximum of 64 colors.

The last video mode, Video S, is only available with the commercial
version of GRASP. Sierra Semiconductor's Hicolor mode (640x480,
32,768 colors) is also supported by the commercial version of GRASP.

you have installed 512K memory on a super VGA card, then you are capable of displaying 256 colors at 640x480 pixel resolution. After squeezing image processing
activity through a narrow range of 16 colors, 256 colors is a luxury! The high-resolution 256-color modes can also display images approaching photo realism.

There is always a trade-off, though, when selecting more colors and higher
pixel resolutions: File size increases dramatically. For example, the 16-color
ROMEBACK.PIC image is 90K in size. At 256 colors it is 356K. At 16 million colors (the original full color scan), the file is close to 1 megabyte in size. Most profes-

sional demos that must be distributed on disk by mail are created in the VGA mode used in this book: 640x480, 16 colors. Fixed installations and trade show programs are created at higher resolutions. Even these shows will use the video adapter's reduced color modes to achieve fast animation speeds. Being able to change video modes at run time is a GRASP advantage!

Working with a Show Palette

When you are preparing a sequence of visuals, making a decision about how the show's picture palettes will be treated should be high on your project's list. You can work with a variety of palettes, even a different palette for each picture. However, if two pictures in a sequence use different palettes, setting the palette each time a picture changes will cause a momentary flash as the second picture's colors are reset. If the first picture has blue in palette slot 10 and the second picture has yellow in slot 10, all the yellow areas in the second picture will be blue until the palette is reset. You can avoid this problem by inserting a black picture between color images. This works well in EGA modes. A little later we'll show you an even better method for VGA modes.

Creating a Blank, Black Image

Let's create a new blank, black picture for this purpose and save it as BLACK.PIC. To do that, click on the black palette slot 0 with the right mouse button. This sets the foreground color to black, the color we want the screen to become. Now click on the File menu and choose New. A dialogue screen pops up. Click on Accept. A blank, black image is created. Now save the file by pressing Ⓢ (for save), clicking on the white text entry box, and typing `black.pic` at the prompt. Click on Save.

Because all the pixels in BLACK.PIC have been set to palette slot 0 (black), you won't see a color flash when you dissolve from a color image to the black image. That's because there are no pixels on the new screen that have been assigned the other palette colors. There is a caveat, however: The two images that are fading one after another must both use black in palette slot 0! It's always a good idea to reserve black for slot 0. Similarly, it's also a good idea to reserve slot 15, the last slot, for pure white, a favorite choice for text and graphic highlights. But how do we alter palettes that have a color other than black in palette slot 0?

Manipulating the Palette

Let's change the palette. Choose Change Colors from the Tools menu in Pictor. A dialogue box pops on the screen. It should look like Figure 4-2.

The Change Colors dialogue box provides the tools for altering the palette. Notice the two vertical columns used for setting the R G B I (Red, Green, Blue,

Intensity) values. These are "sample swatches" that show the effect of manipulating the RGBI values. The left sample swatch corresponds to the left mouse button and the right sample swatch corresponds to the right mouse button. Try clicking on the palette below the swatches with the right and left mouse buttons. The colors represented by the two swatches change. By altering the red, green, blue, and intensity levels of each color in the palette, you can create a 16-color palette from the 256,000 available colors using a VGA card (or 64 colors using an EGA card). Play with the palette colors by altering the RGB and intensity values in the two sample swatches in the Change Colors menu. Notice how the colors of the Pictor main screen and the background image change as you change the colors of the swatches. You can cancel these changes by clicking on Reset or Cancel.

Let's experiment with a few more of the Change Colors menu options. Press Cancel. Let's swap the colors associated with the foreground and the background of a picture. Click on palette slots 0 and 15 with the right and left mouse keys. Choose Swap from the Change Colors dialogue box. The colors trade places. Let's now try altering a range of colors. Click on Spread. A spread of grays is created between the two colors. Click on Default to reset the palette to the default colors for this video mode.

Using the Edit Menu

You can also use the Edit menu at the top of the Pictor screen when altering palettes. For example, you can select a range of colors to copy to the palette clipboard, then

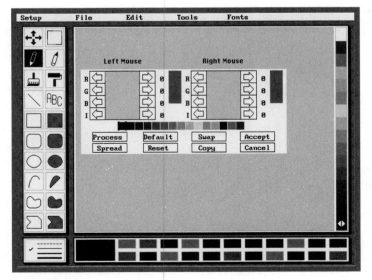

Figure 4-2 Pictor's Change Colors dialogue box

paste them back into the palette at a different location. Select a range of colors by clicking on the palette with the right and left mouse buttons. This places brackets around the selected range. (The left mouse button places a left bracket and the right mouse button places a right bracket.) Once you've selected a range of colors, select the Edit menu and click on Copy. This copies the range of colors you bracketed into the clipboard.

The Change Colors clipboard remains active between pictures. You can copy part of a palette from one picture into the clipboard, load a second picture into Pictor, and paste the colors from the first image's palette into the new picture's palette. Pictor gives you excellent palette editing tools.

Using Gray in Palettes

The background we prepared for the Rome Treasure Tour was created in Pictor's Change Colors dialogue box using the techniques we've just outlined. The range of ten grays provides just enough subtlety in the background to give the image a rich look. We'll be using the gray shades for highlights and shadows as well. Gray is one of the best colors to use in conjunction with other colors because of its neutrality—almost any color will go with it.

Palette Manipulation in GRASP

Let's exit from Pictor and use what we've learned so far. Use (ALT)-(Q) or (CONTROL)-(C) to exit Pictor. Change back into the CHAPT04 subdirectory.

```
cd CHAPT04
```

Type graspc. Press (ENTER) to accept TMPFILE as the default file in the editor. Your screen should look like this:

```
video m

; background image
        pload romeback.pic p1
        palette p1
        pfade 13 p1 200
        pfree p1

waitkey
```

Now fade from ROMEBACK.PIC to BLACK.PIC using fade 5.

```
; TMPFILE.TXT Software Magazine

video m

; Background
```

```
        pload romeback.pic p1
        palette p1
        pfade 13 p1 200
        pfree p1
        waitkey 200

; Transition to blank image
        pload black.pic p1
        pfade 5 p1 200
        pfree p1
exit
```

When you press (F10), there is a 2-second filter fade to the background image. Two seconds later the image filter fades back to black. (We're describing fades in GRASP terms. The (F3) help key lists fades and their definitions.)

Opening and Closing the Software Magazine

We've now created the textured surface over which images will be placed. The gray patterned background is an analog of the paper stock used for glossy magazines. It gives our magazine a rich feel and distinctive character. Let's see if we can improve the way the magazine is opened and closed. Opening a magazine is equivalent to *fading up* our magazine background from black. Closing the magazine is the reverse, *fading down*. These are cinematic terms referring to the practice of increasing an image's brightness from dark to light (fading up) or from full brightness to darkness (fading down).

EGA VERSUS VGA COLORS

The EGA video card's digital 16-color mode draws from a palette of only 64 colors. On the other hand, analog VGA modes can draw from a palette of 256,000 colors. Even though an EGA and a VGA card may have the same pixel resolution (640x480), the color effects you can produce with VGA cards are much more sophisticated than that of the EGA. EGA provides the artist with only two shades of gray along with black and white, so our background would look impoverished on an EGA display system. Color reducing the image with an image processing program like Paint Shop Pro would allow us to simulate grays through dithering, a process where closely spaced clusters of a few colors fool the eye into seeing more colors than exist in the image. However, the limited pixel resolution of EGA systems do not produce entirely satisfactory results. Images with a subtle tonal range displayed on a VGA display system always look better than the same images displayed on an EGA system.

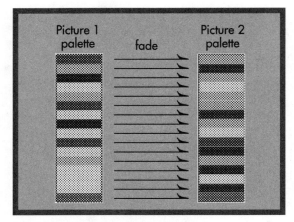

Figure 4-3 The Spread command

We can take advantage of the VGA's greater palette range to simulate a cinematic technique, the gradual fade to black. GRASP has a command called Spread that allows you to gradually change the palette colors from one picture to the next. Figure 4-3 is a conceptual drawing of the process of fading from one picture to another. The columns represent the palettes from two pictures. Notice that each individual palette slot is gradually converted to a corresponding palette slot in a second picture.

If the first picture had black in all its palette slots, then we would be able to create a gradual fade up from those blacks to the colors of the second picture. How do we create a picture with an entirely black palette? We can't create this black palette picture in Pictor, because as soon as we change all the palette colors to black, the screen will black out completely. We need to see the Save menu in order to click on the options for saving. So we can't use Pictor to create an all-black palette. We can, however, use GRASP.

Creating Pictures with GRASP

We can use GRASP to manufacture a picture and save it to disk. What we want to do is create a little utility program that will do the following:

- Set up the video mode as Video M.
- Use a command that changes the system palette to the colors we want.
- Save the screen (with its palette) to a buffer.
- Save the buffer to disk.
- Use the picture's palette in another program.

Figure 4-4 shows you a conceptual drawing of how the commands work.

As you can see, the process of manufacturing an image in GRASP is the reverse of loading an image into GRASP. Let's start by looking at the command that will alter the palette first.

Using Setcolor to Change the Palette

GRASP has a command that directly manipulates the system palette, the Setcolor command. The command Setcolor can only be used in Video M or other 16 color EGA modes. Syntax for the command is:

```
setcolor val0 val1. val2. ... val15
```

All 16 colors must be specified. (Remember that the computer counts from 0 to 15, treating 0 as the first number and 15 as the sixteenth.) The color index values you specify for each of the sixteen palette slots can be any one of the 64 EGA colors. You can find the index values for EGA colors in Pictor's Change Colors pop-up menu. (You don't have to enter Pictor right now. Just consult Figure 4-4.) Choose an EGA-only mode, like Video G, when entering Pictor to do this. When you pop up the Change Colors menu, the screen will look like Figure 4-5.

The color values are shown under the large sample swatches. The white swatch on the right has an index value of 63, and the swatch on the left has a value of 7.

In this case we will assign black to all the palette slots. Black has an EGA index color of 0. We use this index to convert all 16 palette slots to black.

```
setcolor 0 0 0 0 0 0 0 0 0 0 0 0 0 0 0 0    ; sets all palette slots to black
```

Now that we have changed the palette, let's look at the command that will save the screen to a buffer.

Saving the Screen to a Buffer with Pgetbuf

GRASP allows you to save the current screen to a buffer in memory, and then to the disk. The Pgetbuf/Psave command sequence is the reverse of the command sequence that loads images (Pload/Pfade). The Pgetbuf command saves the current screen to a buffer in memory. Pgetbuf's syntax is:

```
pgetbuf buffer [x1,y1 x2,y2]
```

This saves the current screen to a specified buffer. The optional coordinates allow you to save only part of the screen to a buffer. As you will see again and again, Pgetbuf is an invaluable tool in GRASP development, especially when it is combined with the Psave command. During GRASP development it allows you to build up screens using GRASP commands that can be saved to disk and further processed in Pictor.

Using Psave to Save a Buffer to Disk

Once the screen contents have been saved to a buffer in

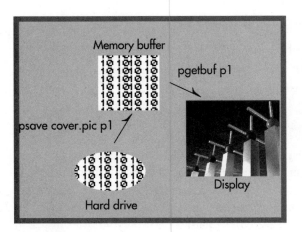

Figure 4-4 Manufacturing an image in GRASP.

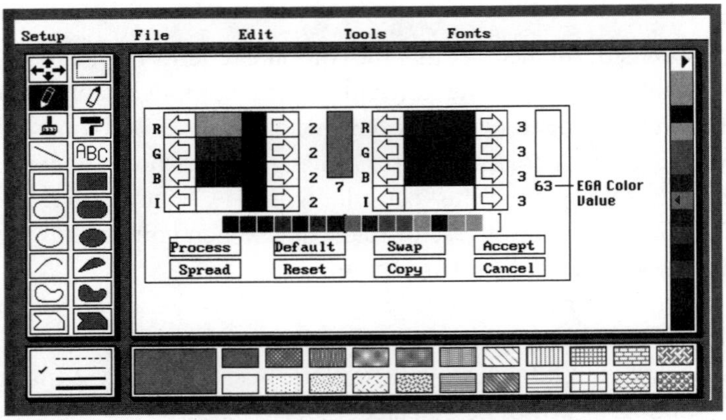

Figure 4-5 EGA color indices displayed in Pictor

memory, we can save that buffer to a disk file. The command Psave saves the contents of the specified buffer to the hard disk. The syntax is:

```
psave name [buffer]
```

Note that you have to include a file extension when you name the file to be saved. If you do not specify a buffer, GRASP will default to buffer 1. The technique for saving the screen to disk can be summarized in this way:

```
pgetbuf p1                   ; saves current screen to buffer 1
psave picture.pic p1         ; saves buffer 1 to disk
```

Now that we've reviewed the commands that will be used to create our all-black palette file, let's create it! (Press (ESC) to exit the editor. Create a new file called BLACK.TXT. Select Create from the File Menu. Type the following lines.)

```
; BLACK.TXT Temporary File for Creating a Black Palette Picture

video m 8,8                       ; sets picture size to 8x8

setcolor 0 0 0 0 0 0 0 0 0 0 0 0 0 0 0 0 ; sets all palette slots to black
pgetbuf p1                        ; saves screen to buffer 1
psave blackpic.pal p1             ; saves buffer 1 to disk
pfree p1

exit
```

When you press (F10), the image is almost instantly created. It's only 8 by 8 pixels, since we used the optional parameter of the Video command to set our screen size to that size. We saved the file with a .PAL extension (for palette). It's an arbitrary naming convention, there to remind us that the file is very small and used solely for its palette. The small 8x8 file we've saved to the hard drive is only 99 bytes in size. It occupies little space on the hard drive, and when we load it into memory, it will occupy little memory in the 640K area of conventional memory. We don't actually fade BLACKPIC.PAL to screen. We load it so we can use the palette attached to it.

Creating the Fade Up from Black

We've just created a picture called BLACKPIC.PAL that has a totally black palette. We're going to use the Spread command to gradually fade up the background image from black. We'll do this by first loading the all-black palette of BLACKPIC.PAL into buffer 1, and then loading ROMEBACK.PIC into buffer 2. Then we'll set the system palette to buffer 1, and fade ROMEBACK.PIC to the screen. Because the palette will be all black, all the pixels on the screen will be black, so we won't see ROME-BACK.PIC at first. We'll use Spread to gradually fade in ROMEBACK.PIC's palette. The black pixels on the screen will gradually change into color.

The Spread command's syntax is:

```
spread [pal1] pal2 [steps]
```

The command gradually alters one palette (pal1) to become another palette (pal2). If you don't specify a palette for pal1, the current palette will be used by default. The default value for the length of the fade (steps) is 64. Let's see how we use the command to fade the background from black to full color. Change TMPFILE.TXT to:

```
; TMPFILE.TXT Software Magazine

video m


; Fade up Background
        pload blackpic.pal p1        ; load palette file into buffer 1
        pload romeback.pic p2        ; load background into buffer 2
        palette p1                   ; set palette to buffer one (all black)
        pfade 0 p2                   ; fade picture to screen (can't see it)
        spread p1 p2 164             ; now reveal the picture by slowing
                                     ; changing to its palette

        waitkey 300

; Fade to Black

        spread 2 1 64                ; spread to all-black palette
        pfree p1 - p2                ; frees buffers 1 to 2, notice dash
        waitkey 100
exit
```

Press (F10) to start the script running. The background gradually fades up from black, holds for three seconds, and then fades down to black again quickly. We add a 1-second wait so that the return to the editor isn't abrupt. Notice that we used a dash to give pfree a range of picture buffers to free. When we free a series of slides (e.g., pfree p1 to p10), we will use this shorthand.

Flipping Pages with spread

The Spread command provides a very gradual fade from one image to another. It's an effect that gives your program a polished look and helps communicate transition points to viewers. We'll be using it a lot in this book. The gradual fade is a nice analog for the flipping of a magazine page. When we turn a page, we take a small mental break, and prepare ourselves for scanning a new page.

Now that we have put the background on the screen with a smooth and polished fade, it's time to add picture elements and text to the cover of our software magazine.

Adding Elements to the Screen

The most inefficient way to create the title screen for the software magazine would be to build it up by sequencing full-screen images. Our background already occupies 90K of hard disk space. We don't want to add 90K to the final program size every time we add a image to the magazine. Wherever possible we want to add small pieces to the parts of the screen that change. It would be much more efficient to construct the screen out of small pieces added to it over time. GRASP excels at storing, displaying, and moving small pieces of the screen called *clippings*. That's why GRASP is so often used for software demos distributed by disk or on bulletin board, where small file sizes are crucial.

Let's add a large visual to the magazine cover background. We're going to use Pictor to prepare the clipping for GRASP's use. Exit GRASP and enter Pictor now. This will require changing into the GRASP directory. Type `pictor`. Select Video Mode M.

Once in Pictor, press the letter (l) (small l) to bring up the File menu. Click on CHAPT04. This selects Chapter 4's subdirectory. Select the file named LION-

---

BITBLT ANIMATION AND MULTIMEDIA

Animating small images on the screen is often called *bitblt animation*. Bitblt animation is an acronym for "bit block transfer." A bit block is a small graphic array in display memory. Bitblt animation makes it easier for the computer to achieve high-speed animation effects because a small rectangular block of pixels on the screen is easier for the computer to load, display, and move than the entire screen. Bitblt animation is sometimes called "sprite animation" or "arcade animation." It's very important to multimedia because high-resolution multimedia picture files are usually quite large. Storing and displaying only part of the screen can help decrease storage requirements for multimedia programs and make animation effects possible.

HEAD.PIC. A lion's head sculpture will appear in Pictor's viewport. (The lion symbolizes Rome's majesty.)

We want to superimpose the head on the gray-textured cover background. There are two ways of cutting out the lion's head from the background. One is by using Pictor's Edit Box and the other is by using Pictor's Seek Edge option in the Edit menu.

Using the Edit Box to Make Clippings

Select the Picture Mover icon (the four-way arrow at the top left of the Tools menu) to drag the viewport so that the entire lion's head appears in the viewport. Select the Edit Box at the top right of the Tools menu. Click on a spot to the top and left of the lion's head. Drag the Edit Box until it surrounds the lion's head. Now press the letter (c) or choose Copy from the Edit menu at the top of the screen. This copies the area you have marked with the Edit Box to the clipboard. This is one way of saving a portion of screen to a buffer in memory. You could now save the clipping to the hard drive by calling up the Save menu, but there's a more efficient way of clipping the lion's head.

Using Seek Edge to Save a Clipping

The alternative method for selecting an area to be clipped and saved into the clipboard is Pictor's Seek Edge option in the Edit menu. Seek Edge finds the edges of objects on solid color backgrounds and places a marquee Edit Box around them. The keyboard alternative is (ALT)-(J). Let's try it.

You must be in full screen mode to find the edges of the complete lion's head. Toggle to the full screen view of the image by pressing (ESC). (You can toggle back and forth between partial and full screen mode with the (ESC) key. Appendix D contains the keyboard alternatives for Pictor commands.) If the Edit Box is active, click on the screen outside of the marquee to deactivate it. Now press (ALT)-(J). The crosshairs shape changes to an hourglass shape as Pictor analyzes the image, looking for the edges of objects. After a few moments, the Edit Box forms around the lion's head, tightly fitted to its perimeter.

The Seek Edge Pictor function is valuable for finding the edge of an object or group of objects. Before saving the clipping, however, we're going to perform one more operation. It's one of the most important processing steps in GRASP programming.

Clipping on Byte Boundaries

Clippings need to be saved in a certain way if they are to be used efficiently in a GRASP program. They must be saved on *byte boundaries*. Byte boundaries have to do with the way an image is stored in memory.

A thorough discussion of the way video memory is organized is beyond the scope of this book. The topic is complicated by the fact that the different video modes (mono, Hercules, CGA, EGA, VGA, and Super VGA) address video RAM (memory on the display card) in different ways. We won't digress too deeply into this highly technical subject. However, how you clip an image in Pictor, store it on disk, and display it in GRASP can have a dramatic effect on the way you use the memory resources in your GRASP programs. Skip the sidebar on video memory if you're not interested in the technical details of memory.

The bottom line on clippings is that they should be created and displayed on byte boundaries. The best way to think about this in a nontechnical way is to imagine that the screen is divided into a series of vertical lines. Clippings on byte boundaries are aligned with these lines; clippings that are not on byte boundaries are not aligned with these lines. Figure 4-6 illustrates this concept.

There is a way to see where the byte boundaries are in Pictor. If you press (ALT)-(F9), you will see the Edit Box jump out horizontally a number of pixels to the left and to the right of the edges of the image you are clipping. (Test this with another image. The lion's head may fall right on the byte boundary.) Press (ALT)-(J) again and watch the Edit Box jump back to the edge of the image. When you press (ALT)-(F9), you are forcing the Edit Box to surround an area of the screen that is on an even byte boundary. Storing a clipping that has been captured in this way uses as much as *eight times*

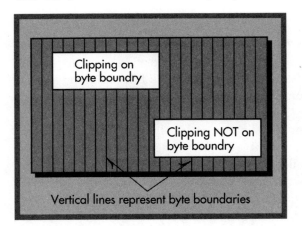

Figure 4-6 Aligning clippings to byte boundaries

less the amount of display memory as an image stored a pixel to the left or right of this boundary. (The clipping that is stored on disk is not eight times bigger; it's the amount of RAM memory that increases to accommodate a clipping that is not on a byte boundary.) This is because of the way memory is organized in certain EGA and VGA modes and cards. How do you know where the byte boundaries on the screen are when you're in GRASP? That's the simple part. Byte boundaries are at the horizontal screen locations that are divisible by eight. Again, it's not really necessary to know the technical aspects of this issue. Just remember that clippings need to be saved and displayed at horizontal (x) screen locations that are divisible by eight. For

HOW VIDEO MEMORY IS ORGANIZED

Video RAM is memory that is physically located on the video card but resides within the computer's address space. In some color modes, such as the 640x480 256-color VGA mode, addressing the video adapter's memory is relatively easy, since in this case video memory is organized a lot like data memory. But in some of the other modes, such as 16-color EGA and VGA modes, memory is organized into *planes*. Each of the planes stores a complete version of the image, one in red, one in green, one in blue, and one storing intensity of the image's pixels. The adapter uses the combination of these four planes to decide what color to make a pixel on the screen. This organization of the image into its separate color values is similar to the way images are separated for printing.

example, putting a clipping up at x,y coordinates of 88,123 puts it up at a byte boundary, 87,123 does not. If you don't save clippings on byte boundaries, they ..ill bloat into memory hogs when you load them into memory for display. If you do save them on byte boundaries in Pictor using the (ALT)-(F9) key combination, and don't display them on byte boundaries in GRASP, the clipping won't display when you run the GRASP program. You won't even get an error message. We'll cover this ground again when we show you how to put up clippings, but the rule is:

When clipping in Pictor, use the (ALT)-(F9) key combination to save clippings on byte boundaries.

Saving a Clipping with Offsets

Often, when you save a clipping to the hard drive, you will want to put it back up at the same spot on the screen in GRASP. Pictor allows you to save the clipping with its *offsets* intact. The x,y offsets are read by GRASP and used to put the clipping back up in the same spot from which it was clipped.

Let's do this with the lion's head. Make sure you've clipped and saved the lion's head using the (ALT)-(J), (ALT)-(F9) key combination. In order to save the clipping you've stored in the clipboard to the hard drive, you must copy it to the clipboard first by pressing the letter (c) or selecting the Copy option on the Edit menu. Then press (s) to pop up the Save menu, or choose Save on the File menu. Select the Clipping option in the Save menu to save the clipboard contents as a clipping. The Text Entry box goes white. Click on it and type in LIONHEAD.CLP and press (ENTER). This places the name of the clipping in the Filename box.

If you click on Save right now, the clipping will be saved without offsets, so that when you display it, it will appear in the bottom left corner of the screen (the origin

USING PICTOR FOR IMAGE PROCESSING

A clipping is simply a portion of the screen saved to disk without palette information stored with it. That's why so many of GRASP's clipping and picture-oriented commands are interchangeable. When you load clippings into Pictor, they take on the color of the current palette. If you need to edit a clipping that is part of a sequence in your script, load a picture from that sequence first, then load the clipping. If you get an error message that says "Clipping too large," try loading the clipping while in full view mode. (Press (ESC) to go from the viewport to the full screen mode. Then press (ALT)-(I) to bring up the File Dialogue box.) You can load pictures without their accompanying palette by loading them as clippings (rename them with the .CLP file extension) or by loading them as pictures while holding down the (ALT) key. This is a quick way of loading and saving images that must have a common palette. Of course, GRASP will not attempt to match the original picture's colors with the colors of the new palette. Use a color processing program (like Paintshop Pro or Image Alchemy) to do that.

When loading a picture into Pictor, you may get a message that says, "Not enough memory for picture." You may be trying to load a high-resolution image into Pictor when it is set to a lower color resolution. Convert the image to the lower resolution first using one of the image processing programs we've recommended (such as Piclab).

point). We want to be able to save the clipping at the exact location on screen we specified with the Edit Box. Pressing the (CTRL) (control) key and clicking on the Save box will save the clipping in the exact position specified with the Edit Box. Do that now. Press and hold down the (CTRL) key and click on Save. The clipping is saved with the correct offsets. Remember, if you Save without simultaneously pressing the (CTRL) key, the clipping will not be saved with its offsets and will appear at x=0 and y=0 location, the screen origin at the bottom left of the screen.

Now that we have saved the clipping to disk, let's return to GRASP to place the clipping over the background. Exit from Pictor and change back into the CHAPT04 subdirectory.

Displaying Clippings

GRASP provides several different methods for displaying images. We've already introduced you to Pfade, which can load and display either full screen images. The Pfade command can also load and display clippings. However there are two commands, Cfade and Putup, that are specialized for displaying clippings. Let's look at the way clippings are loaded and displayed using Cfade first.

The following temporary script loads and displays the clipping we saved in Pictor. Make sure you're in CHAPT04 subdirectory, where the LIONHEAD.CLP clipping is stored. Create a new file in GRASP called TEMP.TXT.

```
; TEMP.TXT Display a Clipping Using CFADE

video m


; Load and display background image.
        pload romeback.pic p1
        palette p1
        pfade 6 p1 200                  ; use a filter wipe to display
        pfree p1

; Load and display clipping
        cload lionhead.clp c1 1         ; load clipping, noshift on
        cfade 6 152,134 c1 200 300      ; display using filter wipe at x,y
                                        ; with 2 sec. delay, then wait
                                        ; 3 seconds

exit
```

When you press (F10), the background first fades up, then the lion's head appears on the screen. Unfortunately, the gray block behind the lion's head also shows up. We'll show you how to get rid of that in a minute.

Notice that Cload and Cfade, which load and display clippings, use "c" as a prefix to the buffer number. Pload and Pfade, which load and display pictures, use "p." This is how to tell GRASP what kind of image you want to work with. Notice also that we've placed a comma after 152 (152,134). Commas are optional when assigning coordinates. We use them to make the code more legible.

Loading Clippings

Let's look at the way images are loaded. The command syntax for Cload is:

```
cload name [buffer] [copy] [tran]
```

You can load either a picture file or a clipping with Cload, but loading a picture with the command will not load the picture's palette. If you omit the file extension, GRASP will assume you mean a file name with the .CLP extension. The *buffer* parameter is optional. If you do not specify a buffer number when loading a clipping, it will load into clipping buffer 1. You can have up to 128 buffers in GRASP.

The *copy* parameter toggles *noshift* on or off. Noshift means "do not create a copy (or copies) that has been shifted over to a byte boundary." It can have a value of either 0 or 1. A 0 directs GRASP to store extra copies of the clipping to ensure that the clipping can be displayed on non-byte boundaries. A 1 directs GRASP not to store shifted copies. If you have created the clipping so that it can be displayed on a byte boundary (by using (ALT)-(F9) in Pictor, for example), then you can turn noshift on by entering a value of 1. GRASP does not need to create a copy—or multiple copies—of a clipping that can be displayed on a byte boundary. The default setting is 0, "create shifted copies." To measure the impact of using this parameter, change the Cload command's copy parameter to 0 ("cload lionhead.clp c1 0") and run the script by pressing (F10). Then exit from the script back to the editor, and look at the blue bar at the top of the editor screen. You will see a memory report of how much memory the small script used when it was run: On our computer it was over 618K! If you don't have at least 618K conventional memory free, the script will not run. Instead, GRASP reports a memory error and drops you back to the line where it attempted to load the clipping.

When the same script is run with the copy parameter turned off ("cload lionhead.clp c1 1"), the clipping loads and displays. Check the memory utilization report again in the editor. On our computer "memory used" dropped down to 337K! You can see why creating clippings on even byte boundaries is so important in GRASP.

Remember: It is RAM memory that is at issue here. The actual size of the clipping does not change. The amount of memory GRASP uses to store the clipping in RAM and display it does change.

Displaying Clippings Using Cfade

Now that we have looked at the way to load a clipping into a buffer, let's review the command for fading clippings to the screen.

```
cfade # x y [buffer] [speed] [delay]
```

The # symbol signifies a fade number. Cfade uses all the same fades as picture fades (listed by the (F3) key), with the exception of fade 0, the instant display fade. (Use Putup for instant display. This command will be reviewed next.) The x,y position refers to the horizontal (x) and vertical (y) position where you want to display the clipping on screen. The bottom left corner of the clipping will be placed at the specified x,y position. The buffer parameter is optional. It defaults to buffer 1. The speed parameter is optional. It is measured in hundredths of a second. The delay parameter tells GRASP to wait, after finishing the fade, before executing the next command. It is also measured in hundredths of a second.

Cfade allows us to add a clipping to the magazine title screen using a variety of wipes. But our example has left a gray border around the lion's head. Is there a way to make the gray border transparent?

Using Putup to Display Images

There is another way to load and display either clippings or pictures: the Putup command. The special advantage of the Putup command is that it automatically displays images using the x and y offsets stored with them. Putup's use of transparency also provides us with a way of getting rid of the gray block around the lion's head. Let's begin by looking at the command's syntax:

```
putup [x,y] [buffer] [delay]
```

Putup without parameters places the clipping currently loaded in buffer 1 on the screen, at the existing x,y offset values stored with the clipping.

If you specify x,y coordinates, these coordinates will be added to the clipping's offsets. This has been the cause of many lost hours for GRASP programmers who saved a clipping with offsets in Pictor, and then attempted to Putup those clippings using additional x,y offsets. Often the clipping is displayed off-screen. GRASP can see it, but you won't. "Putup c1" in effect says here, "Put up the clipping in buffer one, using the offsets (152, 134) stored with the clipping." If you did not save the clipping with an offset (or if you used the Position command to strip it of its offsets) Putup will place the clipping at the bottom left corner of the screen (at 0,0).

Let's now convert theory into practice. Exit from TEMP.TXT and load the TMPFILE.TXT file again. Edit it to reflect the changes we show here:

```
; TMPFILE.TXT Software Magazine

video m

set debug on

; Fade up Background
        pload blackpic.pal p1
        pload romeback.pic p2
        palette p1
        pfade 0 p2
        spread p1 p2 164
        pfree p1 - p2                    ; add this line to free memory!!!!!
        waitkey 300


; Load and Display Lion's Head
        tran on 3                        ; make clipping background transparent
        cload lionhead.clp c1 1 1        ; loads clipping, no-shift, transparent
        putup c1                         ; places clipping on screen
        cfree c1                         ; free up memory
        tran off                         ; turns transparency off again
        waitkey

exit
```

Run the script by pressing (F10). The background image, ROMEBACK.PIC, is loaded and displayed, then the clipping is loaded and displayed. Your screen should look like Figure 4-7.

There are circumstances when you do want to offset a clipping. If you want to shift the clipping to the right 64 pixels and down 10, you would change the Putup

Figure 4-7 The lion's head displayed transparently

command in the script to: "putup 64 -10 1." Try it. Notice that we've made the horizontal x coordinate divisible by eight. Try entering a number that isn't divisible by eight. The lion's head will disappear. That's because you've attempted to put the head up at a non-byte boundary.

Using the Transparency Command

You'll notice that the example script caused the clipping to display without the gray box behind it. The ability to make colors in a clipping transparent to the background is a powerful feature of GRASP. Let's review how the command sequence works.

Here's the method for using the Tran command:

- Turn on Tran and tell it what color to make transparent.
- Load a clipping with the transparency parameter set to 1 (on).
- Use Putup to put the clipping on the screen.
- Turn transparency off.

The Putup command is used in conjunction with transparency. You make parts of a clipping transparent to the screen using the Cload and Putup commands in combination with the Tran (for transparency) command. Syntax for the command is:

`tran [on|off] [color]`

You set the command on or off. Color is the color you want to make transparent. Color here refers to the palette slot color. If gray happens to be in palette slot 3, then all the gray areas in the clipping will be transparent. That's why the gray block behind the lion's head disappeared.

Remember, you must turn on the transparency parameter of the Cload command in order to have the clipping analyzed by GRASP for the presence of the transparent color.

Building Images Off-Screen

Putup does not use fades. It instantly displays images on the screen. Cfade uses a variety of wipes to display clippings over time, but it does not support transparency.

Have we bumped up against a limitation inherent in GRASP? Is there no way to transparently display a clipping that slowly wipes on the screen?

Experienced programmers are often called wizards because the sleight-of-hand they bury in code often appears to be magic. The following method is GRASP magic, although it's very well known to experienced GRASP users:

- Save the current screen to a buffer.
- Redirect screen drawing commands to the buffer.
- Manipulate the buffer while the viewer's attention is on the original (current) screen.
- Replace the current screen with the altered screen.

Figure 4-8 shows the process conceptually.

Here's the process translated into GRASP code:

```
pgetbuf p1      ; save the screen to buffer 1 (or up to 128)
psetbuf p1      ; redirect commands to buffer 1
...             ; do something, such as putting up a clipping
psetbuf         ; reset commands to screen
pfade 0 p1      ; fade the altered buffer to the screen
```

Let's see how we've implemented off-screen magic in the example script.

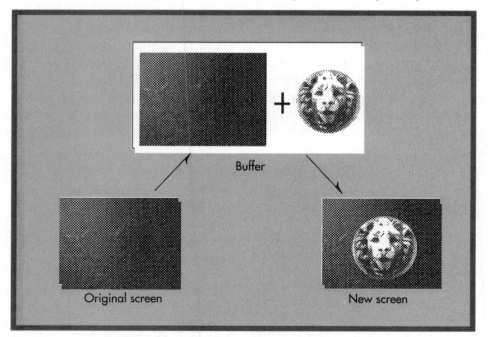

Buffer

Original screen

New screen

Figure 4-8 Building images off-screen

```
; TMPFILE.TXT Software Magazine

video m

; Background and Lion's Head
        pload blackpic.pal p1
        pload romeback.pic p2
        tran on 3                       ; transparency turned on
        cload lionhead.clp c1 1 1       ; clipping loaded
        palette p1
        pfade 0 p2
        spread p1 p2 164
        pfree p1 - p2

; Display Lion's Head
        pgetbuf p1                      ; save screen to buffer 1
        psetbuf p1                      ; redirect screen activity to buffer 1
        putup c1
        psetbuf                         ; redirect activity to screen
        cfree c1
        tran off
        pfade 18 p1 100                 ; assembled image fades to screen
        pfree p1
        waitkey

exit
```

When you press (F10), there is a pause while the picture and clipping are loaded. The background fades on. Then the lion's head wipes on, and the gray block is made transparent to the background. Notice in the script above that we load the clipping and process it for transparency before we display the background. If we loaded the clipping after the background was displayed, there would be a long pause while the processing for transparency and loading of the clipping occurred. Remember, if you include the transparency parameter with Cload (cload lion-

---

USING PNEWBUF IN PLACE OF PGETBUF

You don't necessarily have to save the current screen to buffer one. You could create a blank buffer with the Pnewbuf command (for example, pnewbuf 1) and then add text, clippings, or other items to it before fading it to the screen. The blank picture is created in the currently selected color. Pnewbuf's syntax is:

```
pnewbuf buffer [x,y]
```

where x,y is an optional size of the image in pixels. If you don't specify this parameter, the default is full screen size for the current video mode. The important point is that you have to create a buffer and then use Psetbuf to redirect screen activity.

head.clp c1 1 1), GRASP will process the clipping for transparency. Don't use the parameter if you don't need to display the clipping transparently. Transparency processing can take a long time.

Let's review the new commands. Pgetbuf's syntax was reviewed earlier. Essentially, the command saves the current screen to a buffer. We'll begin with Psetbuf.

Using Psetbuf to Redirect Screen Activity

The Psetbuf command redirects fades, text, and drawing commands to the buffer you specify. You must create a buffer for Psetbuf to point to. You can build up a complex picture off-screen in this way. We used the Pgetbuf command to capture the screen to buffer 1, and then used Psetbuf 1 to direct screen activity to buffer 1. Then we used Psetbuf again (without a buffer number) to redirect screen activity from buffer 1 to the screen.

```
pgetbuf p1                      ; save screen to buffer 1
psetbuf p1                      ; redirect screen activity to buffer 1
putup c1
psetbuf                         ; redirect activity to screen
```

The assembled image in buffer 1 is then faded to the screen.

```
pfade 18 p1 100                 ; assembled image fades to screen
```

Now that we've added the lion's head to the cover background, it's time to step back and admire our work. The effort we've spent in adding a graphic to the screen may seem to you to have been immense, considering the result! But we've learned how to cheat the PC's narrow data path by manipulating only a portion of the screen, and we've taught you some of GRASP's sleight-of-hand. You'll soon learn to apply these techniques quickly to your own work. In the next section we'll add to your toolchest of GRASP tips and techniques.

Coffee Break

This is a good place to take a break away from the computer. When you return we'll be creating another small temporary program.

Enhancing the Cover with an Engraved Effect

Now that we've added the lion's head, let's give the opening screen some extra interest by "engraving" a horizontal groove under the lion's head. A groove in the rock-like surface of the graphic could be simulated by placing a dark horizontal "shadow" line immediately above a light horizontal "highlight" line. On a surface of flat color, this is accomplished by choosing a darker shade of the surface color for the shadow and a lighter shade of the surface color for the part of the groove highlighted by the "virtual" light.

We'll show you what we mean. Create a temporary file called TEMP.TXT. (Choose the Create option of the GRASP File menu.) We're going to create a flat gray background using the palette (but not the picture) from ROMEBACK.PIC. This gives us the range of grays we need to create the effect. Enter the following lines:

```
; TEMP.TXT Routine illustrating a "groove" effect.

video m

set debug on

; Get palette from the background image.
        pload romeback.pic p1
        palette p1
        pfree p1                          ; we don't display it

; Create groove.
        color 4
        clearscr                          ; clear screen to palette color 4
        color 3                           ; set current color to palette 3
        line 0,100 639,100                ; draw line in color 3 (drk gray)
        line 0,-1 0,-1 r                  ; draw 2nd line underneath
        color 5                           ; change to lighter shade gray
        line 0,-1 0,-1 r                  ; draw another line underneath

waitkey
```

When you press (F10), you'll notice that a white band appears at the bottom of the screen. GRASP writes messages about its command activity on this white band. We've used a "debugging" feature of GRASP. Let's review that first.

Using GRASP's Debugging Option

The debugging option places the currently executing command on the screen. You can step through the commands one at a time during execution by pressing the space bar. GRASP will wait until you press the space bar before executing the next command. This is a valuable tool for tracing program execution when something is wrong in the program. It's also a helpful learning tool in this book. You can review long and complex programs one step at a time.

Normally, when you press escape during the running of a program, you are returned to the point where you last edited code. If you have debug set on, you will be placed at the point in the editor where the current command was entered. (Remember, to turn it off you can place a semicolon in front of it.)

With debug on, run the example script and step through it with the space bar. The gray midtone background instantly appears, and a darker shade of gray is used to draw a line 100 pixels from the bottom of the screen. Then the line is thickened by another midtone gray line one pixel below. Finally, a line in a lighter shade of gray is drawn below that. The combination of two dark lines with a lighter line below it produces the "grooved" effect. Your screen should look like Figure 4-9.

Let's review the other new commands in the example code. First note the Color and Clearscr commands.

```
; Create groove.
      color 4
      clearscr                           ; clear screen to palette color 4
```

The Color command tells GRASP what palette slot to use for the current drawing color. Here's the syntax for the command:

```
color color1 [R] [color2]
```

The *color1* parameter sets the current system color. Note that it is the palette slot that you set, not the color index. When the second parameter is specified (R), *color1* is made relative to the current system color. This is a useful feature when you want to *color cycle* the palette.

The last parameter of the Color command ([color2]), is used to determine the color of shadowed text. We'll be using the parameter in a later chapter.

Using Clearscr to Repaint the Screen

Let's turn our attention to the second command in the short example text, Clearscr:

COLOR CYCLING

Color cycling allows you to change the colors on the screen by manipulating the palette. Usually a loop is used to cause colors to shift from one palette slot to the next in a cycle. This type of animation technique is popular in weather shows. It places very little demand on computer resources, since you are manipulating the system palette rather than loading palette or picture files. Here's an application of the technique.

```
video m

color 0

mark 16
      color 1 r
      waitkey 50
      rect 150,100 490,380
loop

exit
```

We'll be introducing you to the command that creates rectangles (Rect) later. The example creates a color rectangle that cycles through all the colors of the default palette, returning to the original black color of palette slot 0.

```
; Create groove.
      color 4                         ; set current color to palette 4
      clearscr                        ; clear screen to palette color 4
```

Clearscr repaints the screen in the current color. Syntax for the command is:

```
clearscr [color]
```

We could have typed in the command as clearscr 4. This would have cleared the screen to palette slot 4 without changing the current color.

Using the Line Command

Let's now review the command that creates the groove on a plain gray background. The groove was created using the Line command. The Line command's syntax is:

```
line x1,y1 x2,y2 [r]
```

where x1 is the beginning horizontal coordinate of the screen, and y1 is the beginning vertical coordinate. The coordinates x2,y2 establish the end point of the line. Figure 4-10 shows how the line is drawn on the screen.

The optional *r* parameter (line x1,y1 x2,y2 [r]) allows you to create a second line whose coordinates are added to (or subtracted from) the previous Line command's coordinates. The relative parameter is useful for creating thick lines by incrementing the line's thickness in loops.

Figure 4-9 Creating a grooved effect on a plain background

The following code fragment shows how you would create a horizontal line 100 pixels from the bottom of the screen 4 pixels thick.

```
line 0,100 639,100               ; line is drawn from 0 to 639 on the x axis
                                 ; at 100 on the y axis
mark 3
      line 0 1 0 1 r             ; adds 0 to x coordinate and 3 to y coordinate
loop
```

Notice in TEMP.TXT we made the dark shadow line one pixel thicker than the lighter highlighted line.

```
      line 0,100 639,100         ; draw line in color 3 (drk gray)
      line 0,-1 0,-1 r           ; draw 2nd line underneath
```

```
color 5                          ; change to lighter shade gray
line 0,-1 0,-1 r                 ; draw another line underneath
```

We've used the subtle color gradations in ROMEBACK.PIC's palette to our advantage. If either of these colors are changed to lighter or darker shades of gray, the realism of the effect is lost.

Adding the Grooved Effect to the Cover

Let's turn back to the software magazine script we are building to apply what we have learned here. Load TMPFILE.TXT back into the editor. Applying the principles we have just learned won't be easy here! Solid lines of colors will not work on this textured background. They'll look like two lines of solid color rather than an indentation in the background. There is a solution, however. We can take two small clippings from the screen and use them to create the lines on the screen. Because the clippings will have the same texture as the background, we'll be able to simulate the look of a real groove. Look at the following code and place it after the display of the lion's head, just before the Waitkey and Exit commands. The file should now look like this:

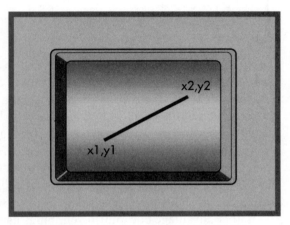

Figure 4-10 The Line command's coordinates

```
; TMPFILE.TXT Software Magazine

video m

; Background and Lion's Head
        pload blackpic.pal p1
        pload romeback.pic p2
        tran on 3                        ; transparency turned on
        cload lionhead.clp c1 1 1        ; clipping loaded
        palette p1
        pfade 0 p2
        spread p1 p2 164
        pfree p1 - p2

; Display Lion's Head
        pgetbuf p1                       ; save screen to buffer 1
        psetbuf p1                       ; redirect screen activity to buffer 1
        putup c1
        psetbuf                          ; redirect activity to screen
```

```
        cfree c1
        tran off
        pfade 18 p1 100                    ; assembled image fades to screen
        pfree p1

; Add Groove to bottom of screen.
        pgetbuf p1 424,103 464,107         ; saves part of screen to buffer 1
        pgetbuf p2 136,198 176,200         ; saves part of screen to buffer 2
        position p1 0,0                    ; sets x,y offsets of p1 to 0,0
        position p2 0,0                    ; sets x,y offsets of p2 to 0,0
        fly 0 52,639 52,32 1 p1            ; creates shadow
        fly 0 49,639 49,32 1 p2            ; creates light line highlight
        pfree p1 - p2
waitkey

exit
```

Here's what we've done. We've used Pgetbuf to capture two small clippings from the background to buffers. We then use them to create the two shadow and highlight lines. One (p1) is cut from a dark area of the screen at the bottom right of the background and the other (p2) is cut from the lighter left side of the screen. It would not have been easier to make the clippings in Pictor and use them for the groove. The advantage of doing them using GRASP commands is that they are never saved as clippings on the hard drive. They won't clutter the hard drive. We save a small amount of time in loading them from the disk as well. GRASP is a real miser when it comes to memory management. Scrooge would approve.

Another advantage of capturing clippings using Pgetbuf is the precision with which we can capture areas of the screen. We can easily adjust the width of the dark and light lines by altering the vertical coordinates used in the Pgetbuf command.

Using Position to Alter Clipping Offsets

Pgetbuf saves the clippings with the offsets intact. This is a problem. If we attempt to use the clippings as they are, we would have to laboriously compensate for these offsets. The Position command allows us to alter the clippings' offsets. Syntax for the Position command is:

```
position buffer x,y [R]
```

Buffer is the buffer number of the picture you want to alter. This can be a clipping or a picture. (Use *c1* for clipping buffer 1 and *p1* for picture buffer 1.) The x,y coordinates determine where on the screen the bottom left corner of the picture or clipping will be placed. The *R* parameter makes the present position command's coordinates relative to a previous position command's coordinates.

Put semicolons in front of the two position commands to see what happens when you display the screen clippings with offsets intact. The clippings do not display properly. That's the reason for using the Position command. Position resets the clippings' coordinates to 0,0.

Using Fly to Animate Clippings

Now that we have created the clippings that we use to etch a groove across the screen, it's time to use them. We use the Fly command to do this. The Fly command animates clippings. That is, it moves a clipping from one part of the screen to another. Fly puts the clippings up between two coordinates that you specify, in the amount of steps you specify, and at the speed you specify. The syntax is:

```
fly x1,ys1 x2,y2 step delay buf [buf] ...
```

You give the Fly command a starting (x1,y1) position and an ending (x2,y2) position. The command works like a loop. The command will keep redisplaying the clipping between the start and end locations. It will use the *step* parameter to determine the distance in pixels between the successive displays of the clipping. It will use the *delay* parameter to determine how long to pause between successive displays of the clipping. You can have the Fly command only animate one clipping (the *buf* parameter), or several clippings (the optional *buf*s). The command will animate each clipping in turn.

The command says, "Put up, between these coordinates, in this amount of steps, with this amount of delay between the steps, the following clipping or clippings." Fly is very closely related to another GRASP command we'll be using presently, Float. While Fly puts up copies of the clippings across the screen, Float "floats" the clipping across the screen. Change the keyword fly in the above script to float to see the effect of this change. You will see the two clippings zoom across the screen, as if floating above the surface. Change the float keyword back to fly again. Figure 4-11 shows the effects of the two commands using a bird as an example.

Fly leaves copies of the bird on the screen. Float does not. As you will see, in the case of Float, it is necessary to Putup the clipping in the final position, otherwise the clipping will float from one spot to another on the screen and disappear. The ability to do sprite or bitblt animation is a key feature of GRASP. Here's how the command was implemented in the example code:

```
; Add Groove to bottom of screen.
        pgetbuf p1 424,103 464,107      ; saves part of screen to buffer 1
        pgetbuf p2 136,198 176,200      ; saves part of screen to buffer 2
        position p1 0 ,0                ; sets x,y offsets of p1 to 0,0
        position p2 0, 0                ; sets x,y offsets of p2 to 0,0
        fly 0 52,639 52,32 1 p1         ; creates shadow
        fly 0 49,639 49,32 1 p2         ; creates light line highlight
        pfree p1 - p2
waitkey
```

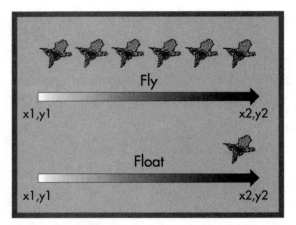

Figure 4-11 Animating a clipping with Fly and Float

By creating the groove this way, we've taken the long road to the end effect: a groove on the screen. However, the underlying graphic, the gray pixelated background, can be used as a background in another part of the program, without the groove. We've saved 90K of space on the hard drive. This makes this method very useful for applications where disk space is critical.

ANIMATING THE LION'S EYES

If our lion were a logo in a corporate presentation, we might decide to add sparkle to it at this point to give our opening screen some visual excitement. Magazine covers rely on unusual images, bright colors and interesting textures to capture the newsstand reader's attention. Let's give our lion some life by animating his eyes! Here's the entire script with the eye sparkle animation added.

```
; TMPFILE.TXT Software Magazine

video m

set debug on

; Background and Lion's Head
        pload blackpic.pal p1
        pload romeback.pic p2
        tran on 3
        cload lionhead.clp c1 1 1
        palette p1
        pfade 0 p2
        spread p1 p2 164
        pfree p1 - p2

; Display Lion's Head
        pgetbuf p1
        psetbuf p1
        putup c1
        psetbuf
        cfree c1
        tran off
        pfade 18 p1 100
```

```
        pfree p1

; Add Groove to bottom of screen.
        pgetbuf p1 424,103 464,107
        pgetbuf p2 136,198 176,200
        position p1 0 0
        position p2 0 0
        fly 0,52 639,52 32 1 p1
        fly 0,49 639,49 32 1 p2
        pfree p1 - p2

; Animate Lion's Eyes
        eyes

        waitkey

exit

eyes:
        cgetbuf c1 258,327 291,346 1          ; left eye saved to buffer
        cgetbuf c2 349,330 370,348 1          ; right eye saved to buffer
        mark 20                               ; outer loop
                color 4                       ; sets/ resets to slot 4
                mark 12                       ; inner loop
                        color 1 r             ; move to next
                                              ; palette slot
                        point 258,327 291,346 ; dots in left eye
                        point 349,330 370,348 ; dots in right eye
                loop
                waitkey 04
                putup c1                      ; restore eye
                putup c2                      ; restore eye
        loop
        cfree c1 - c2
return
```

When you run the modified script, the lion's head appears and the eyes sparkle.

The new script introduces a major new command: Gosub.

Using Gosub for Program Flow

The Gosub command literally means, "*Go* execute this *sub*routine." Unlike the Goto command, which causes program execution to jump to another area of the script and continue execution there, the Gosub command causes execution to temporarily continue someplace else until either a Return or Exit is encountered. Execution then jumps back to the calling point. Syntax for the command is:

```
[gosub] label [val] [val] [val] ...
```

We'll be coming back to the optional *val* parameters. GRASP allows you to send up to 25 values as variables or constants to a subroutine. The subroutine can then use them by employing indirection. The special symbols that access the values use the indirection symbol @ in conjunction with a number: @1, @2, @3 ... and so on.

Use of the Gosub keyword is optional, so in our example instead of using

```
gosub eyes
exit
eyes:
```

we've shortened it to:

```
eyes
exit
eyes:
```

In our example, when GRASP encounters the word "eyes," it knows it's not a re-served keyword, so it looks for a label elsewhere in the script by that name. (Remember that a label is a word with a colon on the end of it.) If it doesn't find the label, GRASP generates an error message ("unknown command") and returns to the editor. Test this by placing a semicolon in front of the eyes: label.

The Gosub command allows us to place the eyes subroutine after the exit point of the script. We place it there for efficiency. Suppose we want to use the eyes sub-routine again. We could type in the eyes code every time we want to sparkle the lion's eyes, but it's more efficient to implement repetitive code as a subroutine. Using a subroutine saves precious memory as well, since we're cutting down on the length of our script. In our example, all we have to do to make the lion's eyes sparkle is use the word "eyes" in the script. Modify the script like this:

```
; Animate Lion's Eyes
        eyes
        waitkey 60
        eyes
```

The eyes sparkle twice.

Placing the subroutine after the exit point also allows other subroutines to call the eyes subroutine. (Subroutines can call other subroutines up to 16 levels deep.) We'll be doing this a little further along when we call eyes from the sound subroutine.

Note that Return hands back control to the script at the line following the Gosub command.

Drawing Points on the Screen

The eyes subroutine makes the eyes sparkle with tiny dots. One of GRASP's advan-tages is that it can draw simple graphics on the screen directly, without loading files from the disk. Graphics primitives like rectangles, boxes, circles, lines, and points can be instantly displayed. One of the these graphic tools is the Point command. We use it to sparkle the lion's eyes.

The syntax for the point command is:

```
point x,y [rx,ry]
```

On its own, without the optional parameter, Point assigns the current color to a precise x,y location on the screen. The point command is of limited use this way—especially in the VGA 640x480 modes, where a point is tiny and hard to see. However, when you add the rx and ry parameters to the command, it takes on an entirely new dimension. The x,y and rx,ry coordinates now describe the opposite corners of an area of the screen where the point is randomly placed (the "r" stands for random). In this case we've created a rectangular area near the edges of each eye within which "sparks" appear:

```
point 258,327 291,346    ; a spark placed randomly in left eye
point 349,330 370,348    ; a spark placed randomly in right eye
```

One spark will not do. That's why we've added a loop:

```
mark 12                      ; inner loop
      point 258,327 291,346  ; sparks left eye
      point 349,330 370,348  ; sparks right eye
loop
```

Each time the loop is processed, it randomly places a spark in each eye. It does this 12 times for a total of 12 sparks. Here's the subroutine again.

```
eyes:
        cgetbuf c1 258,327 291,346 1          ; left eye saved to buffer
        cgetbuf c2 349,330 370,348 1          ; right eye saved to buffer
        mark 20                               ; outer loop
            color 4                           ; sets/ resets to slot 4
            mark 12                           ; inner loop
                color 1 r                     ; move to next
                                              ; palette slot
                    point 258,327 291,346     ; dots in left eye
                    point 349,330 370,348     ; dots in right eye
            loop
            waitkey 04
            putup c1                          ; restore eye
            putup c2                          ; restore eye
        loop
        cfree c1 - c2
return
```

Giving Color to the Eyes with Color Cycling

Because we don't want to fill the eyes with sparks of only one color, we've taken advantage of the "relative" parameter in the color command to cycle the colors.

```
color value [r]
```

The relative parameter tells GRASP how many palette slots to skip over to get to the next color. In this case, we tell GRASP to choose the next higher palette slot color each time through the loop. By setting the starting position in the palette (palette 4 in this case), we cycle through only 12 of the 16 colors in the palette with the

Mark/Loop combination. (The first four slots contain dark grays that don't show up very well on the screen.) To see the effect of changing these values in the example code, alter them and run the script.

More Magic: Nested Loops

The eye sparkle subroutine uses a *nested loop,* a loop-within-a-loop, to put up 12 random sparks in each eye 20 times. Each time the inner loop is processed it exits to a short wait time (Waitkey 03) that leaves the sparks on the screen long enough for our eyes to see them. Then the lion's eyes that were captured with the previous Cgetbuf commands are put up, effectively blotting out the sparks built up by the inner loop. If we hadn't captured the eyes before adding the sparks to them, there would be no way to "erase" the sparks after each cycle, and the sparks would accumulate until the eyes were completely filled in. You can test this by placing semicolons in front of the two Putup commands near the end of the loop. These Putups restore the eyes between each of the eight outer loops. Notice how we indent the loops to clarify their structure. If you step through the script with *debug on*, you will see how the computer processes a nested loop. Restoring screens in nested loops is one of those sleight-of-hands that makes GRASP appear to do magic.

Using Cgetbuf to Preserve Screen Areas

We use Cgetbuf to preserve the eyes of the lion so that we can restore it after each cycle through the sparkle routine. Cgetbuf has a similar syntax to Pgetbuf, but it allows you to save transparent clippings into clipping buffers.

```
cgetbuf buffer [x1,y1 x2,y2] [noshift] [tran]
```

The x1,y1 x2,y2 parameters determine the screen rectangle you want to save. The *noshift* parameter is either 0 (create bit-shifted copies) or 1 (do not create copies). GRASP defaults to creating shifted copies (0), so that you can subsequently put the clipping at any x horizontal position. To save RAM memory, we tell GRASP not to create copies (1) in our example. The optional transparency parameter has a value of 1 (analyze clipping for transparent color) or 0 (do not analyze clipping). We choose not to turn transparency on. (We don't need to put up transparent clippings, since we're pasting the original screen areas over each eye.) This saves processing time.

ADDING TEXT TO SCREENS

Now that we've added the lion head to the screen and sparkled its eyes, it's time to add the magazine title. Let's look at the facilities GRASP provides for adding text to the screen.

We could create the text for the software magazine in Pictor or a program like Corel Draw that has excellent typographical tools. The picture files we create in these programs would have to be saved to disk and clipped for display in GRASP, or sequenced in the case of full frame screens. But this approach has drawbacks. Once type is placed on a background, it is difficult to change without re-creating the electronic slide from scratch. A presentation with a lot of type would soon be filled with picture files, occupying precious hard disk space. If those picture files are high resolution, as they should be if they contained type, they would be large and take a relatively long time to load and display. Also, multimedia programs that use a lot of type will soon annoy users accustomed to fast text display on their computer system.

Fortunately, GRASP allows us to output text directly to the screen. The text is entered in the script along with the other commands that determine the type of font we use, where the type is positioned on the screen, how fast it scrolls, the spacing of characters and letters, and so on. In its simplest form, you can issue a Text command that uses the default system font to write text to the top left corner of the screen. (The default system font is the one built into the ROM of your video adapter.) Here's the simplest use of the text command:

```
text "Hello World"
```

The command is most powerful when it is used with the other commands and controls that give the producer control over the look and layout of the type. Here are the most important commands in the order in which you normally use them:

Color:	for setting the color of the type
Font:	for choosing the style of the type
Fstyle:	for shadowing text
Fgaps:	for setting the gap between letters, words, and lines
Text:	for writing text on the screen

There are also a number of controls associated with type layout on the screen, such as center, justified, and monospace. The summary of commands in Chapter 10 cross-references text commands. See in particular *set(text control)*.

GRASP comes with a number of fonts. Your choice of font for the presentation will be influenced by the same design criteria as other electronic media, the chief among these being the legibility of the type.

Let's see how text is used for the magazine cover. We'll float a red, shadowed title onto the screen from the bottom. Add the following lines to the end of the TMP-FILE.TXT script, placing them just before the Exit command. Don't forget to add the Waitkey command at the end to prevent GRASP from exiting back to the editor.

113

```
; Add title.

        pnewbuf p1                           ; open new buffer 1
        psetbuf p1                           ; re-direct screen activity to p1
        clearscr 1                           ; clear screen to color slot 1
        fload \grasp\squar20.set 1           ; loads font
        color 13 0                           ; sets color for font and shadow
        fstyle 8 20 12                       ; styling: placement of shadow
        fgaps 4 6                            ; spaces between letters, words
        text 150 71 "Rome T~~~reasure T~~~our"   ; title
        ffree 1                              ; frees font buffer
        tran on 1                            ; bkgrd in buffer 1 transparent
        cgetbuf c1 124,062 545,098 1 1       ; capture title to buffer
        psetbuf                              ; resume drawing to screen
        pfree p1                             ; free up picture buffer 1
        float 0 -100 0 0 10 1 1              ; float title from bottom
        putup c1                             ; put title up in final position
        cfree c1                             ; free buffer

waitkey

exit
```

When the script is played, a red title, Rome Treasure Tour, floats from the bottom of the screen, into position above the groove. It casts a black shadow.

Let's walk through the code.

Creating a Buffer Off-Screen

The section of code builds the title off-screen in buffer 1 using GRASP's Psetbuf command (reviewed earlier). First a buffer is created and screen activity is directed to it.

```
pnewbuf p1
psetbuf p1
```

Then we paint the buffer gray (palette slot 1).

```
clearscr 1
```

The background is created in gray to preserve the black shadow we are going to add to the title. The title will be captured to a clipping buffer and floated on the screen. In analyzing the clipping for transparency, GRASP will be told to make gray transparent, so only the red title and the black shadow show up on the cover. This is the reason for making the buffer gray.

Loading a Font

We then load a large, blocky font that harmonizes with the Roman graphics we're going to use.

```
fload \grasp\squar20.set 1
```

114

The command that loads the font, Fload, has the following syntax:

```
fload name [buffer]
```

Fonts can have either a .SET or .FNT extension. GRASP will use the default font for the current video mode (font 0) if no font is loaded before a Text command is issued. You can load up to 128 fonts in buffers.

Using the Font Command

If you have several fonts loaded, you can tell GRASP which font to load by issuing a Font command. It's unnecessary to specify the font in the example code because the text command will default to using the font in font buffer 1. Here's the syntax for the Font command:

```
font [buffer]
```

Omitting the buffer parameter causes GRASP to set the current font to font 0, the default font for the current video mode. Use the Font command with caution. Issuing a Font command causes GRASP to reset the character, word, and line spacing for the selected font to the defaults for that font.

Since fonts occupy about as much buffer memory as disk space, it's not a good idea to load more fonts in memory than you need at any given time. Load them as needed.

Creating a Text Shadow

After loading the SQUAR20.SET font (from the GRASP directory), we created a shadow and selected spacing for the *Rome Treasure Tour* title.

```
fstyle 8 20 12              ; styling: placement of shadow
fgaps 4 6                   ; spaces between letters, words
```

The Fstyle command determines a shadow effect for text. Syntax for the Fstyle command is:

```
fstyle direction offset1 [offset2]
```

The direction of the shadow can have a value from 0 to 8. 0 means no shadow; 8 means a shadow down and to the right. Figure 4-12 shows in what directions the shadow can fall. Television graphics have taught viewers to expect shadows to fall in the direction indicated by the arrow labeled 8.

The offset parameters determine how long the shadow we're creating is going to be. Offset1 determines the distance in pixels the shadow falls horizontally. Offset2 determines how many pixels the shadow falls vertically. If only offset1 value is given, it is used for both the horizontal and vertical offsets. We've chosen to place the shadow 20 pixels down and 12 to the right to make the text look like it is floating above the background.

```
fstyle 8 20 12
```

Fstyle only works in graphic modes. Fstyle 0 turns off shadowing. You determine the color of the text and shadow with the Color command.

```
color 13 0
```

We chose palette color 13 (red) for the text and color 0 (black) for the shadow.

Spacing Text

The command Fgaps determines the character, word, and line spacing for the font. The term *character* refers to the individual letters of the string of text. Command syntax is:

```
fgaps [character] [space] [vgap]
```

The parameters are measured in pixels. Character refers to spaces between letters. *Space* refers to word spacing. *Vgap* refers to line spacing. Fgaps with no parameters resets the spacing to the defaults for the current font. Make sure you issue the Fgaps command after loading a font, or the Font command will reset spacing to the defaults for the font. We chose to space the letters of the title fairly wide apart, and the space between words even wider:

```
fgaps 4 6
```

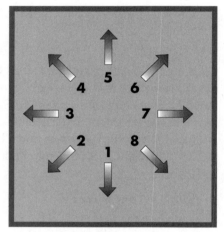

Figure 4-12 Fstyle text shadow directions

Writing Text on the Screen

Now that we've reviewed the commands that set type attributes, let's look at the command that actually places the text on the screen.

```
text 150,71 "Rome T~~~reasure T~~~our"
```

Notice the tilde ("~") marks in the text string. The tildes tell GRASP to move the text one pixel to the left per tilde mark (for a total of three). This adjustment was necessary because of the shape of the letter T. T is one of a number of letters in the alphabet that require manual adjustment because of the space they create around them. Technically, making fine adjustments to individual characters on the screen is called *kerning*.

The syntax for the Text command was provided in the last chapter. Here is the syntax for the command again with an additional comment:

```
text [x,y] string [delay]
```

A string is a series of characters. GRASP uses a space to separate data items in a list, so if your string of characters has a space in it, place quotation marks around the string. Otherwise, GRASP will interpret the word after the space as a command. Quotation marks also allow you to preserve capitalization.

Using Ffree to Release Memory

As soon as we write the text to the screen, we destroy the font buffer, freeing memory for pictures and clippings.

```
ffree buffer [buffer] ...
```

You can unload a font with text on the screen. Currently displayed text will not be altered.

Saving the Title to a Clipping Buffer

Remember that we've written the title and its shadow on a gray background to preserve the text shadow. The viewer cannot see the title yet, however Figure 4-13 shows what the title now looks like in buffer 1.

We put up the title at the exact location where it will finally be displaced on the screen. We'll show you why in a moment. Now that we have the title built on a gray background in buffer 1, we save it to a clipping buffer with the Cgetbuf command and restore screen activity to the viewer's screen.

```
cgetbuf c1 124,062 545,098 1 1   ; capture title to buffer
psetbuf                          ; resume drawing to screen
pfree p1                         ; free up picture buffer 1
```

Saving the title as a clipping will allow us to Float the title onto the screen as a clipping. We use the Tran parameter to tell GRASP to make color slot 1 (gray) transparent. (We turned Tran on earlier.) Cgetbuf saves the title with the offsets intact. Notice that we also turned noshift off (1) so that GRASP does not save extra copies of the title.

Floating the Title on the Screen

Now that we have the clipping saved to a buffer, we can float it onto the screen. The Float and Putup commands use the offsets stored with the title clipping to place the title back at the spot from where it was captured. The method is to tell Float to start the clipping from a position off-screen, and float it to the coordinates where it was originally captured. Figure 4-14 shows the technique.

The Float command's syntax is identical to that of the Fly command, except Float does not leave copies of the clipping in its path:

```
float xstart,ystart xend,yend step delay c1 ...
```

Here's how we apply it using our title clipping:

```
float 0,-100 0,0 10 1 c1          ;float from 0,-100 to 0,0
```

We float the clipping straight up from "below the screen," 100 pixels below its final position on the screen. To move the title clipping from off-screen, we use offsets that are relative (x=0,y=-100) to the final position of our clipping (x=0,y=0). Because Float moves a clipping across the screen without leaving copies on the screen, we must use a Putup to put the title in its final position. Of course, Putup uses the offset information stored by Cgetbuf.

Animating Titles with Autodesk Animator

Autodesk's 2D animation programs, Animator and Animator Pro, simplify the process of clipping (or sprite) animation. Animator is a junior version of the program. It's resolution is fixed at 320x200 256 colors. Animator Pro's colors are also fixed at 256 colors, but this version has an adjustable pixel resolution. The programs allow you to twist, spin, and change the size of clippings as they move from one position to another. The additional depth of effects is purchased at a price in memory, however. In the case of GRASP's Fly and Float commands, you create a very small clipping file and use GRASP's commands to move the clipping on-screen. Animator stores changes to the screen as you move a clipping from one position to another, so the resulting animation file grows rapidly. Also, once the clippings have been generated, you cannot easily change them.

Figure 4-13 The title built in buffer 1

If your program will be installed in a fixed location and your need is for spectacular effects, explore the optical effects menu of Autodesk Animator and Animator Pro. (The Pro version includes additional features.) The commercial version of GRASP will play the FLI and FLC files generated by Animator and Animator Pro respectively. The version of GRASP bundled with this book supports the FLI format only (that is, 320,000 pixel resolution). We'll show you in the next chapter how to convert Animator's 256-color mode images into a form GRASP can display in 16-color modes. The Autodesk animator programs mimic many of the functions of a TV post-production studio and allow you to create television-style effects relatively easily. Figure 4-15 shows a nine-step animation of the title screen created in Animator.

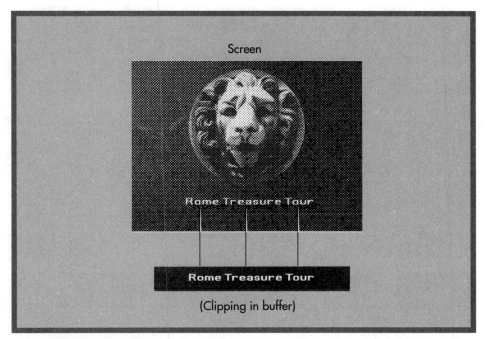

Figure 4-14 Floating a clipping into position on the screen

Screens one through nine are full screen images, shown here reduced. The audience sees the first image in the series enter from the right of the screen. The title screen appears to zoom up to full screen, turning and twisting as it moves. Animator has specialized text animation tools that make creating cinematic text scrolls and other text effects easy.

Animating with GRASP Artools

GRASP comes bundled with software tools that allow you to modify images and create special effects. Merge16 creates cross-fades that resemble cinematic dissolves using Mode l (Mode "L," not the text mode designated by the number one) images. Mosaic "blurs" images by appearing to create a new picture with pixels larger than the pixels in the original image. Transfrm produces clippings that are used to create interesting transformations between images. Txtclp converts screens captured from text programs into Pictor graphic mode images. Warp stretches, compresses, and twists images. The images can then be used to create sequences similar to the sequence shown in Figure 4-15. However, it is much faster and more efficient to create special effects sequences like these in Autodesk 2D animation products.

119

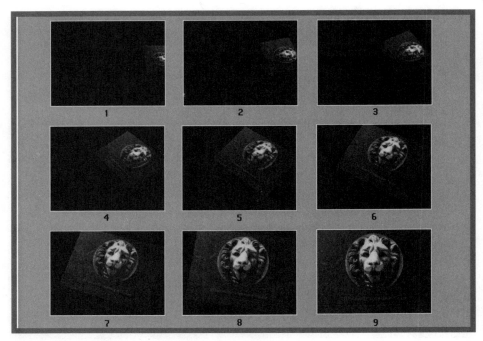

Figure 4-15 Autodesk animator special effect sequence

Adding Sound to the Magazine

Our software magazine will be viewed in the computer environment, which makes it possible for us to use special effect motion sequences. GRASP also makes it possible to use sound cards or the system speaker to play back digitized sound. (Digitized sound is sound converted and stored as digital data by a sound card. It is converted back to analog sound when it is played.) A sound card like the Sound Blaster or its compatibles will provide a much richer sound than the system speaker. We'll be covering sound in detail in later chapters.

We can add to the appeal and interest of the cover by making our lion roar. In making the lion roar, we introduce you to a new command, Merge.

Combining GRASP Scripts

Merge adds another GRASP program to the end of the current program. It is another time-saving GRASP command that helps speed program development and save computer resources. It's very similar in concept to "loadable modules" in other programming languages. Loadable modules are often-used code that act as building blocks for a variety of programs. In the case of a language like C, they are included with the program during the compile phase. Syntax for the Merge command is:

```
merge name
```

The name of the merged file is assumed to have a .TXT extension. Add the file extension if it isn't .TXT, and give the full path and drive if it's not in the current directory. The file must be in ASCII format. Most word processing programs can save in this format.

Adding text or other data, such as help screens, is facilitated by Merge. The merged file exists external to the script you are working on, but when you add it to the end of a GRASP script, GRASP treats it just like it is part of the current script. This makes it possible to use labeled subroutines in the merged script.

In this case we will use a special GRASP script to add digitized sound to the software magazine. Figure 4-16 illustrates the concept of merging a specialized script (sound) to an existing script.

You can examine the external sound script by loading SNDPLAY.TXT into the editor. Don't worry about the intricacies of this file. All that it does is query your hardware for the presence of supported sound hardware, such as the Sound Blaster card. If it finds no supported hardware, it will use the PC's internal speaker. It loads and plays a sound file. It then exits back to the point from which it was called.

Load TMPFILE.TXT back

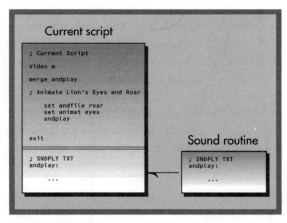

Figure 4-16 Merging a sound script with the current script

into the editor. In order to add sound to the software magazine, enter the line

```
merge \grasp\sndplay
```

right after the Video M command at the beginning of TMPFILE.TXT. This tells GRASP to add SNDPLAY.TXT to the end of TMPFILE.TXT. Note that we've added a DOS path to the file name so GRASP knows where to find SNDPLAY.TXT.

You won't actually be able to see the merged sound file when you use the editor to examine the end of TMPFILE.TXT. But GRASP will treat SNDPLAY.TXT just as if it was typed at the end of the script. That means you can use labels to access the sound playing facilities SNDPLAY.TXT provides. When we want to make the lion roar, all we have to do is tell GRASP to jump to the sndplay: label at the beginning SNDPLAY.TXT file we've tacked on the end of TMPFILE.TXT. Let's do that now. Replace the section that animates the lion's eyes:

```
; Animate Lion's Eyes
        eyes
        waitkey 60
        eyes
```

with the following lines:

```
; Animate Lion's Eyes and Roar
        set sndfile roar
        set animat eyes
        sndplay
```

Make sure that you have merged SNDPLAY.TXT at the beginning of TMPFILE.TXT by adding the line "merge \grasp\sndplay." When you run the script, the lion roars as its eyes sparkle.

Accessing Variables in the Subroutine

The variables we created in our calling script (TMPFILE.TXT) can be accessed and used by the merged sound subroutine. Figure 4-17 illustrates this.

Variables are stored in memory locations. The addresses of those memory locations are the variable's names (in this case sndfile and animat). In using these names, the subroutines can find these addresses in memory and retrieve the values stored there. Let's see how this is done in our example file.

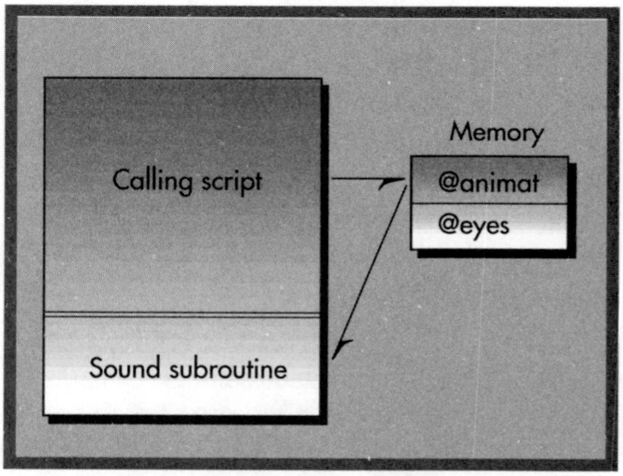

Making the Lion Roar Let's begin with the variable used for the sound file:

Figure 4-17 Accessing variables from subroutines

```
set sndfile roar
```

The lion's roar is a sound file called ROAR.SND that was captured by a Sound Blaster card and converted into a form GRASP's sound playback facility can understand. The line in the SNDPLAY.TXT subroutine that loads the sound file is:

```
load @sndfile$".snd"      ; loads the sound file roar.snd
```

Load is a special GRASP command that loads data into memory. Don't worry if you don't understand this line right now. If you like, you can come back to it in the future when you have a better understanding of GRASP commands. The important point is that we set up a variable in the calling subroutine (sndfile) that is assigned

> **CAUTION!**
>
> A peculiarity of the sound driver (SOUNDPC.GRP) bundled with this book is that digitized sounds cannot be played while the system is accessing the hard disk. That's why the eyes animation is called after the sound begins. The animation must end before the sound subroutine is exited. Several animations can play while a sound is playing, so long as there is no disk access.

the root name of the sound file. The sound routine reads that variable (@sndfile), and adds the .SND extension to it. It loads the file into memory. It starts playing the sound.

Making the Eyes Sparkle We created a variable in the calling routine:

```
set animat eyes
```

that is assigned the name of the subroutine that makes the eyes sparkle. When GRASP executes the SNDFILE subroutine, it encounters @animat, substitutes the value for animat, (eyes) and discovers that it is a label calling another subroutine. GRASP branches to the new subroutine. So, while the sound is playing, the animation occurs. Figure 4-18 shows how the subroutines are called.

You can see that Merge can give your scripts great versatility and economy. All we have to do to change either the sound file or animation variable is to reuse the code in the sound subroutine. The subroutine becomes a kind of black box.

```
set sndfile name
set animat name
```

We can call the sound-playing subroutine by typing sndplay anywhere in the script. The sound-playing subroutine is endlessly reusable. Add another call to the sound-playing subroutine just after the title sequence.

```
; Lion roars again
        sndplay
```

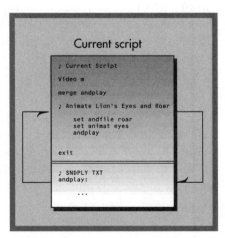

Figure 4-18 The animation subroutine called by the sound subroutine

Take a Break Here

This is a good place to a take a break. In the next section we'll be showing you how to add user interaction to the software magazine.

Flipping Pages with a Mouse

When we reach the end of a page in a magazine, we turn the page. We will make it just as easy for the reader of the software magazine to flip electronic pages. Adding a mouse interface to the magazine is exceptionally easy. All that is required to activate the mouse cursor is to type the line

```
mouse on
```

anywhere within our script. (The command "mouse off" turns the mouse cursor off.) Add this line to the script after the call to the sound subroutine at the end of the title sequence.

```
; Lion roars again
        sndplay

; Turns on mouse
        mouse on
```

Make sure your mouse is installed and working. (If you don't have a mouse, use the keyboard alternatives provided.) Then run the script. After the title floats to its final position, and the lion roars, a red cross-hair appears in the lion's mouth. This is the default mouse cursor. Move it about the screen. Notice how it changes color as it moves over the different color regions.

Creating Custom Mouse Cursors

GRASP allows you to create a custom mouse cursor. We've created an arrow in Pictor and clipped it, using the (ALT)-(J) key combinations to ensure that the clipping is small. We've used a second clipping that is the negative of the first to mask out the background as the arrow moves over different areas of the screen. Here's the syntax for the Mouse Cursor command.

```
mouse cursor shape x,y [mask]
```

Shape is the clipping buffer or clipping file to use for the cursor shape. The mask is optional. The x,y coordinates are offsets into the clipping where you want the cursor's "hot spot" to be located. In the case of the arrow, the hot spot will be the arrow's tip. The custom cursor is installed just before you turn the mouse on. Enter this line before the Mouse On command:

```
mouse cursor arrow 7 17 arrow2
mouse on
```

Arrow is the name of the clipping we created in Pictor, arrow2 is the name of the negative mask we created in Pictor. To make the tip of the arrow the "hot spot" we've used the x,y offsets 7 and 17.

Checking for a Mouse

What if the user doesn't have a mouse installed? GRASP provides a means for checking for the presence of a mouse. When GRASP runs your script, it automatically checks for the presence of a mouse software driver (not hardware!) and creates a system variable (@mouse) where the result of the inquiry is stored. You can check to see if a mouse is installed by querying this variable. The best place to install the query is at the beginning of the script, before it runs. This alerts the user that a mouse is not installed. Place this block of code right after the Video M command at the beginning of the script.

```
; Is there a mouse in the house?
        if !@mouse
                fload \grasp\squar20.set 1
                set center on                            ; centers text horizontally
                text 0,280 "Mouse Driver not present!"
                text 0,240 "Using keyboard alternative."
                set center off
                waitkey 500
                exit
        endif
```

Centering Text

Notice that we've used a command that allows us to center text horizontally on the screen. It's important that you remember to turn text centering off. The command will treat horizontal text coordinates as offsets. Try changing "text 0,280" to "text 300,280" to see what we mean.

Using Operators for Decisions

If and Endif mark off a section of code that GRASP will run if the expression being tested is true. Otherwise, GRASP skips the code and goes to the next command after the Endif. We want the error message to run if it is not true that a mouse is present. Placing an exclamation operator (!) in front of a true value has the effect of making it not true. (Similarly, placing an exclamation operator in front of a false value makes it not false, that is, true.) Since the @mouse variable is true if a mouse is present, we need to place an exclamation mark in front of it to make it not true. Try removing the exclamation mark from the expression to see the effect of the exclamation mark operator.

The warning message advises that a "keyboard alternative" will be used. Throughout the script, wherever a mouse is called for, there will be a test made first to see if it is present. If it is not, the user will be provided with keyboard alternatives.

Now that we have installed the mouse, created a mouse cursor, and turned it on, what do we do with it?

ADJUSTING MOUSE SENSITIVITY

GRASP makes another adjustment available to the producer. The responsiveness of the mouse cursor to movements of the mouse can be altered with the Mouse Sense command.

```
mouse sense [sensitivity] [velocity]
```

Sensitivity is the ratio between movement of the mouse over the desktop and movement of the mouse cursor on the screen. It applies to normal movements of the hand, such as when you are moving from one closely spaced option to another. It can have a value between 0 and 7. Zero is a high degree of sensitivity: a slow hand movement will produce a relatively faster movement of the cursor on the screen; 7 produces the smallest on-screen change relative to hand movement.

The *velocity* parameter controls the speed of the mouse cursor when you move it suddenly from one area of the screen to another. The value can be between 0 and 7. The fastest is 7.

The user will use the mouse to interact with the software magazine. Let's use the lion's nose as the "hot spot," which the user can press to explore Rome's treasures. Before we set that up, let's first send the user a message. We're going to build the message off-screen and then flicker it, using Float.

```
; Build Message to User Off-Screen
        pnewbuf p1                          ; create temporary buffer
        psetbuf p1                          ; redirect drawing off-screen
        clearscr 1                          ; create background color
        fload \grasp\squar15.set 1          ; notice subdirectory
        color 10
        text 190 ,15 "Click on Lion's Nose" ; create title
        ffree 1
        tran on 1
        cgetbuf c1 182,002 487,044 1 1      ; capture title to clipping buffer
        pfree p1
        psetbuf                             ; resume drawing to screen
```

(Don't run the script yet.) Type the following code after the exit point of the script, and after the eyes: subroutine. This section of code will be used as a subroutine.

```
; Signal User
        signal
        mouse off
        mark 8
                float 0 0 0 0 3 10 c1       ; float in one spot
        loop
        mouse on
        goto checkm
```

Again, don't run the script yet. We've created a clipping that will flash a message on and off, just below the engraved groove. The Float command will implement the flicker. The flicker can be adjusted by changing the loop count (8) and the delay time (10).

Now comes the interesting part. Let's make the lion's nose sensitive to our mouse clicks. If the user clicks on the lion's nose, we are going to fade the screen to black and bring up the background again without the lion's head or titles. Before we add the code that checks for a mouse click on the lion's nose, let's first create another file that we are going to load and run when the user clicks on the lion's nose.

Create a new file by exiting the editor to GRASP's main screen. You will be prompted with the message, "Current file has changed. Do you want to save it first?" Answer y for yes. Now choose Create File from the File menu. Call the file TMP-FILE2. Enter the following code:

```
; TMPFILE2.TXT Rome Treasure Tour main screen.

video m

set debug on

start:                                  ; label used by Link command

; Fade to black, then load and fade Main Menu background.
        pgetbuf p1 0,0 8,8              ; captures small bit of screen
        pload blackpic.pal p2          ; black palette for fading to black
        palette p1                     ; current palette
        spread p1 p2 64                ; fades current screen to black
        pfree p1
        pload romeback.pic p1          ; loads background
        pfade 0 p1                     ; fades it, but can't see it yet
        spread p2 p1 64                ; fades it up from black
waitkey
```

Run this script. We've set debug on, so press the space bar right away. Try stepping through the sequence with the space bar. This is the GRASP script that will be loaded and run when the lion's nose is pressed. Later we will develop this script into the Main menu of the Treasure Tour. Because this is going to be the Main menu, we know that we will want to come back to this screen again and again from other GRASP scripts. That's the reason why the debug banner at the beginning of the script appears to fade away. Any image that happens to be on the screen when we link to this script will first fade from the screen before the script runs.

The Pgetbuf command (pgetbuf p1 0,0 8,8) captures a tiny bit of the existing screen to a buffer. Creating a tiny picture uses very little memory. Then we load the palette we created in an earlier chapter, BLACKPIC.PAL, to fade the existing screen to black. We then free up the temporary buffer and load in the background picture. We then cross fade between our black screen and the background image.

Let's go back to TMPFILE.TXT to implement the link to this script. Load it back into the editor.

Checking for a Mouse Click

We're going to give our user a fairly wide latitude in finding the lion's nose with the mouse arrow. Enter the following, just before the Waitkey and Exit commands. (Or you can load MAGAZINE.TXT and have it look at the code there.)

```
; Check for mouse click/enter key.
        checkm:
        if @mouse
                ifmouse 1 continue 236,232 395,379 1 800 signal
        else
                fload \grasp\squar15.set 1
                color 8
                text 230,15 "Press Enter"
                ffree 1
                waitkey
                ifkey enter continue
                goto checkm
        endif

; Link to TMPFILE2.TXT script.
        continue:
        cfree 1                          ; clears eyes clippings
        mouse off
        sndplay
        link TMPFILE2.TXT start
```

When you do run the script, and if you have a mouse installed, you will see the message to the user ("Click on Lion's Nose") flicker momentarily on the screen and disappear. Every eight seconds the message is repeated as part of an endless loop. (If you want to exit the script back to the editor without pressing the lion's nose, press the (ESC) key and click anywhere on the screen.) If you do not have a mouse installed, the message "Press Enter" appears below the groove and the program waits until you press the (ENTER) key. If you click on the lion's nose with the mouse or press (ENTER) (if a mouse is not present), the region around the nose lights up momentarily, then the lion roars (he's upset) and the screen fades to black. Finally, an unadorned ROMEBACK.PIC background fades up from black.

Checking for User Mouse Clicks

The Ifmouse command is complicated, so it's worth looking at in detail. The syntax for the command is:

```
ifmouse button [label1] [x1,y1 x2,y2] [color] [wait] [label2]
```

The command says, "If the user pressed the mouse button in the following region (defined in x,y coordinates), use this color to highlight the area and branch to label

1. If the user does not select this area with the mouse within the specified 'wait' time, branch to label 2."

The button Parameter Ifmouse must be given a mouse *button* to check. The other parameters are optional. GRASP can check for all three (or on two-button mice, any of the two) mouse buttons or a combination of mouse buttons. Mouse button values are provided in the (F2) help screens (last page).

The color Parameter When the user clicks on a test region, the area is highlighted. This gives the user a visual cue that he or she is within the specified region (the lion's nose). You can specify the color to use to highlight the area. We've chosen color 1. Try pressing down on the mouse button and holding it. The area remains highlighted until you release the mouse button. Entering a value of 0 (black is in slot 0 in this case) for the color parameter does not highlight the area.

The label2 Parameter We've placed the Ifmouse command in a loop that continues until a time-out value of 8 seconds is reached. When 8 seconds have elapsed without a mouse click, GRASP branches back to the signal: label and the message to the user is flashed on the screen again. It flickers for a moment and execution continues. The check for the mouse click is once more looped. This endless loop continues indefinitely. If you do not loop the Ifmouse command, it will check for the mouse click only once and faster than you can respond. Place semicolons in front of the "checkm:" and "goto checkm" commands to test this. When you click on the screen—anywhere on the screen—the hot spot is not highlighted, and you continue to the next command, in this case the link to the next script. Remove the semicolons again.

The label1 Parameter If the user does click within the area defined by the coordinates parameter (x1,y1 x2,y2) then execution continues at the label1 parameter, in this case a label called continue:. This is the link to the new script.

Let's now look at the keyboard alternative.

The Keyboard Alternative

Here's the code segment again:

```
; Check for mouse click/enter key.
        checkm:
        if @mouse
                ifmouse 1 continue 236,232 395,379 1 800 signal
        else
                fload \grasp\squar15.set 1
                color 8
                text 230,15 "Press Enter"
                ffree 1
                waitkey
```

```
                ifkey enter continue
                goto checkm
        endif
```

First we check for the presence of a mouse. If there is no mouse present, GRASP ignores the Ifmouse command and proceeds to execute the code after the else statement. It places the message to the user on the screen ("Press Enter") and waits for a keypress. When another key is pressed, Ifkey tests the key and if any other key than the (ENTER) key is pressed, the program seems to do nothing. Actually, the program jumps back to the beginning of the routine, to the checkm label, and cycles back to the Waitkey command. It will keep doing this until Ifkey's test discovers you pressed the (ENTER) key. At that point program execution continues at the continue: label.

The if/else/endif structure implements the program's flexible response to the user's hardware setup. If you have a mouse installed, you can test the keyboard alternative by placing an exclamation mark in front of the variable that returns the result for the test for the mouse (!@mouse). (Paradoxically, this changes the test to read: if the mouse is present use the keyboard alternative.)

Let's now see what happens when program execution branches to the continue label. Here's the code again:

```
; Link to TMPFILE2.TXT script.
        continue:
        cfree cl                        ; clears eyes clippings
        mouse off
        sndplay
        link TMPFILE2.TEXT start        ; link to TMPFILE2.TXT at start: label
```

If the user pressed the lion's nose, execution jumps to the continue: label. There a buffer is freed, the mouse is turned off, the lion roars, and the link is made to another script.

Linking GRASP Scripts

The Link command loads and runs another GRASP script. The existing script is abandoned. This makes Link quite different from Call, the GRASP command that allows you to run an external script and return to a calling script. It's also quite different from Merge, which adds a second script at the end of a first script. Figure 4-19 shows these three different ways of combining GRASP scripts.

Call loads another script, runs it, and returns to the calling script. It's an efficient way of using sections of code repetitively. You temporarily, and completely, abandon the calling script, running the called code as an independent script until an exit or return is encountered. You can, however, pass information to the called script and back to the calling script. We'll be discussing these methods in a later chapter.

Merge is similar to Call, except that the code is actually incorporated into the current script, which means it can branch to labels in the calling program. You cannot do this with Call. Call leaves—and returns to—the same spot in the calling script. Link is valuable because it allows you to break a large GRASP program into smaller, more manageable modules. Scripts occupy memory, just as pictures, clippings, fonts, and other GRASP data. Program files can be a maximum of 24 kilobytes in size. Keeping them as small as possible, through linking and calling, is important for small, efficient programs that occupy less memory and execute faster. The disadvantage of the Link command is that it loads another script from the hard drive, pausing the program—not a big disadvantage with today's fast hard drives.

One more note about the Link command. Local variables remain visible from one script to another. It's better to use variables in subroutines using the Gosub command. Variables used in subroutines are no longer visible upon return to the calling routine. Remember, variables occupy memory. Learn how to manage them.

The sidebar descends into a deeper level of the maze of memory addressing in GRASP. You can skip it now if you like. At some dark hour in the future, when a dread "out of memory" message appears in a white banner on your screen, refer back to the sidebar for a discussion of memory allocation with GRASP.

Now that we've revealed some of the complexities of memory management in GRASP, it's time to return to the pleasure of creating in GRASP. The syntax of the Link command is:

```
link [label]
```

The optional label allows us to avoid a potential problem that occurs when we link to TMPFILE2.TXT. If we had not used the label, GRASP would have run TMPFILE2.TXT from the beginning of the script. It would have encountered the Video M command right away, and blanked the screen as it initialized the hardware to that VGA mode. (The Video M command is necessary during development and testing because we want to be able to run TMPFILE2.TXT on its own.) Branching to a start position below the Video M command is one of those GRASP tricks you soon come to rely on for efficiency.

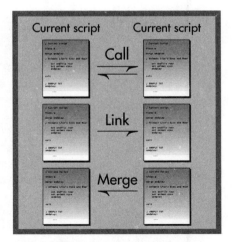

Figure 4-19 Three ways of combining GRASP scripts

One last comment before we leave the opening screen of the software magazine. We turn the mouse off while we fade down the opening screen and bring up the Main menu. This is a subtle way of managing the user's interactive relationship with the program. We're telling the user when the mouse is active, and when it is not. The other point is about the use of sound and visual cues in interactive presentation systems. The lion roars when you press its nose. (And well it should!) This appeals to the child in us. When we use rich, digitized sounds in computer environments, we use the ears as well as the eyes to communicate with the user and open doors to emotions. This is the essence of multimedia: a multisensory computing environment that can convey feeling as well as knowledge. Okay, the lecture's over. Let's have some more fun with the software magazine.

Moving Code Between Programs

We will want to add the engraved "groove" we used for the first screen at the bottom of the next screen. Instead of laboriously copying the code over into the second script, let's use one of GRASP's shortcuts.

We'll save to disk a copy of the code that creates the groove and then insert it in the new script. Position the cursor at the beginning of the section of code that creates the double line and press (F4) (mark the beginning of a block). Then move the

NEAR AND FAR MEMORY

The infamous *segmented memory architecture* of the Intel 8086 family of microprocessors makes memory usage a complicated matter for GRASP programs. The PC has a total address space of 1 megabyte, but only 64K chunks (segments) can be directly addressed at a time. The microprocessor can access data larger than 64K (an example is a 300K picture file), but the addressing scheme is complex. Consequently, the microprocessor uses two ways of addressing data in memory according to whether the data is less than, or greater than, 64K in size. One method uses a single instruction to access data that falls within a single 64K segment of memory. (*Near* pointers in the C programming language take advantage of this fact.) Memory that can be addressed in this way is called *near memory* in GRASP. The more complex method is associated with data that exceeds the 64K limit. It results in more microprocessor instructions and a comparatively slow execution speed. Memory addressed in this fashion is called *far memory.* (Far pointers in the C programming language address memory of this kind.)

(continued from page 132)

GRASP is written in Microsoft C, so it has acquired some of the peculiarities of the way C allocates memory. Near memory is where GRASP program instructions and the data associated with those instructions (such as system variables) are located. It's also the area where the variables you create and the instructions you write as part of a script are located. GRASP allocates 24 kilobytes for you to use for these instructions and data. Other data that you load into memory, particularly picture files, font files, animation (DFF) files, and clippings, are automatically allocated to far memory.

Normally, when you Call, Link, or Merge a script, it is loaded into the area of near memory set aside by GRASP for your program's use. Sometimes your program has grown to the size in near memory such that the called file exceeds this area's limit of 24 kilobytes. GRASP has provided an option that allows you to swap out to far memory the calling routine as needed to make room for the called routine. It's very simple to turn on this option. Just type the following instruction before calling the .TXT file:

```
set maxcall on
```

If far memory is tight turn it off again when your program returns from the called script. (By issuing the command "set maxcall off.") GRASP's editor and the debug system option provide reports on available near and far memory. We'll be using this GRASP system setting near the end of the chapter.

cursor down to the line after the Pfree statements and press (F4) again. This is the section of code that should be highlighted:

```
; Add Groove to bottom of screen.
        pgetbuf p1 424,103 464,107      ; saves part of screen to buffer 1
        pgetbuf p2 136,198 176,200      ; saves part of screen to buffer 2
        position p1 0, 0                ; sets x,y offsets of p1 to 0,0
        position p2 0 ,0                ; sets x,y offsets of p2 to 0,0
        fly 0 52,639 52,32 1 p1         ; creates shadow
        fly 0 49,639 49,32 1 p2         ; creates light line highlight
        pfree p1 - p2
```

The section of code you just marked off should be highlighted. (If it is not, try again.) Now press (F8). At the top of the editor screen, GRASP asks for the file you want to save (Write:). Enter the word `test`. GRASP saves the section of code to disk under that file name. Press (F4) again to un-highlight the text. Then load TMP-FILE2.TXT into the editor.

Now place the cursor on a blank line just before the Waitkey command. Press (F7). At the top of the editor screen, GRASP asks for a file name (Read:). Type the word test at the prompt. The file is inserted at the cursor position. Press (F4) to un-highlight the text. Then run the program. The engraved groove forms on the screen.

The method we have just shown you is helpful for testing code during the development phase of a program. You should, however, look for as many opportunities as possible to implement repetitive code as a subroutine, or a callable text file. If you read the sidebar on near and far memory in GRASP, you know that reducing the length of the code in your programs becomes increasingly important as the complexity of the length of your script and program increases.

Adding a Picture to the Screen

We've prepared an image to help add color and interest to the Main menu. The image originates from a shot taken in the Roman Forum of a red rose with an out-of-focus church in the background. It was scanned and dithered to 16 colors.

We will create a picture frame and a shadow underneath the picture to add to its graphic appeal. The image is built off-screen. Here's the code that creates the image. Enter it right after the section that creates a groove on the background, just before the Waitkey command.

```
; Add frame for picture

        pgetbuf p1                      ; saves current screen to buffer
        psetbuf p1                      ; redirects drawing off-screen

        color 0                         ; black
        rect 052,075 484,360            ; creates black shadow for box
        color 3                         ; medium gray
        box 042,081 477,374 6           ; frame 6 pixels wide
        color 4                         ; lighter gray
        line 042,081 042,374            ; highlight left side of frame
        line 042,374 477,374            ; highlight top of frame
        color 2
        line 042,081 477,081            ; dark edge bottom of frame
        line 477,081 477,374            ; dark edge left side of frame

; Add picture inside frame
        pload rose.pal p2               ; change palette for rose clipping
        palette p2                      ; set palette to buffer 2
        pfree p2                        ; free
        cload rose.clp c1 1             ; load clipping
        putup 48,87 c1                  ; putup inside frame
        cfree c1                        ; free buffer

        psetbuf                         ; resume drawing to screen
        pfade 6 p1 200                  ; horizontal filter wipe new image
        pfree p1                        ; free buffer
```

ALTERNATIVE EDITING KEYS

If you find use of the (F4) key for highlighting editing blocks confusing, you may prefer to use the alternative key combinations (ctrl) (K)-(B) (beginning of block), and Control (K)-(K) (end of block). This is not as convenient as using (F4), but it is less confusing.

Run the script. The Main menu builds on the screen. The framed image of the rose and the cathedral is built off-screen to hide the steps in its construction. (Try commenting out the Psetbuf and Pfade commands with semicolons to see why we have built the image off-screen. The steps in the construction of the picture are disconcerting visually.)

Let's go through the code step-by-step. First we create a black rectangle that will become the shadow for the picture, using GRASP's Rect command.

```
color 0                        ; black
rect 052,075 484,360           ; creates black shadow for box
```

Its syntax is:

```
rect x1,y1 x2,y2
```

The rectangle is drawn in the current color. We set the current color to black to create the black rectangular shadow. The coordinates you supply must lie at opposite ends of the rectangle. It doesn't matter from which corner you start. The offset command can affect these coordinates.

After creating a rectangle, we then create a gray frame 6 pixels wide using GRASP's box command.

```
color 3                        ; medium gray
box 042,081 477,374 6          ; frame 6 pixels wide
```

The Box command's syntax is:

```
box x1,y1 x2,y2 [width]
```

Like the Rect command, the Box command uses the current color to create the hollow rectangle on the screen. We used a gray color. The command includes a parameter that allows you to set the width of the box in pixels. The default width is 1 pixel. We made the frame around the picture 6 pixels wide.

Adding Highlights

Adding subtle highlights to screens helps give them polish and beauty, increasing the viewer's interest in the message you want to convey. Respect is in the details, in other words. We've added a thin, almost imperceptible highlight to the sides of the frame facing the light source (the left side and top of the frame). Using a lighter gray than the gray of the frame, the Line command was employed to create a highlight along the edges of the frame.

```
color 4                        ; lighter gray
line 042,081 042,374           ; highlight left side of frame
line 042,374 477,374           ; highlight top of frame
```

(The Line command's syntax was provided earlier in the chapter.) Similarly, we create a dark, thin edge along the sides of the frame facing away from the light.

```
color 2
line 042,081 477,081           ; dark edge bottom of frame
line 477,081 477,374           ; dark edge left side of frame
```

The eye is very sensitive to the edges of objects. Our highlights help separate the frame from the background.

Palette Sleight-of-Hand

We then put the picture up inside the frame.

```
; Add picture inside frame
        pload rose.pal p2      ; change palette for rose clipping
        palette p2             ; set palette to buffer 2
        pfree p2               ; free
        cload rose.clp c1 1    ; load clipping
```

Note that we load a new palette (ROSE.PAL). Clipping files do not contain palette information. That's why we've had to create a palette for the clipping, ROSE.CLP. ROSE.PAL shares the same first ten color slots with the palette we use for the background, that is, ten shades of gray. It's the last six palette slots that are different. Since none of these colors are on the screen before or after the palette change, the user never sees our sleight-of-palette. You may think that we would not have seen the palette change anyway, since we're drawing off-screen. But even though the palette swapping has occurred while we are drawing off-screen, the system uses the currently selected palette to display colors on-screen, and it's this palette we are changing. You can see the effect of changing palettes while drawing off-screen by changing ROSE.PAL to BLACKPIC.PAL. The screen will go black shortly after the groove builds on, and it will remain black.

The final step in the picture-building process is to add the clipping to the screen.

```
        putup 48,87 c1         ; putup inside frame
        cfree c1               ; free buffer
```

We reset drawing activity to the screen and use fade 6 (horizontal filter fade) to display the completed image on screen.

```
psetbuf                        ; resume drawing to screen
pfade 6 p1 200                 ; horizontal filter wipe new image
pfree p1                       ; free buffer
```

The drawing commands execute very quickly, so the detour we took off-screen is hardly noticeable to the user. Screen magic: the lovely gray-framed rose filter-wipes onto the screen. (By the way, there really is a medieval church in the background.)

Adding the Table of Contents

The main screen is the jumping off point for the Rome Treasure Tour. It acts as the table of contents scanned by the reader of a magazine. We've used Autodesk's 3D Studio to create buttons the user can press to branch to flip the electronic page to an area of interest. Insert the following code after the last section of TMPFILE2.TXT, just before the Waitkey command.

```
; Add buttons
        tran on 1
        cload button c1 1 1
        mark 3
                float 640,80 504,80 8 1 c1
                putup 504,80 c1
                offset 0,90 r
        loop
        offset 0,0
        cfree c1
```

We haven't commented the code because these commands should be quite familiar to you by now. Instead of creating three buttons in 3D Studio, we created one and added a shadow to it in Animator Pro, 3D Studio's companion 2D animation package. (We'll be showing you how to use these programs to generate graphics for 16-color EGA and VGA programs in the next chapter.) By using a gray background (color slot 1), and loading the clipping with the transparency parameter set to on (1), we can float the button plus its shadow onto the screen. The Float command brings the button from off the screen into its final position, but does not leave a copy of the clipping on the screen. It's the Putup command that places the image on the screen. We clipped the button in Pictor with the (ALT)-(J) (ALT)-(F9), key combination to make it byte-wide. We use the noshift parameter when loading the button (cload button c1 1 1). (If this sounds suspiciously like a review of basic commands, it is!) We make sure that we put up the button on a byte boundary (a horizontal position divisible by eight), otherwise it won't show.

The loop we create puts up the same button three times at a distance of 90 pixels from each other, on the vertical (y) axis. The offset command uses the relative switch. This an efficient way to add or subtract buttons from our screen, through increasing or decreasing the loop count. Notice that we set the screen offset back to 0,0 when we exit the loop. If you don't do this, all subsequent screen activity will be affected by offsets.

Adding Titles

GRASP allows you to add titles easily to the screen. This makes GRASP programs very flexible. No need to re-create title slides from scratch, just enter the script and re-type the title. We'll float the Main menu title from the top of the screen and scroll the button titles on.

```
; Add Main Menu Title
        pnewbuf p1
        psetbuf p1
        clearscr 1
        fload \grasp\squar20.set 1              ; notice subdirectory
        color 13 0
        fstyle 8 20 12
        fgaps 10 15
        text 120,410 "Main Menu"
        ffree 1
        tran on 1
        cgetbuf c1 114,400 355,440 1 1
        psetbuf
        pfree p1
        float 0,100 0,0 5 3 c1
        putup c1
        cfree c1

; Button Titles
        fload \grasp\squar10.set 1              ; notice we add subdirectory
        fstyle 8 10 6
        text 537,300 "Slides" 3
        waitkey 02
        text 539,210 "Sites" 3
        waitkey 02
        text 526,120 "Restart" 3
        ffree 1
```

The Main menu title is built off-screen with a shadow, so that we can float it from the top of the screen into position. We turn Cgetbuf's noshift parameter on to make sure that the title is captured on a byte boundary. This is good memory management. So is unloading picture, clipping, and font buffers as soon as they are no longer needed. The button titles scroll on. We've set the speed of the scroll with the optional parameter, in this case, 3. Try changing this number to see the different scrolling rates. The Waitkey commands between the button titles adjust the flow to the animation.

The Lion Again!

If you were creating a software magazine for a company or institution, you would want to add the logo screens in the presentation. A good candidate for the location for a logo would be in the area at the top of the button bar. Since our lion has become our unofficial logo, let's add a lion to this area. The lion we use was shot (no pun intended!) in the same area as the rose and cathedral, at the Forum in Rome. He's more weather-worn than our previous lion, but his roar sounds the same! Let's begin by adding the sound routine to this script. Add the line "merge \grasp\sndplay" after the start: label near the top of the script. (Notice that we give the Merge command a path to find SNDPLAY.TXT. It's located in the \GRASP subdirectory.)

```
start:
merge \grasp\sndplay
```

If we had placed the Merge command before the start: label, GRASP wouldn't see the instruction to merge the sound routines. The Link command at the end of the previous script (link TMPFILE2.TXT start) instructed GRASP to start processing this file after the start: routine.

Remember that Merge adds the SNDPLAY.TXT file to the end of the script we are presently working on.

We are going to create a black box with a small, light gray frame and then float the lion's head up from the bottom of the frame. He'll roar while he does this. Enter the following lines after the last section and before the Waitkey and Exit commands.

```
; Create Box
        pgetbuf p1                      ; save screen to buffer
        psetbuf p1                      ; set screen activity to buffer
        color 0
        rect 514,374 610,468            ; draw black box for lion
        color 4
        box 513,373 611,469             ; put a frame around it

        psetbuf                         ; resume drawing to screen
        window 513,373 611,469          ; place window around frame
        pfade 20 p1 50                  ; sparkle is confined to window
        window                          ; reset to default window (whole screen)

; Lion Rises
        set sndfile roar
        set animat lionrise
        sndplay
        mouse on

waitkey
exit
```

Now add the subroutine after the exit:

```
lionrise:
        cload lion2.clp c1              ; load lion clipping
        window 514,374 610,468         ; create window around lion frame
        offset 0,-120                  ; moves lion head down 120 pixels
        mark 60
        putup 514,375 c1               ; lion head at first can't be seen
        offset 0,2 r                   ; moves lion head up two pixels
        loop                           ; repeats sixty times
        offset 0,0                     ; resets offsets
        cfree c1
        window
return
```

When you run the program, the Main menu should take the final form you see in Figure 4-20.

Once again, we use the Psetbuf command to build the black box and frame off-screen. We could have created the black box on-screen, but we wanted to sparkle fade the box onto the screen, rather than pop it onto the screen. We introduce a new command here that is going to be enormously useful in subsequent chapters. Let's take a moment to explore it.

Altering the Default Screen Window

The Window command confines certain screen activities, such as the effects of drawing commands, to a rectangular area of the screen. When you first start up GRASP, the default window encompasses the entire screen. The command's syntax is as follows:

```
window x1,y1 x2,y2 [r]
```

You must specify the coordinates for the window beginning with the bottom left corner. The second set of coordinates are the top right corner of the window. GRASP will automatically round the horizontal coordinates to the nearest byte boundary. The relative parameter allows you to make the current window's coordinates relative to a previously defined window. This allows you to gradually reveal a window. In this example, the window begins as a thin line (with 0 thickness!) and gradually opens up (or drops) along the bottom to a vertical height of 100 pixels.

```
window 100,100 300,100                 ; window is "shut"

mark 10
        window 0,-10 0,0 r             ; bottom edge moves down
loop
```

We use the Window command in the software magazine code to accomplish something very subtle, but extremely valuable. We use it to confine the sparkle fade (pfade 20 p1 50) to a small area of the screen—to the area where the black box will fade onto the screen.

```
psetbuf                          ; resume drawing to screen
window 513,373 611,469           ; place window around frame
pfade 20 p1 50                   ; sparkle is confined to window
window                           ; reset to default window (whole screen)
```

If you comment out the Window command (by placing a semicolon in front of it), you'll see the reason for doing this. Without the Window command, GRASP must do the fade on the entire screen. With a calculation-intensive fade like fade 20, this can take a long time. By confining the fade to a small area of the screen (the area where the small black box appears), the fade occurs much more quickly.

You'll notice that we typed in the Window command with parameters before the fade and without parameters right after the fade. The second Window command resets the window to the entire screen area. The code skeleton looks like this:

```
window x1,y1 x2,y2      ; screen activity confined to small area
pfade #                 ; fade confined to window area
window                  ; resets screen activity to entire screen
```

Forgetting to reset the Window command is easy to do. When a clipping or a title fails to appear on the screen, look for an errant Window command.

We use the Window command again in the lionrise: labeled subroutine entered after the script's exit point.

Figure 4-20 The Rome Treasure Tour Main menu

```
lionrise:
        cload lion2.clp c1          ; load lion clipping
        window 514,374 610,468      ; create window around lion frame
        offset 0,-120               ; moves lion head down 120 pixels
        mark 60
        putup 514,375 c1            ; lion head at first can't be seen
        offset 0,2 r                ; moves lion head up two pixels
        loop                        ; repeats sixty times
        offset 0,0                  ; resets offsets
        cfree c1
        window
return
```

The window is created just inside the black box's frame. It allows us to create the illusion that the lion's head is rising from behind the screen into the black area of the box.

The Offset command (offset 0,-120) doesn't actually move the lion's head to a position below the frame. It alters the offsets stored with clipping, since a clipping's offsets can be affected by the Offset command. The window's coordinates are not affected by the Offset command. This makes it possible to move the clipping while the window remains static.

The Float command ignores the Window command, so we couldn't use float to move the lion's head into position. It would remain visible throughout the float, rather than just as it entered the window frame. We used the Putup command (which does respect the Window command strictures) to simulate a floating lion's head. (Because the Putups occur on top of each other, we don't see the multiple screen copies created by repeated Putups.) Each time through the loop, we put up the head and change the offsets. The first Putup places the lion's head below the window, so we don't see it. But as the loop progresses, the head does appear and move into position. It's a simple but effective technique you'll use over and over again. Notice that we reset the window to the default screen area at the end of the loop and reset the offset to 0,0.

Adding the Lion Roar

The lion's roar is implemented in much the same way as in the previous script (TMPFILE.TXT). Notice that we assign a new name label to the animation routine variable.

```
; Lion Rises
        set sndfile roar
        set animat lionrise
        sndplay
        mouse on

waitkey
```

142

Giving the Reader Choices

Adding mouse and keyboard interaction allows software magazine viewers to flip the electronic pages. They do this by selecting on of three buttons. First we'll turn on the mouse, and position the arrow cursor. We use the same code as in the previous script with an addition.

```
; Turns on mouse.
        mouse cursor arrow 7 17 arrow2
        mouse position 559,300
        mouse on
```

We've inserted yet another new mouse command, Mouse Position. It's syntax is:

```
mouse position [x,y]
```

The command makes the cursor appear at a specific location on the screen. Issuing the command without the optional coordinates places the cursor at the default screen origin position (0,0). In this case, we place it over the top button. We place the mouse cursor near to the place where the user will employ it. It's these small enhancements that help give multimedia programs a professional look and feel.

Enter the following lines right after the "signal user" section and just before the Exit command.

```
; Check for mouse click/function keys


        checkm:
        if @mouse
                ifmouse 1 slides 531,268 589,338 1 800 signal
                ifmouse 1 sites 531,177 588,247 1 800 signal
                ifmouse 1 opening 531,085 588,157 800 signal
                goto checkm
        else
                color 13 0
                fload \grasp\squar10.set 1
                fstyle 8 10 6
                text 550,281 "F1"
                text 550,191 "F2"
                text 550,100 "F3"
                waitkey

                ifkey f1 slides
                ifkey f2 sites
                ifkey f3 opening
                goto checkm
        endif
exit
```

Don't run the script yet, or you'll get an error message. What we've done is define three areas of the screen as hot spots, one for each button. (For keyboard users, we've made the (F1), (F2), and (F3) function keys available as choices.) We've created labels that GRASP will branch to if one of the buttons are selected or one of the function keys are selected. In the case of the mouse routine, if none of the buttons are selected within an 8 second time-out period, GRASP branches back to the signal label and starts the cycle again.

We're going to create three program branches corresponding to the three button choices.

```
slides:
        mouse off
        cfree c1
        fadeout
        opengl ,, \grasp\chapt03      ; change to chapter 3 subdirectory
        set maxcall on                ; load script into far memory
        local connect 1               ; set variable as flag
        call projecto.txt             ; call slide show
        opengl ,, \grasp\chapt04      ; change back to chapt. 4 subdirectory
        link tmpfile2 start           ; run Main Menu again

sites:
        mouse off
        cfree c1
        fadeout
        link map start

opening:
        mouse off
        when esc
        set esc on
        cfree c1
        fadeout
        link tmpfile start
```

These are the labels the user branches to when any of the screen's three hot spots are clicked on with the mouse. The simplest of the three is the label attached to the Restart button. It causes the program to cycle back to the opening by linking to the beginning of the first (TMPFILE.TXT) script. Notice that we turn off the mouse and free up the clipping buffer used by the message signal before linking to the opening screen. Notice we "turned off" the (ESC) key assignment, and turned (ESC) "on."

Plugging the Slide Projector into the Rome Tour

The most interesting and most complicated choice from a programming point of view is the Slides button choice. When the user selects "slides," the code that follows the slides: label loads the PROJECTO.TXT script and runs the slides you created earlier. (Note: to make sure you have actually created the slides for the software projector, run MAKESLID.TXT from within the CHAPT03 subdirectory.) Because PROJECTO.TXT will look for its files in the current subdirectory, it is necessary to tell GRASP to "change the directory" to the CHAPT03 subdirectory. The Opengl command does this. Syntax for the command is:

```
opengl ,, path
```

The commas instruct GRASP to skip the two options normally specified when GRASP is working with its proprietary library files (GL files). (The version of GRASP that is bundled with this book does not include the library files utility GLIB.EXE.) Using commas in place of options is a common programming convention. Many of GRASP's command options can be skipped in this fashion. The *path* parameter can be any valid DOS path statement. If you have installed GRASP in another directory, or as a subdirectory of another directory, enter the full path name for this option. (An example: `opengl ,, \other\grasp\chapt03`).

If you read the sidebar on near and far memory, then you know what the Set Maxcall On command does. If GRASP runs out of near memory, it will swap the calling routine out to far memory to make room for PROJECTO.TXT in near memory. PROJECTO.TXT has a life of its own, independent of the software magazine. We want to ensure it is free to grow and change.

```
set maxcall on
local connect 1              ; set variable as flag
call projecto.txt            ; call slide show
```

Using Flags in Programming

We've also created something called a *flag* in programming lingo. Flags are used in car racing to give the drivers information about race conditions. Flags perform the same duty for programs. Normally, the projector operates independently of the software magazine. But since we are calling it from the software magazine, we need a way of telling PROJECTO.TXT to return to this script. So we create a variable called *connect* that PROJECTO.TXT can test. When the user presses (ESC) in PROJECTO.TXT, a "when esc goto quit" instruction is executed. Here is the labeled subroutine the program jumps to:

```
; Exit sub-routine.
      quit:
      if def(connect)        ; if the variable connect is defined
            continue         ; jump to continue: label
      endif
      pfree p1
exit                         ; otherwise exit

      continue:
      when esc
      return                 ; return to calling script
```

We tell GRASP to check to see if a variable called connect has been defined. The GRASP function *def(variable)* does this, returning 1 (or true) if the variable is defined, or 0 (false) if it has not been defined. In this case the variable was defined, so the jump is made to the continue: label. (Otherwise, the program would exit to the editor.) As a precaution the (ESC) key is unassigned and return is made to the calling

script. When the return is made to the calling script, the directory is changed back
to CHAPT03.

```
opengl ,, \grasp\chapt04        ; change back to chapt. 4 subdirectory
link tmpfile2 start             ; run Main Menu again
```

Then the Link command is encountered. The command returns us to the top of the
script.

Link to the Sites of Rome

The third and final choice we give the viewer is attached to the Sites button. Instead
of calling MAP.TXT, we pass control completely to it through the Link command. At
the end of the script, another Link command (link romemenu start) will send execution back to the beginning of the Main menu. Note that MAP.TXT links back to
ROMEMENU.TXT not TMPFILE2.TXT. Alter this if you like.

The MAP.TXT script presents a map of ancient Rome during the time of the
Empire. Users select numbers to explore sites. We've just put the names of sites up
on the screen. A more ambitious elaboration would be to branch to other topics or
to in-depth coverage of individual sites. The script shows one way of creating an interactive graphics presentation.

Making the Program Self-Running

We've implemented a feature in the program that would be appropriate if several
people were using the magazine. The magazine will "close" and return to the first
screen (the cover) if nothing happens after a set period of time. If we did not implement this feature, the Main menu would endlessly cycle until a user clicked on a
button. Imagine that the software magazine is in a public space. Wouldn't it be more
effective to have our lion roar to draw attention to the Rome Tour?

Load TMPFILE2.TXT back into the editor. Go back to the section of code where
we signal the user and modify it in the following fashion:

```
; Signal User
        set mcount 0                        ; set counter at 0
        signal:
        mouse off
        mark 20
                float 0,0 0,0 10 10 c1      ; flash message
        loop
                set mcount @mcount+1    ; increment counter by 1
                if @mcount>5 opening    ; does counter exceed 5?
                mouse on
```

We employ GRASP's support of variables and expressions to keep track of how
many times the Main menu cycles without interaction from a user.

A counter is first established (set mcount 0); then, after the message is displayed,
incremented; then compared to a value of 5. If the counter exceeds 5, GRASP

branches to the opening: label at the bottom of the script. There the clipping buffer is freed and we are linked back to the opening screen.

Notice that the "counter" is defined before the signal: label, not after it. If we placed the counter after the label, every time we cycled back to this message routine, the counter would be reset to 0 and we would never get beyond a count of 1!

Touchscreens

It would not be difficult to adapt the software program to work with a touch screen. A touchscreen driver appears as a mouse to GRASP, so when the lion's nose is touched—he roars.

LAST WORDS

We've covered a tremendous amount of ground in this chapter. Most of GRASP's key commands have been covered. Don't worry if you don't remember the syntax for commands. Pressing (F2) while in the editor gives you instant help with commands. Chapter 10 contains command summaries and cross-references. And don't worry if the way that we are using commands seems confusing. The "Ah hah!" that comes with sudden enlightenment will come more rapidly as we develop more robust multimedia applications. This book isn't primarily about GRASP anyway. It's about using GRASP as a tool to learn multimedia.

5
Create an
Animated Demo

THIS CHAPTER brings us to a subject of enduring interest to computer users: Animation. The word contains magic, thanks to Walt Disney's rich legacy of celluloid characters and fantasy worlds that exist far, far away from mundane reality.

GRASP has been an animation program from its inception almost a decade ago (the "A" in GRASP stands for *Animation*). It has been used widely by artists to add movement and color to otherwise static presentations. In the carnival atmosphere of trade shows, chances are the animated demo that caught your eye from a distance was created using GRASP.

Software developers and hardware vendors like to use GRASP to demo their products. Illustrations, animation, text, screens captured from the software product, or photos of the hardware can be woven into a GRASP script for a visual magic carpet ride.

Today's audiences have grown up in front of the TV, and they expect high production values and visual artifice. You communicate excitement about your message or product in the visual dynamics of your presentation. Enhancing your marketing message with graphs that grow and screens that wipe, dissolve, and sparkle keeps the audience attentive and involved with the presentation.

GRASP's support for the Autodesk Animator, Animator Pro, and 3D Studio animation formats (FLI and FLC files) mean you can bring the props, tools, and techniques of a digital production studio to your portfolio or marketing presentation. These programs excel at moving images. Draw and paint programs like Corel Draw, Harvard Graphics, and Zsoft's Paint make images interesting to eyes disenchanted by television. Image processing programs like Paint Shop Pro, Aldus Photostyler, and Handmade Software's Image Alchemy conversion and dithering program help create images that leave lasting impressions with viewers.

Today's True Color display systems, fast microprocessors, and large hard drives have given artists and multimedia producers an excellent playback platform for visually striking presentations. In this chapter we'll show you an image magician's book of spells to wow audiences and influence decision makers.

As in the preceding chapters, we will build an actual application: the floppy-disk demo for *Multimedia Creations*. The demo not only promotes the book, it also demonstrates a number of image processing and animation techniques. We'll dissect its inner workings and lay bare the secrets it buries in code. First, however, we'll show you how the demo was planned.

PLANNING THE DEMO

The first chapter of *Multimedia Creations* outlined the production methods employed by multimedia producers and provided a producer's guide through the hardware obstacle course offered by entry level computers. This chapter will train you in the guerrilla tactics demo producers employ to overcome a hardware platform hostile to the moving image. In your own work, you would do well to consider the challenges that lie ahead before you attempt to storyboard the presentation.

Storyboarding multimedia productions is an onerous task, because it separates you from the joy of making images fly on the screen. However, remember that in animating images you go to war with the stubborn PC. A storyboard allows you to visualize what the demo will look like on the screen. It will help identify the challenges you will run into along the way. No responsible general will toss the troops into a battle that is doomed. Generals like to plan the campaign thoroughly in advance. Ask yourself: How will I actually do this? Will I have enough RAM memory to pull that off? Is that a good visual analogy?

It's a good idea to do a storyboard before visiting the client with the big idea. The storyboard will raise the tough questions you will have to solve back in the studio, and it will help the client visualize what you're trying to portray. That's not all. You know that war analogy you worked and reworked with the storyboard? The client hates it! (Cute ideas are potential mine fields. War is a particularly dangerous analogy to work with in business presentations. You cannot afford to alienate portions of your audience.) Now it's literally back to the drawing board. Even before the big idea arrives, it's a good idea to review design goals for the presentation. Who is the demo's audience? What is the demo supposed to accomplish?

Design Goals

Let's review the design goals for the *Multimedia Creations* demo. First, identify your *intended audience.* In this case it's any person with an interest in creating multimedia productions at their desk on an entry class or better PC.

Now, what do we want the demo to do? These are our *design goals:*

- Make people buy the book.
- Illustrate the audiovisual techniques taught by the book.
- Act as a sample application in the book.
- Show a history of motion and sound on the PC.
- Act as an artistic as well as a business example.

In addition, to reach the maximum audience size, the demo must:

- fit on one high-density floppy uncompressed
- compress to less than 500K
- run on VGA, 16 colors (Video Mode M)
- run on XTs, 286s, or 386s
- run with and without sound cards

Developing a Central Concept (a.k.a. The Big Idea)

In Hollywood the chances for a story's acceptance for production are much reduced if it cannot be encapsulated in a few words, the famous "high concept." Example: "Investigator into JFK's assassination raises conspiracy possibilities." Hollywood built an entire movie around this line. The demo for *Multimedia Creations,* while on a much smaller scale required this kind of intellectual compression.

The central concept that makes the demo work as a unified whole was arrived at almost immediately. Its simplicity spoke well for its power. It also was a lucid communication of the ad's intent. The idea was to spin the Waite Group Press logo (the letter W) on its axis to become the M of Multimedia. Figure 5-1 shows what the logo looks like, and Figure 5-2 shows what the W looks like when it is inverted. Making the client's logo a focal point for the presentation does more then earn kudos in the boardroom. It enhances the logo in the mind of the viewer

Figure 5-1 The W Shape in the Waite Group Logo

and makes it more memorable. Technically, this is called "building awareness."

To make the metamorphosis of the W into the M work, we will spin the W around using 3D animation. In fact, spinning the W in 3D will be easy. Autodesk's 3D Studio will be used to create the outline of the W, extrude it into three dimensions, and animate the spin. It handles this job with aplomb.

The concept develops to: "A print media publisher's logo morphs into the first letter of multimedia." When we add music to that description, we've arrived at our high concept. The concept is a natural way to advertise the book.

Storyboarding the Demo

Now that the concept is nailed down, we turn our attention to cartooning the important actions in the demo. It's time to do a storyboard. Figure 5-3 shows a series of frames from the demo.

This is an excerpt from the entire storyboard. Only the most important frames in the demo are presented here.

You can see that the storyboard helps us develop a visual design for the entire presentation. Like most time-based media, demos are always more pleasing to viewers

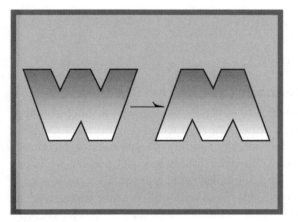

Figure 5-2 The W becomes an M

when the colors, shapes, and visual dynamics exhibit some kind of continuity and unity over time. Even this brief excerpt from the demo gives us a good idea of how the final production will look and how it will evolve visually.

At the heart of the storyboard is the illustration of the central concept. We knew beforehand that the Waite Group logo would not easily spin on its axis as a fully colored, fully textured clipping. The PC's memory space (640K) and internal data rate would not allow a smooth animation. Also, the file size of the animation would be huge.

The solution at the storyboard stage was to reduce the logo to an outline and then spin the outline. Because the outline contains large flat areas of a single color, it places a much smaller burden on computer resources.

You can see the outline of the M in the fifth frame of the storyboard. At this point we were faced with the question: "What do we do with it, once it becomes a bare outline of an M?" "How do we turn it into a more interesting graphic?" It occurred to us to have a little painter pop out of the background. He becomes the "creator" in *Multimedia Creations*. Through his magic, the M is changed into the many textures and colors that symbolize the richness and variety of multimedia.

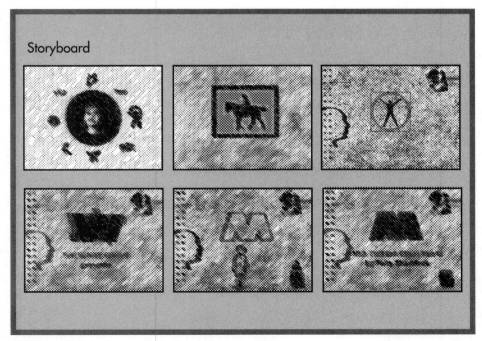

Figure 5-3 The storyboard for *Multimedia Creations*

Okay, so it's not *Ben Hur.* However, what is amazing is that the entire 3-minute demo, including the music and sound effects we will add to it later, will be less than 1 megabyte in size when finished, and it will compress down to about 490K when processed by an archiving utility. Why is this important?

First, it is included with this book, which is distributed on disk and must accommodate the GRASP programs and the other sample applications.

Second, the demo is also distributed in its compiled form so that it will run as a standalone executable file. When GRASPRT.EXE (the run time version of GRASP) is compiled with the demo by GLEXE.EXE (utilities included with the commercial version of GRASP), the size is increased by about 100K. The demo has also been uploaded to bulletin boards. Five hundred kilobytes is already huge by BBS standards. As the demo increases in size, its potential audience decreases. If it was any larger than 1.2 megabytes uncompressed, the demo would have to be compressed before distribution. That would make it difficult to install. These are all reasons for keeping the demo as small as possible.

Other factors determine the design goals for the demo. Because the demo has been created in 16 colors at a spatial resolution of 640x480, it will run on any computer equipped with a standard VGA card. The demo will also run on a computer equipped with only 470K of free memory, as reported by DOS's CHKDSK.EXE program. So we know that people who try to run it on computers linked to local area networks will have a better chance at running the demo.

Structuring the Demo

The multimedia demo rarely has the same structure as a computer program that processes a user's input or gives a user access to data. A demo is meant to be a very short and lively presentation of one, two, or, at the most three ideas. The marketer hopes that the demo's artistry will encourage the audience to seek more information about a product or service. It's not the duty of the demo to sell, but rather to prepare the ground for the sell.

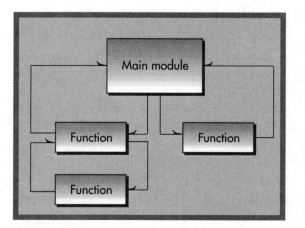

The demo does this by engaging the audience's attention fully. It uses moving images and sounds to capture

Figure 5-4 Classic structure of a computer program

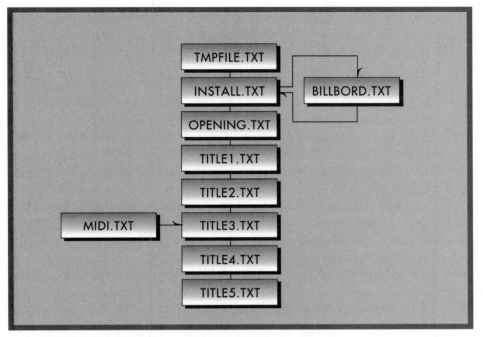

Figure 5-5 Linear structure of the *Multimedia Creations* demo

our naturally short and roving attention. Its choice of colors and visual dynamics communicate excitement. A demo is not a compendium of everything that can be said about, or done with, the product. It appeals directly to the audience's imagination. It says, "Come inside." It doesn't give you an inventory, it just shows you how you are going to feel once you do go inside.

The demo is more akin to a movie than a computer program. It's driven by the need to keep constantly on the move. It grows. It branches. It multiplies. It's organic. Of course, just as movies are made with storyboards and committees, so are business demos. There is no escape from the necessity of planning. However, the demo must ultimately find the path to our imagination. The path is rarely direct, rarely straight.

A well-designed computer program is modular in construction. Usually, it consists of a single main module and subsidiary modules. It employs subroutines to implement a single function or a group of functions. Once the subsidiary module has completed its task, control is passed back to a main module. Figure 5-4 illustrates this modular structure.

Notice how program flow proceeds from a main routine to subroutines. The subroutines may have subroutines, but ultimately program execution follows the ladder back up to a main module. Now compare this with the modular structure of the demo. Figure 5-5 shows the structure of the *Multimedia Creations* demo.

The *Multimedia Creations* demo has a linear structure. One module is merely linked to the next. A specialized routine, the file that implements interaction with a MIDI memory resident player (PLAYD.EXE), is merged to one of the modules. The INSTALL.TXT module calls another subroutine and returns. The demo's structure is closer to that of a movie than a computer program, but it smacks of both.

Here's how the program develops. The first module is TMPFILE.TXT. (Remember that TMPFILE.TXT is the program GRASP looks for when it first starts up.) TMPFILE.TXT checks the hardware to make sure the user has enough free RAM memory, and it also checks the video adapter that supports the demo's video mode. Program execution then proceeds to a sound card install module (IN-STALL.TXT). A module that places opening credits on the screen follows (OPEN-ING.TXT). Then the main modules of the demo follow. The division into modules is fairly arbitrary. It's always a good idea to keep GRASP scripts short to preserve memory. Also, when working on the demo, keeping sections in self-contained modules makes the sections easier to edit. TITLE1.TXT is a countdown sequence. TITLE2.TXT is a starry sky "welcome sequence." TITLE3.TXT illustrates several animation techniques. TITLE4.TXT and TITLE5.TXT animate the Waite Group logo and turn it into the M of *Multimedia Creations*.

That's the structure for the demo. Before we start writing code for the demo, let's visit one more area that we have to consider.

Adding Drama to Presentations with Multimedia

An overview of the planning process would be incomplete if it did not include mention of drama. Drama is as old as the campfire tale of the hunt that held the tribe in captive delight. Drama is the dynamics over time of a story, usually powered by human conflict. The very word "plot" suggests a way of graphing response to a dramatic event over time.

A key feature of multimedia is that it adds drama to computer-based presentations. It does this by adding the dimension of time. When we watch a graphic ani-

---

PEEKING AHEAD

We've provided a complete copy of the demo with the book. Simply type `demo` at the DOS prompt while in the main GRASP directory. The 3-minute demo will play. You will notice that unlike previous chapters, the scripts are quite different than those you enter here. The changes were necessary when sound was added to the demo.

---

mate on the screen, we are caught up in the spectacle of it unfolding. Where is the object going to move? What is the outcome of this series of visual developments? When music is added to the mix, the pace and timing of the presentation are enhanced. Music also helps drive the visuals forward in time, hooked to the rhythmic development of the lyric. Music, even more than the drama inherent in the movement of objects in space, gives the presentation unity and meaning, qualities that are irresistible to human audiences.

CREATING THE MULTIMEDIA CREATIONS DEMO

It's time to get down to business and generate the demo. We're going to start with the opening visuals, rather than the routines that check to make sure users have enough memory free for the program or a VGA card. When creating demos, these routines are always added last. We won't be reviewing the entire demo. By the middle of the demo, all of the new commands and animation techniques will have been discussed. We'll leave the last few scripts for your further study.

As usual, we've provided you with the complete listings on disk (TITLE1.TXT–TITLE5.TXT). However, we recommend that you create a parallel series of scripts (TEST1.TXT–TEST5.TXT) as part of the learning exercise.

Creating an Electronic Academy Leader

We'll honor the principle of drama as it has been embodied in motion pictures by opening our electronic demo with a sequence that mimics what has been called "the Academy Leader." You may have seen the Academy Leader at a 16mm film screening. It's the countdown at the beginning of a film that usually ends on the number two, with a beep. Because the "leader" counts down from eight to two, we'll illustrate the issue of anticipation in drama in a very simple way.

Change to the CHAPT05 subdirectory (cd \grasp\chapt05) and run GRASPC. Make sure you have the DOS environment set (set grasp = c:\grasp). Once at GRASP's menu, create a new file called, TEST1.TXT. Enter the following.

```
; TEST1.TXT An electronic ad for Multimedia Creations

; set debug on

video m

start:


; Load main palette.
        pload greenbck.pal p1
        palette p1
```

```
        pfree p1

; Timer
        timer

; Create circles.
        color 7
        circle 324,257 80 80 10         ; outer light blue rings
        color 10
        circle 324,257 70 70 3          ; inner dark blue rings

; Create cross-hairs
        color 11
        line 322,388 322,370            ; top pink vertical bar
        mark 4
        line 1,0 1,0 r
        loop

        color 11
        line 322,144 322,124            ; bottom pink vertical bar
        mark 4
        line 1,0 1,0 r
        loop

        color 11
        line 192,257 210,257            ; left side bar
        line 0,-1 0,-1 r

        color 11
        line 437,257 454,257            ; right side bar
        line 0,-1 0,-1 r

        color 14
        circle 324,257 40               ; inner circle

; Countdown routine
        pgetbuf p1                      ; save screen to buffer

        set clip 18                     ; set up first clip as 18
        waitkey 60

        mark 7                          ; beginning of countdown routine
                timer
                cload count$@clip c1
                        ;text @elapsed  ; shows clock time on screen
                        ;waitkey        ; remove semicolons to see
                waitkey 40              ; longer for slow hard drives

                timer                   ; reset clock to 0
                putup c1                ; putup number
                cfree c1
                set clip @clip-1        ; advance to next clip file
                waitkey 15
                timer                   ; reset clock
                window 278,214 370,298  ; restricts fade to window
                edge on 15
```

```
              pfade 24 p1
              edge off              ; aperture fade number off
              window                ; restores whole screen
              waitkey 35
              timer                 ; resets clock
              note 40 20 1
              waitkey 10
        loop

        timer

; Clear screen to Black
        cfree c1 - c10
        pfree p1 - p10
        clearscr 0
        note 30 30 15


end:

exit
```

When TEST1 is run, a series of circles forms on the screen, then the number eight appears and the countdown begins. The speaker emits a tick after each number appears and emits a final beep when the number two disappears. This is not exactly the way the Academy Leader works, but it allows us to explore timing issues on the PC, a very important subject for any media that must coordinate visual events to sound events over time. Let's look at the creation of circles first.

Creating the Countdown Circles

We initially create the circles and cross-hairs (vertical bars on the top and horizontal bars on the side of the circles) using GRASP's Circle and Line commands. The Circle command might appear to be simple but its optional parameters allow us to create fairly complex shapes. Here is Circle's syntax:

```
circle x,y xr [yr] [iris]
```

The x,y coordinates determine the circle's center point on the screen. You specify the circle's center and then its horizontal (xr) radius. If you don't specify the circle's vertical (yr) radius, GRASP will make it equal to the horizontal radius. That is, GRASP will create a circle, since a circle's horizontal radius is equal to its vertical radius. This applies to VGA screen modes. Making the vertical and horizontal radii equal doesn't apply to some of the other video modes, like EGA. EGA's screen resolution is flatter than VGA's. It has the same horizontal resolution, 640 pixels, but a shallower vertical resolution, 350 pixels instead of 480. Setting the vertical radius equal to the horizontal radius in EGA produces an ellipse elongated along the vertical axis. To create a circle in EGA modes, you must specify a smaller vertical length than the horizontal length.

The last parameter of the circle command, *iris*, allows you to specify how many inner circles to draw within the initial circle. These circles or ellipses are drawn 1 pixel within the previous one. This produces a rather pleasant looking moiré pattern.

Getting the Timing Right

Now comes the difficult part. A major stumbling block you'll face as a multimedia producer is the disparity in program running times between computers. Hard drive systems vary dramatically in how quickly they allow data to be moved from the hard drive to RAM memory. CD-ROM drives are slow, although they continue to improve. Of course CPU speeds affect performance dramatically. GRASP does not create or manipulate vector objects, so it doesn't use a math coprocessor.

Video systems also vary in how quickly they process information. Because GRASP accesses and manipulates video memory directly, video speed is a factor in program running time. This is why it's always a good idea to run your program on the slowest and fastest computers you can find when you test GRASP programs. Fortunately, for really time-critical parts of your presentation, there is a command that allows you to set the pace of your visuals. (When we add music to the demo, we'll explore a second method of timing your presentation to music. That comes in the next chapter.)

Using Timer to Pace the Script

Notice that we use the Timer command several times in the countdown routine. The Timer command is always paired with a Waitkey. The syntax for the command is:

```
timer
waitkey
```

The Timer command does not have optional parameters. Issuing the Timer command creates a GRASP clock and sets it to 0. GRASP then proceeds to the first Waitkey command it encounters and compares the elapsed time on its clock to the wait time specified by the Waitkey command. If the Waitkey command has a time of 1 second, and only half a second has expired on GRASP's clock, GRASP will wait until a full second has elapsed before executing the next command.

The Waitkey command that follows a Timer command has the effect of turning GRASP's clock off again. That's why we reissue the Timer command after each Waitkey.

The Timer/Waitkey also has the effect of making GRASP run independent of CPU speed. That is, it can slow presentations down on fast machines, and in general provides control over the pace of the presentation. Of course, it can't speed up a presentation on a slow machine.

USING RAM DISKS

Consider using a RAM disk on slow machines. Your DOS manual will tell you how to set aside extended memory as a "virtual hard drive" operating at RAM speed. In the case of presentations that load and display images at a rapid pace, RAM disks can be particularly useful. GRASP's Exec command provides a way of accessing these DOS commands. You can use Exec to copy files to the RAM disk and delete files from it once they have been displayed. For example, to copy a file to another file name and erase the first file:

```
exec c:\command.com "/c copy test1.pic test2.pic >null"
exec c:\command.com "/c del test1.pic >null"
```

This assumes your COMMAND.COM file is in the C: root directory. The redirection to null output ensures that the DOS "file copied" and "file deleted" messages aren't routed to the screen.

We'll cover the Exec command in the next chapter.

Using @elapsed to Time Sequences

There is a way to examine GRASP's "stopwatch" to see how much time has expired since you initiated the clock with Timer. The system variable *@elapsed* contains that information. We used this command with the Text command in the example code, but commented it out with semicolons so it wouldn't interfere with running the show. If you delete the semicolons from the "text @elapsed" and "waitkey" lines, you'll be able to measure how long it takes your system to load the countdown number clippings into memory.

```
timer
        cload count$@clip.clp c1        ; loads clipping into buffer one
                text @elapsed           ; shows clock time on screen
                waitkey
```

GRASP's clock is set to 0 and starts running. The clipping is loaded into a buffer. Then the time that has elapsed is displayed on the screen. On our 386 33-MHz computer with a fast ESDI hard drive, the clipping took a fraction of a second (170 milliseconds) to load into the buffer.

The Timer command helps us to maintain a common execution time for sequences on a wide variety of computers by forcing the computer to wait until GRASP's clock is equal to the wait time specified by a Waitkey command.

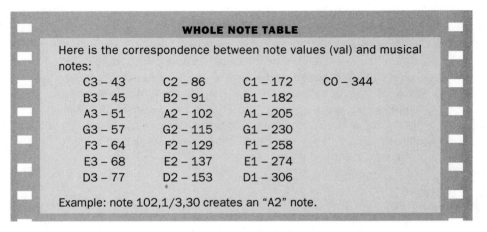

WHOLE NOTE TABLE

Here is the correspondence between note values (val) and musical notes:

C3 – 43	C2 – 86	C1 – 172	C0 – 344
B3 – 45	B2 – 91	B1 – 182	
A3 – 51	A2 – 102	A1 – 205	
G3 – 57	G2 – 115	G1 – 230	
F3 – 64	F2 – 129	F1 – 258	
E3 – 68	E2 – 137	E1 – 274	
D3 – 77	D2 – 153	D1 – 306	

Example: note 102,1/3,30 creates an "A2" note.

Manipulating the Computer System Speaker

When you ran TEST1.TXT, you probably heard a clock ticking noise from your computer's internal speaker. GRASP has a very simple command for generating sound with the system speaker. The syntax is:

```
note val tone time [r]
```

where the value of the first parameter (val) corresponds to its pitch, the value of the second parameter (tone) corresponds to its tone, and the value of the third parameter (time) corresponds to the duration of the sound. The optional relative switch adds the value of the first parameter (the pitch) to a previous Note command. This value does not correspond to sound frequency. Experimentation is the rule when you use the Note command.

Note is a convenient method of generating sound through the system speaker. However, the sounds it creates are not very sophisticated, and the command has a major disadvantage. When the computer is generating the note, it cannot do anything else. We can only create sounds that happen before or after a visual event, never simultaneously with that event. The SNDPLAY.TXT subroutine used in this book plays digitized sound through the speaker, or optionally, through a sound card. Generation of the sound does not tie up the CPU. The SNDPLAY.TXT subroutine allows us to animate visuals and play music at the same time. Of course, the sounds that are generated this way must be initially recorded and stored on disk as digital sound files. GRASP's SOUNDPC.GRP, which is called by SNDPLAY.TXT, drives the system speaker with data from the digital sound files.

Using the Power of Variables to Develop Scripts

We used a loop routine to load in the clippings. Timing the countdown sequence would have been difficult if we had not used variables to load and display these clippings. Reduced to just the commands that load and display the clippings, the routine looks like this:

```
set clip 18                    ; set up a variable for clippings
                               ; and give it a starting value of 18
mark 7                         ; set up a seven times loop
cload count$@clip.clp c1       ; use part of the clipping name (count),
                               ; concatenated to the variable, to
                               ; name the clipping
putup c1                       ; display the clipping
cfree c1                       ; free the buffer
set clip @clip-1               ; decrease the value of variable by 1

loop                           ; loop back to the mark at the beginning
```

This routine loads and displays the following clippings:

```
count12.clp count13.clp count14.clp count15.clp count16.clp count17.clp count18.clp
```

We've used a variable (*clip*) joined ($) to a string (*count*) to name the clippings we want to load and display. This is called concatenation. (We discussed variables in Chapter 3. As you may recall, variables are places in the computer's memory space where data is stored.) The clip variable is decreased by one because we are counting down. GRASP developers use concatenation with variable names regularly in demos.

Sometimes you will find creating lists easier than building a routine like this. However, in this case, the routine would look like this:

```
cload count18.clp c1
(body of routine)

cload count17.clp c1
(body of routine)

...

and so on.
```

You can see that the length of a routine that spells out all the names explicitly makes the use of variables much more efficient, in development time, as well as in memory usage. Adjusting the timing of the sequence would have been cumbersome if we had eight subroutines to modify.

Conserving Disk Space

The 8-second sequence occupies exactly 11,177 bytes on the hard drive and will archive down to 4503 bytes using the archive program ARJ.EXE. Most of the visual dynamics of the sequence have been achieved using GRASP's facilities for directly manipulating video memory, primarily through the Line and Circle commands.

When it comes to visual pyrotechnics, GRASP gives like Santa Claus and saves like Scrooge.

Now that we've gone through the countdown sequence, it's time to begin running the demo. Well, how does the demo begin? It begins deep in time . . . and space.

Creating a Starry Night "On the Fly"

Multimedia's use of drama links it to much older media that stretch back through time. Almost all early cultures attempted to embody their sense of the human drama in petroglyphs, pictures drawn on caves and rocks. Let's suggest multimedia's debt to these ancient traditions. We'll create a dark starry background to suggest time and space. Then we'll create a circle of figures that suggest ancient cultural history. In the middle of our circle of hieroglyphs, we'll surprise the audience with voice and images from the parallel story we're developing: the animated image of a woman, Sylvia, saying, "Welcome." After all, it is the moment when computers begin to speak to us in our idiom that they fully participate in the story-telling traditions of our species.

We know in advance that we will want to display Sylvia's face in a specific range of colors. Sixteen colors does not give us enough colors to realistically portray the human face (it has hundreds of tones), so our approach will be to use a graphical representation. Our choice is to use gray tones for the face with some green high-lights for visual interest. This means using a palette different from the one used for the countdown sequence. The screen is black when we do this, so the switch to the new palette will be easy. Since we are at the end of a sequence and switching palettes, this seems like a good point in our program to link to a new module. By keeping the countdown sequence in its own module, we make it easy to copy and use for other programs. Also, since each GRASP script occupies precious memory, we free up memory by linking to another script and abandoning the present one. We also get rid of other unnecessary baggage.

Enter the following lines just before the Waitkey and Exit commands at the end of TEST1.TXT.

```
; Link to next module
      link TEST2.TXT start

waitkey
exit
```

Now create a new script titled TEST2.TXT.

```
video m

; TEST2.TXT Welcome sequence.

start:

; Switches palettes
        pload gray.pal p1
        palette p1
        pfree p1

waitkey
exit
```

Notice that the Link command specifies that program execution is to start at the "start:" label in TEST2.TXT. This will allow you to run TEST2.TXT as a standalone module. Now create the starry background for this sequence. Enter the following lines before the Waitkey and Exit commands. (If you're comparing this code to the code supplied on disk, TITLE2.TXT, you'll notice that we've moved this and the following code sections into subroutines. That's because of the sound that accompanies the TITLE2.TXT version. Ignore this for now.)

```
; Starry background.

        set cnt 1                       ; set color index count at 1

        mark 300
        color @cnt                      ; set palette at color index
        point 0,0 639,479               ; place point randomly on screen
        set cnt @cnt+1                  ; increment index by 1
        if @cnt==10                     ; when you reach an index of 10
                set cnt 1               ; reset index to 1
        endif                           ; otherwise continue
        loop

        pgetbuf p1                      ; saves screen for use later
```

This code uses the Point command's random feature to generate 300 points on the screen. (The Point command was discussed in the previous chapter.) We use only the first ten colors of the current palette to color the stars. The balance of the palette is a range of grays. We keep the background dark by limiting palette cycling to the dark colors in the first eight palette slots.

The *cnt* variable is used to change the palette color used by the Point command. Remember that a variable is a place in memory where a value is stored. When GRASP sees @cnt, it is directed to an area in memory set aside to store calculations performed on @cnt. (If you remember our discussion of variables in Chapter 3, then you know that the variable *cnt* is actually an address, and @cnt points to the value stored at that address.) GRASP reads the current value stored there (@cnt), and uses that value to set the current system color.

We also use the If/Endif construct to test the *cnt* variable. (If/Endif tests were discussed in Chapter 4.) Each time through the loop, the current value stored as @cnt is tested to see if it is equal to 10. If the count is not 10 (false), the code between the If command and the Endif command is ignored. When the count reaches 10, the If test returns true and the code is executed. The count is reset to 1, so the color index is set to 1.

We've used programming logic and commands to create a background with a few lines of text. These lines occupy 154 bytes on the hard drive. If we had saved this background to the hard drive as a graphics file, it would occupy 2572 bytes. That file would be 16 times larger than the text file containing the instructions for building the background in memory.

We're going to clear the screen to the starry background at the end of the welcome sequence. That's why the Pgetbuf command appears at the end of this fragment of code. The command saves the screen to a buffer for use later.

Adding Comets

Adding comets to the starry background will help give it the feeling of deep space. Again, the strategy is to build the comets in RAM (random access memory) and animate them in RAM.

```
; Comet

        color 15                        ; white
        mark 10                         ; loop moves comet across sky
            line 100,100 105,105        ; 1st comet's body
            point 96,96                 ; comet tail
            offset 10 10 r              ; move comet ten pixels
            waitkey 01
            pfade 0 p1                  ; restore screen
        loop
        offset 0,0                      ; restore offsets

        mark 8
            line 500,100 495,105        ; second comet comes from left
            line 504,96 503,97          ; second comet's tail
            offset -30,30 r             ; moves comet
            pfade 0 p1
        loop
        offset 0,0
```

Both comets travel toward the center of the screen, drawing our eyes to it. Note that the second comet uses a slightly different method of creating the comet's tail.

Now let's add a halo to the sky. The halo will eventually act as a frame for Sylvia's image.

```
; Halo around Sylvia
        color 2
        set radius 0                     ; variable for circle radius

        mark 20                          ; loop routine creating ellipse
            circle 330,268 60 @radius    ; radius is the vertical radius
            set radius @radius+4
            pfade 0 p1                   ; restores screen
        loop

        circle 330,268 60 @radius        ; final position of ellipse

        set cnt 1                        ; resets color index to 1
        color @cnt                       ; resets color to color 1
        set radius 60                    ; resets radius VALUE to 60

        waitkey 50

        mark 2
            set radius @radius+2
            circle 330,268 @radius       ; here radius is the horizontal
            set cnt @cnt+1
            color @cnt
            if @cnt==6
                    set cnt 1
            endif
        loop

        pfree p1

        waitkey
        exit
```

When you run this sequence, you'll see a vertically elongated ellipse along the vertical axis. We create the illusion that the ellipse is unfolding by first saving the starry sky to a buffer and then restoring the saved sky to the screen after each iteration of the loop. We use a Circle command after the exit from the loop. If we hadn't, the last "pfade 0 p1" in the loop would have erased the last circle from the screen.

We then go on to create the inner circles after resetting the color index to 1 and the radius to 1. The radius variable is used for the horizontal radius. Because GRASP defaults to using the horizontal radius if the vertical radius is not specified, we create circles with the second circle sequence. We made sure that the @cnt variable that was used earlier to create colored stars was reset to 1 before using it in a similar way here.

Adding the Petroglyphs to the Sky

We're going to suggest that the cultural roots of representational media finds its ancestry in petroglyphs. Let's now put an arrangement of petroglyphs around the ellipse. Enter the following lines just before the Waitkey and Exit commands.

```
; Load and Display Petroglyphs
        cload symbol10.clp c1 1 1
        cload symbol11.clp c2 1 1
        cload symbol12.clp c3 1 1
        cload symbol13.clp c4 1 1
        cload symbol14.clp c5 1 1
        cload symbol15.clp c6 1 1
        cload symbol16.clp c7 1 1
        cload symbol17.clp c8 1 1

        float 0,0 0,0 5 14 c1 c2 c3 c4 c5 c6 c7 c8
        putup c1
        waitkey 14
        putup c2
        waitkey 14
        putup c3
        waitkey 14
        putup c4
        waitkey 14
        putup c5
        waitkey 14
        putup c6
        waitkey 14
        putup c7
        waitkey 14
        putup c8
        cfree c1 - c8
```

When you run the script, a series of eight petroglyphs appears in a circle around the halo, animating around it for a moment, then settling into place. The Float and Putup commands take advantage of the fact that we saved each of the pictures with the correct offsets in Pictor. Loading the clippings with the noshift parameter off (1) ensures that extra copies of the clippings are not generated and do not occupy additional memory.

Your screen should look like Figure 5-6.

Notice that we load the clippings with the transparency parameter set off. (If you omit the transparency parameter, GRASP assumes you want to set transparency to off or 0.) When the transparency parameter is set on, GRASP processes the clipping to make the specified color transparent to the background. This takes time, especially on slow machines. Here it is not needed because the clippings are floated into position and then pasted on the background.

GIVING YOUR PROGRAM A HUMAN FACE

Now it's time to use GRASP's sound and motion capabilities to give our electronic demo a human face. This is going to take us on a long detour into image processing.

Figure 5-6 Petroglyphs arranged around a halo

Along the way we'll learn how to use images captured from the real world to create animations.

What we'll do is have a face appear in the middle of the halo. The woman who appears will be animated. She will say "welcome." This animation will be fairly easy to create, but time-consuming. Matching lip movements to voice is one of the most difficult and elusive types of animation because humans spend a lot of time unconsciously monitoring the lip movements of other people. Lip movements are highly complex., and it's disturbing when lips and voice are out of synch.

Our method will be use a 35mm camera to capture the animation of Sylvia saying "welcome." The resulting prints will be scanned into the computer and converted into clippings that can be animated. Figure 5-7 shows the steps involved in capturing Sylvia's image.

We shot Sylvia with a camera mounted on a tripod. The camera had a motor winder, and she was instructed to hold still and not move her feet. We captured a series of shots of her saying "Welcome." Keeping her head in fixed relationship to the camera helped us match images in the assembly stage. Our goal was to create an animation that would not consume precious disk space when it was archived for distribution, so we chose flat lighting and a very dark background. (Flat lighting is

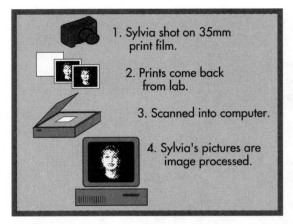

1. Sylvia shot on 35mm print film.

2. Prints come back from lab.

3. Scanned into computer.

4. Sylvia's pictures are image processed.

Figure 5-7 Capturing and scanning Sylvia's image

where the subject is lit by highly directional front lighting. It eliminates shadows on the face and "flattens" the shape of the subject.) To achieve this, we shot Sylvia as the sun was going down. A flash was mounted on the camera. Washing out the detail of the face is usually good practice in "glamor" photography, because a washed-out complexion actually flatters the subject.

We took 48 shots. This guaranteed a range from which to choose the five facial expressions we would eventually use in the animation. A five-part animation is not really adequate for smooth motion, but we had designed a plan for overcoming this. During playback, the images would be overlapped using dissolves. The roll of print film was developed at a local film processing center. The 5x7 size print is adequate for VGA 640x480 screen resolution. That's because the resolution of 35mm print film, even at this small size, greatly exceeds VGA's 640x480 pixel screen resolution.

The prints were than scanned. Since we planned to process the images in Aldus's Photostyler, we scanned the images in Targa format at 24-bit color resolution. Even though we knew that Sylvia's face was eventually going to be displayed using 7 of 16 colors, manipulating 32,000 or 16 million colors gives you a much better chance of

achieving the effect you have storyboarded. More colors in this case meant we were able to selectively remove colors from the image.

Note that we do not need to use a Targa capture board to convert the photographs into digital files. The scanner software supported the Targa TGA format, which has become an industry standard for high-resolution color image files, such as 16-, 24-,

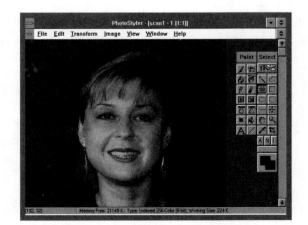

Figure 5-8 Full resolution version of Sylvia

A NOTE ON ALTERNATIVE METHODS OF
CAPTURING MOTION

Gathering and working with still images shot on a 35mm film is a kind of proletariat form of multimedia. On a large budget production, we shoot the images on high-resolution video (like the professional Betacam format), and then use a frame accurate Betacam VCR to capture the images we require for the animation. Betacam is expensive to rent, and editing suites can cost several hundred dollars an hour. The advantage of using Betacam is the ability to capture highly accurate lip movements, as we would have captured her saying welcome at 30 frames per second. There would have been less movement in the head and more even exposure.

Fortunately, inexpensive options are emerging that will allow you to digitize video to the hard drive. An alternative is to shoot her on 8mm video or VHS, and then use a frame buffer (a specialized video card that converts analog video to digital video) to digitize selected frames to the hard drive. We preferred the resolution of 35mm film to the quality of 8mm or VHS.

A third approach would be to use a digital video system to capture and save a series of frames to a digital format in "real time." (Real time means 30 frames per second.) Digital video samples the incoming stream of analog video and saves the resulting digital frames to a hard drive. Once the cost and quality of digital video become acceptable, this will be the preferred approach. (See Chapter 1 for a discussion of digital video.)

As we have said, the proletariat approach was to use a 35mm camera with a motor winder mounted on a tripod. In deciding what images to select from the stills, we used a time-honored approach. We studied live action. The best place to study the movement of lips saying "welcome" is in front of a mirror. The lips purse slightly as they open and widen to voice the first syllable, "well." Then they clamp down to voice the second syllable, "come." This is the movement we want to reproduce.

and 32-bit color files. The format was originally developed by Truevision for its series of highly specialized color display cards under the "Targa" trademark. When you see images with the .TGA file extension, you know that they are probably high-resolution color files. Aldus' Photostyler image processing program supports the Targa format. Figure 5-8 shows a scan of the full color photograph in Photostyler.

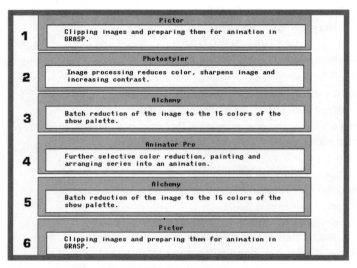

Figure 5-9 The image processing steps

Preparing the Clippings for GRASP Animation

Once the image has been scanned into the computer environment, the ways you can manipulate it are innumerable. Figure 5-9 shows the image processing steps.

Our choice is first to create a palette in Pictor; then to use Aldus's Photostyler to initially process the images; then to use Handmade Software's Image Alchemy to batch reduce the images to 16 colors; then to use Autodesk's Animator Pro to further color reduce and paint the images and arrange them into an animation sequence. Finally, we once more reduce the image using Alchemy and import the images into Pictor for final processing into clippings. We'll explain the process in detail now.

Adjusting Image Contrast and Sharpness

We used Photostyler to adjust image contrast and sharpness. By increasing contrast, we took detail out of the background and washed out the face. The sharpening filter works like the focus ring on a camera, actually making a slightly blurry picture look sharper. Since the image would be reduced to a very small size, we wanted to make sure detail would remain sharp. All these operations were performed on the full color image. Working with high-resolution color in Windows programs does not require a Targa card, a VGA card with a Hicolor chip, or a VGA card with True Color technology, since in a 16- or 256-color mode, the full color resolution image is simulated on the screen with fewer colors. It is much easier, however, to edit the image in full color resolution.

Aldus Photostyler is a professional tool with advanced image processing capability. The Shareware program called Paintshop Pro has much of the functionality of Photostyler. Its image processing tools are not as advanced as Photostyler's, but it supports more file formats. We also prefer to use it for color reduction, because its reduction algorithms produce more accurate results.

Reducing Color Resolution

Our next task was to reduce the image to 16 colors. Color reduction really deserves at least a chapter to itself, if not a book. It's a fine art patiently learned by trial and error. (The Waite Group's PICLAB book treats image processing in depth.) Fortunately, there are several programs that take much of the guess work out of color reduction.

Paint Shop Pro, the Shareware program from JASC, Inc., has excellent color reduction tools. You access these tools in the Colors menu by selecting Decrease Color Depth. If we were working on a single image, we might choose to do our color reduction in Paint Shop Pro. However, our task was to create a series of clippings using a common palette, so we chose to perform color reduction with a program that is batch oriented, Image Alchemy, from Handmade Software, Inc. (A Shareware version is available on CompuServe and many bulletin boards.)

Batch Color Reduction Using Alchemy

Alchemy is a command-line program. All operations are performed at the DOS prompt, or you can write a DOS batch file that will process a series of images. The ability to do batch processing makes Alchemy especially useful for the multimedia producer.

Alchemy allows you to specify a palette from another file as the palette to use in color reducing a series of images. This gives all the files in a series a common palette, which is important for an animated series of images. In this case, we wanted to reduce the Targa 24-bit full color image to 4-bit, 16-color VGA resolution. We created a palette in Pictor. It uses the first seven colors for the background. The balance of the palette slots use a spread of grays. This is the palette you see when you call SHOWPAL.TXT to examine Sylvia's image.

Alchemy has too many parameters to list here. It is an excellent general purpose graphics translation and color-reduction tool and well worth the purchase price. Here's the command we used to reduce our image series:

```
alchemy -g -fgray.pcx scan1.tga
```

This command results in the creation of a GIF file called SCAN1.GIF. The first ("-g") parameter specifies in which image file format you will save the converted file. In this case we want to convert the full color Targa file to a VGA GIF file format. (GIF was developed by CompuServe as a file compression and exchange format.) GIF is the native file format for Animator Pro, the program where the images would be next manipulated.

The second parameter ("-f") specifies that color reduction will be performed using an existing palette. This is a very useful feature of a batch color processing software like Alchemy. It will be much easier to work with the images if they use a common palette. In this case we use the palette we developed in Pictor for our gray-scale images. Alchemy is smart enough to know that this is a 16-color (4-bit) image. Alchemy uses very capable algorithms to decide which of the 16 colors to assign to the translated image.

Here's how it works. It will first analyze the image and decide how to assign the sixteen colors from the palette you specify for the image. It will dither the image where necessary. Dithering is a color reduction method. It works as follows. When color reducing, if Alchemy cannot find a color in the specified palette close enough to the colors in the original image, it will try to simulate the image's color using a combination of two or more colors. In the case of the Sylvia images, Alchemy couldn't find an exact match for the background, so it used the dark colors from the palette (including a dark green and a dark gray) to simulate the dark green trees in the background of the original image. Placing these colors together in close proximity fools the eye into seeing a tone that doesn't exist in the converted image's palette. If you plan to work with reduced color palettes, dithering is something you'll spend a lot of time mastering.

After we color reduced the image, we did further image editing using Autodesk's Animator Pro.

Animator Pro as a Development Tool

Autodesk's Animator Pro or the entry-level version of the program, Autodesk Animator, are invaluable animation development tools. Autodesk Animator has a fixed VGA resolution of 320x200 pixels. Animator Pro's spatial resolution is device independent, meaning it will support whatever pixel resolution your video card is capable of displaying. Color resolution of both programs is 256 colors, and neither supports VGA 16-color modes nor the VGA Hicolor True Color technologies. The strategy will be to import the 16-color images into Animator Pro, alter them, and then export them out of the program as 256-color images. They will then be reduced once more to 16 colors. Creating the palette first in Pictor and using it throughout the image processing cycle is the best approach. Refer back to Figure 5-9 to review the process.

Creating the Flic

We loaded the series of GIF files into Animator Pro, creating a *flic,* the program's nickname for a file containing a sequential series of frames. Being able to work on the images as a series of sequential frames saves time and allows you to keep your images organized. You can easily change the order of the images and preview the animation effect you are trying to create. You can also use Animator's animation tools to create effects not possible with other draw or paint programs.

Altering the Palette

We used Alchemy to give each of the frames the palette we'll ultimately use in the show. Therefore we didn't need to use Animator Pro's palette tools to reconcile the colors between frames. Alchemy faithfully copies the 16 colors of the color-reduced images into the first 16 palette slots, and then fills the balance of the 256 color slots with a random mix of colors. We removed the extra colors and replaced them with black.

Testing the Animation

The five images of Sylvia's mouth moving were rearranged and the flic run at various speeds to see which pictures created the illusion of Sylvia saying "welcome." We found that three images corresponded with Sylvia's mouth opening, and two with her mouth closing. This was the minimum number of images we could use for the animation.

Animating Objects Along a Path

How did we decide how many images to use and how to time them to the sound of Sylvia saying welcome? In motion pictures and professional video, matching individual sounds to individual frames is called lip-synching. It is very difficult to achieve because audiences will immediately detect the slightest time lag between the sound and a corresponding lip movement.

It's difficult to lip-synch in the computer environment. Computers, because they are digital devices, simulate analog patterns with difficulty. It's easy for computers to draw a straight line between two objects; it is much more computer-intensive to draw a curved path. The path of the straight line can be described with two points, the beginning and the end. Curved paths involve much more complex math, since the points along a curve can potentially be infinite. Some animation programs, like Animator Pro and its sister product, Autodesk Animator, assist the animator by calculating the in-between positions as the object moves from A to B along a curved path.

The world is an analog place. Very few moving objects succeed in maintaining straight paths. Only light appears to have any success at traveling at a constant velocity in a straight line. Well, almost straight, considering that space itself is curved!

Remember that by moving objects along a curved path in GRASP animations, you will better simulate realistic action. That's why using only two images for Sylvia's mouth will not produce a very realistic animation. Five positions are not really adequate either. If this animation ran in a fixed installation off a hard drive, we might use more steps to better simulate live action.

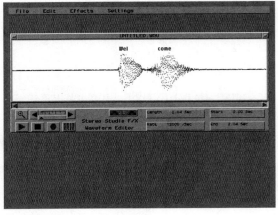

Figure 5-10 Waveform display of Sylvia saying "welcome"

Velocity and Animation

Computers find it much easier to move objects from A to B at a constant velocity. However, few objects in the world travel at a constant velocity. A hand moving from the hip to the mouth slowly accelerates from its starting position, reaches a peak velocity, and then decelerates as it approaches the mouth. If you study your lips saying "welcome," you'll see that they follow this acceleration path. There's an another, more accurate, way of studying velocity. Media Vision's Pro Audio Spectrum 16 sound card has a waveform editor (a program that edits digital sound samples). If we load the digital recording of Sylvia's "welcome" into the program's editor, we will see a visual representation of the sound over time. Figure 5-10 is an actual screen captured from the program.

The horizontal line in the editor's window represents time. The two "bulges" in the line represent the two syllables of the word "welcome." The first bulge, "wel" corresponds to the mouth opening, expelling air. The second bulge, "come," corresponds to the second syllable, where once more air is expelled. Notice how in the case of the first syllable, air is expelled rapidly at first, peaks, and then is expelled less rapidly. The acceleration characteristics of the second syllable are much less pronounced. By paying attention to the way movement occurs in the real world, we can create realistic animations on the computer.

Learning About Animation

We hope we've piqued your interest enough to pursue further research into animation. A few simple rules will get you started. Try recording cartoons off the air with your VCR and playing them back frame by frame. For complex animations we recommend employing a tool dedicated to that task, like Autodesk's Animator products and its 3D modeling and animation companion product, 3D Studio. Both products contain a large library of animations that you can study and imitate.

Reducing the Image in Autodesk's Animator

Our ultimate goal is to remove detail from the five images so that they will be easier to animate and take up less space on the distribution disk. Animator's separation tool, Sep, is extremely useful for this purpose. The separation tool finds and alters either single or related colors in the image. We use it to convert all the dark green and gray colors behind Sylvia's head to black. We also use the separation tool to remove detail from the face by converting the main tones of her face to a single color.

Macro Editing in Animator

One of the most useful features of the program is its macro recording facility, found in the Extra menu at the top right of the screen. When you select Start Record on this menu, subsequent actions you perform on the images are memorized by Animator Pro until you choose End Record. (This is like a macro function in a word processing program.) It allows you to perform identical image processing on each frame of the flic. We used it to remove the detail from the background.

Using Clip to Precisely Line Up the Faces

Adjusting the five faces so that they precisely overlap is made easier by using Animator's clipboard. From the Cel menu at the top of the screen, we selected Clip. Clip works like (ALT)-(J) in Pictor. It seeks the edges of the object (Sylvia's head), and surrounds it with a box. The area inside the box is saved to the clipboard. Here's how: We back up one frame to the previous frame. By making the key color (the black background) transparent, we were able to then use Cel's Move command to place the second frame's image over the first frame's image. Move alters the position of the cel in the clipboard, but does not paste it onto the screen. We then returned to the previous frame, cleared the screen with Pic menu's Clear command, and pasted the repositioned cel back into place using the Paste command on the Cel menu. We followed this procedure for the remaining images in the flic. Then we ran the animation again to check for "wobbly" movement and to make final adjustments.

Using Zoom for Final Touch-Up

Animator's Zoom function allows you to define an area and a level of magnification for editing the fine detail in the image. We did a final edit of the images in Zoom mode and ran the flic again to check for anomalies. Compare Figure 5-11 to the previous images of Sylvia. The detail is progressively removed until a "cartooned" Sylvia remains. Removing information from images makes animation possible with the limited capabilities of today's PC computers. Whether a computer algorithm is performing the image compression and decompression in an automated fashion on dedicated hardware, or the artist is performing the reduction with an electronic brush, the goal is the same: Remove the burden of processing from the CPU, make the images that you are animating smaller and less memory intensive. We've just shown you what we call multimedia's "proletariat" approach.

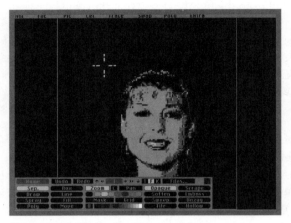

Figure 5-11 Final edited image of Sylvia

Saving and Converting the Flic

If we were working on a 320x200 pixel, 256-color animation, we would simply save the flic to disk at this point and have GRASP run it, using GRASP's direct support for the Autodesk flic formats (FLI or FLC files). However, our animation is in 16-color resolution, so we need once again to save each frame of the animation to disk and use Alchemy to convert the images to 16-color files. For long flics, we use the Macro recorder to save each frame to the hard drive with an incremental file name, such as:

```
pict001.gif pict002.gif pict003.gif ...
```

The [+] button in the Pic save menu adds a number higher by one to the file name. This is useful for creating a set of files numbered sequentially. We can then write a standard batch file that uses Alchemy to convert the image back into the show palette:

```
alchemy -p -fgray.pcx -d pict001.gif
alchemy -p -fgray.pcx -d pict002.gif
...
and so on.
```

The -p parameter tells Alchemy to create a PCX file. The -d parameter tells Alchemy not to dither the file. This is important. Alchemy shouldn't have to perform dithering anyway, because we did not add colors to the image in Animator Pro and the palette colors we used in Animator were the same palette colors as the original palette created in Pictor. Including the instruction not to dither the image is necessary, because Alchemy may develop its own ideas about how the image will be represented!

THE LONG AND WINDING PIXEL EDITING ROAD

We've presented one possible method for creating an animation that was derived from the analog (a.k.a. real) world. If you are blessed with artistic talent, you will probably think of ways to create the "Sylvia" image in Pictor and its variations. You would save yourself the time and effort of entering and exiting programs and the expense of purchasing high-end image processing programs. Digital processing lends itself to alternative methods of creating images and rewards artistic talent. We've shown you one of many ways. For example, you could derive the welcoming face from a clip library and do the mouth movements by hand.

Using Pictor to Convert the Files to Clippings

The final step is to load each of the PCX files into Pictor for conversion to clippings. Since we have already positioned the images in relation to each other in Animator, no further processing of the images is necessary in Pictor. We use the (ALT)-(J) key combination to find the edges around each of the images, then press (ALT)-(F9) to create byte-wide clippings, and finally (ALT)-(F10) to align the clippings to byte boundaries. We press (C) for "copy to clipboard," and (S) for save. In the Save menu, we choose Clipping as the save format and save the five clippings to disk with offsets, by selecting Save and pressing the (CTRL) key simultaneously. This ensures that the clippings can be "putup" in the exact position they were saved in. We then exit Pictor and load TEST2.TXT into the GRASP editor once again. We're ready to animate the welcome sequence.

Animating the Welcome Sequence

Now that we have created the five images that will be animated, it's time to give some thought to the sound that will accompany the animation.

The welcome sequence uses the SNDPLAY.TXT sound file subroutine we used earlier to add sound to the software magazine. Add the line "merge sndplay" at the beginning of the TEST2.TXT script.

```
video m

; TEST2.TXT Welcome sequence.

start:

; Sound subroutine
        merge sndplay
```

As we said earlier, GRASP uses a special file called SOUND.GRP that implements the low-level digital sound support. The file SNDPLAY.TXT is a GRASP interface to that GRP. In order to use the GRP, you must load all images in the series before calling the sound routine. Note also that since the animation is called by the sound subroutine, we must create the animation as a subroutine and locate it after the exit point of the script.

Let's go through the programming steps one by one. First we'll load the Sylvia clippings. Enter the following at the end of TEST2.TXT, just before the Waitkey and Exit commands.

```
; Loads in Sylvia clippings.
        cload syl100.clp c1 1
        cload syl101.clp c2 1
        cload syl102.clp c3 1
        cload syl103.clp c4 1
        cload syl104.clp c5 1
```

This places the clippings in memory, ready for use. We plan to fade Sylvia off the screen after she says "welcome," so we'll save the area where Sylvia will appear in a clipping buffer. Enter the following line next:

```
        cgetbuf c6 287,204 376,329 1        ; saves part of screen
                                            ; to buffer
```

Now we'll fade Sylvia onto the screen. (We introduce a new way of using the Cfade command here. Ignore it for the moment. We'll come back to it presently.)

```
; Fades Sylvia on screen.
        cfade 13 c1->xoff c1->yoff c1 100
```

Next, we'll enter the lines that tell SNDPLAY.TXT where to find the welcome animation and sound.

```
; Animates Sylvia's welcome with sound.
        set sndfile welcome
        set animat sylvia
```

(Don't run the script yet.) We'll add the code that animates the clippings in a moment. First, let's add the line that makes the call to the sound subroutine and the line that fades Sylvia off the screen once the animation runs.

```
        sndplay                             ; calls sound subroutine
        cfade 13 c6->xoff c6->yoff c6 100   ; fades Sylvia off screen
        cfree c1 - c20

waitkey
exit
```

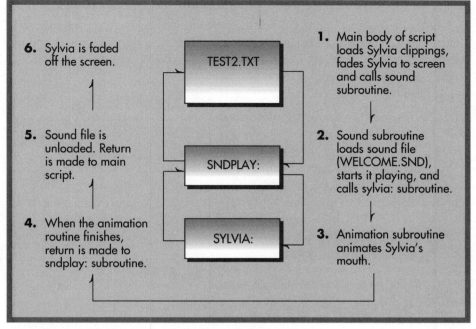

Figure 5-12 Playing sound and animation simultaneously

(Don't run the script yet.) Here's the code you need to enter after the Waitkey and Exit commands to complete the animation. Remember that because the animation is called from the sound subroutine, it uses a label and a Return command, and is located after the exit point of the script.

```
sylvia:
        cfade 13 c1->xoff c1->yoff c1 10        ; smile
        cfade 1 c2->xoff c2->yoff c2 10         ; mouth begins to open
        waitkey 5
        cfade 13 c3->xoff c3->yoff c3 10        ; mouth wide open
        waitkey 10
        cfade 13 c4->xoff c4->yoff c4 5         ; mouth begins to close
        cfade 13 c5->xoff c5->yoff c5 1         ; mouth closed
return
```

Figure 5-12 is a code flow diagram showing you the sequence of commands as executed by GRASP.

When you run the script, Sylvia's face appears, she says,"Welcome," and then her face disappears. The program exits back to the editor. If you do not have a sound card in your system, you will hear Sylvia's voice come out through the speaker of the computer.

Using the -> Operator to Fade Clippings to Precise Locations

Let's now turn our attention to the way that we fade Sylvia's image to the screen. The Cfade command does not normally make use of the offsets stored with a clipping. But GRASP has a special operator, ->, that accesses the offset information stored with a clipping. The command

```
cfade 13 c1->xoff c1->yoff c1 100
```

tells GRASP to retrieve the offset information stored with the clipping and use it to place the clipping on the screen. The images we lined up so carefully in Animator Pro retain their precise positioning on the screen.

We said earlier that five images are not adequate for realistic animation, especially for a complex sequence. Cfade helps us overcome this limitation to a certain extent by allowing us to dissolve the images on rather than instantly displaying them. This creates a kind of overlapping dissolve. Let's take a closer look at the lip-synch subroutine. The first clipping is faded to the screen (the smile). Then the following four clippings animate to "welcome."

```
sylvia:
        cfade 1 c2->xoff c2->yoff c2 10        ; mouth begins to open
        waitkey 5
        cfade 13 c3->xoff c3->yoff c3 10       ; mouth wide open
        waitkey 10
        cfade 13 c4->xoff c4->yoff c4 5        ; mouth begins to close
        cfade 13 c5->xoff c5->yoff c5 1        ; mouth closed
return
```

Unlike the command Putup, which can only quick-snap images to the screen, Cfade allows us to use overlapping fades. In this case we use fade 13, which is a vertical filter wipe, from the top and bottom simultaneously. By *cross-fading* the images in this way, we make it more difficult for the eye to see the jerkiness in the animation.

We also take advantage of the ability to set the length of dissolves with Cfade to approximate the timing of the lip movement animation to the movement of actual lips. The waveform shape depicting "welcome" in Figure 5-10 is approximated in its dynamics by our use of the length of fades and the Waitkey times we introduce between fades. Using Cfade in combination with the -> operator is powerful indeed.

The lip movement animation might be out of synchronization (out of synch) on your machine, because fades are affected by processor speed and video card speed. By adjusting the fade values and Waitkey times, you should be able to create an animation more faithful to the real lip movement. Because each type of fade involves processing data, you might try different types of fades to see which work the fastest, or produce the most accurate results.

After the subroutine runs, we return to the body of the script and fade Sylvia off the screen. It remains to make the transition to the next sequence in our multimedia demo.

Making the Transition to the Next Sequence

The welcome sequence is self-contained. We're about to make a transition to a different background, so it makes sense to create a new script that we will link to. Before doing that, let's remove the petroglyphs and halo from the screen until only the sky remains. You may recall that when we built the sky, we saved it to a picture buffer so that we could restore it later. Here's the section of code again:

```
; Starry background.

        set cnt 1                       ; set color index count at 1

        mark 300
        color @cnt                      ; set palette at color index
        point 0,0 639,479               ; place point randomly on screen
        set cnt @cnt+1                  ; increment index by 1
        if @cnt==10                     ; when you reach an index of 10
                set cnt 1               ; reset index to 1
        endif                           ; otherwise continue
        loop

        pgetbuf p1                      ; saves screen for use later
```

Notice that the last command saves the sky to a buffer. Now let's get rid of our space symbols by fading this buffer onto the screen. Enter the following code at the end of TEST2.TXT, just before the Waitkey and Exit commands.

```
; Dissolves off space symbols.
        pfade 6 p1 300
        pfree p1

waitkey
exit
```

When you run the script, the symbols and halo dissolve off the screen. An empty sky remains.

We're now ready to continue with the story we're building for the demo. Before we do that however, let's take another side excursion. This time, we'll introduce you to a couple of very useful utility scripts.

Examining the Palette

You may wonder how we choose colors when developing a GRASP program. Do we need to exit from GRASP and enter Pictor every time we need to examine the palette?

Included with the disk that comes with this book is a utility called SHOWPAL.TXT. When called from a GRASP script, SHOWPAL will display the current palette in a numbered series of boxes at the bottom of the screen. This allows you to examine the current palette, or choose colors for GRASP commands. It is written so it can be called from your script by entering the line:

```
call \grasp\showpal
```

We've located SHOWPAL.TXT in the main subdirectory so that copies of it do not have to be created in each subdirectory. You can call the SHOWPAL.TXT script from anywhere in your program code, except in a subroutine using sound. Calling SHOWPAL.TXT while sound is playing will cause unpredictable results. For technical reasons you cannot load a file from the hard drive when sound is playing.

Instead of explicitly entering the call to SHOWPAL.TXT in your script, you can use a function key to call it up. This line would be entered at the beginning of your script:

```
when f10 call \grasp\showpal
```

We discussed implementing key assignments using the When command in Chapter 3. Remember that the key must be explicitly unassigned by issuing When without parameters (when f10). Don't forget to remove the command when you distribute the program! Notice that we assigned the call to function key (F10). This frees the first nine function keys for program use.

Figure 5-13 Welcoming visual with palette

Calling SHOWPAL.TXT causes GRASP to temporarily exit the script it is now running, run the SHOWPAL.TXT script, and then return to the calling script to continue executing the script at the point SHOWPAL.TXT was called. Put a pair of Waitkey commands right at the point where you want to display the palette. The first Waitkey will be triggered by pressing (F10). The second Waitkey allows you to examine the palette. You can then exit back to the script to remove the Waitkey commands. Let's examine the palette at the point where Sylvia's face is faded onto the screen:

```
cfade 13 c1->xoff c1->yoff c1 100

call \grasp\showpal
waitkey
```

After running the script, your screen should look like Figure 5-13. On the printed page the whole palette looks as if it is grayscale. However, on the screen the first seven palette slots (0–6) are the colors we use for the background and the balance of the palette slots (7–15) are the grays we use for Sylvia's face. Notice that it conveniently assigns numbers to the palette slots. SHOWPAL.TXT belongs in every GRASPers toolbox.

Finding Screen Coordinates with SHOWCORD

Included on the disk with this book (and installed in the main GRASP directory) is another utility script, SHOWCORD.TXT. The script helps you find screen coordinates during GRASP development. Just like SHOWPAL.TXT, it can be called from anywhere in your script. Try assigning it to the (F9) function key. Enter this right after the Video M command at the top of the script:

```
when f9 call \grasp\showcord.txt
```

By placing a pair of Waitkey commands at the point where you want to examine screen coordinates, you will be able to precisely locate the image whose screen coordinates you want to record. Try placing a Waitkey just after the Cgetbuf command that captures the screen area behind Sylvia's head.

```
    cgetbuf c6 287,204 376,329 0 1
waitkey
waitkey
```

We usually place the Waitkeys in the first column of the screen to make it easy to spot and remove after we've finished with it. You might actually find it more convenient to add the call to SHOWCORD.TXT and a Waitkey at the point in the script where you want to examine screen coordinates:

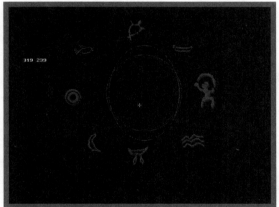

Figure 5-14 Screen coordinates displayed by SHOWCORD.TXT

```
call \grasp\showcord
waitkey
```

This is our preferred method.

Make sure your mouse is installed and working. When you run the script, the screen will pause at the point where you called SHOWCORD. Your screen should look like Figure 5-14.

White cross-hairs will appear at the middle of the screen and a pair of white numbers will appear in the upper left region of the screen. As you move your mouse around, the screen coordinates readout will change, reflecting the coordinates of the cross-hairs. When you click with any of the mouse buttons, the cross-hairs disappear and you are returned to the script. The readout also freezes on the screen. SHOWCORD.TXT allows you to easily find coordinates of objects, points, or areas on the screen.

Animating a Horse, a Bird, and a Man

The next module of our multimedia demo introduces a variety of animation techniques. Let's begin by establishing a new background and introducing it to the reader. First, we'll create the link to the new script. Delete the Waitkey command just before the Exit command and replace it with the following:

```
; Links to next module.
        link test3.txt start
exit
```

Now open a new file called TEST3.TXT and enter the following lines.

```
; TEST3.TXT Racehorse, Parrot and Universal Person Animations.

video m

; Sound routine.
        merge sndplay

; New background.
        pload greenbck.pic p1          ; main palette
        palette p1
        edge on 14                     ; gray leading edge on fade
        pfade 9 p1 150                 ; wipe from top with edge
        pfree p1

; Switches palettes
        pload gray.pal p1
        palette p1
        pfree p1

waitkey
exit
```

When you run TEST3.TXT, the new background wipes onto the screen from the top. It has a leading gray edge. We'll be using sound in this section, so we've added the necessary merge file to enable sound.

The command Edge puts a colored leading edge on horizontal and vertical fades. Syntax for the command is:

```
edge setting [color]
```

The *setting* parameter is the keyword "on" or "off." On turns the edge feature on, off turns it off. The default value for color is the last color in the palette, which is often the color white. It's better to explicitly assign a palette color to the edge. The edge is 1 pixel wide. The command helps create the illusion of shrinking or expanding boxes.

GRASP Palette Magic

When the show palette is restricted to 16 colors, there is a temptation to fade to black between images. Unfortunately, audiences have been conditioned to expect major time or place changes in a movie or television show that fade to black. There is a way around this, however.

The technique is to restrict the colors of the background you're using to as few colors as possible. You then make sure images share the same few colors in their respective palettes. You can then fade to the background between images.

Here's how we used this technique in the demo. The background was created from a full color scan of a scrap art board found at a framing shop. We liked the pattern of dots and the way they were dispersed. The art board's textures gave the background depth and interest. The full color scan was converted to 16 colors with Alchemy using the palette we designed earlier for the show.

We used Animator Pro's separation tool to assign the first seven palette slots to dots in the background. By confining the colors in the background to the first seven palette slots, we ensured that we could use the background for a number of images with different palettes. As long as the new image uses the same seven colors in the first seven palette slots, we can fade images on and off the background without changing the background.

That's what we've done in the code you just entered. We changed the system palette from GREENBCK.PIC to GRAY.PAL, the palette with gray colors in palette slots 8 to 15. (Try using SHOWPAL.TXT to confirm this.)

We did not need to create a new image in order to switch palettes. (We showed you how to create small PAL files in Chapter 4.) GREENBCK.PIC is 90,193 bytes in size. GRAY.PAL uses 99 bytes. Not having to create a new picture for the gray palette saved disk space.

The next block of code floats the moon petroglyph to the top of the screen. We'll be adding these symbols to the screen for visual interest and continuity. The animation is straightforward, so we won't analyze it.

```
; Moon rises.
        tran on 0
        cload symbol15.clp c1 0 1
        float -240,-40 -10,280 15 2 c1
        putup -10,280 c1
        cfree c1
        noise 20 5 3
```

We'll explain the Noise command shortly. The next animation occurs on a white "screen" that drops down over the background. The screen becomes a background for a trotting horse animation.

```
; Screen drops down.
        color 15
        window 208,379 448,379              ; outside dimension of screen
```

```
mark 20
        window 0 -10 0 0 r
        color 10
        box 212,196 444,375 4          ; gray frame around screen,
                                       ; 4 pixels wide
        color 15
        rect 216,200 440,371           ; white screen surface
        noise 10 1 1
loop
window                                 ; restores window to entire screen
```

We use a loop to gradually open a window on the gray-framed white screen. Always remember at the end to reset drawing activity to the entire screen by issuing the Window command without screen coordinates.

Now we'll add more petroglyphs to the screen.

```
; More petroglyphs.
        tran on 0
        cload symbol12.clp c1 0 1          ; person dancing
        float 140,-150 90,-60 20 3 c1
        putup 90,-60 c1
        noise 10 5 3
        cfree c1

        cload symbol17.clp c1 0 1          ; fish
        float -120,-120 -60,-240 20 1 c1
        putup -60,-240 c1
        noise 20 10 2
        cfree c1

        waitkey 10

        cload symbol13.clp c1 0 1          ; ocean waves
        float -420,-190 40,-80 20 1 c1
        putup 40,-80 c1
        cfree c1
        noise 30 5 1
        waitkey 50
```

The petroglyphs (a moon, a person dancing a sacred dance, a fish, and the ocean waves) fill some of the screen's empty space and help communicate our sense that multimedia is a story-telling medium. They also add action to the screen, provide visual interest, and hold the audience's attention. We're now ready to move ahead in time to the dawn of the motion picture era.

Creating the Walking Race Horse Animation

Eadweard Muybridge, the Victorian eccentric, has provided us with a rich source of stop-action photography. His collection of high-speed action photographs is still used today by art students to study the movements of animals and the human figure.

We'll pay homage to Muybridge's work here by animating his study of a race-horse trotting using our own software-created "magic zoetrope." We scanned 12 of Muybridge's photographs and used Photostyler to adjust the contrast and remove detail from the black-and-white pictures. The 12 shots capture the horse's trot.

First, we scanned the 12 shots into the computer. We then used Image Alchemy to color reduce the scans to 16 colors, using the grayscale palette (GRAY.PAL). Then we did final editing in Animator Pro, using its Cel tools to line up the pictures to each other. Figure 5-15 shows a frame from the 12-part series, after it was "cleaned up."

After positioning the sequence of horses so that they precisely overlapped, we saved the series as GIF files. (Animator's macro recorder is handy for this.) Finally, we converted the pictures back to 16 colors, using Alchemy and the grayscale palette.

Normally, we would then clip the pictures in Pictor and load the clippings into GRASP to animate them. However, the 12 clippings Pictor would create would be much too large to be suitable for animation. Especially on systems with slow hard drives, the clippings would take too long to load into memory. And on systems without extended or expanded memory, the clippings would not fit into memory at all. There is an alternative to loading and displaying clippings or pictures. It's a special animation utility called GDFF.

Using GDFF to Create Animations

GDFF stands for GRASP Differential File Format. Included with the disk that comes with this book is a utility program called GDFF.EXE. GRASP's animation utility analyzes a series of pictures, pixel by pixel, looking for the differences between them. It records the differences between frames in this unique file format. GDFF compression works well for a series of pictures that share a common background or share large areas of identically colored pixels, such as flat colored graphics. It saves these differences in a file with a .DFF file extension. (Chapter 1 describes image compression in detail.)

The GDFF file format is similar to Autodesk's FLI and

Fig 5-15 Muybridge's horse processed in Animator Pro

FLC file formats. You can use GDFF.EXE to create a GDFF file from an Autodesk FLI or FLC flic. This will sometimes result in smaller files.

GDFF will not perform color reduction or image resizing. That's why we had to save each frame of the Animator Pro flic (in 640x480, 256-color resolution) as single GIF files and convert them to 16-color files with the same palette before using GDFF to create an animation file.

Syntax for the GDFF utility program can be found by running GDFF without any parameters. Here is the Help screen you'll see when you run GDFF from the command line.

```
GDFF - DFF data generator
        Written by John Bridges - Copyright(C) 1984-1992

To use this utility, execute the following command:

GDFF {/s /x /d:nsector /2} dffname file1 file2 file3...

The parameters are as follows:
/s              - Enable disk swapped for large images (slower)
/x              - Generate XORed DFFs for both forward and reverse playback
/d:nsector      - Make DFF on nsector boundaries
/1              - Include first image as difference with nothing.
/2              - Skip every other image for 2 page animation.
```

GDFF supports a number of file formats, including PIC, PCX, GIF, as well as the FLI, FLC, and DFF animation formats. GDFF will normally load two images into memory and analyze the differences between them. (Remember that the version of GRASP included with this book does not support 640x480 256-color animations.) When images are too large to fit into available memory resources, the /s switch directs GRASP to leave both images on disk while analyzing them. This is much slower than loading two images and analyzing them entirely in memory.

The /x option allows you to create animations that can be run forward or backward. The /D:n parameter is rather specialized. It writes sets of image differences to a specified disk sector boundary. This speeds up disk access. It is only used when you know the animation will be run from a floppy drive.

Normally, GDFF looks only at the differences between images. This means the first image in the series is not saved to the GDFF file. In order for the DFF file to run, you have to put the first image of the series on-screen. GDFF will then play back the changes from that first image. The /1 parameter allows you to get around this problem. Specifying the /1 parameter tells GRASP to include the entire first image in the DFF file. Including the first image in the differential file can increase its size dramatically. If you can bring the animation up from a solid color or an existing background, do so.

The optional /2 parameter does not concern us in this book, which uses VGA modes only. The /2 parameter is used to create images for animations in EGA mode that use the GRASP "2-page animation" technique. Two-page animation is designed to prevent screen flicker in EGA modes.

You can type a list of file names for GDFF to process, but they have to fit on one line. We usually give the files we are going to save as a DFF file sequential file names and use the DOS wild card symbols *.* to tell GDFF what files to include in the DFF. In this case the command was:

```
gdff race.dff horse*.pcx
```

This created RACE.DFF.

Why use GDFF? One big advantage is speed. Because DFF files are much smaller than the files from which they are made, they load quickly into memory and decompress at RAM speed. The second big advantage is the ability to create complex animations. You can have several dozen small objects moving in complex patterns on the screen at once.

Let's create the racehorse animation now. Add the following lines to TEST3.TXT.

```
; Race horse animation.
        dload race.dff 1         ; race horse animation file

        set sndfile horse
        sndplay                  ; animate horse
exit

horse:

        mark 16
        putdff 1 5 0 12 216,200
        loop
        dfree 1
return
```

Notice that the horse: subroutine is entered after the Exit command. That's because the horse subroutine is called by the sound subroutine. When you run the animation, the horse and rider appear and you hear the sound of a horse trotting. Let's look closer at the DFF commands.

The Dload Command

Dload, the command that loads DFF files, is straightforward. You can use it to load either GRASP DFF files or Autodesk Animator files. Dload's syntax is:

```
dload name [buffer] [disk]
```

where name is the name of the DFF file (or Animator FLI or FLC file), and *buffer* is the buffer you want to load the file into. As usual, you can have up to 128 buffers, and buffer 1 is the default if you do not specify the buffer number. The *disk* option gives you a choice of running the animation from the hard drive or from memory. It has a value of 0 by default, which means,"Do not run the animation from disk, but rather play the animation from the memory buffer." If the file is too large to load into memory, you tell GRASP to run the file from the hard drive by entering 1 for this parameter. When creating your own animations, if the animation doesn't run, try entering this parameter (1). The animation will not play back as fast or as smoothly using this parameter, but at least it will run. GRASP reads off images from the disk as it needs them. Consider using a RAM disk in these cases.

The Putdff Command

Syntax for the command that plays a DFF file is:

```
putdff [buffer] [delay] [start] [end] [x,y]
```

The first parameter (*buffer*) specifies a buffer where you have previously loaded a DFF (or FLI or FLC) file. The second parameter (*delay*) specifies the length of time between frames in hundredths of a second (the default is 0). The third (*start*) and fourth parameters (*end*) allow you to play the frames between the frame numbers you designate. The final parameter (*x,y*) allows you to offset placement of the animation on the screen by specifying a value to add to the bottom left corner coordinates of the differential file. We use this offset in the Putdff command to place the horse and rider animation inside the gray frame of the "screen." The differential file keeps an internal record of the individual frames from which it was formed. In other words, what we call frames here were originally individual picture files.

Playing DFF Animations Backward

We don't use an animation that runs backward in this chapter. If you do want to run the animation backward, you would create it with GDFF.EXE using the /x switch and play it back by preceding the Putdff command with a "set" system setting. The playback command looks like this:

```
set xor on
putdff test.fli 1 100 30 20
set xor off
```

This plays TEST.FLI in buffer 1 backwards (from frame 30 to frame 20) with a 1-second delay (100) between frames.

Transforming the Horse into a Bird

Part of the pleasure of working with digital tools is that we can create visual effects on the computer screen that would be difficult and expensive to create in video or in film. Let's do a transformation of the horse into a bird to demonstrate this. Enter the command to load the transformation DFF (dload transfor.dff 2) right after the Dload command for the racehorse DFF.

```
; Race horse animation.
        dload race.dff 1              ; race horse animation file
        dload transfor.dff 2          ; transformation animation

        set sndfile horse
```

Loading two differential files illustrates one of the advantages of the DFF format. Because of the small size of DFF files, we're able to load two into memory very quickly, and have the second DFF file ready to run as soon as the first DFF file has played.

Add the lines that actually call the transformation subroutine.

```
; Transformation to bird.

        set sndfile whinny
        set animat transform
        sndplay                         ; transform to bird
```

(Don't run the script yet.) Now we're ready to add the lines that play the transformation DFF. Enter these lines after the horse subroutine, at the very end of TEST3.TXT. This allows us to call the animation from the sound subroutine. Notice that we blank the screen to white just before transforming the horse into the bird. We do this by setting the system color to white and then creating a (white) rectangle over the screen area.

```
transform:
        color 15
        rect 215,370 440,202
        local cnt 0
        mark 8
                putdff 2 30 @cnt @cnt 216,200
                set cnt @cnt+1
        loop
        dfree 2
        return
```

Here we introduce a slightly different way of playing back a DFF file. Using a loop and a counter (cnt), we play back the DFF one frame at a time, instead of playing the DFF from the beginning frame to the end frame. There is no particular advantage to doing this here. However, if you are creating a program with user interaction (such as a program with a help screen called up with (F1) using the Ifkey command), the user would not be able to interrupt the DFF while it is playing. By playing the DFF one frame at a time, you can have the program check for the (F1) key after each frame is played. The modified code would look like this:

```
        mark 8
                putdff 2 29 @cnt @cnt 216,200
                set cnt @cnt+1
                waitkey 01
                ifkey f1 help
        loop
        dfree 2
        return

        exit

        help:
                help menu goes here
        return
```

193

PARTIAL SCREEN DFF ANIMATION

The racehorse DFF was created with a small utility program available to registered users of GRASP from Paul Mace. The utility program allows you to select an area of the screen that will be stored in your DFF. By creating a partial screen animation, you'll reduce the size of the DFF and create a DFF that can be played anywhere on the screen. Another method of creating partial screen animations is as follows. Load the individual pictures that make up the animation into GRASP one frame at a time. Then use Pgetbuf and Psave commands to save a portion of the screen to the disk. The code looks like this:

```
; Routine for saving portion of screen to disk.

pload horse100.pic p1          ; first frame horse
                               ; and rider

palette p1
pfade 0 p1
pfree p1

pgetbuf p1 245,205 420,350     ; box around horse and
                               ; rider

psave new100.pic p1            ; save smaller pic to
                               ; hard drive


pload horse101.pic p1          ; second frame
...                            ; repeat
```

All twelve pictures are processed this way. The new pictures are much smaller than the originals. As long as you make sure the new series of pictures are all of the same size (by using the same Pgetbuf coordinates), GDFF will process the new series of pictures and create a smaller DFF that has the advantage of being independent of the green background.

Help is a subroutine the program branches to when the (F1) key is pressed. After executing the help subroutine, GRASP returns the user to the point in the DFF animation where it was interrupted.

The transformation from the horse to the bird was created in Autodesk Animator. We captured the horse as a cel, and spun it on its axis over several frames. We then used the Streak tool with the Smear ink to smear and streak the pixels into a spiral. Animator's macro recorder allowed us to perform this action over the entire series of frames. We then saved the frames as GIF files, converted them using Alchemy, and created the differential file using GDFF.EXE.

Animating the Bird Flying Away

Now we'll have the bird appear in the gray-framed screen and fly away. Before it does, we'll make it appear from the mass of dots left at the end of the transformation sequence. Using a DFF to make the bird fly across the background is not as efficient as floating a fixed number of clippings across the screen. Seven clippings are all that are required to make the bird fly wherever we want around the screen. The DFF, on the other hand, would store the bird's (and the background's) every movement as changes. Enter the following lines after the last animation and before the Exit command. Don't run it yet. GRASP will look for and not find the animation subroutines.

```
; Bird flies away.
        window 315,280 315,280            ; reveal window "closed"
        cload parro101.clp c1 0 1
        cload parro102.clp c2 0 1
        cload parro103.clp c3 0 1
        cload parro104.clp c4 0 1
        cload parro105.clp c5 0 1
        sparkle
        cload parro106.clp c6 0 1
        sparkle
        cload parro107.clp c7 0 1
        sparkle
        window                            ; window fully open

        set sndfile birdcall
        set animat birdfly
        sndplay                           ; bird animation
```

The disadvantage of using clippings is in lengthy loading times. Computers vary widely in the speeds of their hard drive systems and in their processing speeds. We need to create a diversion that entertains the audience while the clippings are loaded. As you can see, there is a subroutine called "sparkle" called when loading some of the clippings. Sparkle adds a "pixel sparkle" to the area where the bird is located. It also uses the Window command with a relative switch to open the window and reveal the bird. The sparkle subroutine should be entered at the very end of TEST3.TXT, just after the transform: subroutine.

```
sparkle:
        color 5
        local xmin @minx
        local ymin @miny
        local xmax @maxx
        local ymax @maxy
        window
        mark 20
                local xoff random(-20,20)
                local yoff random(-20,20)
                offset @xoff @yoff
                point 320,280
                offset 0,0
```

```
loop

noise 5 5 5
noise 5 12 5

window @xmin @ymin @xmax @ymax
color 15
window -5,-4 5,4 r              ; open window a little
putup -64,-65 c1

noise 5 5 5                     ; bird chirp
noise 5 12 5

return
```

When the program is run, the area where the bird appears sparkles and the bird is gradually revealed. We use a new set of system variables here to solve a problem. As the bird is revealed, we want the sparkle to occur over the entire area of the bird, not just the area defined by the window. (The window is closed at the beginning, so we wouldn't see the sparkle.) What we do is quite simple. The system variables—@minx, @miny, @maxx, @maxy—contain the bottom right and top left coordinates of the current window. These coordinates define a "closed window." Just before we run the loop that puts random pixels on the screen, we save the current window coordinates by assigning them to the local variables xmin, ymin, xmax, and ymax. We then reset the window to the entire screen. Now we run the sparkle loop. When it is finished, we restore the window coordinates (@xmin, @ymin, @xmax, and @ymax) using the Window command. Then we open the window a little bit for the next call to the sparkle subroutine. As each subroutine is processed, the window gradually opens to reveal the entire bird. Meanwhile, the sparkle subroutine occurs over the entire bird. Each time we Putup the bird clipping, we cover over the previous points created. This creates a sparkle effect.

Using Local and Global Variables

As in the programming language C, GRASP allows you to define the *scope* of a variable. Scope refers to how variables are accessed in programs. Some variables can be accessed at all points in a program. These are called *global variables*. Some variables are accessible from only parts of a program. Local variables created with set or local are available at the level where they're created, and at all lower levels (subroutines). On a return to a higher level, the variable is lost. Defining the scope of variables helps the GRASP programmer use memory efficiently, since the variables that are not needed after they are used are released, and the memory they use is released. GRASP will create local variables by default. You can declare a local variable either by

```
set name [value]
```

or

```
local name [value]
```

A local variable can have the same name as a global variable at a higher level. GRASP will use the local variable until a return to the higher level, when it restores the previous variable.

Global variables, on the other hand, stay in effect as long as your program runs. They are declared by using the word "global:"

```
global name [value]
```

Remember: When you declare a local variable in a subroutine, it is not accessible at a level above that routine, but it is available to a routine below that level. By declaring a global value, you are allowing the variable to be accessed from anywhere in the program. Effectively managing variables is a good way of creating fast, memory-efficient GRASP programs.

Using the Random Function

GRASP supports another feature common to higher level programming languages, *functions*. A function acts like a mailing address that you can get information from or send information to for processing. You can see a list of GRASP functions by paging through the Functions Listing with the (F2) key in the editor. Think of them as little black boxes that perform highly specialized tasks for you. In the sparkle loop that places pixels on the screen, we use a function called random. The syntax is:

```
random(value 1, value 2)
```

The function random returns a random number between value 1 and value 2, inclusive. Let's look at the example code more closely.

```
mark 50
        local xoff random(-20,20)
        local yoff random(-20,20)
        offset @xoff @yoff
        point 320,280
        offset 0,0
loop
```

Each time through the loop, we assign a random number to the xoff and yoff local variables. (Remember that the variables are called xoff and yoff. We access the values stored at the values by using the @ symbol.) We then use the variables to offset a point at the center of the bird (320,280) to a new position and place it on the screen. Then we reset the offset back to 0,0. Each time through the loop, the point is placed in a new, random, position. We repeat the loop 50 times. By placing a bird clipping over the points we've just added to the screen, we cover most of the points we just added. This creates the sparkle effect.

197

Adding a Bird Chirp

At the end of the sparkle subroutine, we add a bird chirp sound effect, created by GRASP's Noise command. Syntax for the command is:

```
noise n m time
```

where *n* and *m* are values used to create a sound wave and time is the duration of the sound wave in hundredths of a second. Specifying different values for *n* and *m* creates complex waveforms rather than smooth glissandos. Noise tends to create sharp, loud, metallic sounds, whereas the Note command reviewed earlier creates more musical sounds. By placing two Noise commands together, we create a more complex sound.

Sound Effects and Animation

Sound effects add "color" to animation. Just as color helps guide our eyes to what is important in a scene, so does sound help us make sense of what we're looking at. It's with a sense of delight that we watch as the bird in the previous animation emerges from the sparkling pixels, and the chirping sound we send out through the PC speaker helps us anticipate the emergence of the bird. Let's now teach our baby bird to fly!

Making the Bird Fly

Our source for the seven-step bird animation is once again Muybridge's excellent work. We scanned seven photos of a parrot's flight and used Photostyler to process the images. We use Photostyler's "sharpening" tool to bring blurry photos into sharper focus. The parrot was processed to sharpen its outlines. Then we saved the series

of seven photos to disk, processed them in Alchemy to reduce them to the 16 colors of our grayscale palette and imported them into Animator Pro. Animator Pro was particularly valuable as a tool for arranging and previewing the seven animation steps. Figure 5-16 shows the seven-step animation as we laid it out in Animator Pro.

We've spread the flight of the parrot over one frame so you can see the individual

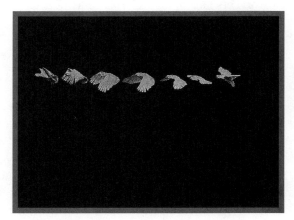

Figure 5-16 The parrot animation previewed in Animator Pro

steps of the animation. When working with the bird clippings, we found that the animation looked the smoothest when we overlapped the birds about three-quarters of their length. Notice that we make the bird fly in a downward arc. We've matched the horizontal position between the first and last bird, so that as the animation is repeated, the last bird of the animation is at the same level as the first bird. This may not be an accurate bird flight path, but the slight bounce helps to give the flight a natural feel. Matching the end point with the beginning point of a looping animation is the key.

After we developed the smooth animation of the bird in Animator Pro, we saved the individual frames to the hard drive and converted them to PCX files using Alchemy. Then we loaded each frame into Pictor and clipped it using the (ALT)-(J),(ALT)-(F9) keystroke combination. We saved the clippings to the hard drive while pressing the (CTRL) key to preserve the offsets.

Let's now make the bird fly and screech. Add these lines after the section that loads the clipping, just before the Waitkey and Exit commands.

```
; Animate bird.
        set sndfile birdcall
        set animat birdfly
        sndplay
```

(Don't run the script yet!) Now add the bird animation subroutine to the very end of TITLE3.TXT, just after the sparkle subroutine.

```
birdfly:

        rect 215,370 440,202                ; blanks screen area

        set xcoord 40                       ; initial bird position
        mark 3
                set parrot 1                ; first clipping
                set xcoord @xcoord-130      ; one cycle to left
                mark 7
                        float @xcoord,-65 @xcoord,-65 10 5 c$@parrot
                        set parrot @parrot+1
                loop
        loop
        cfree c1 - c20

return
```

The white rectangle blanks the area inside the gray frame of the drop-down screen. The bird clippings needed to be moved over to the right by 90 pixels. The initial value of xcoord is +40, then we add -130 to this value for a result of 90 pixels. Since after each loop we want to move all the clippings left by 130 pixels, the "set xcoord @xcoord-130" occurs inside the two loops. Since the bird is flying in a straight path, we keep the vertical offset to a constant 65 pixels (-65). We "float" all seven clippings on the screen. Each iteration of the loop causes the clippings to move to the left by 130 pixels. Meanwhile, the bird screeches as it leaves the screen. In fact, to maintain the illusion, we continue the sound for a few moments after the bird has disappeared.

Testing Code

The next part of the electronic demo uses a true 3D animation sequence created in Autodesk's 3D Studio. We're going to make the job of entering the code for the sequence a lot easier by providing you with a GRASP script that you can work with. On the disk that came with this book, there is a GRASP script called TITLE3.TXT that contains the code for this section. Load the script into GRASP's editor and save it as TEST3.TXT. Change the first commented line

```
; TITLE3.TXT Race Horse, Bird and Perfectly Proportioned Man.
```

to

```
; TEST3.TXT Race Horse, Bird and Perfectly Proportioned Man.
```

This change doesn't affect the running of the script. Our practice is to rename the current file as a "TEST.TXT" script when we want to make a change that we might regret after running it. If we like the change, we'll save it under its original name.

The Perfect Human Form Sequence

The next visual sequence of the demo is reminiscent of a popular artist's icon, Leonardo da Vinci's perfectly proportioned human body. Most of the code we use for the sequence should be easy for you to understand, now that you've worked with GRASP animation. Remove the semicolon in front of the "; set debug on" command at the beginning of the script, allow the animation to run until the bird flies away, and then use the space bar to step through the rest of the animation. Debug puts the currently executing command at the bottom of the screen as the animation progresses.

Here's what happens. After the white screen inside the gray frame shrinks away, a star twinkles at the center of the screen and a white shape appears. The star twinkles again. Then we go through a kind of arcade game sequence that suggests a link between multimedia and parallel developments in the computer game industry. Using the random function, we create laser rays that zap around the screen. The petroglyphs pop off the screen at intervals. Then the shape at the center of the screen zooms out, unfolding into the shape of the "updated" Perfectly Proportioned Man, with arms and legs outstretched.

We introduce no new programming logic or commands in this section. A couple of comments are in order, though.

200

Making the Stars Twinkle

Notice the way the stars are floated on the screen:

```
float 80,-28 80,-28 1 1 c2 c3 c4 c5 c4 c3 c2  ; star sparkle
```

Sparkling stars help give the presentation a "polished" look. The star clippings begin very small and get larger. Notice the pattern we use: tiny star, small star, large star, huge star, large star, small star, tiny star. This pattern mimics the way a spark of light might appear to the eye. If you were to map out the effect on a graph, you would see the shape of an analog wave once again!

Your eyes respond more quickly to very bright objects. Their effect on your eyes takes longer to decay than darker objects. That's what helps "smooth out" the twinkle effect. Change the delay value to 50 in the star sparkle float command. You will see the star sequence in slow motion.

```
float 80,-28 80,-28 1 50 c2 c3 c4 c5 c4 c3 c2  ; star sparkle
```

Notice how we use the shape and colors of the stars to help create the sparkle effect. Darker colors on the tips of the stars simulate a fall-off of light.

Creating the Perfectly Proportioned Man with 3D Studio

The Perfectly Proportioned Man zooms out from the center of the screen, unfolding as it does. It would be difficult, but not impossible, to create this sequence by drawing each of the steps of the animation. To see those steps, change the delay time of the float command that animates him to 120 from 12:

```
float 0,0 0,0 10 120 c1 c2 c3 c4 c5 c6 c7 c8 c9 c10 c11 c12
```

You'll get a much better idea of how the animation was created by examining Figure 5-17.

The screen was captured from the Keyframer module in Autodesk 3D Studio. The Keyframer allows you to animate three-dimensional meshes from one "key" position to another. "Key framing" is a generic animation term for identifying specific frames where some change in the animation occurs. By establishing a key frame for the starting position of an action (like the unfolding of the arms on the man), and another key frame

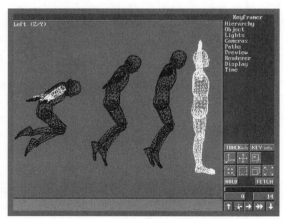

Figure 5-17 Perfectly Proportioned Man animated in Autodesk 3D Studio

for the ending position (the outstretched arms in the last frame), you can have the computer draw the in-between positions. This greatly simplifies the process of creating complex three-dimensional animations. The Perfectly Proportioned Man unfolds from a fetal position to a spread-eagle stance in 12 steps.

Autodesk's 3D Studio is an enormously powerful program for the multimedia artist. The program comes with hundreds of copyright-free meshes (the geometry from which objects are made in 3D Studio). Autodesk calls the CD-ROM disk that accompanies the program the World-Creating Toolkit. There are certainly enough meshes to create an artificial world in 3D.

Mesh objects can be "covered" with a number of different surface shadings, including wire-frame, flat, gourand, and phong shading. Phong shading, which accurately reproduces the effect of light on the surfaces of objects, is the most photorealistic and most computer-intensive. It works well for plastic or metallic finishes and other solid-color surfaces. Flat shading is often a good choice for graphics that will eventually be used in 16-color modes, although dithering can help create the illusion that a phong-shaded object is reflecting light. The man mesh we rendered uses a blue metallic finish rendered with phong shading. (*Rendering* is the term for applying photorealistic surfaces to objects.)

You can edit the properties of the surfaces you apply to 3D meshes as well. Figure 5-18 is a screen captured from the Materials Editor in 3D Studio.

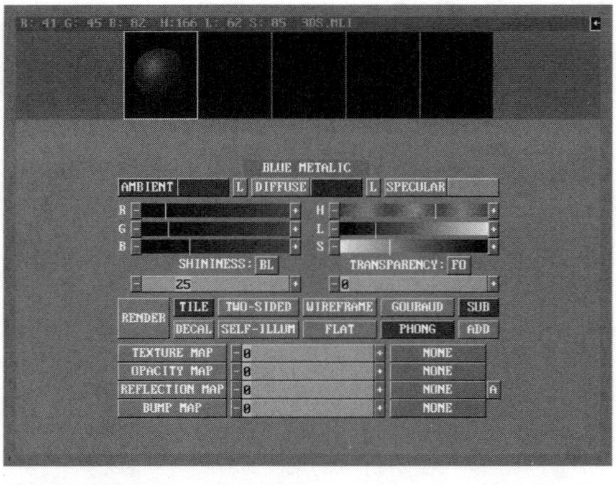

Figure 5-18 Materials Editor in Autodesk 3D Studio

There are controls for adjusting the way surfaces reflect light. This can create very subtle effects, like the sheen of dull metal. You can adjust the transparency of surfaces. You can also do texture mapping in 3D Studio. Texture mapping is the application of bit maps to meshes. For example, rather than trying to reproduce the complex detail of a brick surface, you can scan a brick into Photostyler, touch it up, and export it to 3D Studio as a Targa file. You can then create a material in the materials editor called "brick" and fine-tune its properties. It can then be used as a texture map in the 3D Editor module as a surface for a wall. The Materials Editor allows you to create fairly complex surfaces with its opacity map, reflection map, and bump map controls. The

CD-ROM disk that comes with 3D Studio includes many megabytes of meshes and textures—even a selection of scans of marble surfaces organized according to the Italian quarry they came from! You'll find brick well represented because it is a common building material.

Besides allowing you to create realistic surfaces, 3D Studio also allows you to simulate lighting and camera viewpoints in its Editor. In combination with the controls you have over the lights and camera in the Keyframer, you work as a virtual film camera and lighting crew adding atmosphere and mood to your virtual scene. Figure 5-19 shows camera and lighting in 3D Studio.

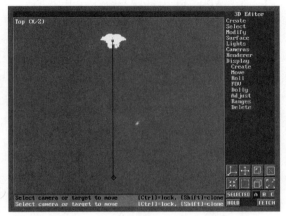

Figure 5-19 Camera and lighting in Autodesk 3D Studio

3D Studio also allows you to create meshes from scratch, using its 2D Shaper and 3D Lofter modules or geometry primitives in its 3D Editor. You can even import objects from other programs through the DXF import filter. We've imported objects originally built in Corel Draw.

The 3D Studio program will generate single or multiple frames in GIF, Targa, color TIF, or mono TIF formats. (TIF is widely supported by desktop publishing programs.) However, the big advantage for the GRASP developer is the ability to create FLI or FLC flics in the Keyframer. Because GRASP directly supports the FLI and FLC animation formats, you can create an animation in 3D Studio and play it back in a GRASP script without having to modify the flic. Of course, 16-color VGA mode is not supported by the Autodesk products. The Perfectly Proportioned Man animation was rendered as a series of GIF files, converted to 16 colors using Alchemy, and then loaded into Pictor for processing into clips.

The trio of products—GRASP, Animator Pro, and 3D Studio—are powerful weapons against the computer's resistance to let graphics images fly. While GRASP is an especially useful tool for creating floppy-disk-based presentations like the electronic ad we've created for this chapter, you may long to create complex, high color-resolution multimedia presentations employing 2D and 3D animation, that run from the hard drive. The commercial release of GRASP supports the 32,000 color mode found on many TSENG 4000 boards with the Hicolor DAC chip. This means that a 32,000 color Targa file generated by 3D Studio can be integrated into a

GRASP presentation. The size of 32,000 color images (600k to 800k on average) makes them impossible to animate with today's PCs. However, GRASP can add text and clip animations with Hicolor images. Because GRASP can switch video modes on the fly, you can create a GRASP multimedia presentation that uses the strengths of each of the different video modes at their color and spatial resolutions. Furthermore, as we will see in the next chapter, adding sound to multimedia presentations is a GRASP strength. Finally, GRASP adds complex user interaction to a presentation. Once the cost of digital video drops to a mass market level (under $500), multimedia really will become the preferred production method for audiovisual communications. Until then, there is no better place to start than the trio of products that was used to create the visuals in this chapter, 3D Studio, Animator Pro, and GRASP.

Completing the Electronic Demo

On the disk included with this book, you'll find the complete set of scripts for the electronic demo you've been creating. They are saved as TITLE1.TXT through to TITLE5.TXT.

What you have learned in this chapter should help you follow the techniques used to create the demo. The 3D sequences were built and animated in 3D Studio. The animated character was created in Animator Pro, animated, and exported as GIF images. It was then clipped in Pictor. By separating out the body parts, we were able to save valuable disk space. Note the subroutines that actually move the arms, head, and feet. They economize on hard disk space by making it unnecessary to move the entire body.

We've added the sound routines to the *Multimedia Creations* demo. If you have a Sound Blaster or a MIDI sequencer, you'll hear the ad as well as see it.

Using GRASP to create multimedia demos is the subject for this chapter. In the next chapter we'll show you how to synchronize visuals and music. We'll be building a virtual VCR using a MIDI memory resident program.

A Final Checklist for Disk-Based Demos

If you plan to distribute your finished work to a wide range of audiences, it's now an accepted assumption that most computer users will at least have a VGA color system with 256K of video memory. VGA cards with 256K (rather than 512K or 1 megabyte of memory) only provide enough video memory in the refresh buffer for 320x200 256-color or 640x480 16-color VGA images, as a maximum. Of course, these boards emulate EGA, CGA, or text modes as well. Less common are 512K VGA cards and 1 megabyte cards that allow you to display Super VGA images. Boards with the Hicolor DAC (digital-to-analog conversion) chips are becoming more common, as are boards with True Color technology. If your presentation is small and you have the space on your floppy disks, you can prepare your presentation in different video modes and write a GRASP routine that queries your user's hardware and runs the appropriate scripts. This is treated in the next chapter.

Continuous-tone images and digitized sound files do not compress as well as files containing large amounts of redundant information, such as graphics with flat areas of color. Use an archiving utility such as ARJ, PKZIP, or LHARC to compress and store the final production. We've found ARJ produces the smallest GRASP archives. Every byte of space you save through compression translates to more action on the disk. ARJ.EXE is available on CompuServe and many bulletin boards.

You will also have to decide whether or not your target audience have mice attached to their systems. The best option is to support either a mouse or function keys. GRASP allows you to provide your audience with keyboard alternatives. This was treated in Chapter 3 (the software magazine).

Finally, if you are distributing your program to a wide variety of users, you will need to set a ceiling for memory usage by your program. Your users may try to run the program from Windows or a shell, or they may be on a local area network. The commercial version of GRASP supports extended, expanded, and virtual memory, but not all users will have this memory available for the program. As a rule, assume your user has a maximum of 450K to 500K of memory. That should leave enough headroom for other programs. If you can push your program headroom down to 450K that would be much better.

Keep in mind as you create your program that hard drives, CPUs, and video subsystems all run at a variety of speeds. Also, laptops are still largely monochromatic. Knowing in advance that the program will run on a laptop with a slow hard drive will influence your design decisions. For example, you'll avoid placing together shades of color that convert to similar grayscale tones. They become indistinguishable when converted to black and white. The best policy is to constantly test your program on the type of computers your users employ.

You need to give some thought as to the palette you are going to create for the presentation. This is not as critical for productions that use the 256-color VGA modes or Hicolor's 32,000 simultaneous colors. Sixteen simultaneous colors on the screen doesn't give you a wide latitude for color in your presentation. Don't fade to black every time you bring up a new visual. This would be disconcerting for viewers. It's a good policy to choose five or six colors for your background and assign them to specific palette locations. You can always fade to the background between images, thereby avoiding the flash that occurs when incompatible palettes are being swapped.

Whether your program runs in a fixed installation or is distributed widely, you will grapple with the issues of color choices, memory usage, and animation speeds throughout the production process. This book is written as a primer on multimedia, and it does not contain all the GRASP tools you will need to distribute your program, nor do we cover the commands that are specific to video modes other than VGA. If you want to distribute your program, purchase the full release of GRASP. It contains utilities for compiling GRASP into a single executable file that runs from the DOS command line and hides the GRASP programming interface from the user. You can also obtain a GRASP utility, WINGRASP, that launches GRASP programs from Windows.

GRASP developers charge from $10,000 to $80,000 for production of a demo. That's because demos blend art and science—and a little sleight-of-hand—to get the right mix onto a floppy disk for distribution. The truly outstanding examples of GRASP multimedia are highly skilled in the way they use memory resources.

In the next chapter, we round out the demo with sound.

Synchronizing
Sight and Sound

HE BIGGEST challenge in multimedia, after data compression, is synchronizing visuals to sound. In audio and video production, tape, film, and audio or videodiscs run on a linear time track. Once synchronized, visuals and music remain in step. The same is not the case for a multimedia production. Because the computer is interrupt-driven, devices literally have to interrupt the CPU to get it to drop its present task and devote time to the request for service . . . until something more important comes along and demands attention. Programmers are very clever at developing contention schemes that make the CPU look like it's devoting attention to several events at the same time, but the inevitable result is that the computer slows down when things get busy as the CPU rushes around trying to service all the requests. When the request involves huge amounts of data, as in the case of CD-quality digital audio and high-resolution graphics, the computer system really slows down. The situation is thoroughly exacerbated by the fact that computer peripherals, and CPUs themselves, run at a wide range of speeds. This offers a major challenge to the distribution of multimedia programs.

The central problem in multimedia can be summarized in one word: time. Computers were not originally created to multitask music and pictures. The central concern is keeping sound and picture in synch.

Here's how the problem is solved in the world of professional video. When a video production is created, visuals and sound may be recorded simultaneously on the videotape in the camcorder, but this is not usually the case. Most professional shoots use sound equipment that records sound on a dedicated tape recorder, while the picture is recorded on a camcorder. The two systems record a reference signal called SMPTE time code. SMPTE stands for the Society of Motion Picture and Television Engineers. SMPTE time code is a continuous series of blips laid down on tape in the format Hours:Minutes:Seconds:Frames. Usually, an external device generates this stream of data while the picture and sound recorder are recording. One track on the videotape and one on the audio tape are assigned to recording this external stream of data. When the audio tape and videotape are later played back, the SMPTE time code acts as a reference for placing the picture and sound in synch. The audio tape is dumped to a video tape with its SMPTE time code and placed on one VTR (video tape recorder). The videotape is put on a second VTR. The editor can line the sound and picture up by telling the two machines to rewind or fast forward to the same "frame" (remember the format of SMPTE time code is Hours:Minutes:Seconds:Frames). This is called *chase and lock*.

Anybody who has tried to use consumer editing equipment knows how important SMPTE and frame-accurate production equipment is to creating a video program. Video and sound playback equipment accurate enough to fast forward or rewind to a specified single frame of video are expensive. Without frame accurate equipment, video editing is a hit-or-miss affair.

Ideally, there should be something in the computer environment that provides the equivalent method of synching the visuals and the sound to the same external reference point. By referencing visual and sound events to this time code, we will have a way of keeping these events in synchronization.

This chapter will show you how to do this. We use FM Software's MIDI player as a kind of control track on a "virtual tape machine." We'll create a software stopwatch for timing sections of a GRASP program. We explore both digital sound and MIDI music. We create a MIDI song in a song-generation program and edit it in a sequencer. A timbre editing program is used to modify the Sound Blaster's FM sounds.

Finally, we'll convert the song for use in GRASP. In the following chapter, we'll show you an alternative method of laying pictures to music.

Producers of time-based media grow very fond of their personal stopwatches. They help them keep track of their place in the linear time domain they work in. Although the GRASP stopwatch will be more awkward to create and use, it lays the foundation for a much more sophisticated method of creating multimedia in the next chapter.

Sound Card Required!

Ideally, you will have a sound card dedicated to producing sound effects and voice (like Sound Blaster Pro or Media Vision's Pro Audio Spectrum series), and a sound card dedicated to quality MIDI music (like Roland's SCC1 or a Roland MPU-401 interface). However, the exercises will work with a Sound Blaster- or Adlib-compatible card. The FM synthesizer chips on these boards are used.

THE MIDI MEMORY RESIDENT PLAYER

Included with the disks for *Multimedia Creations* is PLAY/D, the memory resident MIDI file player from FM Software, written by Kevin Weiner. The program loads as a memory resident program, also called a TSR (terminate and stay resident program). Loading PLAY/D into memory allows it to lurk in the background while GRASP goes about its business. Kevin Weiner has built an interface between this lurker and GRASP that allows the two programs to pass messages to each other.

Installing PLAY/D

In order to use PLAY/D in conjunction with GRASP, you must first load it into memory. You must do this before you start up GRASP. The command-line parameters are:

```
playd -d[dev]:[irq]:[ioaddr] -l
```

The parameters are optional. The -d parameter specifies the MIDI device you are using. For example, the Sound Blaster FM chips (built into the card) are specified as the playback device by including the parameter -dsbf at the command line.

```
playd -dsbf
```

PLAY/D will automatically detect the interrupt and I/O address of the Sound Blaster card or compatible. If it fails to do so, the parameters for the device can be included. For example, if your sound card is at interrupt 7 and at an I/O address of 220H (the H stands for hex) you would enter:

```
playd.exe -dsbf:7:220
```

PLAY/D supports the following MIDI and FM devices:

```
Roland MPU-401 and compatibles    -dmpu
Sound Blaster MIDI interface      -dsbm
Sound Blaster FM interface        -dsbf
Adlib FM                          -dadl
IBM PC Music Feature              -dmfc
Key Electronics MIDIator          -dmid
```

The Roland SCC1 uses the MPU-401 interface. Use the Sound Blaster MIDI interface if you have the Creative Labs MIDI interface attached to your Sound Blaster. Failing that, use the Sound Blaster FM interface. The interface will work with sound cards that are Adlib- or Sound Blaster-compatible. The Media Vision Pro Audio Spectrum 16 supports the FM interface. (Load and run the Media Vision SB_ON.EXE utility.)

You can load MIDI song files into expanded memory by using the -l (small L) parameter. This will free more memory for the GRASP application you build.

The version of PLAY/D that is included with this book is a special version of the program sold with FM Software's MidiTools package. There are a number of other command-line options in the version that comes with MidiTools.

Unloading PLAY/D

PLAY/D can be unloaded by executing the program with the following parameter:

```
playd -r
```

The r parameter "removes" the player from memory.

AUTOMATING INSTALLATION OF GRASP PROGRAMS

This is a good time to take an excursion into the subject of distributing GRASP programs. It is a topic that is more appropriate to distribution of programs created by the commercial version of GRASP, rather than the version bundled with this book. The special version of GRASP bundled with this book cannot be distributed. The commercial release produces standalone executable GRASP programs that run from the command line. These programs can be distributed. However, in adding MIDI music to the *Multimedia Creations* demo program, you must first install PLAY/D before GRASPC.EXE is run. Later we'll show you how to check to make sure users (including yourself!) have done this.

We'll also need to determine before the scripts are played if enough memory is free for the demo. Once PLAY/D is installed, memory will be at a premium.

GRASP includes commands that allow you to query hardware to determine if the user has a video adapter with the correct graphics mode or system memory available to run your program. You place these commands in a module right at the beginning of the GRASP program. The two commands are Ifmem and Ifvideo. Let's look at them in turn.

Using Ifmem to Check Memory Resources

The Ifmem command queries system memory. Syntax for the command is as follows:

```
ifmem mem [label]
```

You give the Ifmem command the total amount in bytes of system memory (the *mem* parameter) the user must have free in order to run your presentation. For example, the "USED:xxxxxx" message at the top of GRASP's editor reports that *Multimedia Creations* uses 453,840 bytes of memory. This is the maximum amount of RAM used by the demo at any given point. Think of it as the high-water mark for memory usage by the demo. Knowing this, we would give a rounded off value of 444K or 444,000 bytes to the mem parameter when we implement the command. That's because there are 1024 bytes in one megabyte of memory. The *label* parameter tells GRASP the name of the label to jump to if the user does have enough system memory free. If the user does not, execution continues at the next line. A simple use of the command would be:

```
ifmem 444000 ok
exit

ok:
     ...
```

(We will see a little later that the memory ceiling should be set higher in actual practice.)

If not enough memory is present, exit is made back to the editor (or the DOS prompt in the case of the commercial release of GRASP). If enough memory is present, execution continues at the commands after the OK: label.

If a label is not used, Ifmem acts like an If command paired with an Endif:

```
ifmem mem              ; if the right amount of memory is present (true)
     ...               ; execute this code
endif                  ; if not skip to the line after this
```

Using Ifvideo to Check the Video Adapter

The command Ifvideo checks to see if the user's system will support a specified video mode.

```
ifvideo mode [label]
```

Ifvideo checks to see if the system supports a specified video mode (the *mode* parameter). If the system does support the mode, execution continues at the label. As in the case of the Ifmem command, omitting the label parameter causes Ifvideo to act like a conditional If statement paired with an Endif.

```
ifvideo mode
        ...
endif
```

We've included a file called CHECK.TXT in the GRASP directory that is a complete implementation of both commands. Change into that directory now and load the file into the editor.

Using CHECK.TXT to Query the User's System

The CHECK.TXT script implements the Ifmem and Ifvideo commands. First we check to see if the user has an adapter that supports the correct video mode. (The demo is written in the standard VGA 640x480, 16-color mode.) If that test fails, we descend down a list of other video modes, checking for support of the next highest mode. We could have simply tested for Video M and issued an error message if the mode was not supported by the user's system. Using the next highest supported mode allows us to put a much prettier and more professional-looking message on the screen. You can also add additional information that will help the user to correct the problem.

Notice that we do not begin the script with the traditional Video Mode command (Video Mode M). This would defeat the purpose of the script. GRASP would put a plain black-and-white error message on the screen indicating the program requires the presence of a VGA adapter. Here's the file that checks memory. Notice that it includes a link to another file, INSTALL.TXT, which we will be discussing shortly.

```
; CHECK.TXT Checks system for video and memory.

start:

; Checks a list of adapters
        ifvideo m vgaok         ; VGA 640x480 16 color
        ifvideo g ega           ; EGA 640x350 16 color
        ifvideo a videoa        ; CGA 320x200 4 color
        ifvideo 2 video2        ; text mono 80 column
        goto anyother           ; any other
```

If Video Mode M is supported, execution jumps to the vgaok: label. There a subroutine checks that the system has the specified memory free. Notice that we have added "headroom" to GRASP's reported memory usage for the demo. This is a good rule of thumb. It means you should give the program a little more space than GRASP says it needs.

212

```
; VGA Adapter checks out, so let's test for memory

vgaok:

ifmem 470000 ok                    ; if there's 470K jump to ok: label

video m                            initialize

; Memory Error Message (test shows there is not enough memory available for demo)
        color 1
        rect 150 100 490 300
        color 3
        box 150 100 490 300

        fload big.set
        offset 0 -10
        set center on
        color 9
        mark 10
                text 0,340 "Multimedia Creations"
                offset 0 2 r
        loop
        color 15
        text 0,340 "Multimedia Creations"
        set center off
        offset 0,0

        fload ibm16.set 1
        window 180 120 470 272
        color 4 0
        fstyle 8 2 2
        fgaps 3 7
text "Sorry, Multimedia Creations requires 470K of free memory."
text " Unload all TSR's or other memory resident software to run the"
text " example scripts. Do not shell out from Windows to run the scripts."
color 14
        text 210 120 "Press Enter to continue."
        ffree 1
        window

        waitkey
exit 1

ok:                                ; everything checked out

link install.txt
```

If everything checks out, the program links to the INSTALL.TXT script, which presents sound card choices to the user. If the user does not have enough memory installed in the system, we put an error message on the screen. You can see what the error message looks like by changing the Ifmem mem parameter to an amount that exceeds your system's memory (e.g., ifmem 999000). Figure 6-1 shows what the memory error screen looks like.

213

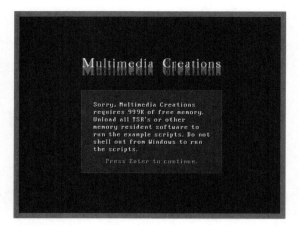

Figure 6-1 Ifmem example error message

This is a much more pleasant and helpful message than the one the user may get from GRASP when a picture or clipping refuses to load "Memory error at line xxx." GRASP will refuse to load the image or clipping and crash back to the editor.

You may have noticed that we added a 1 after the Exit command. The parameter passes an *errorlevel* value back to a program that might have called GRASP. We'll be using this parameter a little later in the chapter.

Now let's see what happens if the user does not have a VGA card installed. What happens if the user has an EGA card installed instead? The line:

```
ifvideo g ega          ; EGA 640x350 16 color
```

causes execution to jump to the ega: label.

```
ega:
        video g                         ; initialize adapter to EGA 16 color mode.
        fload big.set
        offset 0 -10
        set center on
        color 9
        mark 10
                text 0,240 "Multimedia Creations"
                offset 0 2 r
        loop
        color 15
        text 0,240 "Multimedia Creations"
        set center off
        offset 0,0
        color 1
        rect 150 60 490 220
        color 3
        box 150 60 490 220
        fload ibm16.set 1
        window 180 80 470 192
        color 4 0
        fstyle 8 2 2
        fgaps 3 7
        text "We detected an EGA video card in your " 01
        text " system. Sorry, the demo requires a 256K VGA card. Please install one." 01
        waitkey 100
        color 14
        text 210 80 "Press Enter to continue." 04
```

```
        window
        waitkey
exit 1
```

The screen looks very similar in design to the memory error message screen. Here are the error messages for the other common video modes.

```
; CGA 4 color mode
videoa:                         ; test for CGA card
        video a
        clearscr 0
        set center on
        mark 20
        mode 1
        mark 20
        text 0,160 "Multimedia Creations"
text 0,120 "Sorry, demo require VGA."
text 0,100 "Install a 256K VGA video card."
        mode 0
        loop
        mode 3
        loop
        mode 0
        text 0,60 "Press Enter to Exit"
        set center off
        waitkey

        waitkey
exit 1

video2:                         ; text for monochrome adapter
        video 2
anyother:
        set center on
text "




Multimedia Creations
*******************
*******************

This demo requires a VGA color system.

Install a 256 VGA card.

Press Enter to Exit"
set center off
waitkey
exit 1
```

You can see what the other video mode error messages look like by placing semi-colons in front of the preceding Ifvideo commands.

We've checked the system for the correct video mode and the correct amount of free system memory. What about sound?

Configuring for Sound

In Chapter 5 we showed you how to interface GRASP to the GRASP digital sound file player, SOUNDPC.GRP. The accompanying script, SNDPLAY.TXT, provides a programming interface to the digital sound player. As we noted, you merge SND-PLAY.TXT with the current script. The merged file becomes a subroutine (SND-PLAY:) that provides you with access to SOUNDPC.GRP. We created variables that allow you to send the SNDPLAY subroutine the name of the sound file and the animation that you want to play. The subroutine loads the digital file, starts it playing and runs the animation. Then execution returns to the main body of the script.

In Chapter 1 we discussed some of the general limitations of digital sound on the PC, including the demands digital sound files place on computer resources. You'll find additional limitations when working with the version of GRASP bundled with this book. Because of the way the SOUNDPC.GRP works inside the GRASP environment, only short music and effects passages can be played simultaneous with animation. Is there a way around this? Can we play a song that runs the length of the demo?

There is. We can use a memory resident MIDI player to play MIDI songs.

The MIDI Interface to GRASP

FM Software's PLAY/D memory resident MIDI player is included with *Multimedia Creations*. SOUNDPC.GRP plays digital sound files, PLAY/D plays MIDI songs. (Review Chapter 1 if you do not understand the difference between these two sources of music. Basically, digital sounds are digitized to the hard drive from an analog source like a cassette tape, microphone, or CD. MIDI music is synthesized by special chips on sound cards or external synthesizers.)

In the GRASP directory, you will find a script called MIDI.TXT that provides a programming interface to PLAY/D. As in the case of SNDPLAY.TXT, we'll merge MIDI.TXT with the current script, and access its MIDI play facilities through calls to subroutines. We can tell PLAY/D which MIDI songs to play, when to start and stop playing, when to pause, what volume to play the songs at, and so on. It's like having a CD player built into GRASP!

There is a big difference, however, in the way PLAY/D is installed and the way the SOUNDPC.GRP player is installed. As we mentioned before, PLAY/D must be installed before GRASP is loaded into memory. This creates some installation challenges.

What if the user doesn't install PLAY/D? You could create an automatic installation routine that modifies the user's AUTOEXEC.BAT batch file by adding the line that loads PLAY/D at the end of it. This would work for a program created for a fixed installation. But this is not good practice for demos. Demos are meant to be played once or twice and then removed from the hard drive. We don't want to clutter our user's AUTOEXEC.BAT file. It would be much better to write an install routine. This install routine will query the user on the type of sound card installed, if any. The user's response to this query will then be written to a configuration file and saved to disk. When the demo is subsequently run, the batch file that runs the demo will check for the presence of the configuration file. If you ran the demo batch file in the GRASP directory, then you have already configured your system for sound. Here's what happened when you ran DEMO.BAT in GRASP.

Running the Demo

DEMO.BAT makes the configuration and running of the demo fairly easy for the user. It calls a file that checks the video hardware and memory, which in turn configures the demo for sound, loads PLAY/D with the appropriate MIDI device interface, runs the *Multimedia Creations* demo, unloads PLAY/D after the demo is run and exits back to DOS.

Batch file programming is similar to GRASP programming. Let's follow the logic of the process.

Creating the DEMO.BAT Batch File

Let's begin with the DEMO.BAT file. Here is the entire listing for the batch file.

```
rem DEMO.BAT This batch file runs the MULTIMEDIA CREATIONS demo.

cls
@echo off
:again
if exist mpu.cfg goto mpu
if exist sbmid.cfg goto sbmid
if exist sbfm.cfg goto sbfm
if exist adlfm.cfg goto adlfm
if exist midi.cfg goto midi
if exist mfc.cfg goto mfc
if exist no.cfg goto no
call install
goto again

:mpu
playd -dmpu -l
cd \grasp\chapt05
\grasp\graspc check.txt /d
goto alldone

:sbmid
playd -dsbm -l
cd \grasp\chapt05
\grasp\graspc check.txt /d
goto alldone
```

```
:sbfm
playd -dsbf -l
cd \grasp\chapt05
\grasp\graspc check.txt /d
goto alldone

:adlfm
playd -dadl -l
cd \grasp\chapt05 /d
\grasp\graspc check.txt
goto alldone

:midi
playd -dmid -l
cd \grasp\chapt05
\grasp\graspc check.txt /d
goto alldone

:mfc
playd -dmfc -l
cd \grasp\chapt05
\grasp\graspc check.txt /d
goto alldone

:no
playd -dsbf -l
cd \grasp\chapt05
\grasp\graspc check.txt /d
goto alldone

:alldone
cd \grasp
playd -r
```

Consult your DOS reference manual for batch file programming tips. The Rem command works like the semicolon in GRASP. It allows the programmer to add comments to a file. The next command, Cls, clears the screen. The third command, @Echo off, suppresses DOS on-screen messages. The fourth command, :Again, is a label. Labels in batch file programming work exactly like GRASP labels, except the colon is placed before the label rather than after it. The fifth line uses a conditional If statement. If there is a file on the hard drive called MPU.CFG, the batch file branches to the :mpu label. If there is no MPU.CFG file, execution continues on the next line. If no configuration files can be found on the hard drive, the "call install" line is encountered. This calls another batch file named INSTALL.BAT. In batch file programming, Call works like GRASP's Call command. That is, the called file is executed and execution returns to the calling script at the line after the Call.

Calling INSTALL.BAT

Let's see what happens if there is no configuration file on the hard drive. This occurs the first time the demo is run. The call is made to INSTALL.BAT. INSTALL.BAT is a simple batch file that loads and runs the GRASP INSTALL.TXT routine. It contains the line:

```
graspc check /d
```

Notice that we've added the /d parameter. There's a very important reason for this parameter: It causes GRASPC.EXE to return to the DOS prompt rather than to the editor after the specified script is run. The "d" stands for debug. If there were any errors during the running of the program, they will print out to the screen when GRASP exits back to the DOS prompt. In this case, we want to use the parameter to cause execution to return to DOS after the CHECK.TXT and INSTALL.TXT scripts are run. That's because we've called it from the DEMO.BAT file. We want control to return to DEMO.BAT rather than the GRASP editor. For example, if the user does not have enough memory free to run the demo, the error subroutine we looked at earlier in INSTALL.TXT runs:

```
vgaok:

ifmem 470000 ok                    ; if there's 470K jump to ok: label

video m                            ; initialize

; Memory Error Message (test shows there is not enough memory available for demo)
        color 1
        rect 150 100 490 300
        color 3
        box 150 100 490 300

        fload big.set
        offset 0 -10
        set center on
        color 9
        mark 10
                text 0,340 "Multimedia Creations"
                offset 0 2 r
        loop
        color 15
        text 0,340 "Multimedia Creations"
        set center off
        offset 0,0

        fload ibm16.set 1
        window 180 120 470 272
        color 4 0
        fstyle 8 2 2
        fgaps 3 7
text "Sorry, Multimedia Creations requires 470K of free memory."
text " Unload all TSR's or other memory resident software to run the"
text " example scripts. Do not shell out from Windows to run the scripts."
color 14
        text 210 120 "Press Enter to continue."
        ffree 1
        window

        waitkey
exit 1
```

The "1" after the exit command sets the errorlevel to 1 in DOS. Errorlevels allow DOS programs to communicate with each other. The DEMO.BAT batch file looks for this message when control passes back to if from the INSTALL.BAT batch file.

```
call install
if errorlevel 1 goto exit
```

Exit is a label at the end of DEMO.BAT. Execution jumps to the end of the DEMO.BAT file, and the batch file terminates. If we did not include this method of communicating between GRASP and DOS, the batch file would endlessly loop, looking for a configuration file, not finding it, and calling the installation batch file. But it would never create the configuration file, because the user does not have enough memory or the right video adapter.

Let's assume the user does have enough memory and the right video adapter. Execution passes from CHECK.TXT to INSTALL.TXT through a Link command.

Running INSTALL.TXT

INSTALL.TXT is a GRASP script that puts up a message asking the user to indicate what kind of sound equipment (if any) is installed on the system. It then writes the appropriate configuration file to the hard drive. When the user chooses one of the sound card options, the configuration file is written and the user exits from GRASP. Let's look at the INSTALL.TXT script in detail.

We've created a walking billboard in Animator Pro as a background for the install message. "Legs" walks out from the darkness carrying a sign. In order to make the sequence useful for a variety of applications, the action of walking out of the darkness, and later closing the sign and fading to black, is implemented as a separate script. Here's the section of code in INSTALL.TXT that calls the billboard sequence.

```
; INSTALL.TXT Sound Install.

video m

start:

; Calls up installation dialogue box
        call billbord open            ; call walking billboard script
        pfree p1
        pgetbuf p1                    ; save man and billboard to buffer
```

Notice that we branch to the open: label in BILLBORD.TXT. When we "close" the billboard, the branch will be to the close: label in the script. Now here's the BILLBORD.TXT script called by INSTALL.TXT. Notice the way we break the animation up to give the different walking and displaying actions unique timing.

```
; BILLBORD.TXT Walking billboard with legs.

video m

open:

; load legs palette & dff
        pload \grasp\legs.pal p1          ; palette used by billboard animation
        palette 1
        pfree p1
        set xor on
        dload \grasp\legs.dff             ; walking billboard animation

; comes out from darkness and stands
        set cnt 0                         ; counter for loop
        mark 20
                putdff 1 20 @cnt @cnt
                set cnt @cnt+1
        loop

; waits for a moment than pulls sign open
        waitkey 50
        mark 7
                putdff 1 6 @cnt @cnt
                set cnt @cnt+1
        loop
        waitkey 20
        putdff 1 8 @cnt @cnt
        set xor off
        pgetbuf 1
return
```

We created the DFF file with the /x parameter so that we can play the animation
backward or forward. That's why we need to turn the xor setting on before running
the animation.

After this part of the BILLBORD.TXT script is run, execution returns to IN-
STALL.TXT. The next section of code adds a bit of length to the billboard to accommodate all the sound board choices.

```
window 172,275 454,275   ; unfold billboard to full length
        mark 22
                window 0,-4 0,0 r
                color 10
                box 172,190 454,275
                color 7
                rect 173,191 453,276
        loop
        window
```

Now we add the list of card choices to the billboard:

```
        again:
        color 1 0
        fload ibm16.set 1
```

221

```
fstyle 8 1
fgaps 4
set center on
text 0,312 "Music Card Installation "
color 8
fload ibm14.set 1
fstyle 8 0
fgaps 2 2
set center off
color 12 0
text 238,293 "Choose one:"
color 13
text 219,277 "1."
color 12 0
text 238,277 "Roland MPU-401"
color 13
text 219,265 "2."
color 12 0
text 238,265 "Sound Blaster MIDI"
color 13
text 219,253 "3."
color 12 0
text 238,253 "Sound Blaster FM"
color 13
text 219,241 "4."
color 12 0
text 238,241 "Adlib FM"
color 13
text 219,229 "5."
color 12 0
text 238,229 "Key Electronics Mediator"
color 13
text 219,217 "6."
color 12 0
text 238,217 "IBM PC Music Feature"
color 13
text 219,205 "7."
color 12 0
text 238,205 "No Music Card"
```

Notice that there is an again: label at the beginning of the list. The user has been given seven choices. A number from 1 to 7 is selected. If the user presses any other key, the user is returned to the again: label. Here's the code that implements this:

```
.delete(mpu.cfg)              ; deletes previous configuration files
.delete(sbmid.cfg)
.delete(sbfm.cfg)
.delete(adlfm.cfg)
.delete(midi.cfg)
.delete(mfc.cfg)
.delete(no.cfg)
waitkey
ifkey 1 mpu
ifkey 2 sbmid
ifkey 3 sbfm
```

```
ifkey 4 adlfm
ifkey 5 midi
ifkey 6 mfc
ifkey 7 no
fload helvet15.set
set center on
text 0,100 "Choose a number from 1 to 7."
set center off
goto again
```

Pressing a key from ①to ⑦ causes a branch to a specified label. Pressing any other key causes the loop to cycle once again, and the user is prompted with an error message instructing him or her to choose a number from 1 to 7. Notice that we are fairly scrupulous about the system setting that centers text. We turn it on when the text is written and turn it off after it is written. We've spent hours looking for a "set center on" that never got turned off.

The code also contains the commands to delete any previous configuration files that have been written to the hard drive. We'll be covering GRASP file deleting, writing, and appending functions in detail later.

The labeled subroutines that write the user's choice of card to a configuration file follows:

```
; if user has a midi card...
mpu:
                pfade 10 p1 100
                set center on
                text 0,310 "MPU-401 or Roland SCC1 interface."
                text 0,292 "Configured."
                set cfg "mpu.cfg"
                writfile
                color 1 6
                text 0,274 "Press Enter to continue."
                set center off
                waitkey 300
                pfade 10 p1 100
                pfree p1
                call billbord close
                clearscr 0
                video 1
                int 0x21 0x4c00


sbmid:
                pfade 10 p1 100
                set center on
                text 0,310 "Sound Blaster with MIDI option."
                text 0,292 "Configured."
                set cfg "sbmid.cfg"
                writfile
                color 1 6
                text 0,274 "Press Enter to continue."
                set center off
```

```
                    waitkey 300
                    pfade 10 p1 100
                    pfree p1
                    call billbord close
                    clearscr 0
                    video 1
                    int 0x21 0x4c00


sbfm:
                    pfade 10 p1 100
                    set center on
                    text 0,310 "Sound Blaster Compatible FM sounds."
                    text 0,292 "Configured."
                    set cfg "sbfm.cfg"
                    writfile
                    color 1 6
                    text 0,274 "Press Enter to continue."
                    set center off
                    waitkey 300
                    pfade 10 p1 100
                    pfree p1
                    call billbord close
                    clearscr 0
                    video 1
                    int 0x21 0x4c00


adlfm:
                    pfade 10 p1 100
                    set center on
                    text 0,310 "Adlib Compatible FM sounds."
                    text 0,292 "Configured."
                    set cfg "adlfm.cfg"
                    writfile
                    color 1 6
                    text 0,274 "Press Enter to continue."
                    set center off
                    waitkey 300
                    pfade 10 p1 100
                    pfree p1
                    call billbord close
                    clearscr 0
                    video 1
                    int 0x21 0x4c00


midi:
                    pfade 10 p1 100
                    set center on
                    text 0,310 "Key Electronics Mediator MIDI."
                    text 0,292 "Configured."
                    set cfg "MIDI.cfg"
                    writfile
                    color 1 6
                    text 0,274 "Press Enter to continue."
                    set center off
                    waitkey 300
                    pfade 10 p1 100
```

```
            pfree p1
            call billbord close
            clearscr 0
            video 1
            int 0x21 0x4c00


mfc:

            pfade 10 p1 100
            set center on
            text 0,310 "IBM Music Feature Card MIDI"
            text 0,292 "Configured."
            set cfg "mfc.cfg"
            writfile
            color 1 6
            text 0,274 "Press Enter to continue."
            set center off
            waitkey 300
            pfade 10 p1 100
            pfree p1
            call billbord close
            clearscr 0
            video 1
            int 0x21 0x4c00


no:

            pfade 10 p1 100
            set center on
            text 0,310 "No sound card."
            text 0,292 "Configured."
            set cfg "no.cfg"
            writfile
            color 1 6
            text 0,274 "Press Enter to continue."
            set center off
            waitkey 300
            pfade 10 p1 100
            clearscr 0
            video 1
            int 0x21 0x4c00
```

Each of the labeled subroutines first rolls the billboard up by fading buffer 1 (saved earlier) to the screen. We then write a message on this smaller billboard, affirming the user's choice, and we set up a variable that is the configuration file name for the user's choice. We then branch to another subroutine, writfile:, which writes the configuration file.

```
writfile:
            local temp "Remove this file to re-configure PLAY/D."
            local ptr adr(@temp)
            local fs create(@cfg)
            . write(@fs,@ptr,len(@temp))
            . close(@fs)
return
```

Notice that the subroutine uses the variable we just set up (cfg) to name the file being written to the hard drive. The configuration file is a simple text file with the string "Remove this file to re-configure PLAY/D." This is a message to a user who may be familiar with the practice of deleting configuration files to cause a program to go through the installation procedure again. (DEMO.BAT doesn't actually read the configuration file, it just checks for its presence.) GRASP's file writing may look cryptic! Don't worry, we'll be covering GRASP's file functions later.

Now that we've written the configuration file to the hard drive, execution returns to the subroutine that called writfile:

```
writfile
color 1 6
text 0,274 "Press Enter to continue."
set center off
waitkey 300
pfade 10 p1 100
pfree p1
call billbord close
clearscr 0
video 1
int 0x21 0x4c00
```

The user is prompted to press (ENTER) to continue, and exit. After 3 seconds, execution continues anyway. Buffer 1 is restored. The screen is restored in this way because we need to provide the LEGS.DFF with a starting frame for closing the billboard. The call is made to the second half of BILLBORD.TXT, at the close: label:

```
close:
        pfade 10 p1 100
        set xor on
        set cnt 29
        mark 7
                putdff 1 10 @cnt @cnt
                set cnt @cnt-1
        loop
        set xor off

; fade him out
        dfree 1
        pload black.pal p2
        pgetbuf p1
        spread 1 2
        pfree p1 - p2
        dfree 1
        clearscr 0
return
```

Once again we turn xor on to play the sequence backward. When the image fades from the screen, we return to the calling script, INSTALL.TXT. There we encounter the commands that cause an exit to DOS:

226

```
clearscr 0
video 1
int 0x21 0x4c00
```

The Video 1 command switches GRASP into text mode. That's because we want to be in text mode when we exit to DOS. The Int command calls a system interrupt to cause the exit to DOS. It's actually the same interrupt GRASP calls when it exits to DOS. The Int command is very useful in interfacing GRASP to other programs. Syntax for the command is:

```
int num [ax] [bx] [cx] [dx] [si] [di] [ds] [es]
```

The *num* parameter is the interrupt number to call. The other parameters are the values to place in the named registers. Register values must be supplied for all registers, in sequence, up to the last register to be set. The values to be output can be 16-bit values and can be expressed as decimal or hex values. Hex values must be prefaced with Ox (Ox1A is decimal 26). In cases where control passes to GRASP, variable with the names of the system registers are set equal to their contents. These can be referred to as @ax, @bx, and so on. The variable @0 is set equal to the system Flags, for error-checking purposes.

When we exit to DOS, we are returned to DEMO.BAT. Remember that the install sequence was called from this batch file:

```
:again
if exist mpu.cfg goto mpu
if exist sbmid.cfg goto sbmid
if exist sbfm.cfg goto sbfm
if exist adlfm.cfg goto adlfm
if exist midi.cfg goto midi
if exist mfc.cfg goto mfc
if exist no.cfg goto no
call install
goto again
```

Control passes to the line after the Call Install command. There the Goto Again command is encountered, so we're sent back to the conditional If statements that look for and find the appropriate configuration file. This time a configuration file is found. We branch to the appropriate labeled subroutine. Here's the labeled subroutine for the installation of the Roland SCC1:

```
:mpu
playd -dmpu -l
cd \grasp\chapt05
graspc check.txt /d
goto alldone
```

PLAY/D is called. The device driver for the MPU-401 is specified, along with the switch telling PLAY/D to use expanded memory to load song files. Then we change into the subdirectory where the demo is located, and run GRASPC with the /d parameter, which will eventually return us to DOS again. We tell GRASPC to load and run the CHECK.TXT file located in the CHAPT05 subdirectory. This is the file that checks to make sure enough memory is present. We may have bumped up against the user's limited memory space, so running CHECK.TXT here is a good idea. If memory checks out, we link to the script called CHECPLAY.TXT. This file checks to see if PLAY/D has been loaded.

In this case PLAY/D has been loaded, so the demo plays. When the user exits from demo, DOS returns execution to the DEMO.BAT file where the Goto Alldone instruction is encountered. Execution jumps to the :alldone label. There the directory is changed to the GRASP directory and PLAYD.EXE is unloaded from memory using the -r (remove) parameter. We then exit back to the DOS prompt.

```
:alldone
cd \grasp
playd -r
```

You may be wondering why we included the check for the presence of PLAY/D in the demo. After all, once the configuration file is written, won't PLAY/D always be loaded? Not always. As you work through the book, you may enter the CHAPT05 subdirectory after booting up, without running the DEMO.BAT batch file. CHEC-PLAY.TXT lets you know that PLAY/D is not loaded. It advises you to exit from GRASP and type player. Here is CHECPLAY.TXT:

```
; CHECPLAY.TXT Checks to make sure PLAY/D has been installed.

video m

start:

merge \grasp\midi

gosub mfinit

if !@0                              ; if no midi driver installed...
        call billbord open          ; call walking billboard script
        pfree p1
        pgetbuf p1                  ; save man and billboard to buffer

        set center on
        fload \grasp\ibm14.set
        text 0,310 "PLAY/D not installed."
        text 0,292 "Exit and type: PLAYER"
        color 1 6
        text 0,274 "Press Enter to continue."
        set center off
        waitkey
        pfade 10 p1 100
        pfree p1
        call billbord close
        clearscr 0
```

```
        video 1
        int 0x21 0x4c00

endif

return
```

PLAYER.BAT is a slightly altered version of the DEMO.BAT program that checks for the configuration file, installs the appropriate PLAY/D interface, and returns you to the GRASPC editor. We'll be using this batch file for other programs in this chapter; that's the reason why the batch file returns you to the editor rather than the *Multimedia Creations* demo.

Let's go through CHECPLAY.TXT.

First, MIDI.TXT is merged into the file. MIDI.TXT is the interface between GRASP and PLAY/D that we talked about earlier. After we have merged MIDI.TXT with the script, we make a call to a subroutine in MIDI.TXT that checks to see if PLAY/D is installed. If it is not (!@0), the user is advised that PLAY/D is not loaded. The user is told to exit GRASP and run the PLAYER.BAT.

Writing batch files may seem as complicated and as lengthy as writing the program script itself! However, once an install routine is created, you can virtually forget it. And it makes your program a lot easier to use for novices and expert users alike. That's important!

It's finally time to turn to the application we'll be building in Chapter 6. All Chapter 6 program files can be found in the CHAPT05 subdirectory. The example application requires the use of PLAY/D, so if you have not included PLAY/D in your AUTOEXEC.BAT batch file, it's a good idea to do that now. If you would prefer not to alter your AUTOEXEC.BAT file, use PLAYER.BAT in the CHAPT05.TXT subdirectory to install PLAY/D.

If you have PLAY/D loaded and are in the editor, load WATCH.TXT into the editor now. WATCH.TXT is the software stopwatch we talked about earlier.

Creating the Software Stopwatch

Here's the complete script for a software stopwatch we've created using PLAY/D and the MIDI.TXT interface.

```
; WATCH.TXT Creates a Software Stopwatch

;set debug on

video m

start:

; Load main palette.
        pload greenbck.pal p1
```

```
          palette p1
          pfree p1

; Merges MIDI.TXT, initializes MIDI player, zeros the stopwatch.
          merge \grasp\midi
          mfinit                             ; initializes player
          when up gosub disptime             ; up arrow displays elapsed time
          mstimer                            ; reads PLAY/D's clock
          local startime @0+30               ; zeros stopwatch
          disptime                           ; displays current time

; Timer

          timer

; Create circles.
          color 7
          circle 324,257 80 80 10            ; outer light blue rings
          color 10
          circle 324,257 70 70 3             ; inner dark blue rings

; Create cross-hairs
          color 11
          line 322,388 322,370               ; top pink vertical bar
          mark 4
          line 1 0 1 0 r
          loop

          color 11
          line 322 144 322 124               ; bottom pink vertical bar
          mark 4
          line 1 0 1 0 r
          loop

          color 11
          line 192,257 210,257               ; left side bar
          line 0 -1 0 -1 r

          color 11
          line 437,257 454,257               ; right side bar
          line 0 -1 0 -1 r

          color 14
          circle 324 257 40                  ; inner circle

; Countdown routine
          pgetbuf p1                         ; save screen to buffer
      lp:
          set clip 18                        ; set up first clip as 18
          waitkey 60

          mark 7                             ; beginning of countdown routine
          timer
          cload count$@clip c1
               ;text @elapsed                ; shows clock time on screen
               ;wait                         ; remove semicolons to see
```

```
        waitkey 40                      ; longer for slow hard drives

        timer                           ; reset clock to 0
        putup c1                        ; putup number
        cfree c1
        set clip @clip-1                ; advance to next clip file
        waitkey 15
        timer                           ; reset clock
        window 288,288 360,224          ; restricts fade to window
        pfade 24 p1                     ; aperture fade number off
        window                          ; restores whole screen
        waitkey 35
        timer                           ; resets clock
        note 40 20 1
        loop
        timer

; Clear screen to Black
        cfree c1 - c10
        pfree p1 - p10
        waitkey 90
        clearscr 0
        note 30 30 15


; Cycles back to beginning.

        disptime
        stortime
        waitkey
        link WATCH start


; Displays time at bottom left corner.

disptime:
        local tempcol @color            ; preserves current color
        local xmin @minx; preserves window coordinates
        local ymin @miny
        local xmax @maxx
        local ymax @maxy
        local offx @xoff; preserves offsets
        local offy @yoff
        window                          ; clears window coordinates
        offset 0 0                      ; clears offsets
        font 0                          ; specifies system font
        fgaps 1 1 1
        mstimer                         ; reads MIDI player clock for current time
        local time @0-@startime ; how much time has elapsed
                                        ; from beginning
        local time @time; adjust clock

        ; box to display time
        color 14
        box 546 8 637 25 8              ; box for time display
        color 15
```

```
        rect 548 10 637 25

    ; Divides time into units (hrs, mins, secs, hundreds of sec.)
        local hours @time/3600000
        local temp @time%3600000
        local minutes @temp/60000
        local temp @temp%60000
        local seconds @temp/1000
        local temp @temp%1000
        local hundreds @temp/10

        color 0

    ; minutes
        color 14
        window 550 25 637 35                ; window for text
        text "min"
        color 0
        window 550 10 637 20                ; window for text
        text ":"$dec(@minutes,2)            ; displays minutes padded with zeros

    ; seconds
        color 14
        window 580 25 637 35
        text "sec"
        color 0
        window 582 10 637 20
        text ":"$dec(@seconds,2)

    ; hundreds
        window 615 10 637 20
        text ":"$dec(@hundreds,2)

    ; Restores system variables.
        window
        window @xmin @ymin @xmax @ymax
        offset @xoff @yoff
        color @tempcol
return

; Routine to store current stop watch value.

stortime:
        mstimer

        local temp ""$@0-@startime
        local ptr adr(@temp)                ; points to location of variable
        local fs create(stop.dat)           ; names file
        . write(@fs,@ptr,len(@temp))
        . close(@fs)
return

; Zeros stop watch

zero:
        mstimer
```

```
        global startime @0+20
        disptime
return
```

Notice that we call CHECPLAY.TXT at the very beginning of the file to ensure the user has installed PLAY/D.

This script is a modification of the countdown sequence we featured in the last chapter. When you run it, you will see a white box at the bottom right of the screen display the initial stopwatch time of 0 minutes, 0 seconds, 0 hundredths of a second. Whenever you press ⊕ on the keyboard, the stopwatch gives you the elapsed time since the clock was started. When you press the (HOME) key, the stopwatch clock is zeroed. You cycle back to the beginning after each running of the script.

Let's look at the code in detail. As we said earlier, the interface to PLAY/D is in the file MIDI.TXT.

```
; Merges MIDI.TXT, initializes MIDI player, zeros the stopwatch.
        merge \grasp\midi        ; adds MIDI.txt to the script
        mfinit                   ; initializes player
        when up gosub disptime   ; up arrow displays elapsed time
        mstimer                  ; reads PLAY/D's clock
        local startime @0        ; zeros stopwatch
        disptime                 ; displays current time
```

The file is merged with the GRASP script at run time, in effect making the commands that access the MIDI player part of the current script. For example, mfinit is a subroutine in MIDI.TXT that tests for the presence of the MIDI player and makes it active. The mstimer subroutine in MIDI.TXT returns the current time stored by the PLAY/D memory resident timer. This is what is so valuable about PLAY/D. The timer it contains is running independently of the GRASP program and script, so it can act as a valuable reference point for timing events as the program runs. It's like a stopwatch with its own internal mechanism for keeping track of time.

The PLAY/D timer measures time in milliseconds from the moment the program is loaded, not after it is initialized. The mstimer subroutine "returns" (sends back) a variable to GRASP called temp. This variable contains the current value of the millisecond timer. The ability to return a value from a subroutine to the calling program is a powerful programming feature of GRASP. If you examine MIDI.TXT, you'll see that the line

```
return @temp
```

is the command that tells the GRASP calling script where the timer's value is stored. (Remember that variables tell the computer where information is stored.) Because local variables are destroyed when a subroutine is exited, GRASP assigns @temp to the temporary variable @0 in the calling routine.

The @0 Variable

The variable @0 (zero, not the letter o) is a special GRASP variable. It is a temporary storage place for information returned from a subroutine. Each time you return a value to the @0 variable, the value previously stored in @0 is destroyed. We use the value stored at @temp by the mstimer subroutine to set the zero point where the stopwatch is going to start from.

```
local startime @0              ; zeros stopwatch
```

Since PLAY/D is a memory resident program that is installed until we unload it, its timer keeps running regardless of what GRASP is doing, and keeps running even when we exit GRASP to another program. By reading the clock and using the time it reports back as the starting point for our stopwatch, we create a reference point for the GRASP script we are timing.

Accuracy of the Stopwatch

If you run the script continuously, you will notice that the final time displayed on the screen varies as much as 100 milliseconds from one iteration of the script to another. This is a variance of about 12 milliseconds a second, accurate enough for all but the most time-critical applications.

Displaying the Time on the Screen

Let's take a closer look at the routine that displays the stopwatch on the screen.

```
disptime:
        local tempcol @color           ; preserves current color
        local xmin @minx               ; preserves window coordinates
        local ymin @miny
        local xmax @maxx
        local ymax @maxy
        local offx @xoff               ; preserves offsets
        local offy @yoff
        window                         ; clears window coordinates
        offset 0 0                     ; clears offsets
        font 0                         ; specifies system font
        mstimer                        ; reads MIDI player clock
        local time @0-@startime        ; how much time has elapsed
                                       ; from beginning

        ; box to display time
        color 14
        box 546 8 637 25 8             ; box for time display
        color 15
        rect 548 10 637 25

    ; Divides time into units (hrs, mins, secs, hundreds of sec.)
        local hours @time/3600000
        local temp @time%3600000
        local minutes @temp/60000
        local temp @temp%60000
```

```
        local seconds @temp/1000
        local temp @temp%1000
        local hundreds @temp/10

        color 0

    ; minutes
        color 14
        window 550 25 637 35              ; window for text
        text "min"
        color 0
        window 550 10 637 20              ; window for text
        text ":"$dec(@minutes,2)          ; displays minutes padded with zeros

    ; seconds
        color 14
        window 580 25 637 35
        text "sec"
        color 0
        window 582 10 637 20
        text ":"$dec(@seconds,2)

    ; hundreds
        window 615 10 637 20
        text ":"$dec(@hundreds,2)

    ; Restores system variables.
        window
        window @xmin @ymin @xmax @ymax
        offset @xoff @yoff
        color @tempcol
return
```

Notice that we save existing window coordinates, offset coordinates, and the current color on entry to the subroutine, and restore them when we exit the subroutine. When we enter the subroutine, we store current window coordinates, offset coordinates, and color in local variables. This allows us to use unique window, offset, and color commands in the subroutine without disturbing the main program. The original window, offset, and color settings are restored at the exit point of the subroutine. If we had not done this, upon exit from the subroutine, the numbers at the center of the circles would not have wiped on and off the screen properly.

The command Font 0 makes the system font active. (The system font is Font 0 by default.) We don't actually need it here, because we have not made a font buffer active. It's here in case the subroutine is used in another script. One less bug to chase!

After saving the current system state and making the system font active, we measure the time that has elapsed since we originally zeroed the stopwatch by establishing a *start time*.

```
mstimer                        ; reads MIDI player clock
local time @0-@starttime       ; how much time has elapsed
                               ; from beginning
```

This gives us a *local time,* the current PLAY/D time we'll use in the subroutine. By subtracting the start time from the current time, we calculate how much time has elapsed since the stopwatch was zeroed. However, the mstimer subroutine does not return the time in hours, minutes, seconds, and hundredths of a second. It returns the value of the PLAY/D millisecond timer in thousands of milliseconds. We need to convert this number.

The % Operator

Converting the millisecond value to hours, minutes, seconds, and hundredths of a second is accomplished with the modulus operator %. The modulus operator yields the value left over after one value is divided by another. Our method is to reduce the total millisecond count successively to hour, minute, second and fractional second quantities. Here's how the time returned by mstimer is broken down:

```
; Divides time into units (hrs, mins, secs, hundredths of sec.)
        local hours @time/3600000      ; total hours if any
        local temp @time%3600000       ; assign remaining to temp
        local minutes @temp/60000      ; total minutes in temp
        local temp @temp%60000         ; assign remaining to new temp
        local seconds @temp/1000       ; total seconds in temp
        local temp @temp%1000          ; assign remaining to new temp
        local hundreds @temp/10        ; total hundreds of seconds
```

There are 3,600,000 milliseconds in an hour. We first divide the time variable (which is arrived at by subtracting the original start time from the current time) by 3,600,000 to get a value for the hours variable. (We do not display the hours variable in the subroutine, but we might want to use the value in another GRASP program.) Then we use the modulus operator to find out how much time is left after we divide the total time by the amount of milliseconds in an hour. We assign the result to a temporary variable temp. We then use this variable to extract the total amount of minutes in the time value. We repeat this for seconds and hundredths of a second. In order to display hundredths of a second, we divide up the remaining value for temp by a factor of 10. This converts whatever milliseconds are left to hundredths of a second.

Using a GRASP Function to Display the Time

The results of our calculation will be displayed in a small white box at the bottom right of the screen. To display the value for minutes on the screen, we enter:

```
; minutes
        color 14
        window 550 25 637 35           ; window for text
        text "min"
        color 0
        window 550 10 637 20           ; window for text
        text ":"$dec(@minutes,2)       ; displays minutes padded with zeros
```

236

The text command displaying the value for minutes uses a special GRASP function

```
dec(value,width)
```

to ensure that the value is displayed as two digits, with a zero "padding" values that are less than ten. The "width" parameter specifies how many digits will be displayed. In the first minute of the presentation, the value for the minutes display will be 0. We want this to appear as two zeros: 00, so we use a width of 2. We use the concatenation symbol ($) to add the two zeros to a colon.

How the Stopwatch Is Used

Every time we press the (↑), the disptime: subroutine is executed. This allows us to determine the length of sections of shows. We can measure the length in time of specific sections of the show by zeroing the clock (establishing a new start time) at the beginning of the section and calling the disptime: subroutine at the end of the section. This is what we did in the WATCH.TXT script.

When we attempt to time a section of a GRASP program that spans two scripts, we run into problems. Although we can create global variables that can be used by subsequent scripts, they are lost when we return to the editor. During development, we do not want to run the program from the beginning each time we make a change in a subsequent script. The solution is to save the elapsed time on the stopwatch at the end of a script to a file on the hard disk. When we run the next script, we use the value stored in the file to reset the stopwatch. This brings us to GRASP's file writing and reading functions.

Writing Files with GRASP

GRASP provides a number of functions for writing, reading, and appending additional information to disk files. Writing a value to a disk file consists of first telling GRASP where to find that value in memory, then creating a file name, writing the data to the hard drive, and closing the file. Let's create a file called WRITEST.TXT that stores the message, "It worked!"

```
WRITEST.TXT

local temp "It worked!"              ; assigns string to variable
local ptr adr(@temp)                 ; pointer to address of variable
local fs create(writest.txt)         ; opens file, assigns name to fs
. write(@fs,@ptr,len(@temp))         ; writes file to disk
. close(@fs)                         ; closes it

waitkey

text @readfile(writest.txt)          ; displays text read into
                                     ; memory

waitkey
exit
```

237

In this example we create a variable whose content is a string of text. We then use a GRASP function

```
adr(string);
```

to make a copy of the string at a fixed address in memory. This address is used by the write function. The write function

```
write(fs, address, length)
```

requires the address, and the length, of the text string. The address of the string tells GRASP where to find the string in memory. The length of the string tells GRASP how many bytes after the beginning of the address to include in the file written to disk. (A byte is assigned to each letter, symbol, and space in the string.) The GRASP function

```
len(string)
```

returns the number of characters in the string. So the line

```
. write(@fs,@ptr,len(@temp))
```

embeds the call to the len(string) function in the third parameter required by the write function. The period at the beginning of the line tells GRASP that a function follows on the same line. The four file handling functions

```
create(filename)
write(filename)
close(filename)
readfile(filename)
```

are complicated by the fact that we have to give GRASP information about where strings are located in memory, and the length of the strings, but they are otherwise easy to implement.

Reading GRASP Files into Memory

The readfile(filename) function reads the content of a file into memory and tells GRASP where it is located. The line

```
text @readfile(writest.txt)          ; displays text read into
                                      ; memory
```

uses indirection to assign the memory address where the text string is located to a variable. Once the text string is assigned to a variable, it can be displayed.

The WATCH.TXT program includes a subroutine called stortime: that stores the value of the stopwatch in a file on the hard drive.

```
stortime:
        mstimer

        local temp ""$@0-@startime
        local ptr adr(@temp)          ; points to location of variable
        local fs create(stop.dat)     ; names file
```

```
        . write(@fs,@ptr,len(@temp))
        . close(@fs)
return
```

We placed a call to this subroutine at the end of the script.

```
; Cycles back to the beginning.

        disptime
        stortime
        waitkey
        link watch start
```

If you temporarily shell out of GRASP by pressing (ALT)-(F1), and use DOS's type command

```
type stop.dat
```

you'll see the current time on the stopwatch, measured in thousands of milliseconds. This value can be used by a subsequent GRASP script to set the initial value of the stopwatch. All we have to do is add the lines

```
merge \grasp\midi
mfinit
mstimer
global startime @0-@readfile(stop.dat)
disptime
```

to the second GRASP script. The code merges the MIDI interface with the script, initializes PLAY/D, gets the current time, and subtracts the value found in STOP.DAT from the current time to wind back the start position of the stopwatch. Now we can run the second script independently of the first script. The clock will automatically be set back to account for the running time of the first script.

Using the Stopwatch to Add Sound to the Demo

Adding the software stopwatch program to the *Multimedia Creations* demo is relatively easy. First, we'll create one extra feature that will be useful in timing specific sections of the demo. We'll add the ability to zero the stopwatch on demand. You'll find the code that does this at the end of the WATCH.TXT program:

```
; Zeros stop watch

zero:
        mstimer
        global startime @0
        disptime
return
```

In order to make adding the stopwatch routines to GRASP scripts easier, we'll save the disptime:, stortime:, and zero: subroutines to a separate script called TIMESUB.TXT. This is accomplished by highlighting the subroutines in the editor (with the (F4) key or (CTRL)-(K)-(B) and (CTRL)-(K)-(K) key combinations), and writing them to disk with the (F8) key. When GRASP asks for the name of the file, we call it TIME-SUB.TXT. We've done this for you. You'll find TIMESUB.TXT on the disk.

Now all that's required to add the routines to a GRASP script is to merge them. Here are the lines that are added to each script that uses the MIDI.TXT and TIME-SUB.TXT routines.

```
start:

; Adds MIDI player to program and creates software stopwatch

        merge \grasp\midi          ; file with MIDI commands
        merge timesub              ; adds time display and save
        mfinit                     ; initializes player
        when up gosub disptime     ; gives time elapsed on demand
        when down gosub stortime   ; saves current time to disk
        when home gosub zero       ; zeros stopwatch
        mstimer                    ; gets current clock time
        global startime @0         ; sets start time to current time
```

Notice that we assign the clock-zeroing subroutine to the (HOME) key. When you run GRASP scripts using these routines, you can time specific sections of the script by pressing the (HOME) key to zero the clock and either the (↑) or (↓) key to view or save the elapsed time. There is one caveat: At the time this book was written, the digitized sound playback GRP (SOUNDPC.GRP) and the MIDI file player (PLAYD.EXE) both access the computer's system timer. GRASP's SOUNDPC.GRP routine interrupts the clock, making the timing of a section of the show that includes digitized sound playback impossible. The stopwatch routines are only useful for timing sections of the show prior to adding music and effects.

Now that we've created a stopwatch that allows us to time the GRASP script, let's turn to adding digitized sound to animations.

Adding Sound to the Opening Screen of the Demo

Sound adds drama and sets the mood for visuals. The starry night opening sequence of the demo we created in the previous chapter almost demands a sound treatment. Finding the right music and adjusting the timing of visuals to the music is a creative process with fits and starts, false ends, and sudden moments of inspiration. But the result can be spectacular, making the visuals come alive. We're going to choose a somber and mysterious opening to the demo. A single, long synthesizer drone while the stars build up on the screen and while the petroglyphs build on the screen will do nicely.

The first thing to do is to time the opening sequence. We'll change some of the timing of the opening to lengthen it a bit. This will give the synthesizer drone a little extra time to establish itself and develop character. Using the software stopwatch to time the section, we discover that we need about 8 seconds of music.

Recording the Music

We derived our musical drone from a synthesizer. However, if you want to experiment with recording a sound (such as a sound effect) from a CD player, here's how to do it.

Unless the track you want to record is exactly the right length, fading the sound up and down will be necessary. Some CD players come with a programmable fader. The Sony CDP-195 we use has a fader that has a range of 2 to 10 seconds. We found a 3-second fade was exactly right for the synthesizer drone. If your CD player does not have a fade feature, plug its outputs into a cassette deck's inputs. Then plug the cassette deck's outputs into the sound card you are using. You can now use the recording level controls on the tape deck to fade the music up and down.

Failing both of these, you can use the fade in and fade out software options in the various sound wave editing programs. Fading in software is not as effective as using the analog faders on external devices, but it does work.

Using Waveform Editing Software

If your sound card is capable of recording sound to the hard drive, it will include a sound recording utility. The Sound Blaster includes the VOXKIT.EXE program. The Sound Blaster Pro includes VEDIT2.EXE. The Media Vision cards include a variety of sound recording options, including a "Pocket Recorder" that runs under Windows. We've used the STEREOFX.EXE program. Blaster Master, a Shareware waveform editing program available on CompuServe in the MIDI forum and on numerous bulletin boards is another excellent choice. It imports several sound file formats, including the Windows WAV format used by Media Vision products. The most sophisticated and professional tool for sound editing, Recording Studio Professional, is distributed by Turtle Beach Systems. It edits Sound Blaster VOC files, although we've successfully converted Media Vision WAV files to VOC format, put our Media Vision 16 card into Sound Blaster compatibility mode, and fooled the program into believing our card was a Sound Blaster. The program gives you many options to modify samples, plus many interesting sound effects.

Let's look at a sample we recorded using Media Vision's Pro Audio Spectrum 16 and Stereofx. Figure 6-2 shows the captured sample.

The program has a mixer that can be called up from the editing screen. The Pro Audio Spectrum 16 records from an internally connected CD, a microphone, or an external jack. You can also mix these sources. This really does put a recording studio into your PC. Our choice is to use the external line in. We turn down the inputs on the other sound input channels of the mixer to minimize noise, and we also adjust the input level after sampling a portion of the music. If the input volume is too high, the recorded sound will be distorted.

Since many readers of this book will be equipped with first-generation Sound Blaster cards capable of only mono playback, we choose to sample in mono. This is an option in Stereofx. We also set the sampling rate at 5 KHz. This is adequate for the low-frequency synthesizer drone we sample. The recording is noisy at this level and has very little brightness (high-frequency harmonics), but the resulting file size is a lot smaller than a

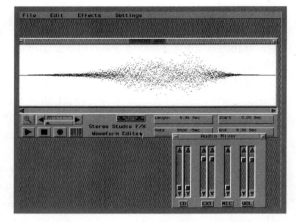

Figure 6-2 Synthesizer drone sampled in Stereofx

sample at the higher rate. We trim the beginning and ends of the file using the Cut choice under the Edit menu.

We then convert the WAV file saved by Stereofx to Sound Blaster VOC format. VEDIT2.EXE, Sound Blaster Pro's waveform editor, adds the VOC header to our WAV file. Finally, we fine-tuned the sample in Recording Studio Professional. Figure 6-3 shows one menu from the program's robust set of tools.

Notice how the display of the sample differs from that of Stereofx. Some of you may prefer this kind of graphic display. It's often a good idea to sample at a much higher sampling rate and then convert the sample to the highest sample rate allowed by your playback equipment. Recording Studio Professional provides this capability, along with a suite of tools with which you can alter the tonal qualities of the sound (equalization), shift the pitch of the sound, invert the sound (play it backward), and so on. Professional studios take into account the acoustic characteristics of the playback system in shaping the sound. For example, the small speaker on a television monitor will emphasize certain frequencies over others. If you know the majority of your audience is going to be listening to the soundtrack through the system speaker on the computer, you'll want to shape the sound accordingly.

Once we are satisfied with the sample, we use GRASP's VOC2SND.EXE utility to convert the VOC file to the SND format required by GRASP's SOUNDPC.GRP sound extension. The program can be found on the disk with this book. You run it from the command line:

```
voc2snd sndfile.voc
```

The sound file (SNDFILE.VOC) must be small enough to fit into available conventional memory (the memory space below 640K, reported by CHKDSK.EXE or DOS

5's MEM command). Practically speaking, the sound file should be less than 150K in size, or smaller if you plan to play back an animation sequence with digitized sound. It's not necessary to specify the output file. GRASP defaults to creating a file with the same root name as the input file, but with an .SND extension.

See the notes of the utility's use in Appendix C: Using GRASP's Utilities for an additional technical requirement.

Adding Digital Sound to GRASP Animations

The script that loads the digitized sound extension to GRASP is merged into the TITLE2.TXT with the command:

```
merge sndplay
```

As we said earlier, disk access interferes with playback of digitized sound, so we must load DFFs, pictures, fonts, and other disk files before executing the sound subroutine.

If you have been running TITLE2.TXT, you have seen— and heard—the effect of adding sound to the opening sequence. It makes the opening much more dramatic. Adding sound makes the au-

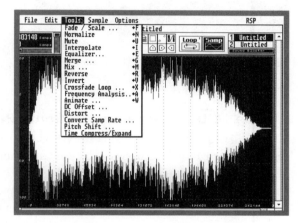

Figure 6-3 Fine-tuning the sample in Recording Studio Professional

dience more attentive. The more senses you stimulate, the more deeply involved your audience becomes in the presentation.

When we created the WELCOME.SND that accompanies the image of Sylvia, we added a muted section of sound after the second syllable. A peculiarity of the SOUNDPC.GRP sound extension to GRASP is that the animation you run concurrently with sound must end before the sound ends. The silent sound was added in Recording Studio Professional. Figure 6-4 shows what the sample looked like after adding silent sound.

If you are planning to do professional-level digital sound playback using GRASP, we highly recommend purchasing the Authentic Audio digital sound playback package. The Real Sound enhancement that comes bundled with GRASP (and is provided on this disk) tends to produce noisy sound playback. Authentic Audio loads compressed sound files into memory and plays them back, whereas Real Sound loads uncompressed sound files. This means longer samples can be used

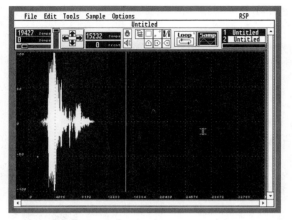

Figure 6-4 Adding silent sound to welcome

with Authentic Audio, and samples load faster. Authentic Audio also permits access to the hard drive while the sound is playing, although you will hear an audible click each time the hard drive is accessed.

In multimedia productions we will always want to add digitized playback to our programs for sound effects, voice over, and short musical sequences. But for music, there is no better solution for sound than MIDI. Let's turn to that now.

Adding MIDI Music to Multimedia Productions

Multimedia authoring tools that allow you simply to attach a digital sound file to a sequence of visuals (usually by selecting and clicking icons) are the easiest and fastest way to add music to visuals. However, this approach does not give us precise control over the sound and picture elements of a production. Precise control is important because television viewers and moviegoers are conditioned to expect the music to complement and enhance the visuals.

In classical animation the development of cartoon action and the soundtrack (effects and music) follows a parallel path. The storyboard identifies the places where music will underscore the action or where an action calls for a sound effect. Peaks and valleys in the cartoon action are matched by peaks and valleys in the music. A sudden and dramatic visual effect is matched with a "music sting," the moment when the music rises to a momentary climax. The next time you watch a music video or a TV ad, look for this correspondence between visuals and music.

Using "Stock" Music

Some companies specialize in supplying music for commercials, audiovisual productions, and multimedia. The music will either be supplied on CDs, cassette tapes, digitized music (in a variety of formats), or MIDI format files (MID or MFF).

If you have a MIDI interface or a card that has a MIDI option (such as the Sound Blaster MIDI option), then you've probably heard the *Multimedia Creations* demo play to music. The song is "Leya's Song" composed by Adrian Scott. It is a demonstration music for Roland Corporations' MIDI sequencers. (Roland Corporation was kind enough to provide The Waite Group Press with permission to use the music

GRASP'S SOUND UTILITIES

Included with the files that came with *Multimedia Creations* is a utility called NEWRATE.EXE, which will change the sampling rate of the sound file after it has been converted to GRASP's sound file format. These programs work from the DOS prompt. Run them without parameters to view their syntax. Local bulletin boards and CompuServe are excellent sources for digitized sounds. However, many of the sounds come from copyrighted materials. Unless you know that the digitized sound is in the public domain, do not use these sounds for work you intend to distribute or play in a public forum. See the sidebar on copyright in this chapter.

for the demo.) We use the song as a kind of stock music piece. "Leya's Song" starts playing when the Perfectly Proportioned Man appears in the demo, and plays through to the end. Even though the visuals in the demo are not programmed to the music, the music works really well with the visuals.

Unfortunately, "Leya's Song" does not sound very good when it is played back through the FM synthesizer technology found on Sound Blasters and Adlib compatibles. "Leya's Song" takes advantage of the advanced technology of Roland and other MIDI equipment, including reverb and chorus effects. (Some external MIDI sequencers may in fact play the song incorrectly. If your sequencer is MT-32 or General MIDI-compatible, you will hear the song as it was composed.) Also, "Leya's Song" uses instruments that simply don't exist on the Sound Blaster and Adlib compatibles.

In order to support Sound Blaster and Adlib FM users, we needed to develop a song especially for them. The song will be written in MIDI and we'll make sure the instruments suit the strengths and weakness of the FM chips. Furthermore, we'll commission a custom song that is synched to the visuals.

Creating Custom Music

We've engaged a Vancouver, B.C. professional musician, John Mitchell, to generate the MIDI song that plays under the 3-minute demo we featured in the last chapter. He works as a musician and also composes jingles for commercials, which gives him an excellent feel for the multimedia medium. We showed him the demo and he interpreted it musically.

His principal suggestion was to allow the music to support the visual changes in the demo. Giving musical emphasis to the visual changes unifies the demo and gives it a polished feel.

Second, in order to synch the music to the visuals, we decided to divide the demo into four musical sections. That way, if the music is played on a slow computer, we have four points in the demo where the music can be realigned with the visuals. (In the next chapter we'll show you a method that provides perfect synch between visuals and music.)

By using the software stopwatch, we were able to identify the precise moments in time when a musical change will occur. John could then create the music on his Atari computer in his studio, using the SMPTE time code of his sequencing program.

SOURCING MUSIC AND MUSIC COPYRIGHT

You should assume that all music is copyrighted unless you know explicitly otherwise: Sheet music is copyrighted. The lyrics are copyrighted; the particular arrangement of a song is copyrighted; the musicians who played the song own the rights to their performances. If you have ever attempted to get copyright clearance for a song, then you know that it is a long and arduous process without any guarantee that the owners of the copyright will finally let you use the song for a fee. So where should you go for music?

The best source of music for multimedia programs is the professional sound studio in your area. The studio often buys the rights to an entire library of music (such as the Network music library). You purchase the rights for a specific use in a specific geographical area. The sound studio can also "cut and splice" the music to the exact length you require. Another source of music is the work of local musicians, especially those who work in MIDI. Place a notice in the local music store that professional musicians frequent.

A third source is a music library targeted to multimedia use, such as Prosonus' MusicBytes, a library of original compositions in various styles, audio formats, and lengths. Each volume comes with 27 original tunes and 107 sound effects. Contact Prosonus at 1-800-999-6191 or 1-818-766-5221. Even more comprehensive are the Valentino sound effects and music libraries. The company sells nine CDs of sound effects and two CDs of music "beds and bits." Once you've purchased the CDs, you own the complete rights—no other clearances are required for their use. Contact Valentino at 1-800-223-6278 or 1-914-347-7878.

Companies like Voyetra Technologies that specialize in MIDI software sell MIDI songs tailored to multimedia productions. Some of these so-called "sequences" are royalty-free. Other companies, like Roland, sell MIDI songs that are for personal use. You'll find many vendors who sell MIDI sequences listed at the back of major music publications, but most of them sell copyrighted material. The use of such material is dangerous.

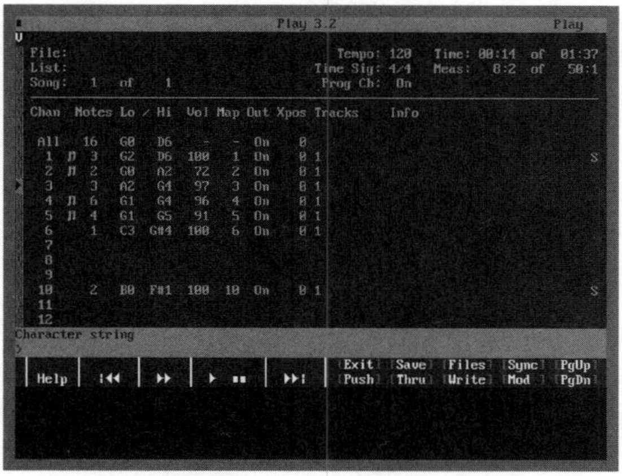

Figure 6-5 FM Software's MIDITools interface

The SMPTE time code gave him a reference point for the music he created in his sequencer. It was much easier for John Mitchell to create the soundtrack this way.

Once John created the music, he brought his Atari to us and we connected the MIDI out from his Atari to the MIDI in of our Roland SCC1 card. We then captured the MIDI data stream from the Atari using FM Software's MIDITools Record utility. The utility is simple and easy. To record the data we type:

```
record testdump
```

That's all there is to it. The utility creates a standard MIDI file we can immediately test by playing it back in MIDITools MIDI player, PLAY.EXE. The program's interface can be seen in Figure 6-5.

Figure 6-5 shows the screen with a song selected from a file list. We use PLAY.EXE, the command line player program supplied in MIDITools for music. FM Software's MIDI player is placed in a subdirectory on the DOS path. This allows us to type PLAY.EXE from any subdirectory in the computer. The interface you see in Figure 6-5 pops up instantly. The Files menu choice at the bottom right of the screen takes us to a second screen, where song files are listed. The screen is reproduced in Figure 6-6.

Most of the playback control you need to audition a MIDI song is provided on the main screen (Figure 6-5). MIDITools Play has a number of simple MIDI processing tools. Any channel can be redirected to another, volume levels can be changed on individual channels, and notes can be transposed. These changes can be saved to disk. We've often found that programs that refuse to accept

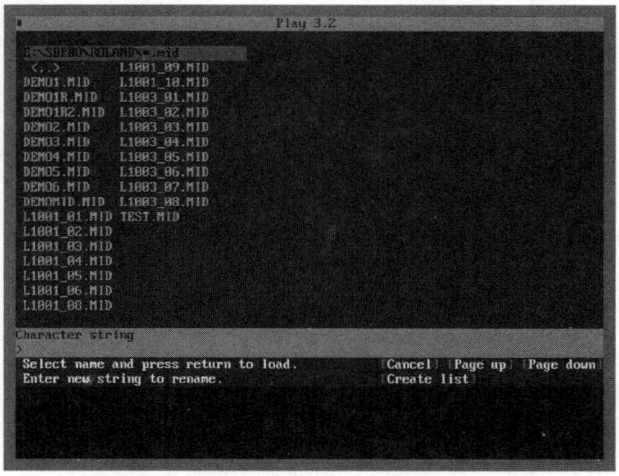

Figure 6-6 The MIDITools player files screen

certain MIDI files load into Play. We've saved them without changing them, and the original, cranky, program has accepted them in their new form. Such player functions as play, pause, rewind, fast forward, skip, tempo control, and song position selection are also available. In fact, PLAY.EXE, which comes with the MIDITools bundle of programs, is very much like the companion PLAY/D program bundled with the book, except that it provides an interactive interface.

PLAY.EXE also has a command-line mode:

`play name.mid`

This will play a song specified at the command line. Think of it as equivalent to DOS's Type command. The MIDITools package really does help you work productively with MIDI files.

The program also includes diagnostic tools that help you determine the hardware configuration of MIDI devices.

Using a Sequencer to Modify a MIDI Song

MIDITools' Play program is an excellent auditioning tool, but you'll need a sequencer for extensive MIDI file modification. A sequencer provides note-by-note, channel-by-channel editing of MIDI songs. A MIDI song is composed of a se-

quence of notes, plus MIDI events. A sequencer loads these notes and events into memory and displays them on the screen, where you can edit them. A MIDI sequencing program does for musical notes what a word processor does for letters of the alphabet. It allows you to write and edit songs.

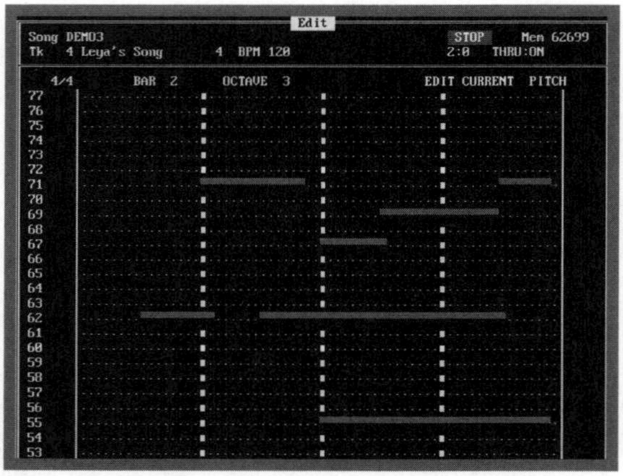

Displaying MIDI Notes

There are two types of MIDI note display systems: piano roll and musical notation.

Figure 6-7 Voyetra's Sequencer Plus Junior piano roll notation

Figure 6-7 shows the piano roll type of display found on many first-generation sequencers and sequencers bundled with most sound cards. This is Voyetra's entry-level Sequencer Plus Junior program:

Voyetra's Sequencer Plus Junior is distributed with the Creative Labs Sound Blaster products. A similar sequencer program is distributed with the Media Vision line of sound cards. The Pro Audio Spectrum 16 comes bundled with SP Spectrum

Sequencer. Most of our comments about the Sound Blaster version of the sequencer will apply to the Media Vision version of the sequencer.

The thick horizontal lines you see in Figure 6-7 represent notes. The length of the note corresponds to the duration they are held. The numbers along the left side (from 53 to 77) represent the MIDI note values. In note edit mode, the individual notes can be raised (higher pitch) or lowered (lower pitch). They can be lengthened (longer sustained note) or shortened (short note). The screen shows a single bar. Other MIDI events can be edited as well.

Piano roll sequencers work well for people who have little or no musical training.

Sequencers that actually display music in traditional notation are favored by musicians. Figure 6-8 shows a screen captured from Musicator.

The song that is displayed on the screen is the same song we just displayed in Voyetra's sequencer program. While the Sequencer Plus Junior screen shows a single bar from a single channel of music (one instrument), the Musicator program displays four channels simultaneously.

John Mitchell's music was brought into Musicator to make subtle changes in notes and to alter music cues. We also used Musicator to assign different patch changes to the song, according to the type of music playback equipment the user would employ. Working with original compositions that are tailored to the visual flow of a multimedia production is a rare and privileged treat. The music helps knit the eclectic image threads together and enhances the rhythm and drama of the presentation. But what if you don't have the time and budget to hire a professional musician? The next section provides an alternate solution for the proletariat multimedia producer.

Figure 6-8 Musicator sequencing using music notation

An excellent music composition program is Power Chords from Howling Dog Systems in Burnaby, B.C. The program runs under Windows and allows you to build up a song from chords through to melody lines. Highly recommended.

Music Generation Programs

On the Starship *Enterprise,* Data, the android ship's officer, has learned to compose music by imitating the styles and methods of the great masters of the past. An artificial person creates artificial music. Science fiction gives us a glimpse of a possibility for computers and music. Few people doubt that some day music programs will be capable of generating very sophisticated compositions that might fool *some* of the people *all* the time into thinking they're hearing a human composition, or fool *all* of the people *some* of the time. The jury is out, however, on the computer's ability to match human creative genius.

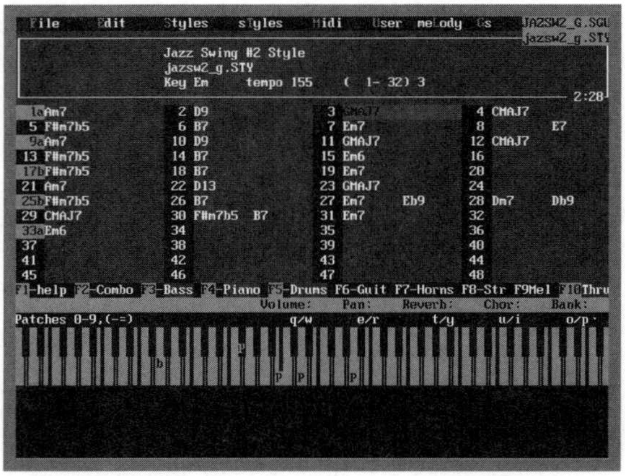

In the meantime there are a number of programs that create artificial music compositions. The most popular of these is a program called Band-in-a-Box, published by PG Music, Inc. The publisher calls the program an "automatic accompaniment program." The program is based on the "music-minus-one" concept, where you choose an instrument and have the program accompany you on bass, drums, piano, guitar, or strings. Band-in-a-Box can generate a wide variety of popular styles of music, including jazz, pop, country, or ethnic. You type in chords to a song, and the song generates an accompaniment in the style you choose. Or you can create your own style. You can then export the song as a MIDI file and import it into a sequencer for further embellishment. That's what we are going to do.

Figure 6-9 Playing a song in Band-in-a-Box

Band-in-a-Box is supplied in two versions: BB.EXE is used with MIDI equipment and BAND.EXE is used with FM sound cards.

We're going to use Band-in-a-Box to create musical accompaniment for the 2-minute demo. When we've finished creating the basic song in Band-in-a-Box, we'll export it as a MIDI file and further enhance it in a sequencer. Figure 6-9 shows you what the program's screen looks like while you're playing a song.

The program has well over a hundred song "styles" to choose from. Here we've loaded a jazz song and used its default style. You can experiment by loading various styles, like "shuffle rock" or "blues straight" with the song. This allows the program to generate hundreds of songs.

In timing the *Multimedia Creations* demo, we discovered that we needed 1 minute and 9 seconds of music from the moment when the perfectly proportioned Man appears until the last image fades from the screen. Our song was too short, so we chose to repeat portions of it. Band-in-Box allows you to specify the song's length through repetition of the main body of the song, the chorus. Or you can add or delete bars by pressing (ALT)-(D) or (ALT)-(I) respectively. The program will prompt you for the number of bars to delete or add. In Band-in-a-Box's song settings (accessed by pressing the (TAB) or (PGUP) key), we changed the default 3 chorus setting to 1 chorus. This shortened the song considerably. The program will automatically generate a two-bar drum lead-in to the song. We chose to begin the song without a lead-in, so we changed the lead-in count to 0. Figure 6-10 shows the song settings dialogue box as it appears after the changes were made.

After exiting the song settings dialogue box, we added eight bars to pad the music out to the requisite length. We moved the highlight bar to bar 21, and pressed (ALT)-(I). A dialogue box prompted for the number of bars to add to the song. We said eight, and eight blank bars were inserted at bar 21. We now had to add chords to these blank bars. You don't have to be a professional musician to generate new music. The program will try to make whatever chords you enter into the bars work with the song. Your back-up band is very patient and very forgiving.

Entering chords in the blank bars we inserted in the song was easy. You merely highlight the empty bar and enter the name of the chord. We chose a shortcut. We copied the previous eight bars into a buffer and then reinserted it at bar 21. You copy bars by pressing (ALT)-(C). This brings up a dialogue box that asks for the point from which to copy bars, how many bars to copy, and where you want to place them. We copied eight bars from bar 13 and placed them at bar 21. We then edited the new bars to vary them from the previous eight bars.

Then we played the song by pressing (F4). We found that adding bars required changing the tag jump point, the point where the song jumps to the ending sequence of chords. We did this in the

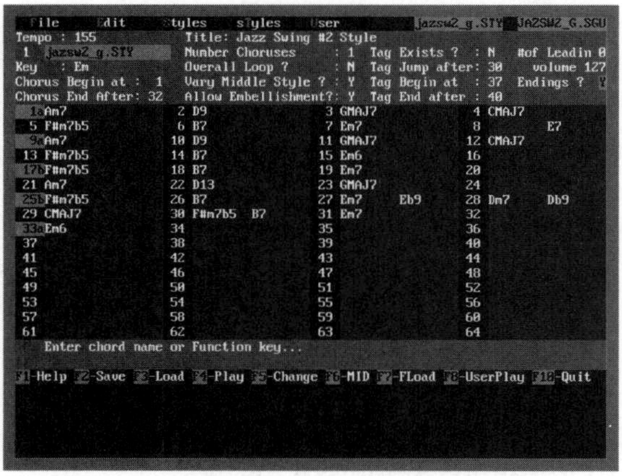

Figure 6-10 Song settings in Band-in-a-Box

Song Settings dialogue box. Our ear also told us our choice of chords was "unmusical" at certain points in the song. We highlighted the offending chords and either changed them, or erased them by pressing the space bar and the (ENTER) key.

Changing Other Parameters of the Song Interactively

Pressing (F1) during play brings up Help Play Mode. Once we were satisfied with our artificial creation, we saved the song as a MIDI file by pressing (F6).

We wanted to know how the song would sound on our MT-32, so we used the MIDITools song player to audition the MIDI song we had saved. We adjusted the relative volumes of the three instruments, bass, piano, and drums. Satisfied, we then imported the song into Voyetra's Sequencer Plus Junior. In Sequencer Plus we were able to audition alternate instrumentation for the song. Figure 6-11 shows the top part of the main screen.

In Sequencer Plus Junior you assign MIDI channels to tracks. You do this in the Chan (Channel) column on the main screen of the program. Tracks are numbered and arranged horizontally on the screen. Sound Blaster's FM synthesizer limits you to 11 instruments. Newer generation sound cards that use the Yamaha OPTI FM synthesizer chip allow for 20 voices. The trick is not to have more voic-

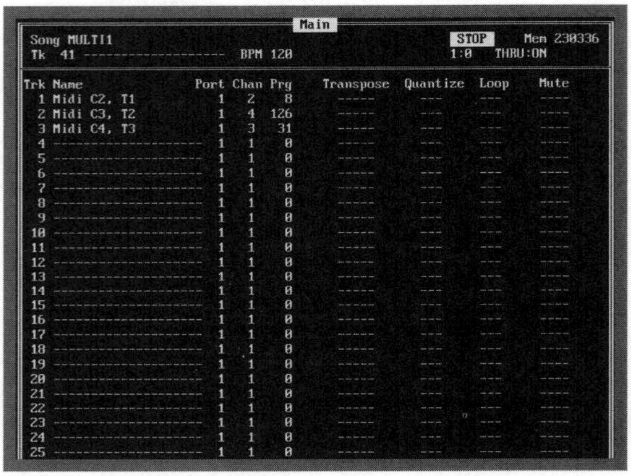

Figure 6-11 Changing instrumentation in Sequencer Plus Junior

es playing simultaneously than the synthesizer chip allows. Theoretically, you could use all 64 tracks this way, although this is improbable. Practically, you use far fewer tracks.

Being able to create separate tracks that use different instruments is a powerful feature of MIDI sequencers. Working with tracks is a lot like working with reel-to-reel tape tracks in a sound studio. You can build up a song in layers, or add "music stings" (short musical sounds, like a tinkling bell) at certain points in the song. Professional MIDI sequencers work with SMPTE to exactly locate music changes or stings in relation to visual events.

Auditioning Selective Tracks

By moving the highlight bar over a track and pressing (M) you can mute a track, so you can hear the effect of the music with that track silenced. Several tracks can be silenced in this manner. Or, by pressing (S) for solo, you can hear a single track playing.

Making Program Changes

A Program Change in MIDI is a change from one musical instrument to another. The vertical column marked Prg contains the Program Change information according to track. By changing the numbers in this column, you change the instrument that will be played. You can do this while the song is playing. Pressing the plus or minus key on your keyboard changes to the next higher or lower instrument. In this way you can step through all 128 MIDI sounds. Page A-3 of the Appendix in the Sequencer Plus Junior manual that comes with the Sound Blaster MIDI

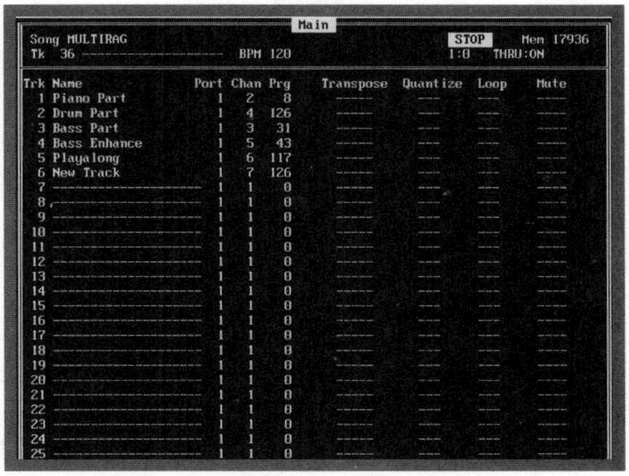

Figure 6-12 Adding tracks to a song

package lists the instruments that are assigned to these MIDI numbers. The FM Synth Program Listing on pages 126–127 of the Pro Audio Spectrum 16's User's Guide lists an identical set of patches for the Media Vision Board. As you can see, there are alternate ways of referencing MIDI instrumentation (Program Changes, patches, MIDI instrumentation, voices). MIDI is not that difficult to understand. Learning MIDI jargon is!

We decide to give the song more "body" by adding a couple of tracks to it. Figure 6-12 shows the screen with the tracks added.

The original song created in Band-in-a-Box had three tracks, which we've named the Piano, Drum, and Bass Parts. The Bass Enhance track is a duplicate of the Bass track. We just renamed it, and altered the instrument assigned to this channel. We looked for a song with a long sustain that complemented the Bass track. This turned out to be 43, a sound called Echo Pan in the Program Listing.

We added two more tracks. New tracks were added by entering the Edit screen (accessed by pressing the letter (e) on the keyboard) and pressing (a) (for Add). The program prompts you for the number of bars to add. We added 43 bars, the length of the song. While in the edit screen you can copy bars into a temporary buffer and reinsert them elsewhere in the song. Sequencers give you a lot of the same editing tools you've become accustomed to in word processing.

Playing Along in Real Time

Now that we had created two new tracks, it was time to play along with the song in real time (while the song is playing). If you have a MIDI keyboard attached to the sound card, you can place the program into record mode by pressing (r). We selected the track we named Playalong, and chose an instrument called Log Drum (MIDI 117). We assigned the track to channel 6. Then we called up the options menu by pressing the letter (o). The metronome was highlighted, so we pressed the (+) key to turn it on. We were now ready to play along with the song.

If you do not have a MIDI keyboard, Voyetra has very thoughtfully provided you with an optional method of recording and playing along with the music. By pressing (SHIFT)-(F1), you pop a "qwerty" (keyboard) synth on the screen. Figure 6-13 shows you what this keyboard synth looks like.

In Figure 6-13 you can see the computer keyboard keys that correspond to the on-screen keyboard at the bottom. The Qwerty synth is primitive but fun! We used it to create a rhythm pattern using the Log Drum sound. It allows you to add a human feel to a very mechanical sounding piece. We did the same thing with the next track, "New Track." We chose MIDI 126, the Analog Synth sound, to add a light, plucked sound pattern to the song.

Once we were satisfied with our creation, we prepared to save the song to disk. When we originally installed Sequencer Plus Junior, we set up our ports differently from that recommended by Voyetra. The Port column on the Main menu allows you to assign tracks to either an external synth (port 1 by default) or the internal FM chips (port 2 by default). We switched this around, assigning the external synth to port 2 and the FM chips to port 1. We knew we were going to be playing the song we created as a Sound Blaster CMF file. The .CMF file extension (Creative Music Format) is Sound Blaster's version of the MIDI file format. We'll be using a utility program available from Creative Technologies to convert our song to this CMF format. The conversion program will only convert tracks that are assigned to Port 1. If

Figure 6-13 Voyetra's Qwerty synth

you don't plan to change the default port assignment in Voyetra's sequencer, then at least change the port assignment from 2 to 1 when you save the song to disk.

Before we do convert the song for use in the *Multimedia Creations* demo, let's take a very brief tour of *timbre editing*.

Editing FM Sounds

Modifying the sounds your synthesizer or sound card is capable of producing is a highly technical subject that really deserves its own chapter, if not book. Fortunately, there is a Shareware program with an excellent interface that allows us to at least experiment with the FM sounds on the Sound Blaster, Adlib, Media Vision boards, or compatibles. It is called SBTimbre from Jamie O'Connell, and is available on the MIDI Forum of CompuServe and on several bulletin boards. Figure 6-14 shows the timbre editing screen.

FM sound technology uses one sound wave to modify a second sound wave. In this case we've selected the acoustic piano sound for modification. The SBTimbre Timbre edit window allows you to modify the characteristics of the two sound waves making up the acoustic piano sound. The basic sound waveform, called the carrier waveform, is modified by the second (modulator) waveform. The numbered fields have spin controls. Clicking on the up or down arrows increases or decreases values. The "Attack" field is shown highlighted here. The Note and chord boxes along the bottom of the Timbre Edit screen allow you to audition changes you make to the FM sounds. Our recommendation for the novice is to play with the various controls until

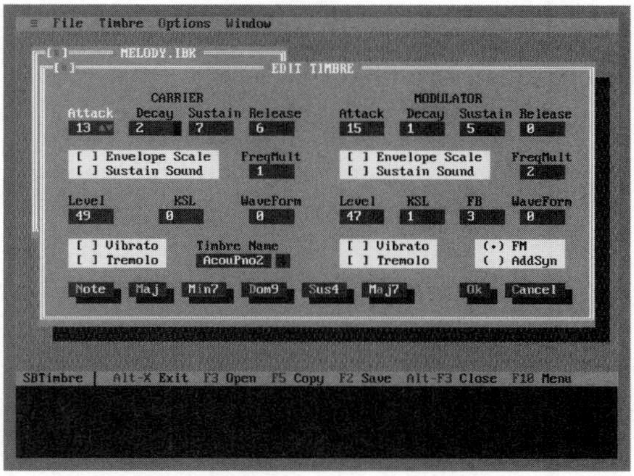

Figure 6-14 Using SBTimbre to modify FM sounds

you've produced the sounds that please you. A basic book on sound shaping using synthesizers will help you understand the effect of changes you are about to make.

When you modify an FM sound, you save it in a file with an IBK extension. The format has been popularized by the sequencing program called Cakewalk from Twelve Tone Systems. IBK files define what sounds are associated with the 128 patches on a sound card with FM synthesizer chips. Figure 6-15 shows you the dialogue box from which to select one of these sounds.

The file shown in Figure 6-15 is called MELODY.IBK. After we used SBTimbre to modify the FM sounds in the Sound Blaster, we saved MELODY.IBK to disk and exited the program.

Converting MIDI Files to CMF Format

Creative Labs publishes a utility program called MID2CMF.EXE. The program converts MIDI files (MID or MFF) to Sound Blaster's proprietary MIDI format (CMF). You simply call the program from the command line. It will prompt you for the name of the MIDI file. You must provide the file extension as well. The utility comes with a MELODY.IBK file, which assigns Sound Blaster FM sounds to the converted file. You substitute the MELODY.IBK file that comes with MID2CMF.EXE with the one you created in the FM timbre editor. This allows you to generate a CMF file with sounds unique to your song. After you type in the name of the MIDI file you want to convert, the program tells you what channels the MIDI file uses, and what instruments. It then prompts you for a CMF file name. You must supply the extension. A CMF file is then created.

Playing the CMF Files in GRASP

We're not actually going to use the CMF song we've just created with the demo. We've used John Mitchell's music instead. Adding support for both MIDI songs and CMF songs has added a level of complexity to the demo. The *Multimedia Creations* demo will run with either no music, MIDI format music (users with a MIDI interface), or CMF music (users with a Sound Blaster or Adlib compatible interface). Not only that, the copyright notices in the opening screens of the show will have to change. When the demo plays with no music, we want only the Waite Group copyright to play on the screen. When the user installs the MIDI interface, we want Adrian Scott's copyright to appear. When the user chooses one of the FM interfaces, we want John Mitchell's copyright notice to appear. We'll also want to load and play the appropriate song (MIDI or CMF) with the appropriate interface.

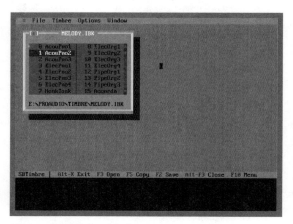

Figure 6-15 Selecting instrument sounds in SBTimbre

Our strategy will be to have GRASP check the configuration file on the hard drive and set up a global variable that will be used to check for the three types of configurations (no sound card, a card supporting MIDI files, or a card supporting CMF files). Then all we have to do subsequent to that is check the global variable to find out what kind of music file to play, if any. The best place to do this is at the beginning of the program, in the script that queries for the presence of PLAY/D, CHECPLAY.TXT.

The first order of business is to write a subroutine that checks the hard drive for the existence of a file. GRASP does not have a command such as the batch file command "if exist filespec" we reviewed earlier. Fortunately, the Int (interrupt) command provides us with a workaround. Here is the file-checking subroutine (cfgexist:) we will add to the end of CHECPLAY.TXT

```
cfgexist:
        int 0x21 0x4e00,,,ofs(@1),,,seg(@1)
        return !(@0&1)
```

The large 0s are zeros and the small os are the small letter o. The subroutine both receives values passed to it by the calling script and sends values back. The @1 values are passed to the subroutine by the calling script. Let's have a look at that now.

```
; CHECPLAY.TXT Checks to make sure PLAY/D has been installed.

video m

start:

cfgexist "\grasp\no.cfg"
if @0
        return
endif
```

We send the file-checking subroutine the name of the configuration file by adding it as a parameter to the subroutine call (cfgexist). The subroutine checks for the file and returns a result. This is the value @0. If @0 has a value of 1 (true), then the next line is executed. The next line is a return. Execution returns to the calling script. We don't need to check for the presence of PLAY/D if the user does not configure the demo for music. If the NO.CFG file does not exist, execution continues with a block of code that checks to see if PLAY/D is loaded. Here it is:

```
merge \grasp\midi

gosub mfinit

error:
if !@0                                  ; if no midi driver installed...
        call billbord open              ; call walking billboard script
        pfree p1
        pgetbuf p1                      ; save man and billboard to buffer

        set center on
        fload \grasp\ibm14.set
        text 0,310 "Sound not configured."
        text 0,292 "Exit and type: PLAYER"
        color 1 6
        text 0,274 "Press Enter to continue."
        set center off
        waitkey
        pfade 10 p1 100
        pfree p1
        call billbord close
```

```
        clearscr 0
        video 1
        int 0x21 0x4c00
```

```
endif
```

(We'll come back to the error: label in a moment.) This code warns the user who has chosen to configure the demo with a sound card that PLAY/D is not loaded. If PLAY/D is not loaded, exit is made to the DOS prompt using the interrupt call. If it is, we then check to see what kind of music file is called for.

```
; checks for a MIDI device

data "\grasp\mpu.cfg" "\grasp\sbmid.cfg" "\grasp\midi.cfg" "\grasp\mfc.cfg"

mark 4
        cfgexist @
        if @0 midi
loop

data "\grasp\sbfm.cfg" "\grasp\adlfm.cfg"

mark 2
        cfgexist @
        if @0 fm

return

goto error

midi:
        global sndcfg "midi"
        return

fm:
        global sndcfg "fm"
        return
```

We use GRASP's Data command to give the @ variable in the loop a series of file names. These are the configuration file names for the four types of MIDI interfaces that will load and play MIDI or MFF MIDI format files. Every time through the loop, the @ symbol is replaced with a name from the list. As soon as GRASP finds a match, execution jumps to the midi: label and the global sndcfg variable is given the string "midi" as a value. The script then returns to the calling script. If GRASP goes through the list and does not find a configuration file that matches an item from the list, the loop is exited and execution continues to a similar loop that tests for FM sound configuration. If none are found, execution proceeds to the "goto error." We jump back to "legs" to advise the reader that sound has not been configured and exit to the DOS prompt.

We have now set up a global variable called sndcfg, which stores information about the user's configuration choice. Because the variable is global in scope, we can access it anywhere within the program. Let's now look at one of the places where the variable sndcfg is used. In the third module of the *Multimedia Creations* demo a song is loaded and played by PLAY/D. Will it be MIDI or CMF? Here's how GRASP uses the sndcfg variable to decide.

```
; section checks to see how playd has been initialized
if def(sndcfg)==1
        if @sndcfg=="midi"        ; MIDI sound card or option
                mfload leya.mid
        else                      ; sound card with FM
                mfload brew2.cmf
        endif
endif
```

We introduced you to the def(variable) function in Chapter 4. The function tests to see if a variable has been defined. If it hasn't, then the section of code that follows is ignored. Remember that we did not create the sndcfg variable if no card was selected by the user. So we don't load a song file if sndcfg returns 0 or false. The song will not be loaded if CHECPLAY.TXT is never run or if PLAY/D is not loaded. If we had not used the def(variable) function and tried to run TITLE3.TXT from the editor, GRASP would have stopped execution of the script when it encountered the sndcfg variable and put up a "Undefined Variable at line 25" message. So the def(variable) function serves double duty here.

If sndcfg has been defined, GRASP then uses the If/Else/Endif structure to determine what kind of file to tell PLAY/D to load.

We use the same approach in the OPENING.TXT file to determine which three copyright options to put on the screen.

Adding Sound to Visuals

In this chapter we explored ways of creating and adding sound effects, voice, and music to the *Multimedia Creations* demo. This follows the method of adding soundtracks to film and video programs. In the next chapter we'll show you how to turn this situation around. We're going to use the code we created for the stopwatch to build a virtual SMPTE tape track, which will then act as our cue list for visuals. It's a powerful new way to create multimedia using FM Software's MIDI tools.

7

Creating a Music Video

USIC VIDEOS offer the producer a different kind of problem than documentaries or dramas. In the documentary process, the soundtrack is usually part of the final stages. The music video producer, on the other hand, receives the soundtrack for the music video as a *fait accompli*.

The music video lays a dance of images over the song—images that enhance and emphasize the rhythm, mood, and character of the piece. If you were a musician standing in the edit suite, you would want to see the visuals placed in a supporting role, not as the main attraction.

The most effective way to make the visuals subservient to the images is to make the music drive the pace and transformation of visuals. When the music is slow and billowy, the images slowly, leisurely dissolve one into the other. When the drummer gives the cymbal a good whack, the visuals should go through a sudden corresponding change.

How does a music video producer attain this perfect correspondence between the visuals and music? After developing rough ideas about how the music will be visualized, the producer will identify the precise points in the music where visuals will change (called *cues*). Some producers will work with a stopwatch, timing the track so that the number and lengths of visual passages are known and can be planned for. Others will work with the SMPTE track.

How would the multimedia producer produce a music multimedia program? In the last chapter we added music to the *Multimedia Creations* demo *after editing the visuals*. By aligning visual changes to music cues, we "bonded" the music and visuals, making them feel as if they belonged to each other. In this chapter, we take the opposite approach. Instead of trying to fit the music to the visuals, we create a vehicle for cueing visuals to music.

CREATING THE MUSIC CUE PROGRAM

The cueing program we create in GRASP interacts with FM Software's memory resident MIDI player. The MIDI player acts as a kind of virtual tape deck. It not only plays the MIDI song (with such tape cassette deck features as rewind, fast forward, pause, and play), it keeps track of the time that has elapsed since it was loaded, much as SMPTE time code allows the editor in the video post production suite to reference sound and visuals to an independent time line.

It's the ability to reference computer events to an independent time line that makes the MIDI player so valuable to us. Cueing—working out the points in the music where visual changes will occur—is integral to any production.

The first module of our GRASP application will be an electronic cue sheet for identifying and storing these sound cues. The second module of our application loads the cues from a stored file on disk into memory and plays them back. Visual changes occur at specified time cues in the music. This process is very similar to the way multi-projector, multi-image slide shows are programmed for entertainment and business shows. In multi-image the soundtrack is recorded on two tracks of a four-track audio tape, along with a third track of proprietary "time code." The time code is fed into a computer as the audio tape rolls. The computer in turn controls slide projectors. The multi-image programmer enters the time cues for slide changes in a computer program. These times are compared to the time code values coming from the audio tape. When they match, the visual change occurs. Our GRASP application reproduces this functionality.

Besides presenting a method for creating music-driven multimedia programs, this chapter teaches you some of the basic design issues raised by any computer application.

Installing the MIDI Player

This chapter requires the use of a sound card. If you have a sound card and ran the demo when you installed GRASP, you should already have the correct configuration file installed in the GRASP subdirectory. If you opted not to install the call to PLAY/D in your AUTOEXEC.BAT file, type player when you are in the CHAPT07 subdirectory. This will install PLAY/D, and change the directory to CHAPT07 and call GRASPC.EXE. You can actually work with the examples in this chapter without a sound card, but you will of course hear no music.

Loading the Program

The program we create in this chapter is on the accompanying disk as MUSIC1.TXT and MUSIC2.TXT. (The second script is linked to the first at run time.) Load MUSIC1.TXT into the GRASP editor and run it by pressing (F10). The background is first cleared to solid blue, then a yellow title forms at the top of the screen ("Music Cue Sheet"), and the first cue is shown. The program now places the current running time on the next line and waits for you to press the (ENTER) key. When you do, the second cue and its time are displayed on the screen, and the program proceeds to the next line. You can repeatedly cue in this fashion until either 266 cues have been recorded or the (ESC) key is pressed. (The cue limit, two full screens of cues, is arbitrary.) If you press the (ESC) key, the program prompts you to save the file. If you choose to save the cues to a file, the program saves the cues and then asks if you want to proceed to the next module (where cues are displayed to the music). Choose (N) for no. We'll review the second module later.

During the running of the program, if you press the space bar, the music and the clock stop. You can then back up through the cues and adjust the current cue by pressing the (+) or (-) key on the numeric keypad. Pressing (ENTER) places the current time value and cue name on the screen, starts the song playing from that point, and resumes displaying the clock on the line below the current line.

Pressing (F1) pops up a Help menu.

The Overall Design

Figure 7-1 provides a code flow diagram of the program. Note that there are three main subroutines that branch off the main routine.

1. If the user presses (E) while in the main routine, a cue is created and stored in memory and displayed on screen. Control then passes back to the main routine.
2. If the user presses the (SPACE BAR) or (B) key, control passes to the pausong: (pause song) routine. There the user has a choice of continuing or backing up a cue. If the user chooses to continue, control passes back to the main rou-

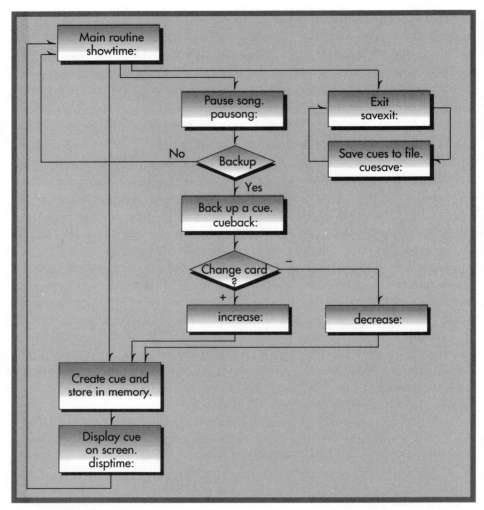

Figure 7-1 Code flow diagram

tine. Users who choose to back up can either change the cue they have backed up to, or go back to the main routine. If they choose to increase or decrease the cue they have backed up to, they can do so. They then go to the cue: subroutine where the cue is created, stored, and displayed, and then control is passed back to the main routine.

3. The user can choose to exit from the program at anytime. The code flow at the exit point has been simplified in the code flow diagram. You may wish to review this code flow diagram as you work through the routines.

Detailed Commentary

Let's look at our GRASP application more closely. The following sections of code establish the initial settings for the program.

```
; MUSIC1.TXT Music Video Cue Sheet

video m


; Check to make sure user has configured sound card and loaded PLAY/D.
        call checplay

;set debug on                            ; remove semicolon to debug script

; Sets up background as blue. Uses default palette.
        clearscr 1

start:

; Software SMPTE routines.
        merge MIDI                  ; loads MIDI interface script
        mfinit                      ; initializes PLAY/D
        set space off               ; turns GRASP pause off
        set esc off                 ; turns GRASP crash exit off
        when end goto done          ; quick exit from program
        when esc goto savexit       ; exit with save option
        when home link music1       ; quick restart
        when f1 gosub help          ; pops up help screen
        offset 0 0                  ; necessary for quick restart

; Loads appropriate song
        if def(sndcfg)==1
                    if @sndcfg=="midi"
                            mfload \grasp\chapt05\leya.mid
                    else
                            mfload brew.cmf
                    endif
        endif

; Titles at top

        color 14 0
        fstyle 8 2
        fload helvet15.set 1
        set center on
        text 0 440 "Music Cue Sheet"
        set center off
        ffree 1

; Help box message
        color 8
        rect 8,450 210,479              ; blanks message area
        color 0
        box 8,450 210,479               ; gray title box
        fload \grasp\helvet15.set 1
```

```
        color 2
        text 18,457 "F1 for Help"

; Initial values
        offset 7,410                    ; output to screen top left
        global name 100                 ; for naming and storing cues
        global cnt 99                   ; for counting cues
        global hilite 8                 ; sets cue highlight to normal

; Gray title at top left
        font 0
        fstyle 8 1
        color 7
        text 4,25 "min"
        text 30,25 "sec"
```

Notice that we've added a call to the routine that checks to make sure the sound card has been configured, and PLAY/D is loaded. This is a slightly modified form of the script we wrote in the last chapter, CHECPLAY.TXT. The routine checks to see if the user has chosen to not configure the program with a sound card. If the user has, he or she is advised to run a batch file in the CHAPT07 subdirectory that calls IN-STALL.BAT. This batch file installs the appropriate configuration file for MIDI or CMF song playback.

Establishing Starting Values

In the "initial values" part of the script, a number of variables are declared and given initial values. We declare them as global variables because they store information we want to access from subroutines. (Remember, global variables are program-wide in their scope. Local variables cannot be accessed by subroutines, unless they are explicitly sent to the subroutine. Also, local variables created in subroutines cannot be accessed by the calling routine, unless they are returned. We'll treat this subject in detail a little further along.) The global variables *name* (cue name) and *cnt* (cue count) are used to create, store, and keep track of cues. Keeping track of cues is one of the main problems we have to solve in this program.

User Interaction and the When Command

An important feature of this script is that it is fully interactive. We use GRASP's When command to manage user interaction. For example, when the user presses the (END) key, this statement:

```
when end done
```

causes the program to branch to the label done:

```
done:
        mfrewind
        exit
```

The command Mfrewind stops the current song, and "rewinds" to the beginning of the song. We then exit to the editor. If we had not issued the Mfrewind command, the song would have kept playing, since PLAY/D is a TSR that runs independently of GRASP. Mfrewind: is a subroutine in the MIDI.TXT interface to the player. (We introduced the MIDI interface in the last chapter.) Let's review the commands that control our virtual tape recorder, since we'll be using them extensively in our program.

```
mfplay                   Plays song currently loaded, or "unpauses"
                         a previously paused song.
mfpause                  Pauses play.
mfrewind                 Rewinds to the beginning of a song.
mfsetpos (+/- val)       Starts song playing from the specified position.
```

Mfsetpos can take a positive or negative value. The value is a time measured in milliseconds. A positive value starts the song playing at the specified offset in milliseconds from the beginning of the song. A negative value, oddly enough, actually skips the song forward from the present position. A value of -1000 would skip the playing position one second further along from the present position. Figure 7-2 shows how this works.

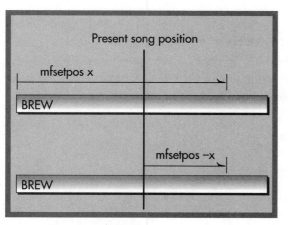

Figure 7-2 Using Mfsetpos to set the song position

The rectangles represent the song loaded by PLAY/D. The figure shows two ways to set the starting position of a song using Mfsetpos. The vertical line represents where we currently are in the song. In the case of Mfsetpos used with a positive value, we specify an offset into the song to get to the new play position. In the case of Mfsetpos used with a negative value, the offset is from the present play position. Refer back to this figure as you work through this chapter.

Altering System Settings for User Interaction

The two commands

```
set space off
set esc off
```

are system control commands. When you first run a GRASP script, the space bar acts as the pause key, freezing playback of the script. Similarly, the default key for quitting the program is the (ESC) key. In most programs, the requirement is for more

> ### PLAYING A SONG LIST
>
> The MIDI player can play songs from a play list. The songs are loaded into memory as needed. We don't cover this function in *Multimedia Creations*. The manual that comes with the commercial release of the program details all the functions of the player, as well as how to access them through the programming interface.

sophisticated interaction than this, since we have a number of events occurring at once: our virtual tape recorder is running, a virtual clock is ticking away, and cues are being recorded and stored in memory. In the case of the (ESC) key, we create a special routine that is executed when the user presses (ESC) to quit the program. We'll look at it a little later, but the essence of it is that it stops the song from playing and queries the user about saving cues to disk. If we did not create this branch to a special exit routine, the script would simply exit back to the editor, and any cues that you have entered would be lost.

Making the Program Interactive

The main loop of the program illustrates another method of implementing user interaction. Just before we enter the main loop, we establish the relationship between the PLAY/D clock and the running time (or song time) that will be shown on the screen:

```
; Set first cue to start of song.
      mfplay
      mstimer
      global startime @0
```

Mfplay starts the song playing. We make a call to PLAY/D to find out the current time. We then "zero" the software clock we'll use to keep track of our position in the song. PLAY/D's timer will keep running regardless of how often we stop, start, or rewind the song. So we display a clock on-screen that reflects the running time of the song rather than the elapsed time on PLAY/D's timer. The main loop of the program implements this logic.

```
lp:
      showtime:
            mstimer
            global songtime @0-@startime
            disptime
            waitkey 0                              ; waitkey with zero
                                                   ;value
            getkey key
                  if asc(@key)==13 continue        ; Check for Enter
                  if asc(@key)==32 pausong         ; Check for Space
```

```
            if asc(@key)==32 pausong        ; Check for Bcksp
      if @cnt==99
            goto continue
      endif

  goto showtime
  continue:
  cue
goto lp
```

The main loop (between the "showtime:" label and the statement "goto show-time") cycles indefinitely, while constantly checking for the press of the (ENTER) key, the space bar or the (BACKSPACE) key. If one of these keys is pressed, the program branches to the specified label. If this is the first time through the loop (@cnt=99), we break out of the loop and go to the continue: label. That's because we want to display the first cue on the screen to mark the beginning of the song. This will be useful for aligning the first visual to the beginning of the song. GRASP does not have a program flow structure such as C's "do while" loop, which loops until a condition is met. The Goto allows us to escape the arbitrary loop.

Using Getkey for User Interaction

Let's take a closer look at the way we use the Getkey command in the loop. Getkey always follows a Waitkey command. Here Waitkey has a value of 0 because we do not want the program to pause at this point—we're using it because the Getkey command demands it.

The syntax for Getkey is:

```
getkey variable
```

where *variable* is any valid variable name. It's usually followed by a conditional if

```
if asc(@key)==val label
```

where val is the ASCII value of the key pressed. The variable you name after the getkey command is used to store the ASCII code of the next key the user presses. Once this is done, you can use the variable name in an if statement to check it against the values of the special keys to which you want your program to respond. The asc(string) GRASP function returns the ASCII value of the specified string. If the key pressed was a function key or (ALT) key combination, two bytes are returned by *Getkey,* the scan code in the first byte and the ASCII value in the second byte. See a DOS reference text for a list of scan codes.

ASCII and GRASP Conversion Functions

A little later in this chapter, we'll encounter another GRASP function

```
chr(value)
```

that translates an ASCII decimal value into an ASCII character. Computer programming languages provide means for storing information in either character or number format. This is a convenience for humans, since at the machine level, the computer is entirely numerical in its operation. A standard has been developed for assigning meaning to the most common symbols stored by computers. The standard is called ASCII, or the American Standard Code for Information Interchange. It is a set of 95 printable characters and 33 control codes. ASCII characters and control codes can be expressed in a variety of notations: octagonal, hexadecimal, character, or decimal. (There is a standard called "extended ASCII," but it is not universally supported.) GRASP provides the following functions that convert ASCII characters and codes from one form to the other:

asc(string)	converts characters to decimal notation
chr(value)	converts decimal notation to characters
hex(value)	converts decimal to Hex equivalent

We could have used the When command in place of the Getkey command, but it's usually good practice to use Ifkey or Getkey in place of the When command. The When command interrupts program flow and causes a branch to another part of the program or another script. This can get you into trouble, because you can't determine beforehand what the system settings are or what pictures, clippings, fonts, or DFFs are loaded in buffers. You can save these settings (as we will show shortly), but it makes your program a lot more complicated than it would be if you used Ifkey or

---

GETKEY AND THE KEYBOARD BUFFER

The computer system keeps information about keypresses in a special area of memory called the *keyboard buffer*. It's this area that GRASP checks to see which key was pressed after the last Waitkey command. It assigns the value of that key to the variable you declare. You can then check that variable to see if it corresponds to the key you want to check for. The command

```
if asc(@key)==13 continue
```

compares the value of the key pressed to ASCII 13, which is the scan code value for the enter key. The function

```
asc(string)
```

converts the value assigned to the variable into decimal ASCII format so that it can be compared to ASCII value 13. There's a list of scan codes and their ASCII values at the back of most MS-DOS reference or programming books.

Getkey in the place of a When command. The Ifkey command is similar to Getkey. It's simpler, although more limited because only certain keys can be associated with the command. Pressing the (F2) key while in the editor lists the special keys associated with these commands. See our coverage of the Ifkey command in Chapter 3.

Here's another potential danger in using When: If you use the command Gosub with When, causing a subroutine to be executed, what may happen is that you will keep branching from subroutine to subroutine. If you descend too deeply (down past sixteen levels) you may crash. If you get the error message:

```
Mark/Loops nested too deep at line (number)
```

it means you have exceeded the limit. The culprit is usually the Goto command, although the Mark/Loop combination will also produce this error message.

Pausing the Song

The Getkey and Ifkey commands also cause program execution to jump to another part of the program without returning. For example, we use them in the main loop of the program. The Getkey command

```
getkey key
if asc(@key)==32 pausong
```

checks for a press of the space bar (ASCII code 32). If the Space Bar is pressed, program execution jumps to the pausong: (pause song) label. Here's what the pause song section of code looks like:

```
pausong:
        mfpause                             ; pauses song
        mstimer
        global songtime @0-@startime        ; current song time
        disptime                            ; calls display subroutine
        waitkey
        getkey key
                if asc(@key)==8 cueback      ; Check for Backspace
                if asc(@key)==43 cueback     ; Check for + key
                if asc(@key)==45 cueback     ; Check for - key

        mstimer
        global startime @0-@songtime
        mfplay
goto lp
```

This section of code causes the song and the "song time" to pause. If the user presses the (BACKSPACE) key, program execution will continue at yet another location in the script (cueback:), without returning.

Good programming design attempts to anticipate user interaction. We implemented additional choices in this routine. In addition to assigning the jump to cueback: to the (BACKSPACE) key, we also made the (+) or (-) keys cause a jump back to this label. When testing the program, we discovered that as users develop the habit of adjusting backed-up cues using the ⊕ and ⊖ keys, they would tend to reach for these keys before pressing the (BACKSPACE) key first. This shows the importance of testing programs. If the user chooses to continue again, a Goto command (goto lp) causes execution to jump back to the main loop.

Managing the Software Clock

We should note in passing that pausing the song was not difficult, we merely issued the call to PLAY/D (Mfpause). But pausing the song does not pause PLAY/D's clock, so we had GRASP store the current song running time at the moment when the clock was stopped. When the song is placed back into play, we establish a new 0 position on the software clock by subtracting the stored value for the software clock from the current PLAY/D clock time stored in the variable *startime*.

```
mstimer
        global startime @0-@songtime
```

No matter where program execution branches to, we just have to subtract the current song time from the current value returned by Mstimer to establish a new reference point for the clock.

Let's return to the main body of the script to see what happens when we call up the Help screen by pressing the (F1) function key. This will show some of the complications involved in using the When command.

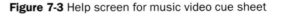

Figure 7-3 Help screen for music video cue sheet

Adding Help Screens to GRASP Scripts

It's a common convention to assign pop-up Help screens to the (F1) function key. Figure 7-3 shows the Help screen that that pops during the running of MUSIC1.TXT up when the (F1) key is pressed.

Here's a case where the When key is indispensable. We want to give the user the opportunity to get help at anytime during the running of the show. The best way to do this is to create a help script that is merged as each script is loaded. (Remember that the Merge command adds code from another GRASP script to the end of the current script.) We won't do that here because the program is very short and only has two modules. Instead, we'll place the help subroutine at the bottom of the script, where it would be placed anyway using Merge. When the user presses (F1), this is the subroutine that is run:

```
help:
          when esc pop out                     ; jump to out: label in
                                               ; calling routine

          mfpause
          mstimer
          global songtime @0-@startime         ; Current elapsed songtime.
          disptime

      ; saves current settings
          local offx @xoff                     ; saves current offsets
          local offy @yoff
          local colr @color                    ; saves current color
          pgetbuf p2                           ; saves current screen
          offset 0 0                           ; resets offsets

    ; builds box for help commands
          offset 3,-3
          color 0
          rect 200,165 440,315
          offset 0,0
          color 8
          offset 0,0
          rect 200,165 440,315
          offset 0,0
          color 7
          line 200,296 440,296
          mark 6
          line 0,-2 0,-2 r
          loop
          color 0
          box 200,165 440,315 3
          color 7
          box 200,165 440,315 2

     ; titles for help screen
          fload \grasp\ibm16.set 1
          color 14
          fstyle 8 2 3
          set center on
          fgaps 10 10
          text 0,285 "Help"
          set center off
          color 14
          fgaps 1 2
          fload \grasp\ibm14.set
          text 240,260 "Esc"
          color 7
          text 290,260 "Exit"
          color 14
          text 240,245 "Home"
```

```
      color 7
      text 290,245 "Start Over"
      color 14
      text 240,230 "Space"
      color 7
      text 290,230 "Pause"
      color 14
      text 240,215 "Bksp"
      color 7
      text 290,215 "Back up a cue"
      color 14
      text 240,200 "+/-"
      color 7
      text 290,200 "Adjust cue"
      set center on
      text 0,174 "Press Enter to continue."
      set center off
      waitkey

  ; restores system settings
      font 0
      offset @offx @offy
      color @colr
      pfade 0 p2
      pfree p2
      mfplay
      mstimer
      global startime @0-@songtime
      mfplay
      when esc goto savexit
return


out:
      pfade 0 p2
      pfree p2
      goto savexit
```

We covered this in the last chapter, but it's important enough to cover in further detail here. Basically, the help subroutine saves current system settings as local variables, saves the current screen to buffer 2, and places a Help box on the screen. It then waits for a keypress. When a key is pressed, the routine restores system settings, restores the screen from buffer 2, and exits. Restoring the screen removes the Help box from the screen.

In the very first line of the main script, we solve a potential problem with the subroutine. In the initial settings for the program, we assigned to the (ESC) key a branch to an exit routine:

```
when esc goto savexit
```

This exit routine saves the current screen as a picture file for review later. If we're inside the help subroutine when the (ESC) key is pressed, the jump to the exit sequence would save the Help screen. We don't want to save this screen. To avoid this, we use GRASP's Pop command to exit the subroutine and restore the screen that was current just before the Help menu popped up.

Using Pop to Exit Subroutines or Programs

Every time you branch to a subroutine, GRASP keeps a record of its position in the script before the subroutine was executed. This information is stored in an area of memory called a "stack." Think of the stack as a stack of plates in a restaurant kitchen. Each time the program branches to a subroutine, it places a plate on the stack. (If the plates grow higher than 16 plates, GRASP halts execution and puts an error message on the screen.) Each time a subroutine is executed and returns to the calling routine, the most recent plate is "popped" off the stack. (After all, in a busy kitchen, who grabs the plate from the bottom of the stack?) So plates are always taken away from the top of the stack.

Normally, the Return command removes the last plate from the stack. But there is a special command that allows you to pop off the stack without an explicit return. That's GRASP's Pop command. Pop's syntax is:

```
pop label
```

which, combined in the example with the When command, becomes,

```
when esc pop out
```

The Pop command causes program execution to exit the subroutine and continue at the specified label in the calling program or routine. It's similar to the Return command, except Pop cannot return values to the calling program. Also, Return continues execution at the point in the calling routine where it was called, whereas Pop jumps to a label, which can be anywhere in the calling routine. In this case we jump to a short routine that fades the screen stored in buffer 2 to the screen, frees the buffer, and then causes program execution to continue at the exit label. The short routine allows us to restore the screen as it was before the Help screen was placed over it.

```
out:
        pfade 0 p2
        pfree p2
        goto exit
```

Pop is a valuable command.

Let's continue reviewing the help subroutine. The commands that follow the opening line of the help subroutine pause the song, and save the current song time. Then the system settings that were active when the (F1) key was pressed are saved to temporary variables.

```
; saves current settings
      local offx @xoff                    ; saves current offsets
      local offy @yoff
      local colr @color                   ; saves current color
      pgetbuf p2                          ; saves current screen
      offset 0,0                          ; resets offsets
```

GRASP automatically creates certain variables that you may check in order to determine the status of system settings. In the listing available by pressing (F2) while in the editor, you'll see a complete list of these global variables. We use the variables for offsets and color here, but another important set of variables are the coordinates for the current window. (We reviewed window coordinates and their use in subroutines in the last chapter.) If you use the help subroutine included in this chapter in other programs, you'll want to include a way of handling window coordinates. Here it is:

```
local xmin @minx                 ; bottom left x position
local ymin @miny                 ; bottom left y position
local xmax @maxx                 ; top right x position
local ymax @maxy                 ; top right y position

window x1, y1 x2,y2              ; new window position in subroutine

window @xmin @ymin @xmax @ymax  ; restores original window
                                 ; coordinates
```

By default, the system window coordinates are equal to the pixel resolution of the current video mode. If you write a test script with the following code:

```
; TEST.TXT Writes maximum window coordinates of the screen.

video m
text @maxx$", "
text @maxy

waitkey
```

The following text will be written at the top left of the screen if you are in Video M mode (640x480, 16 colors).

639, 479

This corresponds to the x,y coordinates of the upper right corner of the screen.

Using the System Font

Notice the Font 0 command in the exit part of the help subroutine. Font 0 specifies the computer system font. We use this font in the time display section of the program for displaying time values.

Let's return to the main loop of the program and follow execution when the
(ENTER) key is pressed.

```
lp:
        showtime:
                mstimer
                global songtime @0-@startime
                disptime
                waitkey 0        ; waitkey with zero value
                getkey key
                        if asc(@key)==13 continue    ; Check for Enter
                        if asc(@key)==32 pausong     ; Check for Space
                        if asc(@key)==32 pausong     ; Check for Backspace
                if @cnt==99 continue
                        endif
        goto showtime

        continue:
        cue
goto lp
```

Notice that the main loop is a loop within a loop. When the (ENTER) key is pressed,
execution jumps from the inner loop to a label in the outer loop (continue:), after
which the cue: subroutine is called.

Creating the Cue Subroutine

The cue: subroutine is called when the user presses the (ENTER) key in the main loop
of the program. The main function of this routine is to update the cue count, display
the new cue number on the screen, and store the latest cue in memory. Upon exit
from the program, the user will be provided with the option of saving all of the cues
to disk. These will be used in the second module. The cue routine is quite long, so
we'll break it down into smaller parts.

When the routine is entered, we read the PLAY/D timer and use that value to determine how much time has passed since the song started.

```
cue:
        mstimer
        global songtime @0-@startime
```

The counter that keeps track of cues is now updated.

```
        ; variable for cue count
                global cnt @cnt+1
```

The next section of code anticipates an error condition and warns the user about it.
We check to see if the user has exceeded the program's arbitrary limit of 266 cues,
or two screens of cues. If the count has been exceeded, the program puts error messages on the screen and exits. The error messages flash, "Too Many Cues!" and
"Press Esc Key!."

```
if @cnt==267
        when esc
        offset 0,0
        fload \grasp\helvet15.set 1

        lp267:
        color 8
        rect 8,456 210,474              ; blanks message area
        color 0
        box 8,455 210,474               ; black outline
        color 4
        text 18,457 "Too Many Cues."
        waitkey 50
        ifkey esc exit                  ; check for Esc key
        color 8
        rect 8,456 210,474              ; blanks message area
        color 15
        text 18,457 "Press Esc Key."
        waitkey 50
                ifkey esc exit          ; check for Esc key
        goto lp267
endif
```

The cue limit of 266 is arbitrary. The cue count allows two screens to fill with cues, providing more than enough cues to time a MIDI song that runs about 3 minutes. You can change the code to specify a higher limit. The real limit to the program is determined by available memory resources in the computer. Setting a limit to cues and generating an error message when that limit is reached is good programming practice because it anticipates and solves a potential problem.

Notice that we unassigned the When key command attached to the (ESC) key at the beginning of the code section. This was not strictly necessary. Because we had earlier assigned to the (ESC) key a jump to the exit label, the Ifkey command (ifkey esc exit) is unnecessary. However, making the jump explicit in this fashion makes the program easier to read. Also, we may later create a condition where (ESC) does not jump to the exit label. The little bit of extra code here can save troubleshooting time later.

Updating Cue Values in the Cue Subroutine

Remember that the cue subroutine's main function is to update the cue count on screen and store cue values in memory. Here's the code that does that:

```
global cuename cue$@name                ; creates cue names
global @cuename @songtime               ; stores song times
fstyle 8 1
color 7
text 100,5 @cuename                     ; puts cue count on screen
global name @name+1                     ; updates cue name value
```

Time cues are stored as a list in memory. First we create a variable name for storing the cue (cuename), then we store the current song running time in that variable. Concatenating the string cue to the variable name (i.e., cue$@name) allows us to display and store the cue name in a legible form. Placing the word "cue" on-screen is an embellishment, but it does make the screen more legible.

The next section of code helps format the information on-screen.

```
if @cnt==120||@cnt==141||@cnt==162||@cnt==204||@cnt==225||@cnt==246
        offset 157 400 r
        pop showtime
endif

if @cnt==183
        pgetbuf p1
        color 1
        offset 0,0
        rect 0,0 639,435
        offset 7,410
        goto showtime
endif
```

We use the cue count variable to determine when we've reached the end of a column. If the count is at 120, for example, we offset cue display by one column (157 pixels) and start at the top of the row (400). These offsets are relative to our present position, at the bottom of the present column. If we've reached the bottom of the last column on the screen (183), we save the screen into buffer 1, cover the screen area under the title with a blue rectangle (effectively removing the last time display or cue from the screen) and position cue display at the first row of the first column (7410). Then we jump back to the main subroutine to display the current song time at the new position.

If neither test of the cue count indicates we've reached the end of a column or page, execution continues, with commands that move text output to the next cue position.

```
        disptime           ; subroutine for displaying songtime
        offset 0,-20 r     ; move down to next cue position
        global hilite 8    ; turn white highlight off if it is on
return                     ; return to calling routine
```

The call to the subroutine that displays the current song time (disptime:) is here because the cue subroutine is sometimes called from a part of the program other than the main loop. When the user pauses the program and backs up through the cues, the cue that is currently selected will have a white highlight around it. The variable hilite allows us to turn the white hilite on (color 15 or white) or off (color 8 or gray). By including the call to disptime here, we ensure hilite is turned off.

279

Displaying the Current Time on the Screen

If you worked through the last chapter, the routine that displays the current time on
the screen should be easy for you to understand. Let's review it.

```
disptime:
        color 7
        box 0,0 93,19 4                    ; gray outline box around time dis-
play
        color 15
        rect 2,2 91,17                     ; white rectangle (background)
        color @hilite
        box 93,2 150,17                    ; outline box around cue name
        color 15
        local hours abs(@songtime/3600000)
        local temp @songtime%3600000
        local minutes @temp/60000
        local temp @temp%60000
        local seconds @temp/1000
        local temp @temp%1000
        local hundreds @temp/10

        font 0
        fgaps 1 1 0
        fstyle 0 0
    ; minutes
        color 0
        text 4,5 ":"$dec(@minutes,2)

    ; seconds
        text 32,5 ":"$dec(@seconds,2)

    ; hundreds
        text 64,5 ":"$dec(@hundreds,2)

return
```

Notice that the color of the box around the cue name is determined by the global
variable hilite we just referred to. The current song time is also determined externally to this subroutine. The current time is measured in milliseconds, so this routine divides the total song time into hours, minutes, seconds, and hundredths of
seconds. The cues are then displayed using the GRASP function that converts variables to decimal numbers and displays them at a specified width:

```
dec(value,width)
```

Increasing or Decreasing a Saved Cue Value

In order to give the user more control over the process of recording and storing
cues, we provide the option of pausing the song, and then backing up through the
list of cues. The user can adjust individual cues by pressing the plus or minus keys.
As a convenience to the user, we've added the ability to pause the program by press-

ing the (BACKSPACE) key, in addition to the space bar. We implemented this after we found in repeatedly testing the program, that the tendency was to reach for the (BACKSPACE) key to pause and back up through the program.

Here's the pause routine again.

```
pausong:
        mfpause                             ; pauses song
        mstimer
        global songtime a0-astartime        ; current song time.
        disptime                            ; calls display subroutine
        waitkey
        getkey key
                if asc(@key)==8 cueback     ; check for Backspace key
                if asc(@key)==43 cueback    ; Check for + key
                if asc(@key)==45 cueback    ; Check for - key

        mstimer
        global startime a0-asongtime
        mfplay                              ; resume playing
goto lp
```

If the user presses any other key than the (BACKSPACE) or ⊕ and ⊖ keys, the program resumes. However, if the (BACKSPACE) key is pressed, execution of the script skips to the cueback: label. Backing up a cue is a lot more complicated than blanking out the current display line and backing text output up one line. All the variables that we have updated need to be decreased by one. Also, backing up a cue means "rewinding" the MIDI song to the specified cue. Let's tackle the problem a few lines at a time. First we blank out the current cue display with a blue rectangle.

```
cueback:
        color 1
        rect 0,0 150,19 ; blanks current cue display
```

Then we check to see if we are at the top of a column. If so, we back up display of the current cue to the bottom of the previous column.

```
; check to see if we are at the bottom of a column
if @cnt==120||@cnt==141||@cnt==162||@cnt==204||@cnt==225||@cnt==246
                offset -157,-420 r
endif
```

If we're at the top of the first column of the second page, we back up to the bottom of the last column of the previous page. Remember the screen we saved to a buffer when we originally cued past the first page? This is why we did it. It allows us to present the previous 183 cues to the user.

```
        if @cnt==183
                pfade 0 p1              ; screen previously saved
                offset 471,-420 r
        endif
```

281

What happens if the user tries to back up past the first cue in the first column of the first page? We warn the user that he or she has backed up to the first cue and then reload and run the program. Reloading the program allows us to reset the start-up settings for the script.

```
; warn the user that they have backed up to the first cue
    if @cnt==100
            when esc                        ; disable current key definition
            fload \grasp\helvet15.set
            fstyle 8 1
            offset 0,0
            color 8
            rect 14,455 209,473
            color 4
            text 18,457 "First cue!"
            waitkey
            link music1                     ; reload and run program
        endif
```

Now here's the main body of the "back up" routine. Backing up a cue means backing up all the values we've been incrementing. Notice the white highlight given to cues that we've backed up to. This is good programming practice, since it gives the user visual feedback on decisions made.

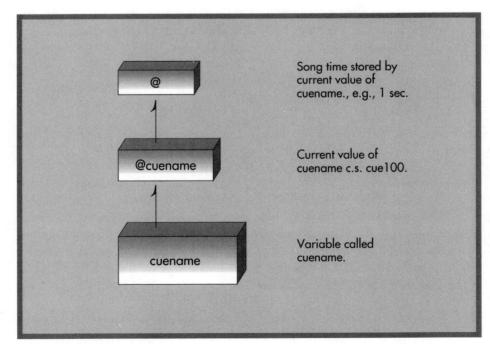

Figure 7-4 Double indirection

```
; decrease current values by one
        global hilite 15                     ; white highlight for cue
        global cnt @cnt-1
        global name @name-1
        global cuename cue$@name
        global songtime @@cuename
        offset 0,20 r
```

Notice that "double indirection" is necessary to access the value stored in the cue we've just backed up to. The variable @cuename stores the cue name, but we want to access the cue time pointed at by the cue name. Double indirection accomplishes this. It says "assign to the variable songtime the variable (@) stored in the variable (@) cuename." That's how we retrieve the cue time stored in our list. It not only gives us the correct time for the cue we've just backed up to, it also tells us where we are in the song we're playing. The variable songtime is used by the MIDI player to set the song position. It might be easier to remember how values are accessed by double indirection if you look at Figure 7-4. Think of double indirection as boxes within boxes. Indirection points to the first inner box. Double indirection points to the second inner box,

Now let's display the current (backed-up to) cue and reset the highlight variable to gray.

```
        disptime

        global hilite 8
        waitkey
```

We'll wait to see if the user wants to adjust the cue.

```
; now check to see if user wants to adjust cue, branch if so
        getkey key
                if asc(@key)==43 increase   ; check for + key
                if asc(@key)==45 decrease   ; check for - key
                if asc(@key)==8 cueback     ; check for Backspace
```

If the user wants to continue cueing, we'll reset our song time, save and display the current cue, set the playing position in the song, resume playing, and exit back to the main loop.

```
; save and display current cue
        mstimer
        global startime @0-@songtime       ; reset start time
        cue
        mfsetpos @songtime                  ; set playing position in song
        mfplay                              ; start playing
goto lp                                     ; return to main loop
```

If our user does choose to alter the cue, then execution continues at one of two labels, depending on the key that was pressed. If the ⊙ key was pressed, the following code section runs.

```
increase:
        global songtime @songtime+50
        global hilite 15
        disptime
        waitkey
        getkey key
                if asc(@key)==43 increase
                if asc(@key)==45 decrease
        global hilite 8
        mstimer
        global startime @0-@songtime
        cue
        mfsetpos @songtime
        mfplay
goto lp
```

We've set the amount incremented every time the ⊙ key is pressed at 25 milliseconds. That's 1/40 of a second, accurate enough for all but the most critical programs. By pressing and holding down the ⊙ key, the user repeatedly cycles through the code incrementing the cue time value. This would not be possible if this section of code were a subroutine. The stack would soon reach its limit of 16 calls. Once the user is satisfied with the change to the cue, the hilite variable is set to "off" or gray, the clock is zeroed, the cue subroutine is run, the song's playing position is offset to the current song time and placed into play. Finally, the program exits back to the main loop.

Let's look at what happens if the user chooses to adjust a cue by decreasing its time value. We need to take into account the case when a cue's value is decreased to the point where it is lower than the previous cue's value. Let's look at the way we solve this problem.

```
decrease:
        global songtime @songtime-25
                check                           ; check previous cue value
                if @songtime<=@0+10             ; if less or equal to,
                        goto cueback            ; jump to cueback: routine
                endif

        global hilite 15
        disptime
        waitkey
        getkey key
                if asc(@key)==43 increase
                if asc(@key)==45 decrease
                if asc(@key)==8 cueback         ; Backspace
                if asc(@key)==92 cueback        ; \
                if asc(@key)==73 cueback        ; PgUp
```

```
        global hilite 8
        mstimer
        global startime @0-@songtime
        cue
        mfsetpos @songtime
        mfplay
goto lp

check:
        local number @name-1
        local cuetemp cue$@number
        return @@cuetemp
```

Essentially, we check the current song time to see if it is less than the earlier song time of the previous cue. If it is, we send program execution back to the section of code that backs up a cue and its associated values. We've used a subroutine to check the time value of the previous cue, because we don't want to alter the values associated with the previous cue. By using temporary variables, we can free the memory they tie up when we exit the subroutine.

Sending Information to a Calling Routine

The check subroutine uses the Return command's ability to return values to send back the previous cue's stored value (return @@cuetemp) to the calling routine. By using the special variable @0 (zero not the letter o) we can use the variable in the expression that compares @songtime to the returned value. But notice that we add 10 milliseconds from the value returned.

```
if @songtime<=@0+10          ; if less or equal to,
        goto cueback         ; jump to cueback: routine
        endif
```

Why did we do this? In the routine that displays time on the screen (disptime), we round off the display of a millisecond value to the nearest hundredths of a second. Potentially two cues could be displayed on the screen with the same values. The cue values are actually different, even though the display of their values is not. We add 10 milliseconds to the value returned from the check subroutine to cause the cue to back up when the cues are within 10 milliseconds of each other. In most cases this will be close enough. If you have a very fast computer, you may want to adjust this value.

Saving the Cue List

There is one last major function to implement in the first module of the Cue Sheet Program. That's the ability to save the cues we've created to disk. We're going to save the cues as an ASCII file and show you the simplest way to do this. Our method involves opening a file and repeatedly appending cues to the file.

285

Let's go over the exit subroutine, where the save option is provided to the user. When the user presses (ESC), program execution jumps to the exit: label.

```
; Exit subroutine
exit:
        when esc goto done              ; redefines esc key
```

The (ESC) key is redefined so that users who want to quickly exit can skip to the done: label.

```
done:
                mfrewind
                exit
```

Here the song is stopped and we exit to the editor. If the user allows the program execution to continue, the message box is cleared and a new message is put up telling the user that the screen is being saved to disk.

```
savexit:

; Blanks message area, creates box, saves screen to disk.
        offset 0,0
        color 8
        rect 8 456 210 474              ; blanks message area
        color 0
        box 8 455 210 474               ; black outline
        fload \grasp\helvet15.set 1
        fstyle 8 1
        color 2
        text 18 457 "Saving cue1.pic..."

        mfrewind                        ; stops song playing
```

First we reset the offsets so we can modify the message box. We clear the message box and announce to the user that we are saving the current screen. Saving the screen to disk allows the user to review the cue list at leisure. First we test to see if the cue list has advanced to the second cue sheet. If it has, then we know that buffer 1 already contains the first screen. We save it to disk. Then we capture the second screen to the same buffer (to save memory) and save it to disk. We also tell the user the names of the files we are saving.

```
; Saves screen to disk.

        color 14
        if @cnt>183                     ; are we on the second page?
                psave cues1.pic p1
                pfree p1
                pgetbuf p1
                color 8
                rect 8,456 210,474      ; blanks message area
                color 2
                text 18,457 "Saving cue2.pic..."
```

```
                        psave cues2.pic p1
        else
                        pgetbuf p1
                        psave cues1.pic p1
        endif
```

The If/Else/Endif construction works well in situations like this. Let's review it.

The If/Else/Endif Construction

We've used the If/Else/Endif routine before, in Chapter 4. Here's the pseudo code:

```
if (value, variable or expression)
        command
else
        command
endif
```

If the condition following If is true, the first command is executed: if it is false, the second command is executed. If both are false, execution proceeds to the line after the Endif. Notice that the statement following else in our example saves the current screen to the buffer before saving buffer 1 to the disk. That's because the command Psave saves the current buffer to the disk. We must update that buffer before saving.

Once the screens have been saved to disk, we query the user about saving cues to a disk file.

```
; Blanks message area, creates box
        color 8
        rect 8,456 210,474              ; blanks message area
        color 0
        box 8,455 210,474               ; black outline

; Save cues to disk file?
        savelp:
                color 2
                text 18,457 "Save Cues? (Y/N)"
                waitkey 10
                ifkey y yessave "Y" yessave n done "N" done
                color 8
                rect 14,457 199,473
                waitkey 10
                ifkey y yessave "Y" yessave n done "N" done
        goto savelp
```

(Notice that we check for both lowercase and uppercase keys. GRASP's Ifkey command is case sensitive. We must surround uppercase letters with quotation marks.) We use the Ifkey command to determine how the user responded, and branch accordingly. If the user chooses to save cues to the disk, program execution jumps to the yessave: label.

```
        yessave:
                color 8
```

```
rect 14,457 209,473
color 4
text 18,457 "Saving cuefile.asc..."
cuesave
when esc goto done
color 8
rect 14,456 209,473
color 2
text 18,457 "Display Cues (Y/N)?"
waitkey
ifkey y cuedisp n done
```

"Cuesave" calls the save routine. Let's step through that routine. The first line redefines the (ESC) key so that program execution continues at the finish: label.

```
when esc goto finish            ; assures file is closed
```

This command *is* necessary, because we don't want the user to exit the cuesave subroutine before closing the file we are about to open. We'll show you that in a moment. Now we set up a local variable, which we will be using a little later in the routine. The name variable will be used to access the cue list by cue name.

```
local name 100                  ; initial cuename value
```

The next line sets up another variable. This variable will allow us to insert a carriage return and new line ASCII character after each cue in the cue list. This effectively places each cue on its own line.

```
local newline ""$chr(13)$chr(10) ; carriage return plus new line characters
```

Notice that we use the GRASP Chr function, which converts ASCII decimal notation to character notation. This is necessary because we are creating a text file. That's also the reason why we've preceded the carriage return symbol with a "null string," created by putting quotation marks around an empty string. This allows us to use the concatenation symbol to append the carriage return and new line characters to the file. We also use this method to create a carriage return to mark the beginning of the file. Here's the code that opens the file and writes a carriage return at the beginning of the file.

```
local add ""$chr(13)            ; creates carriage return variable
local ptr adr(@add)             ; points to location of variable
local fs create(cuefile.asc)    ; names file
    . write(@fs,@ptr,len(@add)) ; writes carriage return to file
```

We've opened the file and written a carriage return to it. Now we move to the next line by using our newline variable and a call to a subroutine that appends that variable to the open file.

```
writefil @newline
```

Here we use GRASP's ability to send variables to subroutines for processing. In this case we send the variable newline to a subroutine that writes it to the current file.

288

```
writefil:
        local ptr adr(@1)              ; pointer to @1 variable
        . append(@fs)                  ; opens filename for appending
        . seek(@fs,0,2)                ; seeks last item from end of file
        . write(@fs,@ptr,len(@1))      ; writes to file
return
```

These lines show the method for appending information to an existing file. The fs (file stream or file name) is the DOS file handle name of the file (CUEFILE.ASC). The Append function is used to open a file for reading or writing. The Seek function requires additional explanation. Here is its syntax:

```
seek(filename, byte position, relative)
```

Seek determines where in the file the new information will be written. If you know the exact byte position in the file where you want to write the information, you can enter its byte offset value as the second parameter. The third parameter, relative, allows you to make that byte position *relative* to either the beginning of the file (0), to the current position (1), or to the end of the file (2). Since we're adding the cue to the end of the file, we specify 0 for the byte position relative to the end of the file. We are by definition 0 bytes away from the end of the file when we are at its end! We then use the Write function (reviewed in the last chapter) to write the information to the file.

The @1 Variable

GRASP assigned @newline to the special variable @1 when it found it after the call to the subroutine. GRASP tells the subroutine how to find the newline variable by pointing at it with the special variable @1. In other words, the line "writefil @newline" told GRASP that @newline was going to be used by the subroutine, so GRASP made a local copy of the *value* of the variable. You might wonder why we didn't declare a global variable that could be accessed by the subroutine. Well, we could have done that. But remember that global variables when declared stay in effect and continue to use memory space throughout the running of the program. This approach allows us to be much more efficient with memory because the variables are destroyed after execution of the subroutine. Also, the unnecessary use of global variables is also considered to be poor programming practice because global variables can sometimes be changed in unpredictable ways by other parts of the program. Here's another example of the method, in this case, writing a text string to the file.

```
local add "cuelist:"
writefil @add
```

We put a label at the beginning of the cue list file because we'll be using the list of cues in the second part of the program. By adding cuelist: at the beginning of the file and dataend at the end of the file, we'll be able to load the file into memory and access the cue list through GRASP's data command, Databegin. It will be used in this form:

```
merge cuefile.asc

databegin cuelist

...     (body of script)

cuelist:
...     (cue times)
dataend
```

Let's continue with the save routine. After adding the cuelist: label to the file, we then run the main loop of the subroutine. This loop writes the cues to CUEFILE.ASC. We access the cue times through the variable @@cuename. By starting at cue100 and incrementing the cue name until we get to the end of the cue list, we'll be able to successfully write the entire list to the file CUEFILE.ASC. How will we know when we reach the end of the list? The global variable cnt tells us how many cues have been added to the list. All we have to do is decrease the value of cnt until we reach a value of 99 for cnt. That means we've written all the cues to the list. (This was the value for the cnt when we began.) Let's look at the loop.

```
again:
if @cnt==99
        finish:
        writefil @newline$"dataend"$@newline
        . close(@fs)
        note 40 20 10
        return
endif

local cuename cue$@name
local name @name+1

writefil ""$@newline$@@cuename
global cnt @cnt-1

goto again
```

Notice that we place each cue on its own line by concatenating the cue song time (@@cuename) to the newline variable. When the count reaches @cnt==99, exit from the subroutine is made. The dataend: label is added, the file is closed, and a note is sounded on the computer's speaker to let the user know that the save operation is finished, and to let you know that you've successfully written the cues to disk. If the user wanted to exit from the save routine earlier, pressing the (ESC) key would have transferred command execution to the finish: label. This allows us to close the file properly. If we had not done this, we would have immediately exited from the program and saved a partial list of cues without the dataend: label. There is no great advantage to saving the dataend label with an incomplete list, it's just good programming practice to explicitly close files that are open.

EXTENDING THE CUE LIST PROGRAM

If you have thoroughly mastered the material so far you will undoubtedly see an opportunity to extend the program by making the cue list easier to edit. It should not be too difficult for you to devise means of stepping back through the list to a previous cue, and either deleting or adjusting it. It will help you understand the art of programming by treating this as an exercise. We encourage you to do so.

As the program is written, it only works in Video M (640x480, 16 color) mode or higher. That's because of the way we determine when we are at the bottom of a column or at the end of a page. An improvement of the program would be to determine the number of cues that fit in a column by using the font and screen resolution rather than "hard coding" numbers like 120,141 and so on. You might also be able to use the modulus (%) operator to simplify this code:

```
colpos = @cnt % 21
        if colpos...
```

and so on.

The Link to MUSIC2.TXT

The user is now given the option of either continuing or exiting from the program. Let's link to the new script. Run the program, save the cues, and answer Ⓨ (*yes*) to the prompt about continuing. The program branches to the dispcue: label:

```
cuedisp:
        pfree p1 p2
        dfree 1
        ffree 1
        link music2 start
```

When the link is made to MUSIC2.TXT, an image wipes onto the screen. You see five columns rising from the bottom of the screen against a red, cloudy sky. There are five balls and piping in a cross shape suspended above the columns. The music begins to play. Individual balls light up according to the timing of the cues in the cue list.

The script MUSIC2.TXT is simple. Let's review it. The following code sets up the default conditions for the script.

```
video m

; MUSIC2.TXT Script for Displaying Cues

;set debug on

call checplay

; set up palette
        pload \grasp\cover.pic p1          ; background picture
        palette p1
        pfade 10 p1 200

; initial settings
        set esc off
        when esc goto exit

; load clippings
        cload bulb01.clp c1 1
        cload bulb02.clp c2 1
        cload bulb03.clp c3 1
        cload bulb04.clp c4 1
        cload bulb05.clp c5 1

; Software SMPTE routines.
        merge \grasp\midi                  ; loads MIDI interface script
        mfinit                             ; initializes PLAY/D
        merge cuefile.asc                  ; cue list built in music1.txt
        mstimer

; initial values
        global startime @0
        global cuetime 0
        global cnt 0

; Loads appropriate song
        if def(sndcfg)==1
                        if @sndcfg=="midi"
                                mfload \grasp\chapt05\leya.mid
                        else
                                mfload brew.cmf
                        endif
        endif
```

It's very simple to add the ASCII file we saved in MUSIC1.TXT to this script. All we do is use GRASP's Merge command, which effectively adds CUEFILE.ASC to the end of MUSIC2.TXT. The file already has the cuelist: label we'll use with the Databegin command, as well as the Dataend statement at the end of the list to tell GRASP where the cue list ends.

The main loop of the program cycles endlessly until we reach the end of the cue list. It consists of calls to three subroutines.

```
; Main loop of program
        lpcue:
```

```
        waitfor               ; wait for next time cue
        action                ; light a bulb
        update                ; move to next cue
        goto lpcue
```

When the script runs, a bulb lights when the current running time is greater than or equal to the first cue time on the cue list. Each time this condition is met, the script proceeds to the next cue on the list and waits until the current running time is once more greater than or equal to the cue time.

Here's the waitfor: subroutine.

```
; routine cycles waiting for next cue
        waitfor:
        mstimer
        local time @0-@startime
        if @cuetime>=@time
                goto waitfor
        endif
        return
```

The subroutine reads PLAY/D's timer, compares that to the time at start-up, and assigns the difference to a local variable called time. Earlier we declared the variable cuetime and gave it an initial time of 0. The cuetime variable is subsequently drawn from the cue list. Because on the first pass cuetime is less than the current running time, program execution exits from the subroutine back to the main loop. But on subsequent loops, the cuetime variable will exceed the current running time, in which case the subroutine will repetitively cycle until running time catches up with cue time. At this point, program execution returns to the main loop.

When the return is made to the main loop, the action subroutine is encountered.

```
; lights "bulbs"
        action:
        putup random(1,5)
        pfade 0 p1
        return
```

When the cuetime value equals or exceeds current running time, a lightbulb is lit. We let the random function pick which of the five clippings will be put on the screen, lighting the bulb. As soon as that is done, we turn the lightbulb off again by using pfade 0 p1 to snap wipe the original screen. Then we return to the main loop, where the update: subroutine is encountered.

```
; routine for stepping through cue list
        update:
        databegin cuelist              ; merged cue list from cuefile.asc
        global cnt @cnt+1
        dataskip @cnt                  ; moves pointer along list
        global cuetime @
;       pfade 0 1                      ; un-comment this line
```

```
;          text @cuetime              ; un-comment this line
           if @cuetime=="dataend" exit ; exit if at end of cue list
           global cuetime @cuetime-700 ; adjust cuetime
           endif
           return
```

Retrieving the Cue List

We introduced the Databegin command in an earlier chapter. Essentially, the command tells GRASP to seek a data list at the specified label. In this case the Databegin command seeks and finds the cue list we merged into the script by loading CUEFILE.ASC. This is a good way of adding short ASCII text to screens as well. Merge them as ASCII files, then use the Databegin command to access the text. If you un-comment the two lines in the subroutine shown above (by removing the semicolon at the beginning of the line), you'll see the cue times displayed on the screen as each bulb lights up. The times are displayed in milliseconds.

We use the Dataskip command to step through the cue list. Recall that dataskip moves a pointer around in a list of data items. Initially, we set up a global variable (cnt). Each time through the loop, the variable is updated. This approach was not really necessary, since the pointer is automatically moved to the next item on the list every time we use the @ variable to read a cue time from the list. However, it's good practice to do it this way. It makes the program easier to understand and easier to modify later. In developing programs that may use several lists, you will need to explicitly refer to Databegin labels and their data items.

We've used a simple method for determining when we are at the end of the cue list. If the item we've just read from the cue list is the text string "dataend," we exit.

Notice that we've adjusted the actual cue time read in from the cue list.

```
global cuetime @cuetime-700      ; adjust cuetime
```

We've done this to more precisely align the time cue to the bulb flash. When running the first script, we tended to hit the (ENTER) key seven-tenths of a second after we heard the cue in the music.

The exit routine pauses the song and slowly fades the screen to black.

```
exit:
       mfrewind
       pload \grasp\black.pal p2           ; black palette for fade out
       spread 1 2

exit
```

A slow fade to black is more pleasing than a sharp cut to black.

Enhancing MUSIC2.TXT

Our script is very simple. At the heart of it is the comparison between the current running time and the current cue from the cue list. By adding to the program the capability of adjusting, inserting, or deleting cues, the program will acquire the flexibility it will need to be a truly interactive multimedia production tool. A simple but cumbersome and time-consuming method is to use an ASCII editor (or word processor that saves in ASCII) to edit the CUEFILE.ASC file. Alternately, you could cue to the beats in the entire song, and then use the Dataskip command to jump to those cues you wanted to "hit" with visual changes.

TIMING MULTIMEDIA PRESENTATIONS

The primary benefit of the approach we've outlined in this chapter is the creation of programs that are independent of hardware running times. Even the world of professional video production is not a perfect world. Tape machines run at slightly different speeds. "Frame accurate" is not quite as precise as computers can get. Engineers have developed SMPTE time code as a solution to timing problems. It's not a perfect solution, but it's close enough to perfect for imperfect human perception. In this chapter we developed a solution for multimedia production, which is much more complex. Computer systems can run at vastly different speeds. Even the same computer can run at different speeds when processing demands vary.

We developed a kind of virtual tape deck using FM Software's memory resident MIDI player. PLAY/D's timer runs independently of the script and the computer hardware, much as SMPTE time code on a track of tape acts as an independent reference point. The program is forced to wait until the current running time derived from PLAY/D is equal to or greater than the cue time recorded in the cue list. If you're distributing multimedia programs across a wide variety of PCs, you'll probably want to develop a strategy for developing machine-independent programs. This chapter has helped prepare you for that challenge.

GRASP can be used not only to make interesting presentations, but to create useful tools to aid in program development. That's an important point and a good benefit!

PART THREE

Deeper into the Mix

8

A Game for Computer-Based Training

IN LEARNING GRASP, you've trodden the path taken by the early multimedia pioneers. You've learned to wrestle with the stubborn blocks and difficult passages the Intel-based PC offers to the novice animator and multimedia explorer. You've also learned how to create programs that are interactive. It's the data processing capability of the computer and the possibilities it holds for sophisticated interaction that set computer-based multimedia apart from the other media.

In this chapter, we will put you in the company with those masters of the language who are pushing the envelope on what GRASP is capable of creating. The applications and techniques they reveal here indicate just how powerful GRASP can be as a programming language. The programs we present can be modified and extended for your own

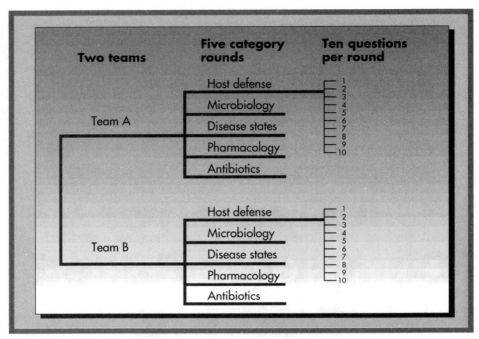

Figure 8-1 "The Final Challenge"

use. We certainly encourage experimentation! It's the best way to really master a programming language.

A Game for Computer-Based Training

"Stealth learning" is the high-tech way of describing computer-based learning that is a by-product of fun. Whether the student is a lone student or part of a group, games are a wonderful way to take the drudgery out of the learning process. Computer games are especially fun because they have the potential of being highly interactive. The user gets a response to his or her answer almost immediately. Also, it's much easier to suffer through being wrong when the opponent is silicon-based! In this chapter we're going to build a product knowledge game that has all these benefits built in. Product knowledge games test the participants' knowledge and encourage group dynamics, especially competitiveness. The multiple-choice format can be used for testing knowledge acquired from print materials or from computer-based training.

We'll use GRASP's advanced programming features to keep track of questions, answers, and scores. We'll develop methods for formatting text on-screen and pro-

THE AUTHOR

The author is Mabyn Martin from Reeves Technologies, Waban, Massachusetts (617) 969-2863. Reeves Technologies was founded in 1989. Mabyn has been designing instructional software since 1980. Mabyn uses GRASP for custom computer-based training software and demo disks. "The Final Challenge" originated with CBE Services, Inc., as a variation on its Knowledge Quest software for schools. It was originally programmed in C. Mabyn converted the game to GRASP, a natural for a program of this type. It makes changing the program easier and makes the addition of multimedia sound and moving image potentially much simpler.

viding interactive feedback to team players. We'll use GRASP's graphics programming features to create backgrounds and display questions and results.

THE OVERALL DESIGN

The game is played by two teams, Team A and Team B. The game is divided into five category rounds. Each round has ten questions each. Figure 8-1 shows the layout of the game.

Only the first round (Host defenses) is presented in this chapter. (As you will see, adding more rounds and questions is easy.) The game has provisions for a timer (60 seconds per question), but it is disabled here. You can activate the timer by removing the semicolons that comment it out. Figure 8-2 shows the code flow of the program.

The program is composed of three scripts. The main routine (in GAME.TXT) initializes the variables used in the program, introduces the game, puts up the main scoreboard, and calls the second script (CATEGORY.TXT). The second script, CATEGORY.TXT, displays questions and checks user answers, scores answers, and returns to the calling script (GAME.TXT). (The questions and answers were stored in simple ASCII data files. Only the data file associated with the first category, HOST.TXT, is provided here. It is merged with CATEGORY.TXT at run time.) At the end of the game, the grand total is posted and the winning team is named. Notice how the first script calls the second and the third is merged into the second.

The program shows its roots in the C language in its structured, modular format. The program is divided into subroutines that are devoted to specific functions. Variables are created and their values are passed back and forth between routines. Mabyn's program is an excellent follow-up to our last chapter and is worthy of study for its efficient design and sophisticated use of variables.

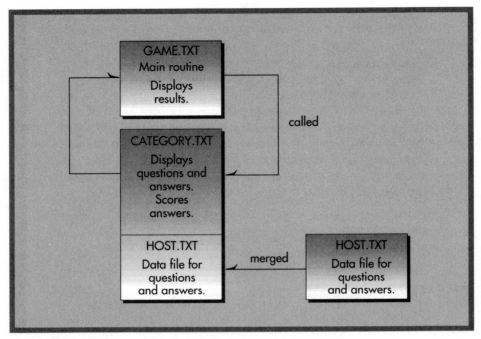

Figure 8-2 The three scripts of "The Final Challenge"

KEEPING TRACK OF GAME INFORMATION

You'll find the script for GAME.TXT in the GRASP directory. Load and run the program.

The video mode employed by the game is CGA (320x200, 4 colors), a mode we haven't used in the book. This makes the program very fast, and highly portable. It can be modified for high-resolution display. (We tell you how in the accompanying box.) At the time the game was created, the common denominator among client machines at business meetings was CGA. Also, CGA has very large text that makes small monitor screens easier to read at a distance. The main routine is found in the first of three scripts, GAME.TXT. The program begins by setting the video mode, and the CGA colors used for the background and foreground.

```
; GAME.TXT Product Knowledge Game main script.

    video a             ; CGA 4-color mode
    mode 0 3            ; sets the background and foreground colors
                        ; in CGA

    pfree p1            ; precaution: frees memory
```

Then variables are declared and given values.

```
set catnum 0          ; variable indicating category number (example uses only one)
set score 0           ; variable used for keeping total of correct answers
set ctr 0             ; variable used in different routines for "counting"
set qnum 0            ; variable used for numbering questions
set rndcnt 0          ; variable for numbering category rounds
;set totsec 60        ; beginning time for each round in seconds (not used)
```

Keeping track of categories, questions, answers, scores, and totals is the central problem a game of this kind must solve. The program does this elegantly. Refer back to Figure 8-1 to keep track of the structure of the game. Sequentially numbered variables are created for storing and displaying team scores for each category round. You can get another view of the structure of the game by looking at the main scoreboard put up by GAME.TXT. Figure 8-3 shows this screen.

We only play the first category round (Host defenses), but it does take us through the entire cycle of the game. The category round scores that are tallied at the end of the game are put on this screen.

CHANGING THE RESOLUTION

The program would not be too difficult to re-create at a higher resolution. Besides changing the video mode letter from Video A to one of the higher-resolution modes, the pictures and clippings in the program have to be created at the higher video resolution. Some of the commands refer specifically to locations on a CGA resolution screen, such as the command in GAME.TXT that establishes the initial settings for where text is put up:

```
local x 101 y 101 x2 151
```

Video A's spatial resolution is 320x200. It would have to be scaled up to VGA's 640x480 spatial resolution. Coordinates ultimately will depend on how you lay out the screen for your game. Of course the program's color choices would have to be mapped for the video mode you select. Your choice of text will also affect the layout and spacing of text. For example:

```
set y @y-15
```

is the line in the main script (GAME.TXT) that moves text output down a row during play. You might have to increase the 15 to 20 or 30 to accommodate a large VGA font.

The program also contains commands that blank out previous scores on-screen with color rectangles generated by GRASP's Rect command. There are other Text and Box commands that are specific to Video A's screen resolution.

303

The next section of code in GAME.TXT creates the variable that will hold the score for each of the category rounds. It's these scores that are put up on the screen you see in Figure 8-3.

```
mark 5
   set ctr @ctr+1          ; number created for each of 5 categories
   set "a"$@ctr 0          ; "a" team scores, initialized to zero
   set "b"$@ctr 0          ; "b" team scores, initialized to zero
loop

   set ctr 0               ; set counter back to zero
```

The loop uses concatenation to create the variables assigned to each team's category scores (Figure 8-4). If you look at Figure 8-1, you can see what the loop is effectively doing. It's taking the team's letter (A or B) and adding another variable (1 through 10) to it through concatenation. The first variable is surrounded by quotation marks to tell GRASP that the expression should be evaluated as a string. The second variable, ctr, is updated each time the loop is processed. Because the first variable is a string, the second variable is converted to a string by GRASP. The first string variable created by the loop is *a1* and the last one is *b10*. Remember these are variables that will eventually store the each team's score at the end of a round. That's why they are explicitly given a value of 0 at this point.

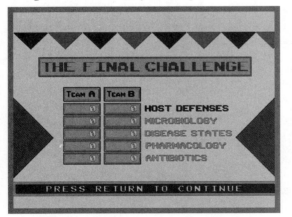

You'll see these variables listed at the end of the program as @a1, @a2, @a3, @a4, @a5, @b1, @b2, @b3, @b4, @b5. By creating the variables this way, we can expand or shorten the game easily—all we have to do is change the loop count (mark 5).

Figure 8-3 The main scoreboard of "The Final Challenge"

Storing Category Names in a List

Next, category names are assigned to variables. By concatenating category names with numerical values, we are able to use loops and expressions to keep track of where we are in the program. This is important because the program creates many loops, loops within loops, and branches to subroutines that have loops. This is a good use of GRASP advanced programming features. Here's the routine that creates the list of category names.

```
databegin labels              ; data list below: HOST MICRO DIS PHARM ANTIB
mark 5
  set ctr @ctr+1              ; local counter created for concatenating...
  set "cat"$@ctr @            ; category number created and assigned label
                             ; e.g. "HOST" for the first round
loop
set ctr 0
```

By using loops to define variables, Mabyn has made the program flexible, and reusable! We can easily change the category names by changing the data list. Here's the data list GRASP finds further along in the script.

```
labels:
    "Host" "Micro" "Dis" "Pharm" "Antib"
dataend
```

Now that GAME.TXT has created the variables required for the game, we start by putting up the introductory screens for the game.

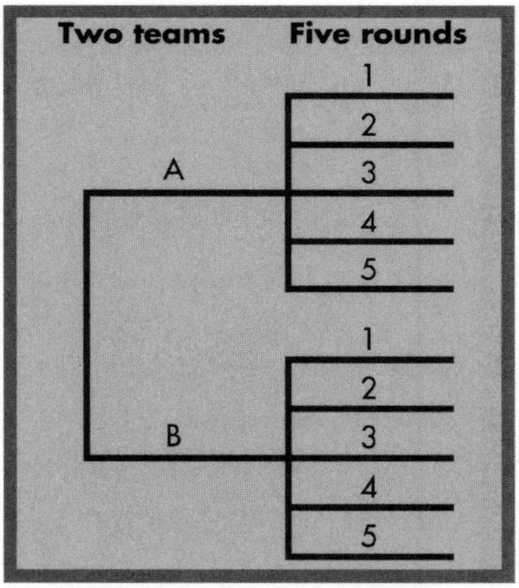

Creating the Game Introduction Screens

The screens that introduce the game to participants are processed by a subroutine.

```
gosub intro
```

Figure 8-5 shows the game's title screen.

Here's the subroutine found after the exit point in the script. Notice how the text is formatted. The text is "poured" into a window, which confines it to an area of the screen.

Figure 8-4 Organization of the game

```
INTRO:
    pfree p1                           ; precaution
    pload fctitle.pic p1               ; "The Final Challenge" title screen
    pfade 22 p1 100

    waitkey
    pfree p1
    getkey k name                      ; pressing F1 allows reviewer to test game
    if @k==F1
        call category quesbegin "test" ; branches to category script
                                       ; sends test variable
            pop alldone                ; returns from branch and pops to exit routine
    endif

    pload patt p1                      ; pattern around text box
```

```
    pfade 23 p1 100
    pfree p1

    window 53,40 266,166                    ; confines text to window in text box

;The text that is flowed into the window now follows.

    color 3
    text "Welcome to The Final Challenge.
Your team will answer 10 questions in a round and score points. If your answer is
correct, your score will increase by 100 points.

If your answer is not correct, your score will decrease by 50 points.

The score will display on each screen."

    waitkey

    color 0
    rect 53 40 266 166                      ; blanks out text screen
    window 53 47 264 161
    color 3
    text "At the end of the round, the next team will have a chance to compete.

In every topic, each team will compete twice.

The game will stop after each topic and report the scores for both teams."

    waitkey

    color 0
    rect 53,47 264,161
    window 53,47 264,161
    color 3
    text "The questions in the final topic will be worth 200 points.

After all 5 topics are completed by both teams, total scores will be reported.
The team having the most points wins the game.

        GOOD LUCK!"
  waitkey
return
```

After the return to the main body of the script, GRASP proceeds to the next section of code. It's the main loop of GAME.TXT.

Creating the Main Loop Routine of the Game

The main loop originally had five loops that processed five categories. The principal function of the loop is to update the current category number, display accumulated category scores, and branch to category questions, answers, and scores. When return is made to this loop from CATEGORY.TXT script, exit is then made to done: label. There a final tally is made and the winner is announced.

```
mark 1                          ; Original game had five loops/categories.
   set catnum @catnum+1         ; increments category number
   window                       ; ensures window is set to full screen
   gosub dispscore              ; subroutine displaying current score
   gosub qscreen                ; displays questions bkgrd screen
   call category quesbegin      ; Branches to category script at label.
loop

   gosub done                   ; goes to exit routine after last loop

exit
```

This loop is similar to the main( ) function in a C program, although the analogy is not perfect because program execution at run time begins at the first line in a GRASP script, while in C program execution at run time begins in the main( ) function. However, the GRASP program is similar to a C program, in that the flow of the action of "The Final Challenge" game is controlled by a main routine and specific functions are assigned to subroutines. This divides the program into manageable portions.

Figure 8-5 "The Final Challenge" title screen

The first thing that happens in the loop is the category number is updated. This is redundant in our example, since the first category is the only category functional. However, you can see how categories can be added or subtracted from the game by increasing or decreasing the loop count. The @catnum variable that is updated will be used by the called script, CATEGORY.TXT, to determine what category questions and answers to process. First we issue a Window command. This ensures that a previously issued Window command is not still active and is a useful precaution.

Calling the Routine Displaying the Score

After the Window command, the dispscore: subroutine is called. This subroutine posts the current accumulated scores for the category. The first line in the subroutine uses the list of category names created earlier to process the category statistics. Notice that because the catnum (category number) variable is updated each cycle through the loop, we'll be assured of selecting the right category name from the original data list.

```
dispscore:
    set cat @("cat"$@catnum)        ; Accesses list of categories set up earlier.
                                    ; E.G. First category named "HOST."
    window
    pfree 1
    pload fcselnew.pic 1            ; category selection/score board screen
    pfade 23 1 100
    pfree 1
    color 0
    local x 101 y 101 x2 151        ; initial settings for where text is put up
    local ctr 0
```

Refer back to Figure 8-3 to see the screen where scores are displayed. The background image is a GRASP PIC file that can be created in other styles and resolutions. The dispscore: score display subroutine has its own loop:

```
; Initially all scores are zero.
    mark 5                          ; five categories
      set ctr @ctr+1                ; counter number for each category
      local ln len(@(a$@ctr))       ; figures out width of "a" team score
      text @x-@ln*8 @y @(a$@ctr)    ; where to put category "a" team score
                                    ; uses indirection to access team score
      local ln len(@(b$@ctr))       ; figures out width of "b" team score
      text @x2-@ln*8 @y @(b$@ctr)   ; where to put category "b" team score
      set y @y-15                   ; move down a row to next category
    loop
```

In the full version of the program, the loop is processed five times to reflect the five categories of the game. Each loop cycle puts each category's score up on the screen. Notice how scores are lined up in columns by first determining their length and then subtracting that from the default x position. Recall that the Len(string) function returns the number of characters in a string. The expression @x-@ln*8 is an example of GRASP's use of precedence in determining what part of the expression is processed first.

Here the number returned by the Len ( ) function (in the first loop the 0 score has one character) is multiplied by eight first, and the result (8) is subtracted from the x variable (101). The text is therefore put up at 93, 101. If the score was 50, the

---

OPERATOR PRECEDENCE

Precedence is the order in which GRASP will evaluate an expression. When GRASP encounters the expression @x-@ln*8, @ln will be multiplied by 8 and then subtracted from @x. That's because the * symbol has precedence over the - symbol. While in the GRASP editor, press (F2) and page down to the Operators Listing to see the listing for GRASP operator precedence.

Len ( ) function would have returned 2, GRASP would have multiplied this figure by 8, and subtracted the result (16) from the x position (85). Since the width of the font is 8 pixels, this would cause the score of 50 to be shifted over to the left by one character, so that if it followed a 0 score, the zeros would line up in the column. The same method is followed in putting up B Team's score, only a different default x position is used, x2. This places B Team's score in a different column. Finally, the y position is decremented by 15 pixels, to move text output down one row to the next category's level. Here's the code again.

```
; Initially all scores are zero.
  mark 5                        ; five categories
    set ctr @ctr+1              ; counter number for each category
    local ln len(@(a$@ctr))     ; figures out width of "a" team score
    text @x-@ln*8 @y @(a$@ctr)  ; where to put category "a" team score
                               ; uses indirection to access team score
    local ln len(@(b$@ctr))     ; figures out width of "b" team score
    text @x2-@ln*8 @y @(b$@ctr) ; where to put category "b" team score
    set y @y-15                 ; move down a row to next category
  loop
```

The variable a$@ctr stores the current score for A Team's category questions. Notice how it is enclosed in brackets when the indirection symbol @ is employed: @(a$@ctr). This ensures that GRASP processes the expression properly. You'll get an error message if you enter @a$@ctr, since GRASP will think that you are concatenating @ctr to @a (the variable a) instead of concatenating the variable ctr (@ctr) to the letter a.

The name of the category is placed on the screen using a clipping. Then return is made to the main loop of GAME.TXT.

```
cload @cat c2 1 0          ; clipping highlighting category name
                          ; e.g. "HOST"

putup 0 0 c2
cfree c1 c2

waitkey

return
```

Generating the Question-and-Answer Screen

Processing continues in the main loop. The next command encountered is the qscreen: subroutine that displays the background screen for the question and answer rounds.

```
gosub qscreen          ; displays questions bkgrd screen
```

Figure 8-6 shows what that screen looks like. The first question is on the screen. The code that displays this screen is simple:

```
qscreen:
  pfree p1
  pload qscreen p1
  pfade 23 p1 100
  pfree p1
return
```

Branching to the Second Script

The next line in the main loop routine branches to the label quesbegin: in CATE-GORY.TXT.

```
call category.txt quesbegin
```

Creating the Test Subroutine

This is the beginning of CATEGORY.TXT.

```
; CATEGORY TEXT Script for category question and answers.

;video a                      ; used in development only
quesbegin:

if @1=="test"
  gosub test
endif
```

When GRASP loads and begins processing CATEGORY.TXT at the quesbegin: label, it first checks to see if a parameter (@1) has been passed to it by GAME.TXT. If the program is being tested by a reviewer, the (F1) key would have been pressed

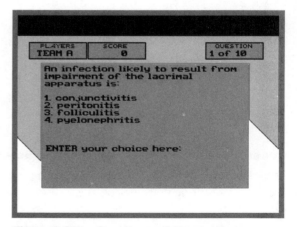

when the title screen to the game is up and this parameter would have been passed. This allows the game to be reviewed during development without actually being played. If the parameter is present, GRASP will branch to the test: subroutine at the end of CATEGORY.TXT. The test routine is shown below. We've commented out the other four category choices.

Figure 8-6 The Question-and-Answer screen

```
test:
clearscr 3
color 0
window 40 50 300 150
text " Which category do you wish to
```

```
test?

 1. Host defenses "
; 2. Micro                           ; other categories disabled in this version
; 3. Disease States
; 4. Pharmacology
; 5. Antibiotics
text "


Please press a number."
waitkey
getkey k name
;set catnum @k                       ; original version looked for nos. 1 - 5
set catnum 1                         ; added for this version
;set totsec 600                      ; disabled for this version
return
```

The routine takes the user through a mock session of the game. If the test for the
(F1) parameter indicates that the key was not pressed, processing continues.

Accessing Category Name Variables

The next line selects the appropriate category name from the list created earlier in
GAME.TXT.

```
set cat @("cat"$@catnum)             ; in our example finds "HOST" in data list
```

Notice that here the current category number @catnum is concatenated to the string
"cat" (short for category). Since we are currently at the first category, the expression
concatenates 1 to the string cat. Therefore @("cat"$@catnum) evaluates to @cat1.
The indirection symbol @ points to the value stored in the cat1 variable, which is
the text string HOST. When the names of the categories were originally created in
GAME.TXT, a counter variable was used to create the variables referencing category
names. Here's the code from GAME.TXT.

```
databegin labels                     ; data list is "host, micro, dis, pharm, antib"
  mark 5
    set ctr @ctr+1                    ; local counter created for concatenating...
    set "cat"$@ctr @                 ; category number created and assigned label
                                     ; e.g. "HOST" for the first round
  loop
```

In the first loop of the program, the original value of the counter (0) is incremented
to 1. Then the number 1 is concatenated to the string cat to produce the variable
cat1. It's this variable that is referenced by both sections of code.

Merging Questions and Answers with the Script

The next line encountered in processing uses the variable we've just created to load
and merge the appropriate list of questions and answers.

```
merge @cat$".txt"              ; This is text file (e.g. "HOST.TXT") with
                               ; questions and answers. Merges with this file.
```

The questions and answers for this category are merged as an ASCII text file. (In the last chapter, we loaded the cue list this way.) The questions and answers for each category can be easily created in an ASCII editor or word processing software that optionally saves in ASCII format. Each question and answer begins with a label and ends with a dataend statement. This allows each question, its parameters and answers, to be accessed in a loop. Here's what the first question looks like.

```
q10:
4 1 100
"An infection likely to result from impairment of the lacrimal apparatus is:

"
"conjunctivitis"
"peritonitis"
"folliculitis"
"pyelonephritis"
"Lacrimal glands produce tears to remove microorganisms and other eye
irritants.  Most often, pneumococci and staphylococci cause bacterial
conjunctivitis."
dataend
q11:
4 3 100
"Epithelial cells of the upper respiratory tract contain microscopic
hair-like projections called:

"
"fimbriae"
"flagella"
"cilia"
"pseudopodia"
"Smoking and air pollution inhibit the motion of respiratory cilia,
increasing the likelihood of respiratory tract infections."
dataend
```

Creating the Questions-and-Answers Loop

Now here's the loop that displays and processes questions and answers. First we set up variables we'll need in the loop. Teams A and B get one round each of ten questions.

```
set ctr 9                      ; Counter set at 9. Used for numbering
                               ; questions. Questions begin at ten and go
                               ; up. This avoids sorting problem.
set rndcnt 0                   ; Used to keep track of which round and
                               ; team we processing. This version has
                               ; only two rounds.
```

The question counter is initially set to 9 and incremented to 10 when the main body of the loop is entered. We start numbering questions at 10 because of the way numbers are sorted and incremented on a computer. If we had started at 1, instead of ten, the numbers would be sorted in this way by the computer.

1 10 2 3 4 5 6 7 8 9

instead of

10 11 12 13 14 15 16 17 18 19 20

Keeping Track of the Round

The round count (*rndcnt*) variable keeps track of which round of questions we are processing. It's initially set at 0 and updated to 1 when we enter the main loop. It is used in subroutines that determine the current team, such as the one that posts the current team's name on the screen:

```
tmlabel:
        color 0
        if @rndcnt==1||@rndcnt==3          ; round three applies to original game
                text 24 174 "TEAM A"
        else
                text 24 174 "TEAM B"
        endif
return
```

The example code uses only two rounds, so the second part of the expression is evaluated but never found in our example.

Creating the Main Loop of the Script

Now we enter the main loop of CATEGORY.TXT. The main loop processes each set of 10 questions, scores correct or incorrect answers, and keeps a tally of each team's score for the category. The loop is processed twice, once for each team. Let's look at the first part of the loop.

```
; two loops, one for each team
mark 2
  ;mark 4:              ; original version has 4 category rounds
  set qnum 0            ; sets question number at 0 at beginning of
                        ; category round
  set score 0          ; sets score at 0 at beginning of round
  gosub doscore        ; displays accumulated score on screen at
                        ; beginning of round
  set rndcnt @rndcnt+1 ; increments round count
  window
  color 3
  rect 235 174 295 182 ; blanks box at top right showing question
                        ; count (i.e. which question of ten)
  color 0
```

Displaying the Current Score

At the beginning of each round of questions, the routine first zeros the variable that counts questions (qnum). This is used to actually number the questions and answers on screen. The score is now set at 0 for the round. The doscore: subroutine places these statistics on the screen.

```
doscore:
        window
        local ln len(@score)           ; finds number of characters in score
        color 3
        rect 92 174 150 182            ; blanks current score box
        color 0
        text 135-(@ln*8) 174 @score    ; uses character count to determine
                                       ; horizontal position on screen
return
```

The score is 0 the first time through the loop.

The Loop within the Loop

Now execution progresses and encounters a loop within the first loop. This loop cycles through the ten questions that make up each round.

```
;inside loop where questions/answers/results/feedback are processed
        mark 10                        ; there are ten questions
            window
            set qnum @qnum+1           ; increments question number/count
            color 3
            rect 20 174 79 182         ; white rectangle for main question area
            rect 235 174 295 182       ; blanks question count box
            gosub tmlabel              ; places name of team at top left
            color 0
            text 235 174 @qnum$" of 10"  ; displays question number/count in box
            set ctr @ctr+1             ; starts at question 10
            gosub ques                 ; routine where question/answers/result
                                       ; are processed
        loop
```

Each time the loop is processed, the question counter is updated, the main question area is blanked, the question count box is blanked, the new team's name is posted, the new question count is posted, and the question counter is updated. Then the subroutine that places questions and answers on the screen is called. The branch to the subroutine is a good example of the way Mabyn approaches game design. The approach is "divide and conquer." Each major function of the program is isolated in its own subroutine, allowing the game to be easily modified and updated.

The Question Processing Loop

The call to the ques: now places the current question and possible answers on screen and tests for and scores correct answers. It then provides feedback to the user by highlighting the correct answer and commenting on it. We go through the routine twice, once for the question and once for the answer. This is the program's longest and most complicated loop. Let's review each part of the loop in turn.

ACCESSING THE QUESTIONS IN HOST.TXT

Earlier, we showed you part of the list of questions stored in the HOST.TXT text file and merged with the script. The Databegin command (used with a label) accesses the list of questions and answers. There are ten questions. The questions are labeled as q10: to q30:, with the first ten questions assigned to Team A and the second ten questions assigned to Team B. Dataend statements mark the end of each block of text associated with a question. The first line in the ques: subroutine uses a counter variable to determine which question will be processed in the loop.

```
ques:
;
set dat q$@ctr                    ; question label in HOST.TXT
```

The first time through the loop the expression q$@ctr is evaluated as q10, because the counter variable (ctr) was previously incremented from 9 to 10. The variable dat will be used by the Databegin command to find the current question label.

```
set flag 0
```

This command sets a flag. Flags are variables that can be checked in subsequent code to see if a certain condition is true. In this case, the flag will be used to determine whether this is the first or second time through the loop. If it is the first time through the loop, we know this is the question part of the round, rather than the answer part. When the flag is set later to 1, execution will be sent back to the doques: label rather than the ques: label. You'll see why later.

The next part of the routine prepares the screen for displaying a question and its possible answers by creating a box to place questions into, a box we'll call the main question area. (In subsequent passes through the loop, the Rect command will act to blank the previous question out.)

```
doques:                          ; we return to here in answer phase
window
color 3
rect 29 12 283 165               ; blanks main question area on screen
color 0
box 29 12 283 165 1              ; border around question area
local x 33 y 13 x2 279 y2 162    ; text area inside question area defined here
window @x @y @x2 @y2             ; uses preceding coordinates
```

Displaying the Questions and Answers

Now the question and the possible answers are accessed by the Databegin statement.

```
databegin @dat              ; accesses data block at label in
                            ; HOST.TXT e.g. first one is q10:
```

The following list uses the special GRASP "@" variable to read in the labeled data block piece by piece.

```
local num @                 ; first data item is number of answers in block
local corr @                ; second item is the right answer
local value @               ; third item is the score for correct answer
color 0
set count 0                 ; initialize element count
text @                      ; fourth data item is text block in HOST.TXT
                            ; that places question on screen
```

If we look at the first part of HOST.TXT, we'll understand what Mabyn is doing with the data command here.

```
q10:
4 1 100
"An infection likely to result from impairment of the lacrimal apparatus is:

"
"conjunctivitis"
"peritonitis"
"folliculitis"
"pyelonephritis"
"Lacrimal glands produce tears to remove microorganisms and other eye
irritants.  Most often, pneumococci and staphylococci cause bacterial
conjunctivitis."
dataend
```

The first data item GRASP discovers after the q10: label is the number 4. The second is the number 1, and the third is the number 100. Each of these data items is read from the data block in turn, through the use of the special @ parameter. Remember that the @ symbol here does not stand for indirection. When it is used on its own after a databegin command, it is interpreted by GRASP as a pointer to the items in a data list. Each time the data list is accessed, the pointer moves to the next item. Each block of text enclosed in quotation marks is treated as a separate data item. So the fourth @ sign refers to the question ("An infection likely to result from impairment of the lacrimal apparatus is:"). Note that the data block in HOST.TXT includes the space between the question and the possible answers. The quotation marks demarcate the data item here.

Displaying Answers on the Screen

The following loop displays the possible answers on-screen. Notice that the loop count used to put each answer on the screen employs the *num* variable.

```
mark @num                        ; sets loop equal to number of answers
  set count @count+1             ; used for numbering answers
  text @count                    ; puts answer number on screen
  text ". "                      ; adds period after answer number
loop
```

The *count* variable was created earlier for numbering questions.

Creating Window Coordinates for Text Formatting

The program makes clever use of a couple of system variables for formatting text on-screen.

```
window @textx @y @x2 @texty+@fontysize-1
```

The @textx and @texty system variables contain the current "cursor coordinates" on the screen. We don't actually see a cursor, but if we did, it would be located at this x,y position on the screen. Since the last x,y cursor position was the period mark we just put up on the screen, we have an excellent reference point for determining the left x coordinate of a text window. We then use the current y coordinate (decremented at the end of the round to move text output down one row) to determine the bottom left corner's y position. To determine the top right corner of the window, we use the current righthand limit to the text window, established earlier. Finally the window command uses the system variable @fontysize, which provides the current font height, to determine the height of the text window.

This may seem laborious, but after the algorithm is worked out for one passage through the loop, all the other text positions fall into line. And converting the program to use a higher video resolution is made easier.

Highlighting the Correct Answer

The next section of code is executed only on the second cycle of the loop, during the answer phase of the subroutine. (Note: as usual the spacing is important.)

```
  if @count==@corr&&@flag==1      ; ignored in question phase
    color 2
else
    color 0
  endif

  text @                          ; Answer from data block.
```

In the answer phase, the right answer is highlighted in red. Let's walk through the logic. All statements must be correct in a logical comparison that uses the logical and (&&) operator. The first part of the expression is evaluated to see if the current answer (@count) is equal to the correct answer (@corr). If it is, the expression continues to evaluate the expression on the right of the && operator. The value of the

317

flag variable (0 in the question cycle and 1 in the answer cycle) is compared to 1. If it is 1, then we are in the answer cycle. If both evaluations are true then the answer will subsequently be displayed in red. If one or both of the conditions are false, the default black color is used to put the answer up. In other words, the answer is not highlighted in the question cycle (@flag==0). The answer is only highlighted when this is the correct answer. GRASP's programming logic is used to add the highlight to the correct answer in the answer cycle of the loop. This makes the code economical indeed.

In the next lines of the ques: subroutine, the color is reset to the default of black, and text output is moved down to the next row.

```
color 0                          ; reset color to color 0
window @x @y @x2 @texty-2        ; moves text window down to next question
loop                             ; loops back to mark
```

When all the answers have been put up on the screen, the current cursor is saved for use later in the feedback routine.

```
local xsave @textx ysave @texty    ; saves text cursor coordinates for feedback  routine
```

Then the last block of text accessed by the data command is assigned to a variable used in the feedback routine. This text is the explanation associated with the correct answer.

```
set fb @                 ; assigns next text block (correct answer)
                         ; to fb variable for feedback routine
```

Another test is made to see if this is the answer cycle. If so, program execution branches to the feedback routine.

```
if @flag==1               ; Checks flag to see if we are in answer
  goto feedback           ; phase of routine, if so jumps to
                          ; routine where results are posted
                          ; for this question/answer.
endif
window
```

Testing for Valid Keypresses

If the previous test of the flag indicates we are still in the question cycle, then we need to prompt the user to respond to the question with the correct answer. Two variables are initially created and assigned null (or empty) strings. These will be used to check for valid keypresses when the team responds to the questions. Assigning null text strings to these variables is similar to "type casting" in the C language. It's a way of telling GRASP that the variables store text strings rather than binary numbers. The prompt label is where program execution will return to if user responses are invalid.

```
prompt:
set ans ""
set k ""
color 0
text 35 57 "ENTER your choice here:      "
```

The next line saves the current text cursor position for determining where to display the user's answer, i.e., after the semicolon.

```
local x @textx y @texty
```

The next line uses the current text coordinates and font size to create a rectangle that blanks out any previous responses that were incorrect, therefore causing program execution to jump back to the prompt: label. Note that the font size system variables are used for creating the rectangle.

```
color 3
rect @textx-(2*@fontxsize) @texty-2 @textx+@fontxsize @texty+@fontysize
color 0
```

The original version of the program gave the user 8 seconds to respond.

```
waitkey ;800
```

After waiting for user response, the key that was pressed is tested.

```
getkey ans name                ; assigns key pressed to ans variable
window
if @ans>0&&@ans<(@num+1)
```

The test checks to see if the answer is between zero and the total number of answers for this question; in other words, in the 1–4 range in the case of the first question (q10:). If so, the answer is placed on the screen. It is also stored in the ans variable for use later in the feedback routine.

```
   text @x-16 @y @ans               ; puts answer on screen
```

If not, a warning beep is sounded and processing jumps back to the prompt: label.

```
else
   note 100 40 50               ; warning beep
   goto prompt                  ; if answer not in range, redisplays
endif
```

Now that the answer is on the screen, it can be changed by pressing the (BACKSPACE) key. Pressing the (BACKSPACE) key redisplays the sequence from the prompt: label, effectively blanking out the current answer. Pressing the (ENTER) key continues execution. Pressing any other key causes a warning beep to sound and execution jumps back to the prompt: label. This prevents double-digit answers or other incorrect answers from being entered. Mabyn has done the kind of error-checking programs like this demand.

```
waitkey
getkey k name
if @k==backsp              ; If user presses back space go back
  goto prompt              ; to prompt. Allows user to correct answer
                           ; before pressing return.
else
        if @k<>return      ; If user presses any other key than return
          note 100 40 50   ; sound warning beep and return to prompt:
          goto prompt
        endif
endif
```

Note the <> symbol. The symbol is a comparison operator that says "not equal to."

Now that a valid (but not necessarily correct) answer is on the screen, processing continues. Here the flag is "flipped" to the answer cycle value and processing is sent back to the doques: label near the beginning of the ques: cycle.

```
if @flag==0                ; Are we in question phase?
  set flag 1               ; If so set flag to 1 and
  goto doques              ; jump back to label for answer phase.
endif                      ; Otherwise, ignore.
```

The cycle is now once again processed, this time with the flag set to 1.

Evaluating the Answer

At the end of the answer cycle of the loop, program execution jumps over the prompt section of code to the feedback: label. Here the answer selected and stored in the ans variable is compared to the value for the correct answer (stored in the corr variable). The routine assigns the result of the test in the stat (status) variable. The score is then updated.

```
feedback:
if @ans<>@corr             ; Compares the key just pressed to correct
                           ; answer. If not correct...
  set score @score-50      ; decreases score by fifty...
  set stat "w"             ; Status set to w (wrong). Used below.
else
  set score @score+@value  ; ...if correct, adds current answer correct
                           ; value to score.
  set stat "r"
```

Then the score is placed on the screen using the doscore: subroutine Mabyn created earlier.

```
  gosub doscore            ; Display accumulated score in box at top
                           ; of screen.
```

Giving the Team Feedback

The next section first blanks the area below answers, then tells the team if their answer was correct or incorrect, and finally displays an explanation of the correct answer on the screen.

```
window
color 3
rect 30 13 282 @ysave            ; Blanks area below answers.
color 0
window 33 12 280 @ysave          ; Window for text area.
if @stat<>"r"
  text @xsave @ysave-@fontysize "Incorrect.  " ; Placed in front of feedback.
else
  text "Correct.  "
endif
text @fb                         ; The block of text from HOST.TXT that
                                 ; was assigned to this variable earlier.
lp3:
waitkey
return                           ; end of ques: subroutine, returns
                                 ; to main loop for the team's round
```

At the end of the of the feedback loop, processing goes back to the main loop. Here it is again.

```
mark 10                     ; there are ten questions
      window
      set qnum @qnum+1      ; increments question number/count
      color 3
      rect 20 174 79 182    ; white rectangle for main question area
      rect 235 174 295 182  ; blanks question count box
      gosub tmlabel         ; places name of team at top left
      color 0
      text 235 174 @qnum$" of 10" ; displays question number/count in box
      set ctr @ctr+1        ; starts at question 10
      gosub ques            ; routine where question/answers/result
                            ; are processed
   loop
```

Upon reentry to the loop, processing is sent back to the mark label at the beginning of the loop, the question number is updated, and the cycle begins again. When the loop is finally complete, execution exits to the following command.

```
gosub round
```

The first part of the round subroutine blanks the screen area and announces the score for the round.

```
round:
window
color 3
rect 29 12 283 165                          ; blanks question box
color 0
box 29 12 283 165 1                          ; highlight around question box
local x 33 y 13 x2 279 y2 162                ; determines coordinates for text
window @x+20 @y @x2-20 @y2-10                ; window coordinates
text "Your score for this round was "$@score$", Team "
```

The next line tests to see if Team A has just played. If it has, it appends Team A's name to the preceding line and announces the next team's turn.

```
if @rndcnt==1||@rndcnt==3
  text "A.  The next team up is B."
```

Then Team A's current total for the category is updated.

```
set "a"$@catnum @("a"$@catnum)+@score
```

This looks complicated, but if the current round is round one, and Team A scored 100 points, the expressions would evaluate to "set a1 @1+100." In other words, "Update the score assigned to the first category to 100 points."

If this is Team B's round, the same calculations are made.

```
else
  text "B.  The next team up is A."
  set "b"$@catnum @("b"$@catnum)+@score
endif

Then the next team is prompted to play when ready.

text "

Press ENTER when you are ready to begin."
waitkey
return
```

Finally, processing returns to the main routine. This time a loop is encountered.

```
gosub round
loop
```

The loop takes us back to the outer loop. Remember that the outer loop controls which team is up. Here's the beginning of the outer loop again.

```
mark 2
  set qnum 0                    ; sets question number at 0 at beginning of
                                ; category round
  set score 0                   ; sets score at 0 at beginning of round
  gosub doscore                 ; displays accumulated score on screen at
                                ; beginning of round
  set rndcnt @rndcnt+1          ; increments round count
  window
  color 3
  rect 235 174 295 182          ; blanks box at top right showing question
                                ; count (i.e. which question of ten)
  color 0
```

At the end of the second loop, when both teams have played, exit is made to another routine. This is the wrapup: routine. This routine posts the final results for the category on the screen.

```
wrapup:

color 3
rect 29 12 283 165                       ; blanks main question area
color 0
box 29 12 283 165 1                       ; places highlight around question area
local x 33 y 13 x2 279 y2 162             ; text window coordinates
```

```
window @x+20 @y @x2-20 @y2-10              ; window for text
text "RESULTS FOR THIS CATEGORY"

text 53 120 "Team A:      "$@("a"$@catnum)  ; Posts accumulated score in
                                            ; variable set up to hold team A's
                                            ; category score.

text 53 100 "Team B:      "$@("b"$@catnum)
text 53 60 "Press ENTER to continue"
waitkey
return                                     ; returns user to point in GAME.TXT
                                           ; where this script was called
```

The final return marks the exit point back to the calling script. Let's look at the point in the main routine in GAMES.TXT where we originally came from, and to which we now return.

```
mark 1                            ; Original game had five loops/categories.
    set catnum @catnum+1          ; increments category number
    window                        ; ensures window is set to full screen
    gosub dispscore               ; subroutine displaying current score
    gosub qscreen                 ; displays questions bkgrd screen
    call category quesbegin       ; Branches to category script at label.
  loop

gosub done
```

In the original version of the game, processing would be sent back to the mark point four times for a total of five category cycles. Each of these cycles would branch to the category script to process questions and answers and update category scores. At the end of these cycles, program execution exits the subroutine and encounters the call to the done: subroutine. This is where the game's final results are posted and the winner announced. The code is relatively simple here—especially when compared to the deft coding of earlier routines!

```
done:
    gosub dispscore               ; display current score
    local x 101 y 26 x2 151       ; where to display exit key message
    window

    cload f10exit 1 1 0           ; Message clipping: F10 to exit
    putup 0 0 1
    cfree 1

    cload grdtot 1 1 0            ; grand total clipping
    putup 0 0 1
    cfree 1

    set agrand (@a1+@a2+@a3+@a4+@a5)  ; Tallies scores for A Team.
                                      ; Remember seeing the
                                      ; @(a$@ctr) variable earlier?
                                      ; This is another way of referencing
                                      ; the variables.
    set bgrand (@b1+@b2+@b3+@b4+@b5)  ; tallies scores for b team

    local ln len(@agrand)             ; Measures width of grand total score.
```

```
    color 0
    text @x-@ln*8 @y @agrand                ; Displays A Team's Grand Total
    local ln len(@bgrand)
    text @x2-@ln*8 @y @bgrand               ; Display's B Team's Grand Total

    if @agrand==@bgrand                      ; determines if scores equal
       cload tie1 1 1 0                      ; tie message
       cload tie2 2 1 0                      ; tie message highlight

    else
       if @agrand>@bgrand
           cload awin1 1 1 0                 ; A Team wins!
           cload awin2 2 1 0                 ; highlight
       else
           cload bwin1 1 1 0                 ; B Team wins
           cload bwin2 2 1 0                 ; highlight
       endif
    endif

mark 2                                       ; Special effect on tie or win title.
  cfade 5 28 145 1 100 40
  cfade 5 28 145 2 100 40
loop

cfree 1 2

almostdone:                                  ; loops until f10 is pressed
waitkey
getkey k name
if @k=="f10"
   goto alldone
else
   goto almostdone                           ; user didn't press f10 - send them back!
endif

alldone:
exit
```

SUMMARY AND EXTENSIONS

Mabyn Martin's product knowledge game readily demonstrates how powerful GRASP can be as a programming language. If you can master programs like this, you can make multimedia programs highly interactive.

The game can easily be modified to support higher video resolutions. Adding music and special effects (like a ticking clock for the timed version of the game) would add tension, heighten team involvement, and introduce more fun. The scripts could be incorporated in a larger training package that first taught the concepts and then tested the learner's comprehension of the material. Mabyn's use of GRASP's advanced programming features contains many nuggets that can be quarried and used in other interactive programs, such as her method of testing for valid keystrokes.

Creating an
Interactive Kiosk

In Chapter 4 we presented an interactive graphical menu system for the user who wants to browse through a software magazine at a leisurely pace. In some situations however, the speed of the magazine software interface would appear glacial to users. If the application doesn't have a captive audience (a kiosk rather than a software magazine, for example), speedy responsiveness is needed to keep the user's attention. A wait of more than a couple of seconds for the next screen feels sluggish and unresponsive.

In this chapter we'll present a menu system that will act as an extremely fast, highly interactive front end to an interactive kiosk.

THE AUTHOR

Murry Christensen, Art & Science, Inc., 34 Coryell Street, Lambertville, NJ 08530. Murry comes to multimedia design and programming from traditional media. His background is in typography and print advertising production, commercial graphics, multi-image and industrial theater (trade shows, conventions, meetings), corporate videotape and local-market TV commercials. Murry is a consultant and interactive media designer. He can be reached on Compuserve: 71521,2515

OVERVIEW

Murry's solution for a dynamic, resolution-independent menu system has the advantage of being highly portable across projects. In many cases only the video mode needs to be set for the menus to work in either CGA, EGA, or VGA modes. Screen coordinates and colors are adjusted accordingly.

The menu buttons do not use clippings, but rather GRASP's fast screen drawing features.

We've slightly modified Murry's system to show you how it can be used. We're going to create a simple kiosk that might be used at a zoo to help visitors browse the zoo's attractions before exploring the zoo in depth.

To Murry's graphical menu system, we've added a title (Sandpiper Zoo) and a clipping (a Sandpiper bird) to illustrate the theme. Even with the addition of the clipping of the bird, the menu forms quickly on the screen. We've also made the menu buttons active. Pressing a button causes a branch to a menu choice. Figure 9-1 shows what the menu looks like.

OVERALL DESIGN

Figure 9-2 shows how the scripts for the system are organized.

The menu system proper is composed of four scripts that divide the work of setting up the screen menus, evaluating user choices, and linking to four user "choices." (We've also included an Exit option.)

Figure 9-1 The menu

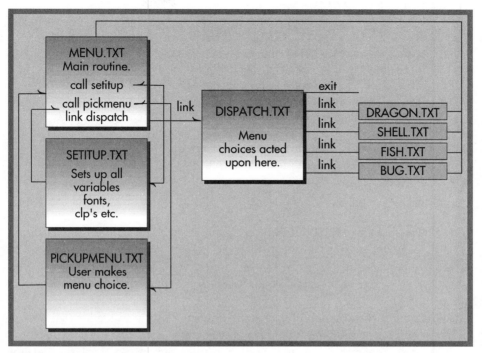

Figure 9-2 Organization of the the menu system

The main routine is found in MENU.TXT. It calls another script, called SETIT-UP.TXT. SETITUP.TXT sets up variables, fonts, video modes, and other system settings. PICKMENU.TXT contains the routines that check for user menu choices. DISPATCH.TXT evaluates choices made in PICKMENU.TXT and takes the appropriate action. DISPATCH.TXT becomes the hub point for the other parts of the application. From this point the user can choose one of five menu choices. Choosing one of the menu choices causes a branch to the specified script or an exit to DOS. It's a very well organized and thoughtful approach to menu design.

The main features of the menu system include:

- horizontal or vertical screen orientation of the menu buttons
- definable number of buttons
- definable spacing between buttons (fixed or equally spaced)
- definable origin for fixed-space buttons
- definable text on each button (single-line)
- definable screen resolution (standard CGA, EGA, and VGA)

The code is liberally commented and broken into multiple sections for easy comprehension and maximum utility. All variables have informative names, and the

PEEKING AHEAD

When you run MENU.TXT, the menu appears almost instantly. The background is blue. The Sandpiper bird appears. The title "Sandpiper Zoo" appears. Five buttons form on the screen: Bug, Fish, Shell, Dragon, and Exit. Normally an Exit choice would not be offered to a user. We include it here for your convenience. Selecting any of the other four menus causes the accompanying animation to run. After the animation runs, return is made to the Main menu. Notice how responsive the system is to choices.

code is designed for easy modification and maintenance. All buttons and labels are generated by code—not CLP or bitmap based—for compactness and speed of screen display and quick response to user interaction. Places in the code where you can add your own enhancements are indicated. Some suggestions for enhancements are included.

The modular construction of the system limits the overhead it adds to a GRASP program, since code is loaded into memory only when it's needed. It's a textbook example of good program design and excellent documentation. As usual, the code for the menu system can be found on the accompanying disk. The main script is called MENU.TXT.

CREATING THE INTERACTIVE KIOSK

The interactive kiosk for the Sandpiper Zoo gives visitors instant access to information about the zoo, its seashell collection, its "dragon," it's beetle collection, and its aquarium. We'll use Murry's code to implement the kiosk.

Like Mabyn Martin's product knowledge game in Chapter 8, the major functions of the menu system are called from one script, MENU.TXT. The loop draws a menu on the screen with either a horizontal or vertical orientation. One to six buttons are drawn on the screen. (We use five of them.) They can be equally spaced or fixed space. You can also control at which margin button columns begin.

Detailed Commentary

The first command we encounter when we run MENU.TXT is the call to the script that sets up the screen and program variables.

```
;==============================================================
;                         MENU.TXT
;==============================================================
```

```
        call SetItUp SetUp              ; set all variables, load font
```

In centralizing all variables, clippings, and font loading, SETITUP makes it easier to modify the system. The first command encountered in SETITUP.TXT is the one that sets up a variable for the screen mode.

```
;=====================================================================
;                         SETITUP.TXT
;=====================================================================
Setup:
        set ScreenMode G                ; specify video mode — note how
                                        ; other related vars are set later
                                        ; in this block
```

Mode G is the digital EGA 640x350 16-color mode. Note that this command does not actually set up the screen mode, it merely assigns the letter g to the variable ScreenMode. Later in the script, the following variables will be created and assigned values.

```
ModeG:
        global ScreenMode G
        global HRes 639
        global VRes 349
        global NumColors 16
        goto Next
```

These variables will be used in subsequent routines to determine screen drawing coordinates and palette colors. Try changing the "set ScreenMode G" command to other video modes, such as Video Mode M.

```
set ScreenMode M
```

Notice that the Sandpiper changes shape as you change modes. That's because of the different screen ratios of the different modes. The lines that divide the screen into four rectangles help us visualize the shape of the screen in the various screen modes. Video M creates a much more square screen than Video G's flatter shape. Incorporating pictures or clippings in the menu system reduces its flexibility somewhat. By changing the placement of the titles, size of buttons, and the size of the clipping, you can adjust the menu system to the video resolution you want to specifically support. See the end of the chapter for hints on how to make the menu system work with graphics in different screen modes.

After selecting the screen resolution, we now load the fonts we will need for text display.

```
; load clippings, fonts
        ; fonts
        fload \grasp\normal.fnt,1              ; button text
        fload \grasp\normal1.fnt,2
        fload \grasp\bold.fnt,3
        fload \grasp\bold1.fnt,4
```

The program loads four fonts. Next, we assign the clippings that will be used for the mouse arrow and its mask to global variables. (We covered mouse cursors and masks in Chapter 3.) Because it is the name of the cursor that is being assigned here, adding the .CLP extension is important.

```
        global shape arrow.clp        ; the cursor
        global mask arrowm.clp        ; XOR mask
```

Getting mouse cursors to work in all video modes is problematic, especially if you use custom palettes. You may have to store different versions of the cursor for different video modes and palettes. Again, at the end of the chapter we'll show you how to query the current video mode and load the appropriate clipping. As a rule, try to use palette 15 for white and palette 0 for black. You will also have to adjust the hot spot definition for some video modes. (The hot spot definition pinpoints the arrow tip as the "pick point.")

After loading the shapes for the mouse cursor, we now set mouse sensitivity:

```
; set mouse sensitivity
        mouse sense 6 6
```

In Chapter 3 we discussed mouse sensitivity. Remember that a value of 6 for the first parameter sets the speed for slow mouse movements, and the second parameter (also 6) sets the velocity for fast mouse movement.

Next we set up the origin point of the screen. In GRASP this is the bottom left corner of the screen. Explicitly setting the origin point of the screen allows us to reference all screen drawing commands to the same point.

```
; screen origin
        global OrgX 000
        global OrgY 000
```

Variables for the menu choices buttons are created.

```
; define Button variables
        global ButtonColor 7
        global EdgeLite 15
        global EdgeDark 0

        global ButX_Size 100              ; size of button
        global ButY_Size 035
```

```
global BaseLine 040              ; spacing from edge of screen
global XOR_Color 15              ; color for button XOR's
```

The program creates a color for the button and the edges around the button. The size of the button can be adjusted, and its distance from the edge of the screen can also be adjusted. We adjusted the spacing from the edge of the screen (BaseLine) for the kiosk screen layout. GRASP's XOR command was covered briefly in Chapter 5. Besides allowing you to play DFF animation files backward, XOR makes the drawing and text commands semitransparent. XOR is off by default. You turn it on by entering the command:

```
set xor on
```

Now we set up the variables that are associated with the screen mode we set earlier. The screen mode letter we assigned to the variable ScreenMode is used to create a label. That's how we determine which set of video mode-specific commands to run.

```
goto Mode$@ScreenMode
```

Here's a list of all the video modes supported by the menu system.

```
;Screen resolution is 320x200
ModeA:
        global ScreenMode A
        global HRes 319
        global VRes 199
        global NumColors 4
        goto Next

ModeB:
        global ScreenMode B
        global HRes 319
        global VRes 199
        global NumColors 16
        goto Next

ModeJ:
        global ScreenMode J
        global HRes 319
        global VRes 199
        global NumColors 16
        goto Next

ModeL:
        global ScreenMode L
        global HRes 319
        global VRes 199
        global NumColors 256
        goto Next

;Screen resolution is 640x200
ModeC:
        global ScreenMode C
        global HRes 639
        global VRes 199
```

```
        global NumColors 2
        goto Next

ModeD:
        global ScreenMode D
        global HRes 639
        global VRes 199
        global NumColors 16
        goto Next

;Screen resolution is 640x350
ModeE:
        global ScreenMode E
        global HRes 639
        global VRes 349
        global NumColors 2
        goto Next

ModeF:
        global ScreenMode F
        global HRes 639
        global VRes 349
        global NumColors 4
        goto Next

ModeG:
        global ScreenMode G
        global HRes 639
        global VRes 349
        global NumColors 16
        goto Next

ModeI:
        global ScreenMode I
        global HRes 639
        global VRes 349
        global NumColors 16
        goto Next

;ModeR:
;        global ScreenMode R
;        global HRes 639
;        global VRes 349
;        global NumColors 256
;        goto Next

;Screen resolution is 640x480
ModeO:
        global ScreenMode O
        global HRes 639
        global VRes 479
        global NumColors 2
        goto Next

ModeM:
        global ScreenMode M
```

```
        global HRes 639
        global VRes 479
        global NumColors 16
        goto Next

;ModeS:
;       global ScreenMode S
;       global HRes 639
;       global VRes 479
;       global NumColors 256
;       goto Next
```

The special version of GRASP bundled with *Multimedia Creations* does not support the higher resolution modes (ModeR and ModeS). We've commented out the lines that set up these modes.

Once the variables associated with the video mode we've selected are set up, we're ready to return to the calling script, MENU.TXT. There follows a jump to a label (goto Next:). The Exit command found there sends us back to the calling script.

```
Next:

exit


; ======================= end of file SETITUP ============================
```

DRAWING THE MENU ON THE SCREEN

We now return to the main script (MENU.TXT). The next command encountered initializes the screen mode.

```
        call SetItUp SetUp      ; set all variables, load font
        video @ScreenMode       ; set video before beginning
```

Setting Up the Background

The next command calls the subroutine that creates the background for the menu.

```
        Background                       ; blank colored screen
```

Let's look at that now:

```
;   Creates background for menu.

Background:
        clearscr 1

        ; just for orientation we draw V&H center lines
                offset 000,000
                color 0
                line @OrgX,@VRes/2,@HRes,@VRes/2
```

```
        line @HRes/2,@OrgY,@HRes/2,@VRes

; add some visual interest to screen
        cload piper.clp c1 1
        putup 256,0 c1
        cfree c1
        fstyle 8 2 2
        color 7 0
        text @HRes/2+70 @VRes/2+70 "Sandpiper Zoo"
        fontstyle3
return
; ------ end of Background
```

Notice that we use the global variables for the screen resolution to determine placement of the title on the screen. Murry adds lines to the screen that draw the vertical and horizontal lines for the current screen mode. This helps us visualize the shape of the screen. As you can see, Video G is a lot wider than it is tall.

Adding Visual Interest to the Menu

We've added the clipping and "Sandpiper Zoo" title to make the screen visually interesting and to simulate the opening screen to a kiosk. Normally, you either add a Help button or instructions on the screen for using the interactive menu. We've found that a sign mounted beside the kiosk works well for users who like to maintain a distance from computers! Ideally, the interface should be a touchscreen. Contact Paul Mace Graphics Software for recommendations on touchscreen hardware and software.

Using GRASP's Programming Flexibility

Processing now returns to the main part of the script. The next command is another call to a subroutine:

```
DrawMenu 5,1,0,0,"Bug","Fish","Shell","Dragon" "Exit"
```

Here we see GRASP's flexibility as a programming tool. The line of parameters that follows the call to the subroutine (DrawMenu) puts the options we'll use to define the layout of the menu in one place that's easy to modify and update. The variables sent to the subroutine can be summarized as follows:

```
DrawMenu #buttons orientation start spacing text1 text2 ...
```

Here's how the parameters are communicated to the subroutine. When GRASP encounters the command DrawMenu, it looks for a labeled subroutine called DrawMenu:. It will then treat the parameter items after the DrawMenu command as variables. The special symbols @1, @2, @3, @4, @5, and so on allow the subroutine to access the values stored by the variables. The first item of the parameter list is treated as @1, the second is treated as @2, and so on. Here's the way the variables are used in the DrawMenu subroutine:

```
@1 #buttons -    number of buttons to draw, range = 1 to 6
@2 orientation - 0 = horizontal
                 1 = vertical
@3 start -       positioning of buttons according to...

                      start = 0              start = 1
                 *--------------------*--------------------*
orientation = 0 (h)  |     LEFT       |       RIGHT        |
                 *--------------------*--------------------*
orientation = 1 (v)  |     TOP        |      BOTTOM        |
                 *--------------------*--------------------*

(@3 only has effect if @4==1 is TRUE)

@4 spacing -     0 = equally-spaced across screen.
                 1 = fixed number of pixels (half current size of button).
@5 text1 -       Text to be written on button #1 (using the current
                 screen origin).
@6-@10           Text written on subsequent buttons.

                 (NOTE! number of text strings must equal number
                 of buttons. This is the user's responsibility.)
```

Creating the Buttons

Processing continues at the DrawMenu: label. First the current offset is made equal to the screen origin. This is a safety trap.

```
; -------------------- DrawMenu code begins ----------------------

DrawMenu:

  offset 000,000              ; make sure we know where we start
```

Next we set up variables that will be used to determine where the buttons will be placed on the screen. Note that the global variable Increment is passed back to the main part of the script. This and other global variables created in the DrawMenu subroutine will be used in the PICKMENU.TXT to determine which button the user has selected. The Increment variable determines spacing between buttons. The variables we set will depend on whether we chose vertical or horizontal menu buttons and equally spaced or fixed-space buttons. Let's go through each scenario.

Creating Equally Spaced Buttons

Let's create equally spaced horizontal buttons. (We create equally spaced vertical buttons in a very similar manner, so we'll review only the former.) First, we'll calculate the distance between buttons, and use this distance for the origin point of the row of buttons. The vertical position of the horizontal row of buttons is the same for all the buttons, but the horizontal position of each button is different. Figure 9-3 shows a horizontal arrangement of buttons. The baseline is indicated.

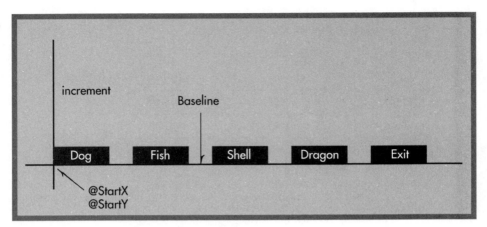

Figure 9-3 A horizontal arrangement of buttons

```
if @4==0                              ; equally spaced buttons

    if @2==0                          ; orientation is horizontal
      set Size @ButX_Size
      global Increment (@HRes-(@Size*@1))/(@1+1)
      global StartX @OrgX+@Increment
      global StartY @OrgY+@Baseline
    endif   ; if @2==0
```

First, a local variable size is created and assigned the previously set value for the button size (@ButX_Size). This allows us to use the value for the horizontal button size in the subroutine without modifying the original button size variable. The distance between buttons (Increment) is calculated using the value assigned to the HRes (horizontal resolution) variable created in SETITUP.TXT. The horizontal size of the button (@Size) is multiplied by the number of buttons selected by the user (@1) and subtracted from the horizontal resolution of the screen mode (@HRes). If we used horizontal buttons for the kiosk example, these values would be:

639-(100*5)

or 139. This gives us the space between the buttons. Since there is one more space than there are buttons (because of the space-button-space layout), we add 1 to the number of buttons and divide 139 by that number.

139/6

This gives us the value of 23. (The remainder after the division, 1, is thrown away.) The value given to Increment is 23, the space in pixels between buttons. (Increment is shown in Figure 9-3 as the space between the edge of the screen and the first but-

ton.) If you change the menu orientation to horizontal in the subroutine call
DrawMenu:

```
DrawMenu 5,1,0,0 "Bug", "Fish", "Shell","Dragon","Exit"
```

and then use SHOWCORD to measure the distance between horizontal buttons,
you will discover that they are exactly 23 pixels apart.

The next line

```
global StartX @OrgX+@Increment
```

calculates the horizontal starting position (StartX) for the row of buttons. (See
Figure 9-3.) The variable @OrgX is the horizontal screen origin point that we explicitly assigned in SETITUP.TXT (global OrgX 000). We add the space between the
origin point (000) to the value we have just assigned to the spacing between buttons
(@Increment). This is 23 pixels in our example.

The vertical position (StartY) of the row of horizontal buttons:

```
global StartY @OrgY+@Baseline
```

is arrived at by adding the vertical screen origin point to the value we gave to the
Baseline variable in SETITUP.TXT. Moving the buttons to the top of the screen is
just a matter of altering the Baseline variable.

Fixed-Space Menu Buttons

The menu system is using algorithms to figure out where to place buttons on the
screen. This makes it a lot easier to develop graphical menu interfaces for a variety
of video modes. It also makes it easier to alter the placement of the buttons on the
screen.

Fixed-Space Buttons

In cases where you want to arrange the buttons horizontally or vertically with fixed
spacing, the code is as follows. Let's begin with horizontal buttons. First we create a
local variable for the button horizontal size.

```
if @4==1                          ; spacing is fixed

    if @2==0                      ; orientation is horizontal...
      set Size @ButX_Size
```

In this example, we set the spacing at half the width of the button.

```
global Increment @ButX_Size/2  ; ...so spacing is 1/2 WIDTH
```

This can be changed to any value that will accommodate the amount of buttons
you've selected. If the value is too large and one or more buttons are placed beyond
the edge of the screen, GRASP will generate an error message.

Next, we set the origin point for the first button. The @3 parameter in the subroutine call determines which side of the screen the starting position is on. A value of 0 means start at the left corner, and a value of 1 means start at the right corner. If we start at the left side of the screen (@3==0), the spacing from the edge of the screen to the first button (Increment) is the original value we gave in SETITUP.TXT for the screen origin (000), plus the fixed value we've just given for button spacing:

```
if @3==0                            ; start at left corner
        global StartX @OrgX+@Increment
```

The vertical starting position of the row of menu buttons is determined by adding the value we gave to the screen origin (000) to the value we gave to the baseline variable (40).

```
        global StartY @OrgY+@Baseline
    endif
```

The other screen positions are worked out in similar ways.

```
    if @3==1                                ; start at right corner
            global StartX @HRes-(@ButX_Size*@1+@Increment*@1)
            global StartY @OrgY+@Baseline
        endif
    endif   ; if @2==0

    if @2==1                                ;orientation is vertical...
        set Size @ButY_Size
        global Increment @ButY_Size/2       ; ...spacing is 1/2 HEIGHT

        if @3==0                            ; start at screen bottom
                global StartX @OrgX+@Baseline    ; vertical
                global StartY @OrgY+@Increment
        endif
        if @3==1                            ; start at top
                global StartX @OrgX+@Baseline
                global StartY @VRes-(@ButY_Size*@1+@Increment*@1)
        endif
    endif   ; if @2==1
endif   ; if @4==1
```

Drawing the Buttons on the Screen

Now that we have created the variables that will be used to create the buttons on the screen, it's time to draw the menu. The basic strategy is to move a "screen pointer" to the spot where a button will be drawn. The StartX and StartY variables we created earlier define the origin point for the row of buttons.

```
offset @StartX,@StartY          ; move the screen position pointer
```

Then we use a loop to create the buttons. We use the first parameter of the DrawMenu subroutine (which tells us how many buttons to create) to determine how many loops to process.

```
mark @1                                 ; going to draw #buttons
```

Then we make a call to another subroutine.

```
DrawIt
```

This subroutine determines the look of the buttons. In our example, the buttons are drawn with rectangles and straight lines. You could replace the Line and Rect commands with a command that loads a clipping. The routine uses the variables for button sizes, button color, and the button "edge" colors established in the SETITUP.TXT script.

```
DrawIt:
        color @ButtonColor
        rect 000,000 @ButX_Size,@ButY_Size      ; draw the basic button

        color @EdgeLite
        line 000,000 000,@ButY_Size             ; 3D the button
        line 000,@ButY_Size @ButX_Size,@ButY_Size
        color @EdgeDark
        line 000,000 @ButX_Size,000
        line @ButX_Size,000 @ButX_Size,@ButY_Size

return
; ------ end of DrawIt
```

Processing returns to the DrawIt subroutine, where the next command checks the DrawMenu parameter that determines if the menu is horizontal or vertical. It generates the appropriate offset relative to the previous Offset command.

```
        if @2==0                                ; horizontal
                offset @Size+@Increment,000,r
        endif
        if @2==1                                ; vertical
                offset 000,@Size+@Increment,r
        endif
    loop
```

The offset command uses the horizontal or vertical size of the button (@Size), plus the distance to the next button (@Increment) to determine the next position of the button. We then loop back to the subroutine that draws the button on the screen (DrawIt).

Adding the Text to the Buttons

The next section of the script adds text to the buttons. First we call a subroutine that selects a font and a style for that font.

```
; label the menu buttons, using the text strings handed in as parameters
  FontStyle1                            ; contains the values for X_Step/Y_Step
```

Here's the subroutine for FontSytle1. Recall that we loaded the font in SETIUP.TXT.

```
fontstyle1:
        font 1                  ; normal text
        color 15,0
```

```
        fstyle 8,1                  ; drop shadow
        fgaps 2,06                  ; gaps between letters, words
        global X_Step 020           ; these control how the text is positioned
        global Y_Step 015           ; on the button surface
return
```

The X_Step and Y_Step variables establish positions for text on the button surface. These positions are relative to the button itself, so we still have to calculate where we are relative to the entire screen. On return to the text part of the DrawMenu subroutine, there is a command that determines this for us.

```
local Text_X @StartX+@X_Step
local Text_Y @StartY+@Y_Step
```

We set up two temporary variables that store the text position relative to the current x and y button origin coordinates.

```
offset @Text_X,@Text_Y
```

The next section of code is at first a bit tricky to make sense of until you release that the value you give to the variable *count* refers to the items in the parameter list handed to the subroutine by DrawMenu. Count is at first given a count of 5, which indexes the fifth item in the parameter list, "Bug."

```
(DrawMenu 5,1,0,0,"Bug","Fish","Shell","Dragon" "Exit"

set count 5                         ; where the text strings start

mark @1                             ; same # as we drew
     text 000,000,@@Count
       if @2==0                     ; horizontal
            offset @Size+@Increment,000,r
       endif
       if @2==1                     ; vertical
            offset 000,@Size+@Increment,r
       endif
     set count @count+1
loop
```

Double indirection (@@Count) points to the string "Bug." Each time through the loop, the count variable is updated and we move along the list of button titles. The offset positions determine where the next title is placed on the screen. They use the size of the button and the size of the space between the buttons to move the screen pointer along to the next position.

We're nearly finished processing the DrawMenu subroutine. We have one more task to perform: We have to set a couple of global variables that will be used when we test for user mouse clicks in PICKMENU.TXT. We use the parameters originally passed to DrawMenu by the main script to assign values to the two global variables.

```
        global NumButtons @1
        global Orientation @2

return
; ----- end of DrawMenu
```

At the end of the DrawMenu subroutine, we return to the main body of the script, only to encounter a call to another script.

```
        call PickMenu Entry
```

Determining User Menu Choices

Again, Murry keeps the components to his menu system separate in order to facilitate future changes or to create special applications. The PICKMENU.TXT script displays the mouse cursor and loops, checking for mouse clicks, until a selection is made. The global variable Index is created to store the user's selection. Then we exit the routine, returning to the calling level.

```
;===========================================================
;                        PICKMENU.TXT
;===========================================================
;
; Variables used on input:
;       @Orientation
;       @HRes, @VRes
;       @StartX, @StartY
;       @ButX_Size, @ButY_Size, @Increment, @NumButtons
;
; Variables set and returned on exit:
;     @Index    - this variable is used to communicate the button selected
;                   by the user.
; ---------------------- code begins ----------------------------
```

Upon entry to the script, the current offset status is reset.

```
Entry:

  offset 000,000               ; always a good idea to know where you start
                               ; from when manipulating screen coords
```

We've adapted the mouse-checking code from Chapter 4 to check for the presence of a mouse driver. If we do not have a mouse driver installed, and we run the code without error-checking, GRASP will report an error that will be puzzling at first. The Getmouse command (which we are about to introduce) sets a variable that provides mouse status information. GRASP will report that the variable was not created, an error message that will puzzle users. Here's the mouse-checking routine.

```
; Is there a mouse in the house?
        if !@mouse
                offset 0,0
                font 3
```

```
                color 15
                offset 10,-10
                color 0
                rect @HRes/2-160 @VRes/2-30 @HRes/2+160 @VRes/2+30
                offset 0,0
                color 8
                rect @HRes/2-160 @VRes/2-30 @HRes/2+160 @VRes/2+30
                set center on
                color 14
                text 0,@VRes/2+12 "Mouse driver not present!"
                text 0,@VRes/2-2 "Install mouse and run again."
                color 15
                text 0,@VRes/2-20 "Press Enter to Exit"
                set center off
                waitkey
                exit
        endif
```

If the mouse is present, we create the interface to the mouse. (We covered mouse interfacing in Chapter 4.)

```
mouse cursor @Shape,15,20,@Mask         ; cursor specification
mouse on
mouse position @HRes/2,@VRes/2          ; now put it where it'll be seen
```

The shape and mask variables were set in SETITUP.TXT. Recall that the command Mouse Cursor creates a custom mouse cursor using a clipping. The 15,20 parameter is the offset into the clipping from the lower left pixel for the mouse hot spot. (This may have to be adjusted for other video modes.) The mouse will appear in the middle of the screen, which is determined by the Mouse Position command by dividing the horizontal and vertical screen dimensions in half.

We now branch to the appropriate button layout scheme.

```
if @Orientation==0                      ; horizontal menu
  goto Horiz_Menu                       ; make your selection
endif
if @Orientation==1                      ; vertical
  goto Vert_Menu                        ; ditto
endif
```

We'll follow the horizontal menu structure. We need to develop a strategy for finding where on the screen the user clicked. If the user clicked within a button area, we need to know which button was selected. We used the Ifmouse command in Chapter 4 to check for mouse clicks. The Ifmouse command checks for mouse clicks in specific areas:

```
ifmouse button label [x1,y1 x2,y2] [color] [wait] [label2]
```

If the user clicks within the x1,y1 x2,y2 rectangle, then there is a branch to label; if not, there is a branch to label2. This will not work for us here, because we do not know beforehand where the buttons will be located. The command that tells us exactly where the mouse click occurred is the Getmouse command. This command reports on mouse status and position, and is useful in a loop. The difference between Ifmouse and Getmouse can be summarized as follows: Ifmouse is in the specified region and branches accordingly. The Getmouse command is issued *before* a mouse click. After a mouse click, it files a report on which mouse button (if anything) the user pressed and where the user clicked.

The command will also give you the current status of the mouse. Its syntax is:

```
getmouse butn [x,y] [test]
```

The but parameter is the name of a variable that stores the information about which mouse button was pressed, if any, since the last Getmouse command was issued. A value of 0 indicates no button was pressed, and a value of 1 indicates the left mouse button was pressed. You can also test for right mouse button clicks or combinations of mouse buttons. There is a table of mouse button values in the (F2) online help guide.

The x,y optional variables store where the user clicked on the screen or what the current mouse cursor position is.

The third parameter, test, is also optional. It refers to a test for a button. If it is not used, GRASP reports the current status of the mouse: Is a button currently being pressed down? Where is the current mouse cursor? If the mouse button is not currently being pressed, a 0 is returned.

If the test parameter is given a value of 0, GRASP returns information about the most recent button click (press). When the user presses the button, GRASP stores mouse status information. If a 1 is used for test, GRASP returns the information about the button and screen location at the point where the button is released. This allows the user to drag the mouse cursor around before releasing it. If no button was pressed since the last time a Getmouse command was issued, @butn has a value of 0.

Here's how the Getmouse command is typically used:

```
mouse on                      ; turn the mouse on
lp:                           ; loop label
      getmouse butn x,y test; issue the command
if @butn>0                    ; any value > 0 indicates the mouse was pressed
      text @butn              ; print the mouse click value on screen
      text @x                 ; print x position
      text @y                 ; print y position
endif
goto lp                       ; repeat
exit
```

Let's now see how the program uses Getmouse.

The next section checks horizontal menus. First, we assign the current origin point for the buttons to temporary variables. This allows us to alter these values without changing the original global values.

```
Horiz_Menu:
  local LocalX @StartX           ; start position
  local LocalY @StartY
```

Then we initialize a counter. This counter will be used to set a global variable called index. The @Index value will be used by a routine in DISPATCH.TXT to determine which button was selected by the user. The first button has an index value of 1, and the next 2, and so on. During the loop the first button will be given a count value of 1. As buttons are checked with each pass through the loop, the count value is incremented. Finally, when a button tests true, the current value of count is assigned to the index global variable.

Processing begins with the initialization of the counter.

```
local Count 1                         ; initialize counter
```

The loop is now entered. A Getmouse command is issued.

```
LoopH:
        getmouse Click,X,Y,1            ; read position on button RELEASE
```

The button that is pressed by the user is assigned to the variable click. The x and y positions where the click occurred is assigned to the variables X and Y, respectively. The 1 parameter specifies that the Getmouse variables will be assigned only when the user releases a mouse button.

First we check to see if the user clicked with the left mouse button. If not, we return to the top of the loop.

```
        if @Click<>1                   ; only accept L button selection
          goto LoopH
        endif
```

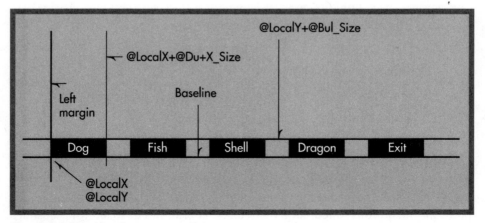

Figure 9-4 Checking for a mouse click

Now we check to see if the vertical mouse position is greater than or equal to the baseline.

```
CheckY_H:                               ; first check for Y restriction
            if @Y>=@LocalY              ; above the baseline, therefore
                goto NextY_H            ;  may be a valid selection
            endif
            goto LoopH                  ; failed test
```

If it is not, it means that we are below the row of buttons and we return to the top of the loop. Figure 9-4 will help you visualize this. If it is above the baseline, we jump to the next label. There, we will check to see if the user clicked within the band marked by the top of the buttons in the horizontal row of the buttons (see Figure 9-4).

```
    NextY_H:
            if @Y<=@LocalY+@ButY_Size   ; within the button Y band
                goto CheckX_H           ; so now we check X-area
            endif
            goto LoopH
```

If the test failed, we return to the top of the loop. If we passed, then we know that the user clicked somewhere within the horizontal lines marking the band of buttons. We now check to see if the user clicked on the area to the right of the left margin of the first button. (Figure 9-4 shows where the left margin is located.)

The next section of code loops, checking each button in turn. We use the global variable NumButtons passed to this script by MENU.TXT to determine how many buttons there are and therefore how many times to go through the loop.

```
    CheckX_H:
    mark @NumButtons                    ; step thru buttons - 1 cycle
```

First, we check to see if the user clicked to the right of the left edge of the button.

```
            if @X>=@LocalX              ; to the right of the left margin
                goto NextX_H            ; ...yes, now let's check button area
            endif
            goto LoopH                  ; failed...
                                        ; start over
```

If the user clicked in the area between the screen edge and the edge of the button, the user missed the first button, so we return to the top of the loop to check for the next valid click. If the user clicked to the right of the left margin of the button, then processing continues at the NextX_H: label.

```
NextX_H:
            if @X<=@LocalX+@ButX_Size   ; within button width, so...
                goto Selected           ;   bingo!
            endif
```

This label checks to see if the click was to the left of the right edge of the first button, that is, within the first button area. If the test is evaluated as true, we jump to the Selected: label. If the click was not within the first button's area, we know that the user must have tried to click on one of the other buttons. The next routine updates the counter and moves the screen pointer to the next button position.

```
SkipIt_H:                          ; no hit, so set up for...
  local Count @Count+1
  local LocalX @LocalX+@ButX_Size+@Increment
```

Then we are sent back to the beginning of the loop. We continue to loop until we reach the last button.

```
loop                               ; ...and check next button position
```

If the text fails for the last button, we know that the area between the last button and the right edge of the screen was selected. This is an invalid selection, so we fall through to the command that sends us back to the beginning of the routine.

```
goto Horiz_Menu                    ; continue to loop until we make a
                                   ;    valid selection
```

The process of checking for a valid mouse click begins again.

The vertical menu choices work in a very similar way to the horizontal menu choices, so we won't review them here.

Processing the User Selection

Once the user makes a valid selection, we jump to a label that creates a global variable called index.

```
Selected:
        global Index @Count        ; all that work just to do this!
        mouse off
        goto Page$@Index
```

This variable stores the information about which button was selected. It will be used by DISPATCH.TXT to determine the appropriate action. The jump to the Page$@Index label allows us to carry out whatever other action we might want to take as a result of the user's selection. For example, we may have a bell that rings when the user makes a correct selection. In this case we do nothing.

```
Page1:
      return

Page2:
      return

Page3:
      return
```

346

```
    Page4:
          return

    Page5:
          return

    Page6:
          return

exit      ; a safety trap

; ==================  end of file PICKMENU ====================
```

Processing now returns once again to MENU.TXT. The next command is processed:

```
    Link DISPATCH.TXT Start
```

We're now ready to proceed to the final script. DISPATCH.TXT acts as the hub that launches the balance of the application we're creating. We could incorporate DISPATCH.TXT into PICKMENU.TXT to keep things simple. However, keeping it separate keeps us better organized in large, complex applications.

EVALUATING MENU CHOICES

DISPATCH.TXT evaluates the selection made in PICKMENU.TXT and initiates the appropriate action. We returned from PICKMENU.TXT with the variable index set. The values stored in the variable indicate the button selected. Here's the table:

```
    value                 Goto
      1               BUG.TXT
      2               FISH.TXT
      3               SHELL.TXT
      4               FISH.TXT
      5               EXIT
      6               N/A
```

In our example we do not use a sixth button. We can add as many possibilities as you want.

Here's the entire listing for DISPATCH.TXT. Notice the exit point. This is a safety trap. The user exits back to DOS if the linked file cannot be found.

```
; ------------------  code begins  -------------------------


Start:
        if @Index==1
                link bug.txt              ; bug menu choice
                exit
        endif
```

347

```
        if @Index==2                  ; goto Main Menu level
                link fish.txt         ; fish menu choice
                exit
        endif

        if @Index==3                  ; forward one chunk
                link shell.txt        ; shell menu choice
                exit
        endif

        if @Index==4                  ; exit
                link dragon.txt
                exit
        endif

        if @Index==5
                color 0
                pnewbuf p1
                pfade 20 p1
                exit
        endif


;
; --------- below is currently not used. For now we leave it here
;               so you don't have to reenter it for 6 button menus.


        if @Index==6
                endif

Exit    ; safety trap

; ====================== end of file DISPATCH ===========================
```

SUMMARY AND EXTENSIONS

As a rule, you should give the user no more than five menu choices. If your information system requires additional choices, placing another layer of menus below
one of the buttons helps keep the interface uncluttered and less confusing for users.
However, try to keep the program from going deeper than three layers of menus.
The temptation is to create a labyrinth, but users quickly get disoriented.

An enhancement to Murry's program would be automatic checking for the current video mode. The vmode system variable returns information on the current
video mode selected by the Video command. By testing for this variable, the program could load the clippings or pictures appropriate to a specified video mode. For
example, the Sandpiper clipping appropriate to the current video mode could be
loaded. Here's how you would write a program to support either 16-color EGA or
VGA modes. It queries the current video mode and loads the appropriate picture.

Change the Video command to Video M to see the effect of changing video modes. Notice that a quirk of this command is that the video mode letter you test for must be capitalized and placed in quotation marks.

```
video g                    ; selects EGA mode

if @vmode=="G"             ; note video mode capitalized and in
                           ; quotation marks
        cload piper.clp 1
else
        pload fish.pal p1
        palette p1
        cload fish.clp 1
endif
putup c1
waitkey
exit
```

The test reveals that Mode G is currently selected. The picture of the piper is loaded and displayed. If the mode is changed to Video M, the fish clipping is loaded and displayed. Note that we have to load a palette with the fish clipping to display its colors properly. You can avoid this when you build menus by using a standard palette for all clippings used on the main menu screen. Of course, if you want to support two-color or four-color modes, this means confining the colors in the clipping to the first two or four palettes respectively.

Another enhancement to Murry's program would be automatic checking of video modes supported by the user's system. If the menu system is used to distribute a program to a wide variety of computers, you would have GRASP check for the highest valid video mode on the user's system and automatically branch to the appropriate routines for setting video modes and drawing menus in the right colors and resolutions. (We discussed installation routines in Chapter 6.)

Because Murry's system is written in GRASP, it's easy to add pictures, animations, and sound to the basic menu system to create a full multimedia interactive display system. Of course, adding pictures and clippings to the menu adds memory overhead. You may elect to keep the menu system itself simple for information kiosks where speed of system response is important.

Our visit to the Sandpiper Zoo using Murry Christensen's interactive menu system has been brief. However, his system gives us a very flexible system to build on. It's the jumping-off point for highly interactive sound and sight extravaganzas.

EXIT

This brings us to the jumping-off point in the book. The chapter that follows provides a summary of the GRASP commands that we have covered in *Multimedia*

Creations. We've included a few others that you might find solve a particular problem as you work through your own scripts.

GRASP is a wonderful entry into the entire world of multimedia. It gives you the tools to challenge the PC's internal data rate with animations and music that delight and educate. The DOS environment is still the environment of choice for animators and multimedia producers who want to attain maximum warp speed and take audiences on a visual high-tech magic carpet ride. GRASP puts you at the controls. Now it's up to you. There's a brand new frontier to be conquered by today's multimedia producers. Go where no programmer has ever gone before.

PART FOUR

Reference

10
GRASP
Help and Commands

The first part of this chapter is a guide to GRASP's on-line Help listings. The rest of the chapter is devoted to a review of GRASP commands.

ON-LINE HELP

Here's a quick tour of GRASP's on-line help: Press the (F1) function key while in the editor to find help on editing keys. Press (F2) to bring up summaries of GRASP commands, functions, variables, and operators. Press (F3) for a listing of GRASP fades and video modes. When accessing on-line help, use the (PGUP) and (PGDN) keys to step through the "pages." Press (ENTER) to step forward to the next page; press (ESC) to return to the editor.

Operators Listing

Operators are listed on pages 7 to 9 of the editor's on-line (F2) Help listings. Operators determine how GRASP evaluates expressions. The order of precedence of operators is on page 9 of the listing.

An expression is a combination of values and operators that evaluates to a value. Commands are processed from left to right. For example:

@eg+4*6/2

evaluates to:

@eg+((4*6)/8) or @eg+12. Order of precedence dictates that the multiplication is performed first, then division, then addition. You multiply 4 by 6, divide the result by 2, and add the result to the value stored at @eg. Placing parentheses around the operations you want GRASP to evaluate first is not only a valid way of coding expressions, it's recommended!

GRASP Functions

You'll find GRASP functions on pages 9 to 11 of GRASP's (F2) on-line Help listings. Think of functions as little black boxes where you can send information to be processed. For example, the function Open(fname) opens a DOS file and returns its DOS file handle. Like GRASP commands, functions encapsulate low-level coding, freeing you to concentrate on the broader aspects of your program. You will often see functions used this way:

```
. read(@fs,@buf,@len)
```

The period mark instructs GRASP not to capture the return value. In effect, the period mark turns this function into a GRASP command that "reads" disk files.

GRASP Variables

Variables are listed on pages 12 to 15 of the (F2) listings. GRASP "read only" global variables cannot be modified by your program. The global variables are accessible from anywhere in your program, and they give you a lot of useful information about the computer system and the status of such things as the current color. There are a number of places in *Multimedia Creations* where we show you how to use these variables. For example, in Chapter 7 we show you how to preserve system offsets when the user pops up a Help screen. The strategy is:

```
set offx @xoff        ; save the x offset as a temporary variable
set offy @yoff        ; save the y offset
offset 0,0            ; reset the system offsets
...                   ; do the help screen
offset @offx @offy    ; when finished, restore original offset
return                ; and return to the main script
```

This is an indirect way of modifying system variables.

The read and write variable values can be directly modified. For instance, to center text we change the value of the variable that centers text (@center) from its default condition (off) this way:

```
set center on
```

Now text will be centered in the active window.

GRASP Key Names

Special keys used with the When, Ifkey, and Getmouse commands are listed on page 15 of the (F2) listings. For example, to make pressing the (←) key cause a branch to an exit: label, we would enter this:

```
when left goto exit
```

When the user presses the (←) key, program execution continues at the exit: label.

Mouse Button Values

The Ifmouse and Getmouse commands test for a mouse button click. If the user does not press a mouse button, GRASP assigns a value of 0 to the variable that reports back on the user's mouse click. A value of 1 indicates the left mouse button was clicked. The other mouse buttons have various values, depending on whether the user's mouse is of the two-button or three-button kind. The last page of the (F2) listings provides a table listing values for the these buttons.

GRASP Fades

GRASP's fades are listed on pages 1 and 2 of the (F3) function key listing. We've prepared a little utility program called FADES.TXT in the \GRASP\UTILITY subdirectory. Load it and play it to see the effect of GRASP's 25 fades and wipes.

GRASP Video Mode Listing

Find page 3 of the listings by pressing (F3). It provides a guide to the video modes supported by the special version of GRASP bundled with *Multimedia Creations*.

GRASP'S COMMANDS LISTED BY FUNCTION

Here are GRASP's commands listed by function. Remember that the picture and clipping commands are largely interchangeable. For example, you can load a picture as a clipping in the following manner:

```
cload cover.pic c1 1
putup 1
```

Of course, this does not load the palette, because the difference between Cload and Pload is that Pload loads the palette with the picture, Cload does not. Clipping (CLP) files contain no palette information. You can Pload them, but a subsequent Palette command will do nothing.

Picture Display, Save

Loading and displaying	Pload, Palette, Pfade, Pfree
Saving	Pgetbuf, Psave
Adding an edge to a fade	Edge
Creating a new buffer	Pnewbuf
Redirection to buffer	Psetbuf (buffer #)
Redirection to screen	Psetbuf
Clearing screen	Clearscr
VGA palette fading	Spread

Clipping Display, Save

Loading and displaying	Cload, Cfade, Putup, Cfree
Transparent display	Tran
Saving to a buffer	Cgetbuf
Tiling screen	Tile

Animation

Moving a clipping	Float, Fly
DFF animation	Dload, Putdff, Dfree

Drawing and Color

Shape creation	Box, Rect, Circle, Line, Point
Changing colors	Color, Chgcolor, Getcolor, Setcolor, Setrgb, Set xor on

Text

Loading, selecting	Fload, Font, Ffree
Typographical control	Fgaps, Fstyle, Text
	Set (text control)
Pouring text into window	Window
Loading text from disk	Merge, Load

Screen Layout

Offsetting	Offset, Position
Restricting activity	Window

Data

Defining data	Data, Databegin/Datend, Databegin, Label
Moving data pointer	Dataskip

Variables

Defining variables	Set, Local, Global

Controlling Program Flow

Controlling timing	Waitkey, Timer
Branching	Goto, Gosub Link, Call, Merge
Decisions	If (jump), If (If-Else-Endif) When, Ifkey, Getkey
Looping	Mark/Loop, Break
Returning, exiting	Return, Exit, Pop

Input/Output and Memory

External calls	Exec, Int
Loading GRPs	Load
Send to a DOS device	Send
System Sound	Noise, Note
Testing memory/video	Ifmem, Ifvideo
Changing directories	Opengl

Mouse

Interfacing	Mouse (on/off, cursor, position, Sense, Window)
Program flow	Ifmouse, Getmouse

GRASP COMMAND SUMMARY

Once you become familiar with GRASP, you'll find that pressing (F2) to access the Command Summary listing quickly reminds you of the syntax of GRASP commands. It's so easy and quick to review commands by popping the Command Summary on-screen, there is little need to commit the syntax of commands to memory.

This section is a slightly more detailed review of the commands than you will find in on-line help. We also guide you to the pages where the syntax for GRASP commands are provided in detail. Not all GRASP commands are included here. Commands specific to other video modes are not fully covered. In particular, we do not cover two-page animation, a method of achieving flicker-free animation on digital EGA cards. If you plan to use GRASP for commercial work, purchase the commercial version. It provides an exhaustive reference text that covers commands and their syntax.

Notes on Command Conventions

The following conventions apply to all commands:

- Commands can be entered in either uppercase or lowercase.

- Brackets [ ] indicate optional parameters. All other parameters must be entered, or GRASP will return an error message.

- Options can be separated by spaces, commas, or slashes (/). Use commas to skip options you do not want to enter. Two commas are necessary to skip the first command option.

- Ellipses indicate that the last option can be repeated indefinitely, or until the end of the line in the editor is reached.

Box

Draw an unfilled rectangle on the screen.

```
box x1,y1 x2,y2 [width]
```

Parameters

x1,y1   The coordinates of the first corner of the box.

x2,y2   The coordinates of the second corner of the box.

width   The width of the line used to draw the box.

Comment

The Box command uses the current color to create a hollow rectangle on the screen.

Break

Break halts execution of a loop and transfers control to the specified label.

```
break label
```

Parameters

label   The point in the script where execution continues.

Comments

Use Break to exit out of a Mark/Loop structure. See the command Mark/Loop.

Call

Load and execute another GRASP script and then returns to the calling script.

```
call name [label] [parameters]
```

Parameters

name   Name of script.

label   Optional label in the called script where execution begins.

parameters   Optional parameters that can be sent to the called script.

Comments

Parameters sent to a called script are read by the called script as @1,@2,@3, and so on. See Chapter 9's discussion of the DrawMenu subroutine ("Using GRASP's Programming Flexibility") for a more extensive example of parameter passing using the Gosub command. Using "set maxcall on" before the Call command causes GRASP to swap the parent file to far memory as needed to make room for the child. (See "Near and Far Memory" in Chapter 4.) This is recommended for long scripts. Either a Return or an Exit command can be used to end processing of the called script. Called text files can't return a value, Gosub routines can. See the Return command for this. Also see the Link and Merge command summaries. See the section in Chapter 4 called "Linking GRASP Scripts" for a comparison of Call with other program control commands.

Cfade

Add a clipping to the screen using a variety of wipes or fades.

```
cfade # x,y [buffer] [speed] [delay]
```

Parameters

The # symbol signifies a fade number. Cfade uses all the same fades as picture fades (listed by the 3 key), with the exception of fade 0, the instant display fade. Use Putup for instant display.

x,y The horizontal (x) and vertical (y) position where you display the clipping on screen. The bottom left corner of the clipping will be placed at the specified x,y position.

buffer The buffer parameter is optional. It defaults to buffer one.

speed Speed of the fade in hundredths of a second.

delay A wait time after finishing the fade, before executing the next command. Measured in hundredths of a second.

Comments

See the commands Cfree and Putup. You can Cfade a picture to the screen by preceding the buffer number with a "p." See Chapter 4's treatment of "Clipping on Byte Boundaries." See "Displaying Clippings" in Chapter 4. See Chapter 5, "Using the -> Operator to Fade Clippings to Precise Locations."

Cfree

Free a clipping buffer.

```
cfree buffer [buffer] [buffer] ...
```

Parameters

buffer Clipping buffer number. Optionally, a series of buffers can be freed by using a dash. For example:

```
cfree 1 - 10
```

frees buffers 1 through 10 inclusive.

Comments

Good memory management dictates that you unload a clipping right after it is displayed. See the summary for the Cfade and Putup commands, both of which use the Cfree command.

Cgetbuf

Save an area of the screen into a clipping buffer.

```
cgetbuf buffer [x1,y1 x2,y2] [noshift] [tran]
```

Parameters

buffer   Buffer number from 1 to 128.

x1,y1   Bottom left corner of screen rectangle to save.

x2,y2   Top right corner of the screen rectangle you want to save. These are added to the clipping so that you can put it back up in the same position.

noshift   Either 0 (create bit-shifted copies) or 1 (do not create copies). GRASP defaults to creating shifted copies (0), so that you can subsequently put the clipping at any x horizontal position. To save RAM memory, tell GRASP not to create copies (1).

tran   The optional transparency parameter can have a value of 1 (analyze clipping for transparent color) or 0 (do not analyze clipping).

Comments

Cgetbuf has a similar syntax to Pgetbuf, but unlike the latter, it allows you to save transparent clippings into clipping buffers. If you are not displaying transparent clippings, leave Tran off (or assign 0 to it). This saves processing time. The Position command can be used to clear the offsets stored with the clipping. See Position. The system option cgetshift allows you to save a clipping that is not on a byte boundary. The clipping will be saved without shifted copies:

```
set cgetshift off
cgetbuf 1 100,100 110,110 1
psave test.clp c1
```

This saves the clipping TEST.CLP to the hard drive. See Chapter 4's "Clipping on Byte Boundaries."

Circle

Create an ellipse.

```
circle x,y xr [yr] [iris]
```

Parameters

x,y   The x,y coordinates determine the circle's center point on the screen.

xr   The circle's horizontal radius.

yr   The circle's vertical radius. If you do not specify this parameter, GRASP will make the vertical radius equal to the horizontal radius.

radius
Iris allows you to specify how many inner circles to draw within the initial circle. These circles or ellipses are drawn one pixel within the previous one. This produces a moiré pattern.

Comments

See the discussion of the Circle command in Chapter 5, "Creating the Countdown Circles."

Clearscr

Clears the screen to the current color or the color specified.

`clearscr [color]`

Parameters

color
Repaints the screen in the specified color. If you do not specify a color, Clearscr uses the current system color.

Cload

Loads a clipping into a buffer.

`cload name [buffer] [copy] [tran]`

Parameters

name
Clipping or picture name.

buffer
The buffer parameter is optional. If you do not specify a buffer number when loading a clipping, it will load into clipping buffer 1. You can have up to 128 buffers in GRASP.

copy
The copy parameter toggles noshift "on" or "off". Noshift means, "Do not create a copy (or copies)." It can have a value of either 0 or 1. A 0 directs GRASP to store extra copies of the clipping to ensure that the clipping can be displayed on non-byte boundaries. A 1 directs GRASP *not* to store shifted copies.

tran
Tran turns transparency processing for the clipping on (1) or off (0). See the Tran command summary for details on its use.

Comments

You can load either a picture file or a clipping with Cload, but loading a picture with the command will not load the picture's palette. If you omit the file extension,

GRASP will assume you mean a file name with the .CLP extension. See Chapter 4, "Loading Clippings," for a detailed discussion of this command. See Cfade and Cfree for the commands associated with Cload.

Color

Set the current color.

```
color color1 [R] [color2]
```

Parameters

color1   The color1 parameter sets the current color.

R   When R is specified, color1 is made relative to the current color. This is a useful feature when you want to color cycle the palette.

color2   Color2 is used to determine the color of shadowed text. Default value of 0.

Comments

Note that it is the palette slot that you set, not the color index. When GRASP starts, the last color in the palette (15 in Video M mode) is the default color.

Data

Create a list of data items on a single line in the editor.

```
data item item item ...
```

Parameters

data   Data items can be numeric values, file names, or text strings. Commas or spaces divide data items. Enclosing quotation marks around a text string creates a single data item. This also preserves capitalization.

Comments

Data creates a list of file names in memory that GRASP can access sequentially. The @ symbol is used by GRASP to access a data list one item after another. See Chapter 3, "Using The Data Command," for a detailed discussion of the data command and its use. See the Dataskip command summary.

Databegin/Dataend

When the data item list exceeds a single line, the Databegin and Dataend
commands are required to define the boundaries of your list.

```
databegin
...
dataend
```

Comments

Databegin and Dataend act like brackets enclosing the data items. Databegin
instructs GRASP to keep reading data until GRASP sees a Dataend demarcation.
The special symbol @ is used to access items from the list one item at a time. See
Chapter 3, "Using the Data Command," for a detailed discussion of the command.
See the Dataskip command summary.

Databegin Label

When used with a label, the Databegin command looks elsewhere in your program
for the data list.

```
databegin label
...                        ; program code uses @ symbol to access list

label:
...                        ; data items
dataend
```

Comments

See the previous command summaries for the various ways of accessing data lists
in GRASP using the @ symbol. There is a detailed discussion in Chapter 3. Labeled
lists are usually placed after an exit point so that program execution does not
encounter the data list out of context. See the Dataskip command summary.

Dataskip

Move a pointer about a data list.

```
dataskip number
```

Parameters

num   Number can be positive (go forward) or negative (go back). Dataskip
            moves GRASP's internal pointer forward or back in the data list.

Comments

One important caveat: You must ensure that Dataskip does not step beyond the boundaries of the list. Doing so will produce an error message. See the Data, Databegin/Dataend, and Databegin Label commands. See, "Creating a Remote-Control Switch with Dataskip" in Chapter 3 for an example of the command's use.

Dfree

Frees differential animation file buffer.

```
dfree buffer [buffer] ...
```

Parameters

buffer   Differential animation file buffer.

Comments

See the Dload and Putdff commands.

Dload

The command that loads DFF files. You can use it to load either GRASP DFF files or Autodesk Animator files.

```
dload name [buffer] [disk]
```

Parameters

name   The name of the DFF file (or Animator FLI).

buffer   The buffer you want to load the file into.

disk   The disk option gives you a choice of running the animation from the hard drive (1) or from memory (0). It has a value of 0 by default.

Comments

Chapter 5 provides extensive coverage of this command. The command Putdff plays the animation. The command Dfree unloads a DFF animation file.

Edge

Put a colored leading edge on horizontal and vertical wipes.

```
edge setting [color]
```

Parameters

setting   The setting parameter is the keyword "on" or "off." "On" turns the
             edge feature on, "off" turns it off.

color   The default value for color is the last color in the palette, which is
             often the color white. It's better to explicitly assign a palette color to
             the edge.

Comments

The edge is 1 pixel wide.

Exec

Executes an external DOS program and returns.

```
exec name ("options")
```

Parameters

name   Name is the full name of the program you want to load, including its
             extension.

options   Options are the optional parameters required by the external DOS
             program.

Comments

The command should not be used to load TSRs (memory resident programs).

Exit

Halts execution of the current program and returns control to a previous calling
program.

```
exit [value]
```

Parameters

value   The optional value is used when GRASP has been called from
             another program. It is a number that can be used to set the DOS
             errorlevel value.

Comments

Control returns to the editor when using GRASPC.EXE. GRASP programs loaded
and run by GRASPRT.EXE (the commercial version of GRASP) return control to

DOS. In both cases, if the script was called by another script, control passes back to the calling script. See the Return and Pop command summaries. See Chapter 7's "Using Pop to Exit Subroutines or Programs" for a review of the different ways to end a subroutine.

Ffree

Unload fonts from memory buffers.

```
ffree buffer [buffer] ...
```

Parameters

buffer   The designated font buffer.

Comments

See the Fload, Fgaps, Font, Fstyle, and Text commands. See the Set (Text Control) command for additional typographical controls.

Fgaps

Sets the gaps between text characters and the words.

```
fgaps [character] [space] [vgap]
```

Parameters

character   The spaces between letters.

space   Word spacing.

vgap   Line spacing.

Comments

The parameters are measured in pixels. Fgaps with no parameters resets the spacing to the defaults for the current font. Chapter 4's "Adding Text to Screens" provides information on formatting text displays. Also see the Fload, Ffree, Font, Fstyle, and Text commands. See the Set (Text Control) command for additional typographical controls.

Fload

Loads a font into memory.

```
fload name [buffer]
```

Parameters

name   The file name of the font.

buffer   The buffer into which a font is loaded.

Comments

Fonts can have either a .SET or .FNT extension. GRASP will use the default font for the current video mode (font 0) if no font is loaded before a Text command is issued. See Chapter 4 for an extensive discussion of Text commands. Also see the Fgaps, Ffree, Font, Fstyle, and Text commands. See the Set (Text Control) command for additional typographical controls.

Float

Floats a clipping between two locations on the screen.

```
float xstart,ystart xend,yend step delay buf[buf]...
```

Parameters

xstart,ystart   The starting (x1,y1) position.

xend,yend   The ending (x2,y2) position.

step   The Step parameter determines the distance in pixels between the successive displays of the clipping.

delay   Determines how long to pause between successive displays of the clipping.

buf   You can have the Fly command only animate one clipping (Buffer.), or several clippings. The command will animate each clipping in turn.

Comments

See Chapter 4, "Floating the Title on the Screen" for an example of the command's use. Compare this command to the Fly command. While Fly puts up copies of the clippings across the screen, Float "floats" the clipping across the screen. The clipping is pasted into the final position with the Putup command.

Fly

Paste clippings between two specified locations on the screen.

```
fly xstart,ystart xend,yend step delay buf[buf]...
```

Parameters

xstart,ystart   The starting (x1,y1) position.

xend,yend   The ending (x2,y2) position.

step   The Step parameter determines the distance in pixels between the successive displays of the clipping.

delay   Determines how long to pause between successive displays of the clipping.

buf   You can have the Fly command only animate one clipping (buf), or several clippings. The command will animate each clipping in turn.

Comments

See Chapter 4 ("Using Fly to Animate Clippings") for an extensive discussion of this command and the related Float command. Fly pastes up copies of the clippings across the screen, while Float "floats" the clipping across the screen.

Font

Select a previously loaded font.

`font [buffer]`

Parameters

buffer   The buffer where the font was previously loaded

Comments

Omitting the buffer parameter causes GRASP to set the current font to Font 0, the default font for the current video mode. Use the Font command with caution. Issuing a Font command causes GRASP to reset the character, word, and line spacing for the selected font to the defaults for that font. A guide to text attributes and typographical controls can be found in Chapter 4's "Adding Text to Screens." See the list of typographical controls in the command summary Set (Text Control). Also see the Fgaps, Ffree, Fload, Fstyle, and Text commands.

Fstyle

Choose a shadowing style for text.

`fstyle direction offset1 [offset2]`

Parameters

direction The direction of the shadow can have a value from 0 to 8: 0 means no shadow, 8 means a shadow down and to the right. Figure 4-12 (Chapter 4) shows in what directions the shadow can fall.

offset1 Offset1 determines the distance in pixels the shadow falls horizontally.

offset2 Offset2 determines how many pixels the shadow falls vertically.

Comments

If only offset1 value is given, it is used for both the horizontal and vertical offsets. A guide to text attributes and typographical controls can be found in Chapter 4's "Adding Text to Screens." Fstyle 0 turns off shadowing. Also see the Fgaps, Ffree, Fload, Color, Font, and Text commands. See the Set (Text Control) command for additional typographical controls.

Getcolor

Assigns the color of a designated point on the screen to a variable, or sets current color to equal a specified point on the screen.

```
getcolor x,y [variable]
```

Parameters

x,y Coordinates of the designated point.

variable Any valid variable name. GRASP will assign the color at x,y to this variable. If the variable is not given, GRASP will change the current color to the one found at x,y.

Comments

The command provides a convenient way of setting the current color using a point of color on the screen.

Getkey

Assigns the user's last keystroke to a variable.

```
getkey variable
```

Parameters

variable Any valid variable name.

Comments

Getkey is preceded by a Waitkey. It's usually followed by a conditional If.

```
waitkey
getkey key
if asc(@key)==val label
```

where val is a decimal value assigned to the key. See Chapter 7 ("Using Getkey for User Interaction") for a thorough discussion of this command.

Getmouse

This command reports on mouse button status and mouse cursor position.

```
getmouse butn [x,y] [test]
```

Parameters

butn   The butn parameter is the name of a variable that stores the information about which mouse button was pressed, if any, since the last Getmouse command was issued. A value of 0 indicates no button was pressed, and a value of 1 indicates the left mouse button was pressed. See the on-line reference ((F2)) for other mouse clicks.

x,y   The x,y optional variables store where the user clicked on the screen or what the current mouse cursor position is.

test.   If test is not used, GRASP reports the current position and button status of the mouse. If the parameter is given a value of 0, GRASP returns information about the most recent button click (press). If a 1 is used for test, GRASP returns the information about the button and screen location at the point where the button is released.

Comments

See Chapter 9, "Determining User Menu Choices" for a detailed discussion of Getmouse and a comparison between Getmouse and Ifmouse.

Global

Create and set values for variables that stay in effect throughout the running of a program.

```
global name value [name value] ...
```

Parameters

name   Variable name.

value   A variable, character string, or expression. An expression is a combi-
            nation of values and operators that can be evaluated to yield a value.
            The editor's on-line (F2) Help key lists operators.

Comments

The use of variables in a GRASP program is discussed in Chapter 4. The discussion
of the "scope" of variables is in Chapter 5 "Using Local and Global Variables." The
values of global variables can be changed using either the set or global key names.
See the discussion of the GRASP function that checks for the presence of variables,
def(variable), in Chapter 4, "Using Flags in Programming." See also the command
summaries for Set (variables) and Local variables.

Gosub

Causes a branch to a labeled subroutine.

```
[gosub] label [val] [val] [val] ...
```

Parameters

label   A label marking another part of the script where execution
            continues. (A label is a word with a colon tacked on the end.)
            Execution returns to the main body of the script when a return is
            encountered.

val   Up to 25 values can be passed to a subroutine. The subroutine reads
            the values as the special symbols @1, @2, @3, ..., @25.

Comments

See Chapter 3, "Branching with Goto," for a the review of the difference between a
Gosub and a Goto. Chapter 9's DrawMenu subroutine (in the section "Using
GRASP's Programming Flexibility") is an excellent example of parameter passing
between a main script and a subroutine. The keyword Gosub is optional. See the
following command summary for Goto.

Goto

Causes a jump to another part of a GRASP script where execution continues. Does
not return.

```
goto label
```

Parameters

label   Word with a colon tacked on the end that denotes a block of
               commands.

Comments

See Gosub. Goto is discussed in Chapter 3.

If (if-else-endif)

Tests an expression. If the expression is true, executes command. If false, executes
second set of commands.

```
if expression
        command
else
        command
endif
```

Parameters

expression   A GRASP expression, a value, or a variable. An expression is a
               combination of values and operators that can be evaluated to yield a
               value. The editor on-line (F2) Help key lists operators and their
               precedence.

Comments

If both expressions are false, execution proceeds at the line after the Endif.

If (jump)

Causes a jump to another part of the program if an expression tests true, otherwise
execution continues with the next command.

```
if expression label
```

Parameters

expression   A GRASP expression, a value, or a variable. An expression is a
               combination of values and operators that can be evaluated to yield a
               value. The editor on-line (F2) help key lists operators and their
               precedence.

label   Word with a colon tacked on the end that marks a block of
               commands.

Comments

See the next command summary for a comparison between If(jump) and If (If-Else-Endif). If the expression evaluates to 0 (the number zero), than the expression is false. If the expression evaluates to 1, the expression is true. If an expression is true, execution jumps to the label. If an expression is false, execution continues with the next command.

Ifkey

Test key pressed after a Waitkey. If specified key is pressed, jump to another part of the program, otherwise continue execution on the next line.

```
waitkey
ifkey key [label] [key label] ...
```

Parameters

key   Key is the key or key combination to check for.

label   If a label is supplied, GRASP will branch to the label specified elsewhere in the program. If a label is not specified, Ifkey works like a conditional If programming statement.

Comments

See Chapter 3 for commentary on this command. The Ifkey command is similar to the When command. The When command continues looking for a keypress until it is turned off; the Ifkey command only looks for the specified key during the last Waitkey. To test for uppercase keystrokes, use quotation marks around the letter. See the on-line reference ((F2)) for special keys for which you can test.

Ifmem

Check system memory.

```
ifmem mem [label]
```

Parameters

mem   The total amount in bytes of system memory the user must have free in order to run your presentation.

label   If the user has the required memory, execution jumps to a label (word ending with colon) in another part of the program.

Comments

See Chapter 6 for an extensive treatment of the command.

Ifmouse

Tests the user's mouse click after a Waitkey command.

```
waitkey
ifmouse button [label1] [x1,y1 x2,y2] [color] [wait] [label2]
```

Parameters

button
: The mouse button to check for. Designated by a number. 0 tests for no buttons pressed. A 1 tests for left button presses. See the table in the on-line help ((F2)) for a table of mousebutton values.

label1
: GRASP label to jump to if user selects test region.

x1,y1 x2,y2
: Test region.

color
: Color used to highlight the test region. If selected, the test region is highlighted when mouse button is released. Entering 0 does not highlight test region.

wait
: Specifies how long GRASP waits for the user to click. Measured in hundredths of a second.

label2·
: Label (word with colon on end) where program execution jumps to if the user does not click within specified wait time.

Comments

Chapter 4 gives extensive coverage to mouse interfacing. The mouse must be turned on with the Mouse command. See the summary for the Mouse command.

Ifvideo

The command Ifvideo checks to see if the user's system will support a specified video mode.

```
ifvideo mode [label]
```

Parameters

mode
: A specified video mode. See video mode listings by pressing (F3) while in the editor. If the system does support the mode, execution continues at the label.

Comments

See Chapter 6 ("Using Ifvideo to Check the Video Mode") for extensive coverage of this command.

Int

Calls a system interrupt. Especially useful for low-level DOS operations such as disk access.

int num [ax] [bx] [cx] [dx] [si] [di] [ds] [es]

Parameters

num   The num parameter is the interrupt number to call. The other parameters are the values to place in the named registers. Register values must be supplied for all registers, in sequence, up to the last register to be set. The values to be output can be 0 to 65,535 and can be expressed as decimal or hex values. Hex values must be prefaced with Ox (Ox1A is decimal 26). In cases where control passes to GRASP, variables with the names of the system registers are set equal to their contents. These can be referred to as @ax, @bx, and so on. The variable @0 is set equal to the system Flags, for error-checking purposes.

Comments

See Chapter 6 for an example of the command's use.

Line

Draw a line between two screen coordinates.

```
line x1,y1 x2,y2 [r]
```

Parameters

x1,y1   The beginning horizontal coordinate (x1), and the beginning vertical coordinate (y1).

x2,y2   The end point of the line.

r   The optional r parameter (line x1,y1 x2,y2 [r]) allows you to create a second line whose coordinates are added to (or subtracted from) the previous line command's coordinates.

Comments

Chapter 4 ("Using the Line Command") provides extensive commentary on this command.

Link

Load and pass control to another GRASP script. Do not return.

```
link [label]
```

Parameters

label   Branch to a label (word with colon on an end) in another script.

Comments

See section in Chapter 4 called, "Linking GRASP Scripts" for a comparison of Link with other program control commands. See the Call and Merge command summaries.

Load

Load disk files into a memory buffer.

```
load [path]file
```

Parameters

path   Valid DOS Path statement (e.g. c:\).

file   Use the file's extension to load the file.

Comments

The command is used to load GRPs into memory. (GRPs are special files that extend GRASP's functionality.) The command offers an alternate way of loading text files into memory for display. Here's an example:

```
video m
load words.txt          ; loads ASCII text
text @@words            ; displays it on screen
waitkey
.farfree @words         ; free up memory
exit
```

The Farfree function is similar in operation to Pfree and Cfree. It frees memory assigned to the text file. Note that we use double indirection to refer to the content of the buffer. Large text files that exceed memory resources cannot be loaded this way.

Local

Create and set a local variable. You declare a local variable using either of the following:

```
set name [value]
```

or

```
local name [value]
```

Parameters

name   Name of the variable.

value   A character string, expression, or variable. An expression is a combi-
              nation of values and operators that can be evaluated to yield a value.
              The editor on-line (F2) Help key lists operators and their precedence.

Comments

See the discussion "Using Local and Global Variables" in Chapter 5. See also the
Global and Set Variables command summaries. See the discussion of the GRASP
function that checks for the presence of variables, def(variable), in Chapter 4,
"Using Flags in Programming."

Mark/Loop

The Mark/Loop structure causes a section of code to be repeated a specified
number of times. Here's the structure of the loop:

```
mark count
...                              ; body of loop
loop
```

Parameters

count   The number of times the loop is executed. The value can be 1 to
              65,535.

Comments

A Mark must be paired with a Loop. See Chapter 3, "How a Loop Works," for a
detailed discussion of the structure of a loop. You can nest loops inside loops, but
each Mark command must be matched by a Loop command. To stop a loop before
reaching the counter value, use the Break command.

Merge

Merge adds another GRASP program to the end of the current program.

```
merge name
```

Parameters

name   The name of the merged file is assumed to have a .TXT extension. Add the file extension if it isn't .TXT. The file must be in ASCII format.

Comments

The merged file exists external to the script you are working on, but when you add it to the end of a GRASP script, GRASP treats it just as if it is part of the current script. This makes it possible to use labeled subroutines in the merged script. See "Combining GRASP Scripts" in Chapter 4. See the Call and Link command summaries. Chapter 8, "Merging Questions and Answers with the Script," provides an example of using Merge to load disk files into the current script for display as text on the screen.

Mouse Cursor

Create a mouse cursor shape using a clipping.

```
mouse cursor shape x,y [mask]
```

Parameters

shape   Shape is the clipping buffer or clipping file to use for the cursor shape.

x,y   The x,y coordinates are offsets into the clipping where you want the cursor's hot spot to be located.

mask   The mask is a second clipping that prevents the background from showing through.

Comments

See the extensive discussion of mouse interfacing in Chapter 4, particularly "Creating Mouse Cursors." See the following mouse commands as well.

Mouse On/Off

Turn display of the mouse cursor on and off.

```
mouse setting
```

Parameters

setting   Either "on" or "off."

Comments

See the Mouse Cursor command for determining the mouse cursor shape. See the following mouse commands. Mouse interfacing is covered in Chapter 4.

Mouse Position

Place the mouse cursor at a precise location on the screen.

```
mouse position [x,y]
```

Parameters

x,y   Location of the mouse cursor hot spot on the screen.

Comments

Default mouse position is 0,0. Chapter 4 covers mouse interfacing in depth.

Mouse Sense

Changes the sensitivity of the mouse cursor to hand movements.

```
mouse sense [sensitivity] [velocity]
```

Parameters

sensitivity   Sensitivity is the ratio between movement of the mouse over the desktop and movement of the mouse cursor on the screen. It applies to normal movements of the hand, such as when you are moving from one closely spaced option to another. It can have a value between 0 and 7: 0 is a high degree of sensitivity (a slow hand movement will produce a relatively faster movement of the cursor on the screen); 7 produces the smallest on-screen change relative to hand movement.

velocity   The velocity parameter controls the speed of the mouse cursor when you move it suddenly from one area of the screen to another. The value can be between 0 and 7 inclusive. The fastest is 7.

Comments

Chapter 4 covers mouse interfacing extensively. See the other mouse commands as well.

Mouse Window

Restrict movement of the mouse to an on-screen window.

```
mouse window [x1,y1 x2,y2]
```

Parameters

x1,y1 x2,y2   Coordinates of the window, beginning with bottom left corner.

Comments

The mouse will jump to the area inside the window when it is first turned on. Use the command without the coordinates to reset the window to the entire screen.

Noise

Generate a tone on the system speaker.

```
noise n m time
```

Parameters

n m   Values used to create the sound wave.

time   The duration of the sound wave in hundredths of a second.

Comments

Specifying different values for n and m creates complex waveforms rather than smooth glissandos. Noise tends to create sharp, loud, metallic sounds, whereas the Note command creates more musical sounds. By placing two Noise commands together, we create a more complex sound. See "Adding a Bird Chirp" in Chapter 5 for an example of the command's use.

Note

Uses the system speaker to create tones.

```
note val tone time [r]
```

Parameters

val   The pitch of the sound.

tone   The tone of the sound.

time   The duration of the sound.

r   Adds the value of the first parameter (the pitch) to a previous Note command.

Comments

See "Manipulating the Computer Speaker" in Chapter 5 for a discussion of the command's application. A table of notes is also provided.

Offset

Displays screen activity by a specified amount for selected commands.

`offset x,y [r]`

Parameters

x,y   Displaces the coordinates for subsequent commands by the specified amounts. The x,y values are added or subtracted to the subsequent command's values.

r   Relative switch. Add or subtract x,y values to the previous offset command.

Comments

Offsets are most often used with loops.

Opengl

Changes the current directory.

`opengl ,, path`

Parameters

,,   The commas instruct GRASP to skip the two options normally specified when GRASP is working with its proprietary library files (GL files).

path   Any valid DOS Path statement.

Comments

The version of GRASP that is bundled with this book does not include the GL library files utility, GLIB.EXE. The command is discussed in Chapter 4 ("Plugging the Slide Projector into the Rome Tour").

Palette

Change the current palette to that of the specified picture.

`palette [buffer]`

Parameters

buffer   Buffer containing the picture.

Comments

If the palette command is not used, or is used without the buffer parameter, the palette is set to the default palette for the current video mode.

Pfade

Fades a picture onto the screen.

```
pfade fade [buffer] [speed] [delay]
```

Parameters

fade   Fade number. The editor's (F3) key lists 26 fades.

buffer   Number of buffer. Default buffer is 1.

speed   Speed of the fade in hundredths of a second.

delay   Pauses the specified time before executing the next command.

Comments

The command does not support transparency. See Pfree, Pnewbuf, Psetbuf, and Pload.

Pfree

Unload a picture from a specified buffer.

```
pfree buffer
```

Parameters

buffer   Number of buffer. Default is 1. A series of picture buffers can be freed by using a dash between values, e.g., pfree p1 - p10.

Comments

See Pfade, Pgetbuf, Pload, and Psetbuf command summaries.

Pgetbuf

The Pgetbuf command saves the current screen to a buffer in memory.

```
pgetbuf buffer [x1,y1 x2,y2]
```

Parameters

buffer   A specified buffer.

x1,y1 x2,y2   The optional coordinates allow you to save only part of the screen to
                a buffer.

Comments

See the section on "Saving the Screen to a Buffer" in Chapter 4. There we present
the technique of saving the screen to a file on the hard drive using the Psave
command in combination with Pgetbuf.

Pload

Loads a picture into a memory buffer.

```
pload name [buffer]
```

Parameters

name   Use the full name with extension if the picture is not in GRASP's PIC
                format.

buffer   A number from 1 to 128. Default buffer is 1.

Comments

GRASP supports Pictor (PIC), CompuServe (GIF), Bsave (PIC), and Zsoft (PCX)
picture formats. You can load a picture into a previous picture's buffer, but it is
good practice to free an existing buffer first.

Pnewbuf

Create a buffer containing a blank picture in the current color.

```
pnewbuf buffer [x,y]
```

Parameters

x,y   Optional size of the image in pixels.

Comments

If you don't specify a screen size, the default is full screen size for the current video
mode. See the section "Building Images Off-Screen" in Chapter 4.

Point

Sets the color of an individual pixel on the screen.

`point x,y [rx,ry]`

Parameters

x,y   Assigns the current color to a precise x,y location on the screen.

rx,ry   In combination with the x,y coordinates, creates a rectangular area
                inside which the point is randomly placed.

Comments

See "Drawing Points on the Screen" in Chapter 4.

Pop

Causes a subroutine to stop executing. Branches to a label in the calling routine.

`pop label`

Parameters

label   A label (word with a colon on the end) in the calling routine.

Comments

See the extensive review of the Pop command in "Using Pop to Exit Subroutines or
Programs," Chapter 7. Compare Pop to Exit and Return commands.

Position

Alter the position of a picture or clipping relative to the screen.

`position buffer x,y [R]`

Parameters

buffer   Buffer number of the picture you want to alter. This can be a
                clipping or a picture.

x,y   Determines where on the screen the bottom left corner of the
                picture or clipping will be placed.

r   Makes the present position command's coordinates relative to a
                previous position command's coordinates.

Comments

See an example of the use of the command to alter clipping offsets in Chapter 4,
"Using Position to Alter Clipping Offsets."

385

Psave

Save a picture in a buffer to the disk drive.

`psave name buffer`

Parameters

name   Name of the file to save. You must include the file extension. Use
            .PIC for pictures and CLP for clippings.

buffer   Buffer number of the picture or clipping (e.g., "psave new.clp c3"
            saves a clipping to disk).

Comments

The section "Saving the Screen to a Buffer with PGETBUF" in Chapter 4 describes
the method for saving a buffer to the disk. See the Pgetbuf command.

Psetbuf

The Psetbuf command redirects fades, text, and drawing commands to the buffer
you specify.

`psetbuf [buffer]`

Parameters

buffer   Buffer number to which screen activity will be directed. When the
            parameter is omitted, activity is restored to the screen.

Comments

You must create a buffer for Psetbuf to point to. You can build up a complex
picture off-screen in this way. See Chapter 4, "Building Images Off-Screen." See
Pnewbuf, Pgetbuf, Pload, and Psave.

Putdff

Plays a DFF (differential) animation previously designated by the Dload command.

`putdff [buffer] [delay] [start] [end] [x,y]`

Parameters

buffer   A buffer (or disk file) you have previously loaded. Can be a DFF or
            Animator FLI file.

delay   Specifies the length of time between frames in hundredths of a second (the default is 0).

start end   Allows you to play the frames between the frame numbers you designate.

x,y   Offset into the screen from the bottom left corner where the animation will play.

Comments

The commercial version of GRASP supports the FLC (high-resolution) animator format. If you did not create the DFF animation with the /1 parameter, use the Pfade command to display the first of the series of pictures from which the animation was made. See the extensive comments on GDFF in Chapter 5, "Using GDFF to Create Animations." See also Dfree and Dload.

Putup

Method for displaying clippings at a precise location on the screen.

```
putup [x,y] [buffer] [delay]
```

Parameters

x,y   If you specify x,y coordinates, these coordinates will be added to the clipping's offsets.

buffer   Previously loaded buffer.

delay   Specified pause in hundredths of seconds until next command is executed.

Comments

The special advantage of the Putup command is that it supports transparency and automatically displays images using the x and y offsets stored with them. See "Using Putup to Display Images" in Chapter 4 for an example of the use of the command with transparency.

Rect

Create a filled rectangle on the screen.

```
rect x1,y1 x2,y2
```

Parameters

x1,y1 x2,y2   Coordinates describing opposite corners of the rectangle.

Comments

The rectangle is drawn in the current color.

Return

End execution of a subroutine and return control to the calling routine.

`return [value]`

Parameters

value   A value or string passed back to the calling routine. The calling
                 routine reads the return variable @0. See "Using The @0 Variable" in
                 Chapter 6.

Comments

Compare return to the Exit and Pop commands. See Chapter 7's "Using Pop to Exit
Subroutines or Programs" for a review of the different ways of ending a subroutine.

Set (system control)

Provides additional control over the system.

`set function setting`

Parameters

function   The system attribute to change.

setting   Either "on" or "off".

Comments

The following is a select list:

```
set abort on/off          on:    Default. Allows keys to cancel Waitkeys.
                          off:   Prevents keys from canceling Waitkeys.
set cgetshift on /off     on:    Default. Used with Cgetbuf.
                                 Rounds coordinates to nearest byte boundary.
                          off:   Clipping taken from exact screen location
                                 specified.
set debug on/off          on:    Displays commands on bottom of screen as
                                 they are executed.
                          off:   Default.
set esc on/off            on:    Default. Terminates program.
                                 Can make equal to another key.
```

388

```
set space on/off          on:    Default. Pauses program. Enter resumes.
                                  Can make equal to another key.
set retrace on/off        on:    Slows down animation to avoid flicker.
                          off:   Default.
set xor on/off            on:    Makes drawing commands semitransparent.
                                 Allows DFFs to play backward.
                          off:   Default.
```

Note: (ESC) and (SPACE) keys can be reassigned to other keys:

```
set (ESC) (ALT)-(S)
set (SPACE) (CONTROL)-(P)
```

Set (text control)

Provides typographical control over the display of text.

```
set feature setting
```

Parameters

feature   The text attribute to change.

setting   Either "on" or "off."

Comments

The following text attributes can be set:

```
set center on/off         on:    Centered on screen or in window.
                          off:   Default.
set cliptext on/off       on:    Window clips text at right edge.
                                 Turn wrap off first.
                          off:   Default.
set left on/off           on:    Left-justifies text.
                          off:   Default.
set monospace on/off      on:    Fixed letter spacing. Handy for charts.
                          off:   Default.
set right on/off          on:    Right-justifies text.
                          off:   Default.
set wrap on/off           on:    Default. Ignores return/line feeds in blocks of text.
                          off:   Preserves line breaks in blocks of text.
                                 Text still wraps if it is too long for window.
```

See Fgaps. Fload, Font, Fstyle, Text, and Window command summaries. A guide to text attributes and typographical controls can be found in Chapter 4's "Adding Text to Screens."

Set (variables)

Change the values of global and local variables. Create local variables.

```
set variable value [variable value] ...
```

Parameters

variable GRASP variable name.

value   A character string, expression, or variable. An expression is a combination of values and operators that can be evaluated to yield a value. The editor's on-line (F2) Help key lists operators.

Comments

Creates local variables only, but can change either local or global variables. The use of variables in a GRASP program is discussed extensively in Chapter 4. The discussion of the "scope" of variables is in Chapter 5, "Using Local and Global Variables." See the discussion of the GRASP function that checks for the presence of variables, def(variable), in Chapter 4, "Using Flags in Programming." See also the command summaries for Global and Local variables.

Setcolor

Directly manipulate the system palette. The command can only be used in Video M or other 16-color EGA modes.

```
setcolor val0 val1 val2 ... val15
```

Parameters

val0 ...val15 A value from 0 to 63. All 16 colors of the palette must be specified.

Comments

The color index values you specify for each of the 16 palette slots can be any one of the 64 EGA colors. Setcolor is reviewed in Chapter 4, "Using Setcolor to Change the Palette."

Spread

Gradually alter one picture's palette (pal1) to become another picture's palette (pal2). Requires a VGA adapter.

```
spread [pal1] pal2 [steps]
```

Parameters

pal1   The current palette.

pal2   The destination palette.

steps   Number of palette changes between pal1 and pal2. Default is 64 steps. A negative number will multiply each of the 64 steps by the specified number of times. E.g., -2 causes each step to be multiplied by 2, lengthening the time of the fade.

Comments

The (ESC) key will not arrest a spread.

Text

Text puts a string (series of characters) on the screen at the specified screen location.

```
text [x,y] string [delay]
```

Parameters

x,y   If you do not specify an x,y (horizontal, vertical) position for text to appear on the screen, the default position is in the top left corner of the screen or a window. Additional text is added to the point where the last text stopped.

string   A series of characters. If there are spaces, the string must be enclosed in quotation marks. This preserves capitalization and allows text to be spread over several lines.

delay   Time it takes to print the line on-screen in hundredths of a second.

Comments

See the Text command's explanation, "Displaying Text on the Screen," in Chapter 3. A guide to text attributes and typographical controls can be found in Chapter 4 "Adding Text to Screens." See the list of typographical controls in the command summary Set (text control). Setting the xor setting on (set xor on) causes the text to be displayed semitransparently. To confine text to a rectangular area of the screen, define a window. Text will begin to appear at the top left corner of the window. If the text command uses the x,y parameters and a window is active, only the text that falls within the window will display. Text color is set by the Color command. If you specify a second color (e.g., color 15 0), The second color will become the shadow color. (The Fstyle command turns on shadowing.) See the Merge and Load commands for ways of putting disk file text on the screen.

Tile

Wallpaper the screen with clippings.

```
tile buffer [bleed]
```

Parameter

buffer   Buffer number of the clipping to use.

bleed   Default is 0 (off). Setting to 1 starts the tile at the bottom left corner and fills the screen, allowing the clippings to overlap (bleed) on the edges. Setting to 0 centers clippings on the screen.

Comments

If the clipping does not have an even number of bytes, load the clipping with shifted copies. If the clipping was loaded with transparency set to "on," the clipping will be displayed transparently.

Timer

Issuing the Timer command creates a GRASP clock and sets it to 0. GRASP then proceeds to the first Waitkey command it encounters and compares the elapsed time on its clock to the wait time specified by the Waitkey command. It waits until the time specified by the Waitkey command has elapsed before proceeding to the next command.

```
timer
waitkey
```

Parameters

None.

Comments

The Waitkey command that follows a Timer command has the effect of turning GRASP's clock off again. The Timer/Waitkey also has the effect of making GRASP run independent of CPU speed. See Chapter 5's treatment of the command, "Using Timer to Pace the Script." See also "Using @elapsed to Time Sequences."

Tran

Process clippings so that a specified palette color is transparent to the background.

```
tran set [color]
```

Parameters

set   Either "on" or "off". Default is off. When turned on, analyzes clipping for transparent color.

color   Palette color slot to make transparent.

Comments

See the extensive explanation of this command in the section "Using the Transparency Command" in Chapter 4.

Video

Sets the video mode.

```
video mode [x,y] [int]
```

Parameters

mode   A letter designating the video mode. See the list of video modes on Page 3 of the editor's (F3) on-line Help.

x,y   The horizontal and vertical size of the screen.

int   Optional DOS interrupt call (10h) value.

Comments

Use the command to establish an initial video mode and to change it subsequently.

Waitkey

Pause program execution until a key is pressed or until a specified time has elapsed.

```
waitkey [time] [label]
```

Parameters

time   Time in hundredths of a second.

label   Label (word with a colon on end) to branch to if the user presses a key.

Comments

When used without parameters, Waitkey suspends program execution until the user presses a key. You can optionally specify a wait time. Program execution will continue after the wait time has elapsed.

When

Assign commands to specified keys.

`when key command (parameters)`

Parameters

key   The key GRASP checks for constantly, even while the computer is doing other things. For a list of special keys and key combinations used with the When and Ifkey commands, press (F2) while in the GRASP editor and cycle to the last page.

command   The command to be executed including its options if any.

Comments

The When key assignment stays in effect while the program runs. The key assignment can be canceled at any time by issuing a When command without a key assignment. See "Using When to Implement User Interaction" in Chapter 3.

Window

Confines screen activity to a rectangular area of the screen.

`window x1,y1 x2,y2 [r]`

Parameters

x1,y1 x2,y2   A rectangular area beginning at the left bottom coordinates.

r   Adds the coordinates to previously issued window coordinates. Can be negative.

Comments

When you first start up GRASP, the default Window encompasses the entire screen. Make sure you define the window beginning with the bottom left corner. When used with no coordinates, the window is reset to the default resolution for the current video mode. See the discussion of the Window command in "Altering the Default Screen Window," Chapter 4. See the discussion of the system variables minx, miny, maxx, and maxy in the "Animating the Bird" section of Chapter 5. The section shows how to preserve and restore system window settings.

Appendix A:
Multimedia Creations Disk

This appendix lists the contents of the *Multimedia Creations* disks. The Install program on the Install disk (INSTALL.EXE) automates the installation of the files onto the hard drive. The files are organized into a master directory (GRASP) and a number of subdirectories (CHAPT01 to CHAPT09 and UTILITY). These subdirectories correspond to the chapters in the book. Chapter 6 files are actually found in the CHAPT05 subdirectory. The CHAPT06 subdirectory is omitted. Chapters 1 and 10 do not have example files. Chapter 2 example files are found in the main directory (GRASP). Most of the utility files are found in the GRASP directory, although some of them can be found in the UTILITY subdirectory.

FILE LISTINGS

Here are the file listings for the subdirectories as reported by DOS's DIR command:

Directory of C:\GRASP

```
Directory of C:\GRASP
[.]             [..]            [CHAPT03]       [CHAPT04]       [CHAPT05]
PICTOR.EXE      [CHAPT07]       [CHAPT08]       [CHAPT09]       [UTILITY]
README.TXT      DEMO.BAT        INSTALL.BAT     PLAYER.BAT      README.BAT
BELLO1.CLP      BELLO2.CLP      BELLO3.CLP      BELLO4.CLP      BELLO5.CLP
BELLO6.CLP      BREW1.CMF       CAP.COM         LEGS.DFF        CONVPIC.EXE
GRASPC.EXE      PLAYD.EXE       SHOWPIC.EXE     TXTCLP.EXE      WHATPIC.EXE
LIBRO.FLC       BOLD.FNT        BOLD1.FNT       BOLD2.FNT       ORMAL.FNT
NORMAL1.FNT     NORMAL2.FNT     OLDENG.FNT      OLDENG1.FNT     OLDENG2.FNT
ROMAN.FNT       ROMAN1.FNT      ROMAN2.FNT      SPECIAL.FNT     SPECIAL1.FNT
SPECIAL2.FNT    SOUNDPC.GRP     BREW1.MID       GRHELP.OVR      PCTRCGA.OVR
PCTREGA.OVR     PCTRHI.OVR      PCTRPSLO.OVR    PCTRRS.OVR      PCTRVID.OVR
```

395

```
PICTOR.OVR      BLACK.PAL       LEGS.PAL        BLACK.PIC       COVER.PIC
BIG.SET          HELVET15SET    HELVET20SET     HELVET25.SET    HELVET30.SET
IBM14.SET       IBM16.SET       IBM8.SET        ROME15.SET      ROME25.SET
SQUAR10.SET     SQUAR15.SET     SQUAR20.SET     BILLBORD.TXT    CHECK.TXT
CHECPLAY.TXT    COVER.TXT       INSTALL.TXT     MIDI.TXT        SHOWCORD.TXT
SHOWPAL.TXT     SNDPLAY.TXT
      82 file(s)
```

Directory of C:\GRASP\CHAPT03

```
[.]             [..]            SLID003.CLP     SLID004.CLP     SLID005.CLP
SLID006.CLP     MAKE003.PAL     MAKE004.PAL     MAKE005.PAL     MAKE006.PAL
BLACK.PIC       MAKE000.PIC     MAKESLID.TXT    PROJECTO.TXT    SLIDES.TXT
      15 file(s)
```

Directory of C:\GRASP\CHAPT04

```
[.]             [..]            ARROW.CLP       ARROW2.CLP      BUTTON.CLP
LION2.CLP       LIONHEAD.CLP    MAP1.CLP        MAP2.CLP        MAP3.CLP
ROSE.CLP        BLACKPIC.PAL    RED.PAL         ROSE.PAL        BLACK.PIC
LIONHEAD.PIC    ROMEBACK.PIC    ROAR.SND        BLACK.TXT       MAGAZINE.TXT
MAP.TXT         ROMEMENU.TXT
      22 file(s)
```

Directory of C:\GRASP\CHAPT05

```
[.]             [..]            PLAYER.BAT      ARMLFT.CLP      ARMRTHIP.CLP
BRINBUCK.CLP    BRUSH1.CLP      BRUSHL2.CLP     BRUSHL3.CLP     BRUSHR2.CLP
BRUSHR3.CLP     COUNT12.CLP     COUNT13.CLP     COUNT14.CLP     COUNT15.CLP
COUNT16.CLP     COUNT17.CLP     COUNT18.CLP     DOT.CLP         HEAD.CLP
HEADDOWN.CLP    HEADPROF.CLP    HEADUP.CLP      MAN100.CLP      MAN101.CLP
MAN102.CLP      MAN103.CLP      MAN104.CLP      MAN105.CLP      MAN106.CLP
MAN107.CLP      MAN108.CLP      MAN109.CLP      MAN110.CLP      MAN111.CLP
MULTI1.CLP      MULTI2.CLP      PAIL01.CLP      PAIL02.CLP      PAIL03.CLP
PAIL04.CLP      PAIL05.CLP      PARRO101.CLP    PARRO102.CLP    PARRO103.CLP
PARRO104.CLP    PARRO105.CLP    PARRO106.CLP    PARRO107.CLP    POINT.CLP
SQUARES.CLP     STAR1.CLP       STAR2.CLP       STAR3.CLP       STAR4.CLP
STATUE.CLP      SYL100.CLP      SYL101.CLP      SYL102.CLP      SYL103.CLP
SYL104.CLP      SYMBOL10.CLP    SYMBOL11.CLP    SYMBOL12.CLP    SYMBOL13.CLP
SYMBOL14.CLP    SYMBOL15.CLP    SYMBOL16.CLP    SYMBOL17.CLP    TAPDOWN.CLP
TAPUP.CLP       TURN.CLP        TURNARM.CLP     TURNHEAD.CLP    UMPEX100.CLP
UMPEX101.CLP    UMPEX102.CLP    UMPEX103.CLP    UMPEX104.CLP    UMPEX105.CLP
UMPEX106.CLP    UMPEX107.CLP    W.CLP           WAVE101.CLP     WAVE102.CLP
WAVE103.CLP     WAVE104.CLP     WAVE105.CLP     WAVE106.CLP     WAVE107.CLP
WAVE108.CLP     WGLOW.CLP       WOUT1.CLP       WOUT2.CLP       WOUT3.CLP
PAIL04.CLP      PAIL05.CLP      PARRO101.CLP    PARRO102.CLP    PARRO103.CLP
PARRO104.CLP    PARRO105.CLP    PARRO106.CLP    PARRO107.CLP    POINT.CLP
SQUARES.CLP     STAR1.CLP       STAR2.CLP       STAR3.CLP       STAR4.CLP
STATUE.CLP      SYL100.CLP      SYL101.CLP      SYL102.CLP      SYL103.CLP
SYL104.CLP      SYMBOL10.CLP    SYMBOL11.CLP    SYMBOL12.CLP    SYMBOL13.CLP
SYMBOL14.CLP    SYMBOL15.CLP    SYMBOL16.CLP    SYMBOL17.CLP    TAPDOWN.CLP
TAPUP.CLP       TURN.CLP        TURNARM.CLP     TURNHEAD.CLP    UMPEX100.CLP
UMPEX101.CLP    UMPEX102.CLP    UMPEX103.CLP    UMPEX104.CLP    UMPEX105.CLP
```

```
UMPEX106.CLP    UMPEX107.CLP    W.CLP          WAVE101.CLP    WAVE102.CLP
WAVE103.CLP     WAVE104.CLP     WAVE105.CLP    WAVE106.CLP    WAVE107.CLP
WAVE108.CLP     WGLOW.CLP       WOUT1.CLP      WOUT2.CLP      WOUT3.CLP
RACE.DFF        TRANSFOR.DFF    W2MSPIN.DFF    LEYA.MID       BLACK.PAL
GRAY.PAL        GREENBCK.PAL    M1.PAL         M2.PAL         M3.PAL
PALETTE.PAL     COVER.PIC       GREENBCK.PIC   BIRDCALL.SND   HORSE.SND
SAM.SND         SYNTH.SND       WELCOME.SND    WHINNY.SND     BILLBORD.TXT
CHECK.TXT       CHECPLAY.TXT    OPENING.TXT    TIMESUB.TXT    TITLE1.TXT
TITLE2.TXT      TITLE3.TXT      TITLE4.TXT     TITLE5.TXT     TMPFILE.TXT
WATCH.TXT       WFORM.TXT       BREW2.CMF      BREW.CMF
         129 file(s)
```

Directory of C:\GRASP\CHAPT07

```
[.]             [..]            INSTALL.BAT    PLAYER.BAT     BULB01.CLP
BULB02.CLP      BULB03.CLP      BULB04.CLP     BULB05.CLP     BREW.CMF
CHECPLAY.TXT    MUSIC1.TXT      MUSIC2.TXT
          13 file(s)
```

Directory of C:\GRASP\CHAPT08

```
[.]             [..]            AWIN1.CLP      AWIN2.CLP      BWIN1.CLP
BWIN2.CLP       F10EXIT.CLP     GRDTOT.CLP     HOST.CLP       TIE1.CLP
TIE2.CLP        FCSELNEW.PIC    FCTITLE.PIC    PATT.PIC       QSCREEN.PIC
CATEGORY.TXT    GAME.TXT        HOST.TXT
          18 file(s)
```

Directory of C:\GRASP\CHAPT09

```
[.]             [..]            ARROW.CLP      ARROWM.CLP     BUG.CLP
DRAG01.CLP      DRAG02.CLP      DRAG03.CLP     FISH.CLP       HELPWIN.CLP
PIPER.CLP       SHELL.CLP       BUG.PAL        FISH.PAL       SHELL.PAL
DRAGON.PIC      BUG.TXT         DISPATCH.TXT   DRAGON.TXT     FISH.TXT
MENU.TXT        PICKMENU.TXT    SETITUP.TXT    SHELL.TXT
          24 file(s)     161411 bytes
```

Directory of C:\GRASP\UTILITY

```
[.]             [..]            FADES.TXT      VOC2SND.EXE    ORDER.FRM
GDFF.EXE        ORDER.TXT
           7 file(s)
```

Appendix B:

GRASP Editor Help

This appendix provides basic help for beginning computer users in using GRASP's Editor.

STARTING THE EDITOR

If you installed GRASP correctly, you can start GRASP from any directory. (See the Installation Note at the beginning of the book if you run into trouble running GRASP.) To start GRASP type:

```
graspc
```

at any DOS prompt. If you do not understand what we mean by a DOS prompt, then you should consult a beginner's guide to navigating the MS-DOS operating system.

When you type graspc, you enter GRASP at the menu screen. GRASP has only one menu. We cover its use in Chapter 2, Using GRASP's Digital Studio.

Make sure that the red highlight is on the Edit menu choice. If it is not, use the ↑→↓← keys to move the red highlight onto the Edit choice. Then press ENTER.

INSIDE THE EDITOR

The sign-on screen disappears and you are placed "inside" the GRASP editor. If you are new to computers, you may experience a moment of terror. You are faced with a black screen with a blue ribbon on top. On the blue ribbon is the cryptic message:

TMPFILE   COL:1 LINE:1   FREE:4224 USED:969952 INSERT ON

The numbers that follow FREE and USED may be different on your computer. They report how much memory has been used (USED) so far in your program and how much is left or free (FREE). Ignore this for now.

Note the INSERT ON message. By default the (INS) key located on your keyboard is "on." This means text will be inserted at whatever spot you place the text cursor on the screen. The text cursor is that blinking dash up in the corner of the screen. Leave Insert "on" for now.

ENTERING TEXT

GRASP's editor works just like a primitive word processing program. In fact, if you've worked with the grandfather DOS word processing program, Wordstar, then you already know most of GRASP's editing keys. Like the original Wordstar program, the GRASP editor does not support a mouse.

By default, the script you are now working on is called TMPFILE.TXT. (If there happened to be a TMPFILE.TXT script in the directory where you ran GRASP, then you will see a screen full of text. GRASP loads the file TMPFILE.TXT in the editor by default. Exit GRASP and start it in another directory that does not contain TMPFILE.TXT. A DOS DIR command will tell you if the current directory has a file by that name. Chapter 2 shows you how to use GRASP's file functions.)

You enter text into TMPFILE.TXT simply by typing. Try that now. Type anything you like on the screen. When you get to the end of the line, GRASP will signal the fact by sending a high-pitched sound out through your system speaker. GRASP is a line-oriented editor. It gulps down text one line at a time. You must press (ENTER) (or (RETURN) on some keyboards) to get to the beginning of the next line. Pressing (ENTER) moves the cursor down the screen. GRASP interprets everything to the left of the cursor as program data.

Notice that as you type, the COL and LINE values at the top of the screen change. GRASP tells you exactly where you are on the screen. GRASP organizes the screen into 80 columns (COL) and 24 lines (LINE). If your script exceeds 24 lines, the line count continues to increment indefinitely, or until you run out of memory. Remember, every letter and every space you enter into a script occupies memory.

When you make a mistake in entering a command, GRASP will tell you the exact location of that mistake. Let's pretend that the first line you type was meant to be a GRASP command. Press (F10), GRASP's action key. The editing screen disappears and a white banner appears at the top of the screen.

Unknown command at line 1
Press Any Key to Continue

That's an error message from GRASP, telling you that it does not understand the command you just entered at the first line of the TMPFILE.TXT script. It also tells you at what line GRASP ran into trouble (1). Press any keyboard key to return to the editing screen.

CHANGING TEXT

You alter the text on screen by moving the text cursor to the line and text character that you want to change and inserting or deleting text. Use the ⊕⊖⊙⊖ keys to move to one of the characters you entered a moment ago and press the (DEL) key, once, quickly. (If you keep pressing on the (DEL) key, the next letters and the letters after that are deleted.) The letter disappears from the screen and the text to the right moves over to cover up the deleted character. Now press any of the letter keys. The text obligingly opens up to accommodate the new letter.

Now press the (ENTER) key. The line splits at the point where the cursor is placed. The part of the line to the right of the cursor moves with the cursor to the next line. Now press the (BACKSPACE) key. (It's either labeled "BackSpace" or it's the arrow at the top right of the letter keys that's pointing to the left. Don't confuse it with the arrow key.) The line moves back up to its previous position.

Pressing (ENTER) always moves the part of the line to the right of the cursor to the next line. Use it at column one (the far left) to open up spaces in your sript.

The (BACKSPACE) key always erases the letters or spaces to the left of the text cursor. Use the arrow keys to move about the screen without altering the text.

You can "type over" text on the screen by turning the (INS) key "off." The (INS) key is an example of a toggle switch. This means that it can be switched to its opposite condition by pressing it: If it is on, pressing it turns it off. If it is off, pressing it turns it on. Try typing over the lines that you entered by pressing the (INS) key to turn it off. Check that you have done so by looking at the top right corner of the screen. You should see INSERT OFF.

NAVIGATING THE EDITOR

You do not have to memorize the keys that will allow you to move about a GRASP script while in the editor. Pressing (F1) at any time while you are in the editor brings up the editor Help screen. Do that now. You will see the following screen:

```
TMPFILE      COL: 1   LINE:   1   FREE:42224   USED:934608      INSERT ON
```

```
  GRASP – Editor Help Screen                          Page 1 of 3

  F1 – Help with editor            ALT-F1  – DOS Shell
  F2 – Help with GRASP commands    ALT-F2  – File selection lists
  F3 – Help with GRASP fades       ALT-F3  – User defined help screens
  F4 – Block Mark – toggle on/of   ALT-F4
  F5 – Block Copy                  ALT-F5
  F6 – Block Move                  ALT-F6
  F7 – Read block from file        ALT-F7
  F8 – Write block to file         ALT-F8
  F9 – Save/run from current line  ALT-F9
  F10 – Save/run from top of file  ALT-F10 – Quick jump into Pictor

       ESC – Return to menu          ARROWS – Move around in editor
      HOME – Beginning of line    CTRL-HOME – Go to top of file
       END – End of line           CTRL-END – Go to bottom of file
  CTRL-LEFT – Left Word               ALT-D – Delete line
 CTRL-RIGHT – Right Word             INSERT – Insert mode toggle on/off
```

The screen lists the Help screens that are available by pressing the function keys at the top of your keyboard (labeled F1, F2, and so on). At the bottom of the screen are special keys that help you navigate the editor. If you press the (ENTER) key or the (PGDN) key, you'll see that there are other "pages" in the help listings. We'll return to these in a moment. Press (ESC) to exit from the Help screen.

THE MOST COMMON KEYS

You will develop personal preferences for how you work in the editor. Here are the most common kinds of activities and their associated keys.

Moving Around a Line:

(END)	Move to the end of the line.
(HOME)	Move to the beginning of the line.
(CONTROL)-(→)	Move right one word.
(CONTROL)-(←)	Move left one word.

Moving Around a Script:

(PGUP)	Move up 20 lines.
(PGDN)	Move down 20 lines.
(CONTROL)-(HOME)	Move to beginning of the file.
(CONTROL)-(END)	Move to end of file.

Deleting Text:

(ALT)-(D)	Delete a line.
(DELETE)	Delete one or more characters.

The dash between two names means to press two keys simultaneously. (CONTROL)-(→) means press down the (CONTROL) key and the (→) key. (ALT)-(D) means hold down the (ALT) key and either the uppercase or the lowercase (D) key.

These are all the keys you will need to know to begin writing GRASP scripts. You may find the other keys listed on the other pages of the editor Help screen useful. Don't try to memorize them at this time.

SEARCHING FOR TEXT OR REPLACING TEXT

Like most word processing programs, GRASP's Editor can search through a file looking for a string of characters and optionally replacing them. GRASP's editor includes this capability. Use (CONTROL)-(Q)-(F) to search for text in a long script. You will find the command documented on the second page of the editor Help screen.

```
^Q F    - Search for string
```

The ^ symbol stands for the (CONTROL) key. You must press the (CONTROL) key and either the uppercase or the lowercase (Q) key at the same time. Then you release the two keys and press the uppercase or lowercase (F) key. The other key combination that is quite useful is (ALT)-(S). This key combination allows you to search for a character or a series of characters and replace them. Both (CONTROL)-(Q)-(F) and (ALT)-(S) will prompt you for an option. Enter one of the following.

W	find whole words only
G	global search from the beginning of the script

The (ALT)-(S) combination has these additional options:

N	nonstop search and replace
#	number of replacements to make

Appendix C:

Using GRASP's Utilities

This appendix contains programs that will help you work with GRASP and GRASP scripts. The everyday utility programs are in the main \GRASP directory; specialized programs have been placed in the \GRASP\UTILITY subdirectory. These programs are provided as a service to our readers.

UTILITIES IN THE GRASP DIRECTORY

The following utilities can be found in the GRASP main directory. When you run some GRASP utilities without parameters, a Help screen with a summary of command options appears.

CAP.COM

Nobody has yet invented the Swiss Army knife of screen capture programs. The GRASP CAP.COM capture utility is provided as a service to our readers, with two caveats: Don't expect it to capture all the screens in all your applications, and remember that it can get cranky at times and lock up your computer. (In other words, we do not provide tech support for this program!) In particular, CAP won't capture Windows screens. We suggest you use Windows' own facilities to do that. Save the Windows screen in PCX format. You can then use GRASP's CONVPIC.EXE utility to convert the PCX file into Pictor PIC format.

CAP.COM saves screens in GRASP PIC format. You install it as a memory resident program (TSR). Just type the program's name at the DOS prompt. The program has four options:

```
cap [/K:xx] [/I:5] [/V:m] [name]
```

Parameters

/K:xx   Sets the hot-key combination used to call CAP. ReplaceX with one of the
following letters: A (Alt), C (Ctrl),L (Left-shift), or R (Right-Shift).
Default key is (A)(R).

/I:5   Causes (SHIFT)-(PRTSC) (Shift-Print Screen) to call CAP.

/V:m   Forces CAP to capture in the specified video mode.Replace m with a
GRASP video mode. (See the listings for these by pressing (F3) and
paging down in the GRASP editor.)

name   Saves the screen with the designated name. Successive screens add an
incremental number to the file name.

Comments

Assigning a new hot-key combination may be required because some programs may
already use the default GRASP hot-key combination ((ALT)-(RIGHT SHIFT)) for program
functions. Don't call CAP twice, you may hang the computer. Try calling it up with
the hot-key combination to see if it is loaded.

Using Cap

Load CAP, then run your application. CAP is called by pressing the hot-key combination. If CAP is successfully installed, you will see a flashing + at the center of the
screen. Pressing the (ENTER) key selects the current screen for capture. At the top left
of the screen a prompt appears asking for a PIC (picture) name. When you enter the
name and press (ENTER), the screen is saved to the disk. GRASP adds the file
extension .PIC to this disk file. Press (ESC) to remove the flashing + from the screen.
Choose the next screen for capture and repeat the process.

Unloading Cap

Call up CAP with the hot-key combination. When the flashing + appears, press
(ALT)-(Q). CAP.COM is removed from memory. You may have to reboot the computer
if CAP does not uninstall.

Other Features

Capturing screens can be a very tricky business. The commercial version of GRASP
contains an updated version of the program and documents additional features that
will improve your chances of capturing screens from programs that do not work
with CAP.COM. We use a number of screen capture programs for our work.

CONVPIC.EXE

This utility converts picture files from one mode to another and from PCX, GIF, and Bsave to GRASP's PIC format. The utility does not scale the image to the new video mode, so an EGA 640x350 pixel resolution image will appear smaller on a VGA 640x480 screen. Syntax for the command is:

```
convpic vmode imgname [imgname ...]
```

Parameters

vmode   The video mode of the resulting (not original) picture.

imgname   File name (including extension) of the original picture. The new file
         overwrites the old file.

Example

```
convpic m test.pic
```

If the original TEST.PIC was in Video Mode G (EGA), the new TEST.PIC file would be converted to Video Mode M (VGA).

Text screens cannot be converted with this utility. See TXTCLP.EXE for a utility that converts text files to graphic files. We often use Pictor as a file conversion program. Load the pictures into Pictor and save them as PIC files.

PLAYD.EXE

PLAY/D is the memory resident MIDI player provided with *Multimedia Creations*. It is part of the MIDITools package available from FM Software. Its use is documented in Chapters 6 and 7. We recommend that you purchase MIDITools. (A coupon at the back of this book provides information on how to do this.) Purchasing MIDITools entitles you to tech support. Kevin Weiner from FM Software also provides additional GRASP interfacing information.

SHOWPIC.EXE

Use SHOWPIC.EXE to view the pictures and clippings in the current directory.

```
showpic file [file] ...
```

Parameters

file   File or files. Can use wildcards. Shows CLP (clippings), PCX, GIF, IMG,
         and Bsave formats.

Example

```
showpic *.clp
```

This will show a list of clippings in the current subdirectory. Because clippings are not stored with palettes, the colors will not be correct. Pressing (ENTER) advances to the next clipping. You may find that some files will hang the computer system when loaded by SHOWPIC.EXE. Again, this utility is provided as a service to our readers. Please do not ask for tech support if it does not work for you. Use the Shareware program VPIC.EXE in its place.

TXTCLP.EXE

TXTCLP.EXE is one of the utilities from the Artools package that comes bundled with the commercial version of GRASP. It converts text screens to graphic screens. Use CAP.COM to capture a text screen from your application. Remove CAP.COM before running TXTCLP.EXE. Running CAP.COM and the conversion utility at the same time might hang your computer system.

When you call the program without parameters, it puts an interactive menu on the screen. Supply the program with the name of the source file and the name of the destination file. You can optionally include a GRASP font file name. The default font is the default font for the new video mode. You tell GRASP in what video mode to create the destination file name. Press return. The text screen is converted to a graphic file.

TXTCLP.EXE will also run in batch mode at the command line:

```
txtclp /v:vmode imgname [imgname] ...
```

Parameters

vmode   The graphics video mode in which you want the destination files created.

imgname   The name of the source file or files.

Example:

```
txtclp /v:m test01.pic test02.pic test03.pic
```

The example converts a series of text screens to Video Mode M graphic screens.

WHATPIC.EXE

List file sizes, offsets, and video modes for pictures and clippings.

```
whatpic file [file] ...
```

Parameters

file   Use the wildcard to list files, or supply a specific file name with an extension.

Example:

```
whatpic *.pcx
```

Lists all the PCX format files in the directory, their size, and colors. This is a valuable utility for examining GRASP pictures and clippings.

UTILITIES IN THE UTILITY DIRECTORY

The UTILITY directory is a subdirectory off the main GRASP directory (\GRASP\UTILITY).

GDFF

GDFF (GRASP Differential File) creates differential animation (DFF) files. See Chapter 5, "Using GDFF to Create Animations," for a tutorial on the use of the utility. Use the program name without parameters for a quick review of its options.

FADE.TXT

To view all 26 GRASP fades, load and run FADE.TXT. To run the file from the DOS prompt, type:

```
cd \grasp\utility
\grasp\graspc fades
```

VOC2SND.EXE

This utility converts Sound Blaster VOC files to GRASP SND file format. SND sound files are used by the digital sound playback facilities of GRASP (SOUNDPC.GRP). The script that loads and plays sound (SNDPLAY.TXT) expects to find files in the SND format. Only short files that fit into available memory can be converted by the utility. If you have Windows WAV sound files, convert them first into VOC format. You can adjust the sampling rate of the sound file with NEWRATE.EXE.

VOC2SND.EXE will only successfully convert VOC files that are composed of a single data block. SoundBlaster's recording programs create a series of 32K blocks when recording to disk. You must either record the sound entirely in memory and then save it or use a utility to convert the sound file into a single block.

NEWRATE.EXE

NEWRATE.EXE allows you to alter the sampling rate of the GRASP SND file. The best time to do this is before the file has been converted to GRASP's SND file format. Your VOC editing program provides much finer control over the sound file's characteristics. See Chapter 6, "Using Waveform Editing Software," for a discussion of sample rates.

Appendix D:
Pictor Keyboard Alternatives

The following keys can be used in place of choosing options with the mouse in GRASP's Pictor paint program.

(ESC)   Toggle between full screen and viewport (partial screen) mode.

(F1)	picture mover	(SHIFT)-(F1)	open rounded box
(F2)	edit box	(SHIFT)-(F2)	filled rounded box
(F3)	pencil	(SHIFT)-(F3)	open oval
(F4)	eraser	(SHIFT)-(F4)	filled oval
(F5)	paint brush	(SHIFT)-(F5)	open curve
(F6)	paint roller	(SHIFT)-(F6)	filled curve
(F7)	line	(SHIFT)-(F7)	open shape
(F8)	text	(SHIFT)-(F8)	filled shape
(F9)	open box	(SHIFT)-(F9)	open polygon
(F10)	filled box	(SHIFT)-(F10)	filled polygon

Capitalized items are menu options.

A	Change Colors		N	New
B	Control Box		O	outline
C	copy to clipboard		P	paste from clipboard
D	drop shadow		Q	quit
E	erase edit box		R	rotate
F	Fill Options		S	Save
G	grid on/off		T	transparent on/off
H	flip horizontal		U	undo
I	invert colors		V	flip vertical
J	seek edge		W	Tools menu
K	cut to clipboard		X	Fonts menu
L	Load		Y	clear clipboard
M	make pattern		Z	zoom (magnify x4)

(CONTROL)-(F) keys work in VGA modes only.

(ALT)-(F1)	same as (F1)	(CONTROL)-(F1)	less red
(ALT)-(F2)	select viewport	(CONTROL)-(F2)	more red
(ALT)-(F3)	magnify	(CONTROL)-(F3)	less green
(ALT)-(F4)	clear viewport	(CONTROL)-(F4)	more green
(ALT)-(F5)	Set Brush	(CONTROL)-(F5)	less blue
(ALT)-(F6)	Fill Options	(CONTROL)-(F6)	more blue
(ALT)-(F7)	same as (F7)	(CONTROL)-(F7)	darker
(ALT)-(F8)	Font Options	(CONTROL)-(F8)	brighter
(ALT)-(F9)	make Edit Box even byte width	(CONTROL)-(F9)	less contrast
		(CONTROL)-(F10)	more contrast
(ALT)-(F10)	align Edit Box on byte boundaries	*	restore palette

Keyboard Mouse Equivalents

(INS)	left mouse button click
(DEL)	right mouse button click
(←)(↑)(→)(↓)	move mouse cursor
(HOME), (END), (PGUP), (PGDN)	move cursor diagonally
(1),(2),(3),(4),(5) ... (9),(10)	set cursor movement rate
(+)	start/end left button drag
(-)	start/end right button drag
(ENTER), (SPACE)	accept dialog box choices
(ESC)	cancel dialog box

Appendix E:

Printing a Form with GRASP

This appendix contains a simple entry form that runs as a GRASP script. The user enters information into an on-screen form. After the user fills in the blanks, the form is output to the printer attached to the computer system.

The program Don Magnusson has written is composed of a script and a data file. The script (ORDER.TXT) processes keyboard input from the user and outputs the user's information to the printer. The script employs the data file (ORDER.FRM) to format the information sent out the printer and to add additional information to the form.

The order form is loaded into a buffer in memory with the Load command. Here's what ORDER.FRM looks like:

```
                     Sample Order Form

                       Company Name
                         Address
                      City, ST  01234
Customer Name:    XXXXXXXXXXXXXXXXXXXXXXXXXXXXXXXXXXXXXXXXXX
Customer Phone:   YYYYYYYYYYYYYYYYYYYYY
                   Misc. other text goes here...
```

THE AUTHOR

Donald E. Magnusson, 2290 Pernoshal Crt., Dunwoody, GA. 30338, (404) 452-1578. Don is a true GRASP wizard who can usually be found on CompuServe's GRASP forum dispensing advice and giving a programmer's peek into the internal working of GRASP. Don is the author of the GRASP Multimedia user's manual and technical reference book.

413

The information the user enters is stored as two variables, VAR1 and VAR2. Don's replace_txt subroutine replaces the XXX's and YYY's with these two variables.

Here's ORDER.TXT, documented by Don.

```
video g

set quicktext on clearkey off      ; needed for text input routine

set space off esc ctrl-q           ; allow space char in text input

clearscr 1                         ;
color 15 1                         ; sample screen display
text 40,240 "Name    :"            ;
text 40,220 "Phone   :"            ;

global var1 "" var2 "" order ""    ; initialize global variables

get_string var1 40 120 240 15 4    ; get name (var1)

get_string var2 20 120 220 15 4    ; get phone (var2)

set clearkey on                    ; reset clearkey function

get_active_printer                 ; check for active printer
if !@0                             ; abort if no printer found
    text 80,140 "Cannot find active printer !!!"
    waitkey
    exit
endif

load order.frm                     ; load order form template
replace_text                       ; put entered text into template

text 120,140 "Sending form to printer on "$@printer

send @printer @@order              ; print it

exit

; ------------------------- end of program -------------------------


; ------------------------------------------------------------------ ;
;                                                                     ;
;   get_string @1 @2 @3 @4 @5 @6                                      ;
;                                                                     ;
;   Allows simple string input.  Simulates a flashing cursor in       ;
;   graphics modes.  Must use an 8 pixel wide font (the ROM font       ;
;   will do) in QUICKTEXT mode.  Subroutine will return to caller      ;
;   if ENTER or ESC keys are pressed.                                  ;
;                                                                     ;
;   @1 = name of variable containing string to be edited              ;
;   @2 = max length of field to be edited                             ;
;   @3 = starting x-coordinate                                        ;
;   @4 = starting y-coordinate                                        ;
;   @5 = foreground color                                             ;
;   @6 = background color                                             ;
; ------------------------------------------------------------------ ;
```

```
get_string:

dummy_lp:
    getkey dummy                              ; throw away keystrokes
    if len(@dummy) dummy_lp                   ; in keyboard buffer

    local edit_str @@1                        ; make copy of current string
    color @5 @6                               ; set text color
    text @3,@4 string(@2+1," ")               ; print spaces for max length +1
    text @3,@4 @edit_str                      ; print current string

getk:
    text "_"                                  ; show cursor
    offset -8 0 r                             ; reset text location
    waitkey 15                                ; wait 15/100ths
    getkey k name                             ; get keypress
    if asc(@k)==0                             ; if no keypress
        text " "                              ; hide cursor
        offset -8 0 r                         ; reset text location
        waitkey 15                            ; wait 15/100ths
        getkey k name                         ; get keypress
        if asc(@k)==0 getk                    ; if no keypress, loop
    endif

    text " "                                  ; hide cursor
    offset -8 0 r                             ; reset text location
    if @k==space                              ; convert "space" string
        set k chr(32)                         ; to space char
    endif
    if len(@k)==1                             ; if not extended keystroke
        if asc(@k)>31                         ; if not a special char
            if len(@edit_str)<@2              ; if string is not yet max length
                text @k                       ; show key pressed
                local edit_str @edit_str$@k   ; append to string
            endif
        endif
    else
    if @k==backsp&&@edit_str<>""              ; if backspace was pressed and
        offset -8 0 r                         ; at least one char has been entered
        text " "                              ; back up over last char and erase it
        offset -8 0 r                         ; reset text location
        local edit_str left(@edit_str,len(@edit_str)-1)
    else
    if @k==return||@k==esc
        offset 0 0                            ; reset offset to 0,0
        if @k==return                         ; if RETURN was pressed
            global @1 @edit_str               ; set passed variable name to string
        endif
        return                                ; return to caller
    endif
    endif
    endif
    goto getk                                 ; go back and get another keypress

; ----------------------- end of get_string -----------------------
```

415

```
; ----------------------------------------------------------------    ;
;   get_active_printer      (no parms)                                 ;
;                                                                      ;
;   Checks for an active printer on parallel ports.                    ;
;   Returns 0 (FALSE) if no printer is available.                      ;
;   Else returns non-zero (TRUE) and sets the global variable          ;
;   @printer equal to "LPTx" where x = 1, 2, or 3                      ;
; ----------------------------------------------------------------;
get_active_printer:
    global printer " "
    mark 1 3
        chk_printer @loop
        if @0
            global printer "LPT"$@loop
            break got_it
        endif
    loop
got_it:
    return !(@printer==" ")

chk_printer:
    int 0x17 0x0200,,,@1-1,,,,
    return ((@ax&0x9000)==0x9000)

; ------------------- end of get_active_printer -------------------


; ----------------------------------------------------------------    ;
;   replace_text    (no parms)                                         ;
;                                                                      ;
;   Replaces strings in loaded text file with var1 and var2.           ;
;   Subroutine allows creation (and destruction) of local vars.        ;
; ----------------------------------------------------------------    ;
replace_text:
    local pointer instr(@@order,"XXXXX",0)
    local rep_text @var1$string(40-len(@var1)," ")
    movemem adr(@rep_text) @order+(@pointer-1) 40
    local pointer instr(@@order,"YYYYY",@pointer)
    local rep_text @var2$string(20-len(@var2)," ")
    movemem adr(@rep_text) @order+(@pointer-1) 20
    return

; ---------------------- end of replace_text ----------------------
```

The two program files can be found in the UTILITY subdirectory.

Appendix F:

GRASP Error Messages

GRASP displays its error messages at the top of the screen. It uses the first color in the palette slot for text display, and the last color in the palette slot for background. If you cannot see the error message, modify the palette slot colors in GRASP with the Mode (CGA), Chgcolor (EGA), or Setrgb (VGA) color commands.

When GRASP displays an error message, it pauses. When you press (ENTER) to continue, GRASP takes you to the exact spot where the command caused the problem. If the problem occurred in a merged text file, the cursor may appear at the end of the current script, not at the faulty command in the merged script.

GRASP's debug command:

```
set debug on
```

allows you step through the script one command at a time. Enter "set debug on" at the beginning of the script. When you run the program, pause the script by pressing the space bar. Then step through the program one line at a time using the space bar. Every line executed, including those belonging to a called or merged script is displayed on the screen. This is a good way to track down an errant command.

ERROR LISTING

Command not available in this video mode

The command is mode-sensitive. It cannot be used in the current mode. See the summary of the command in Chapter 10.

Duplicate label

The same name is used more than once as a GRASP label. All labels must have unique names.

Error in loop count

The loop value in the Mark/Loop structure must be greater than 0.

Error in name

The file name contains invalid characters, or the file doesn't exist in the current directory or library file. Dashes are not allowed in file names unless they are given in quotation marks.

Error in packed clipping

The file does not exist or is corrupt, or there is a disk problem. Check the clipping with WHATPIC. It will probably have to be replaced.

Error in X coordinate

The horizontal value used is outside the range for this video mode. Check to see if an Offset command has placed your coordinate out of range. Negative numbers will also generate this error.

Error in Y coordinate

Similar to "Error in X coordinate," above, but in a command specifying a vertical coordinate.

Error loading DFF *or* Error loading font *or* Error loading picture *or* Error loading text

There was an error loading the file with the designated extension. The file may be corrupt.

Illegal argument(s)

An invalid character or value has been given for one or more command parameter. Check command syntax and variable values. The (F2) key in the editor provides quick reviews of command syntax, or check the command summary in Chapter 10.

Illegal buffer

The buffer number was out of range. Buffer number can be 1 to 128.

Illegal character at line x

Check that the program is not a formatted document. Also check for unbalanced quotation marks anywhere in the program. Once it encounters a quotation mark, GRASP treats everything up to the next quotation mark as text.

Illegal color

The value given for the color exceeds the range for the current video mode.

Illegal fade

The value given for a fade is out of the range of 0 to 25.

Illegal palette

The value given for a CGA palette is out of the range of 0 to 5.

Illegal speed

The value given for a fade speed is out of the range of 0 to 10,000 (100 seconds).

Invalid font style

The value given for an Fstyle command is out of the range of 0 to 8.

Invalid gap value

The value given for font gaps is out of the range of 0 to 255.

Label not found

A command tried to jump to a nonexistent label. Check for colons after labels and check for spelling.

Loop without Mark

A Loop command has been encountered, but no matching Mark command has set up a loop. Check for balanced Mark/Loop commands.

Mark/Loops nested too deep

Check that the maximum of 16 levels of Mark/Loop nesting has not been exceeded. Note also that the use of Goto to exit a loop will fail to pop a loop off the program stack. Use the Break command to exit a loop.

Memory error

The file is too large to load. Check to make sure all fonts, pictures, clippings, and DFFs are unloaded. (Use Ffree, Pfree, Cfree, and Dfree respectively.) Make sure there are no TSRs (terminate and stay resident programs) loaded. Make sure enough conventional memory is free for GRASP's use. (Use DOS's CHKDSK utility to check free memory.) Make sure you have not used (ALT)-(F1) to shell out to DOS and then failed to use the DOS Exit command to exit from the shell and return to the editor. That is, you may have started up a second copy of GRASP in memory. (Try quitting GRASP and typing "exit" at the DOS prompt.) Load clippings with noshift "on." See the command summary for Cload for further information on this.

No data setup before use of @

Before the data variable @ can be used, a data structure must be defined with the Data, Databegin (label), or Databegin/Dataend commands. Check the command summaries.

Not enough arguments

One or more of a command's required parameters is not given. Check the command summaries. Only parameters in square brackets are optional. You can skip parameters with commas. See the Opengl command in Chapter 10 for an example of this usage.

Return without a Gosub

A return command has generated the error message. The current code has not been called as a subroutine. You may have omitted an Exit command in the main script causing GRASP to fall through to a subroutine.

Too many loops

Mark/Loop pairs have exceeded the maximum of 16 levels deep. Or too many calls to subroutines with loops. Or subroutines are being called by subroutines without returning to the original calling script.

Too many marks

Mark/Loop pairs can be nested to a maximum of 16 levels. This includes calls to subroutines with loops.

Undefined variable

A variable has not been created with the Set, Local, or Global commands. Or the program has returned to a higher level and the local variable definition has been destroyed. See the command summaries for local and global variables.

Unknown command

A line doesn't make sense as a command. Check for misspellings, labels without colons, and data that wasn't preceded by a Databegin command or a label.

Index

Books have a substantial influence on the destruction of the forests of the Earth. For example, it takes 17 trees to produce one ton of paper. A first printing of 30,000 copies of a typical 480 page book consumes 108,000 pounds of paper which will require 918 trees!

Waite Group Press™ is against the clear-cutting of forests and supports reforestation of the Pacific Northwest of the United States and Canada, where most of this paper comes from. As a publisher with several hundred thousand books sold each year, we feel an obligation to give back to the planet. We will therefore support and contribute a percentage of our proceeds to organizations which seek to preserve the forests of planet Earth.

FRACTAL CREATIONS

Explore the Magic of Fractals on Your PC

by Timothy Wegner and Mark Peterson

Over 40,000 computer enthusiasts who've purchased this book/software package are creating and exploring the fascinating world of fractals on their computers. **Fractal Creations** includes a full color fractal art poster, 3-D glasses, and *Fractint*, the revolutionary software that makes fractals accessible to anyone with a PC. *Fractint* lets you zoom in on any part of a fractal image, rotate it, do color-cycle animation, and even choose accompanying sound effects and a 3-D mode. PC Magazine said "**Fractal Creations**...is a magical ride...guaranteed to blow your eyes out." Winner of the 1991 Computer Press Association Award for "Best Non-Fiction Computer Book." For MS/PC DOS machines; best with a VGA video board and a 286/386 processor.

ISBN 1-878739-05-0, 315 pp., 1 5.25" disk, color poster, 3-D glasses, $34.95 US/$44.95 Can., Available now

VIRTUAL REALITY PLAYHOUSE

by Nick Lavroff

Jack-in to the world of Virtual Reality with this playful new book and disk package. Virtual Reality is a new interactive technology which creates the convincing illusion that you are completely immersed in worlds existing only inside your computer. **Virtual Reality Playhouse** lets you enter those worlds and even create your own personal digital dimension. Expand the parameters of your mind as you move rapidly from an introduction of virtual reality's basic concepts to visual explorations illustrating real-life applications. Demo programs include a 3-D simulation that puts you inside a robot which travels through a computer-generated city. Or, you can play a game in a 3-D room that can be tilted, spun, and twisted in near impossible ways. Put on the enclosed 3-D glasses and jump right into any one of 8 startling VR simulations. There are even plans for building your own LCD shuttering VR glasses and power glove to manipulate objects in a VR world. For MS/PC DOS machines.

ISBN 1-878739-19 -0, 146 pp., 1 3.5" disk, 3-D glasses, $22.95 US/$29.95 Can., Available now

RAY TRACING CREATIONS

Create 3-D Photorealistic Images on the PC

by Drew Wells

With the **Ray Tracing Creations** book/disk combination, you can immediately begin rendering perfect graphic objects like the ones in computer movies. Using the bundled powerful shareware *POV-Ray* program, you'll learn to control the location, shape, light, shading, and surface texture of all kinds of 3-D objects. *POV-Ray*'s C-like language is used to describe simple objects, planes, spheres, and more complex polygons. Over 100 incredible pre-built scenes are included that can be generated, studied, and modified any way you choose. This book provides a complete course in the fundamentals of ray tracing that will challenge and entice you. Contains 386 and 286 versions of *POV-Ray;* VGA display required. For MS/PC DOS machines.

ISBN 1-878739-27-1, 400 pp., 1 HD 3.5" disk, 3-D glasses, $39.95 US/$49.95 Can., Available January 1993

Send for our unique catalog to get more information about these books, as well as our outstanding and award-winning programming titles, including:

Master C: Let the PC Teach You C and **Master C++:** Let the PC Teach You Object-Oriented Programming. Both are book/disk software packages that turn your computer into an infinitely patient C and C++ professor.

Workout C: Hundreds of C projects and exercises and a full-featured C compiler make this an unbeatable training program and value.

C++ Primer Plus: Written by Stephen Prata in the same style as his C Primer Plus, which won the Computer Press Association's coveted "Best How-To Computer Book" award and sold over 400,000 copies.

Object Oriented Programming in Turbo C++: Robert Lafore, master teacher of the programming art, takes the prospective C++ programmer from the basics to the most complex concepts, and

provides anyone with C++ programming experience a comprehensive reference.

Windows API Bible: The only comprehensive guide to the 800 instructions and messages in the Windows Application Programming Interface.

Visual Basic How-To and **Visual Basic Super Bible.** Both books cover the unique Microsoft language that makes Windows programming much more accessible. **How-To** provides solutions to VB programming questions. **Super Bible** is the ultimate compendium of reference information on VB.

Turbo Pascal How-To: Everything you need to know to begin writing professional Turbo Pascal programs.

IMAGE LAB
Explore, Manipulate, and Create Images on Your PC
by Tim Wegner

Image Lab is a complete IBM PC-based "digital darkroom" in a unique book disk package that covers virtually all areas of graphic processing and manipulation, and comes with the finest graphics shareware available today: *PICLAB, CSHOW, IMPROCES, Image Alchemy,* and others. The software included in Image Lab lets you size images, remove colors, adjust palettes, combine, crop, transform, ray trace, convert from one graphics file format to another, and render your images. Graphics expert Tim Wegner shows how to make 3-D fractals and combine them to make photorealistic scenes. The powerful POV-Ray program and clever examples are worth the price of the book alone. Full color stereo glasses are available along with detailed directions for making your own stereoscopic full color images. Best on MS/PC DOS 386 machines with a VGA video board.

ISBN 1-878739-11-5, 350 pp, 1 HD 3.5" disk, color poster, $39.95 US/$49.95 Can., Available now

FRACTALS FOR WINDOWS
The Magic of Fractals Becomes Even More Accessible
by Tim Wegner and Bert Tyler

This is a perfect companion to **Fractal Creations**, but it probes deeper. It is bundled with *WINFRACT*, a powerful Windows program which enables you to play with over 80 fractals, or create totally new fractals, controlling your experiments simply with a zoom box, buttons, dialog boxes, menus, and a mouse. And because *WINFRACT*'s core technology is the latest version 18 of *FRACTINT* for DOS, it's faster than lightning at computing fractals. Plus you can generate fractals in the background! If you don't have any programming experience, that's ok. We've designed this package so you can still climb on board. But if you are a programmer, you'll love this rich resource of spectacular images you can use with other Windows programs.

ISBN 1-878739-25-5, 350 pp, 1 HD 3.5" disk, color poster, 3-D glasses,
$34.95 US/$44.95 Can., Available December 1992

WAITE GROUP PRESS™

Save 30% in this special offer for readers of Multimedia Creations....

You have seen how the Play/D demo driver accompanying Multimedia Creations lets you easily add MIDI music to your GRASP programs. Now you can obtain the complete MidiTools package including Play/D and much more! MidiTools has something for every MIDI user—from amateur to professional. If you are a programmer, it lets you add MIDI support to programs written in virtually any language, with ready-made libraries for C, Pascal, Basic, and GRASP. But programming is just a small part of what MidiTools offers. There are 20 MIDI utility programs of all kinds that you will find indispensable while working with music in multimedia applications. Some of these programs include: a sophisticated MIDI song file player with numerous options for setting up playback, a memory-resident player with pop-up display for background music, a MIDI data stream analyzer and patch bay utility, powerful filtering utilities for quickly adding or removing MIDI file information, a pair of programs for converting MIDI files to text and back again, plus many more unique programs! MidiTools will run on any MS-DOS 3.0 or greater system, and supports all popular MIDI interfaces. Although MidiTools programs are DOS-based, they can be used in conjunction with Microsoft Windows, and will even help you run other DOS MIDI programs under Multimedia Extensions.

If you already use one of the many fine MIDI sequencing or scoring programs available today, you will still find many features in MidiTools which complement and extend what you already have. So take advantage of this special no-risk offer and get a head start in multimedia with these powerful music tools.

Yes! Please send my copy of MidiTools right away.

I understand that I need send no money now, and that I will be billed with shipment. I will have 15 days to evaluate MidiTools, and if I am not satisfied, I may return the package and owe nothing; otherwise, I will pay the special low price of $59.50 (plus shipping, handling, and applicable sales tax).

❏ Please bill me (Domestic orders only)

❏ Payment enclosed $ _____ (All foreign orders must include full payment in US dollars only, plus $7.00 shipping and handling. Shipping is free for prepaid domestic orders. PA residents add 6% state sales tax.)

Disk size: ❏ 3.5" ❏ 5.25"

Return this order form to:
FM Software
P.O. Box 5098
Bethlehem, PA 18015

Name _____

Address _____

City _____ State ____ Zip code _____

Country _____

This is a legal agreement between you, the end user and purchaser, and The Waite Group®, Inc., and the authors of the programs contained in the disk. By opening the sealed disk package, you are agreeing to be bound by the terms of this Agreement. If you do not agree with the terms of this Agreement, promptly return the unopened disk package and the accompanying items (including the related book and other written material) to the place you obtained them for a refund.

SOFTWARE LICENSE

1. The Waite Group, Inc. grants you the right to use one copy of the enclosed software programs (the programs) on a single computer system (whether a single CPU, part of a licensed network, or a terminal connected to a single CPU). Each concurrent user of the program must have exclusive use of the related Waite Group, Inc. written materials.

2. Each of the programs, including the copyrights in each program, is owned by the respective author and the copyright in the entire work is owned by The Waite Group, Inc. and they are therefore protected under the copyright laws of the United States and other nations, under international treaties. You may make only one copy of the disk containing the programs exclusively for backup or archival purposes, or you may transfer the programs to one hard disk drive, using the original for backup or archival purposes. You may make no other copies of the programs, and you may make no copies of all or any part of the related Waite Group, Inc. written materials.

3. You may not rent or lease the programs, but you may transfer ownership of the programs and related written materials (including any and all updates and earlier versions) if you keep no copies of either, and if you make sure the transferee agrees to the terms of this license.

4. You may not decompile, reverse engineer, disassemble, copy, create a derivative work, or otherwise use the programs except as stated in this Agreement.

GOVERNING LAW

This Agreement is governed by the laws of the State of California.

LIMITED WARRANTY

The following warranties shall be effective for 90 days from the date of purchase: (i) The Waite Group, Inc. warrants the enclosed disk to be free of defects in materials and workmanship under normal use; and (ii) The Waite Group, Inc. warrants that the programs, unless modified by the purchaser, will substantially perform the functions described in the documentation provided by The Waite Group, Inc. when operated on the designated hardware and operating system. The Waite Group, Inc. does not warrant that the programs will meet purchaser's requirements or that operation of a program will be uninterrupted or error-free. The program warranty does not cover any program that has been altered or changed in any way by anyone other than The Waite Group, Inc. The Waite Group, Inc. is not responsible for problems caused by changes in the operating characteristics of computer hardware or computer operating systems that are made after the release of the programs, nor for problems in the interaction of the programs with each other or other software.

THESE WARRANTIES ARE EXCLUSIVE AND IN LIEU OF ALL OTHER WARRANTIES OF MERCHANTABILITY OR FITNESS FOR A PARTICULAR PURPOSE OR OF ANY OTHER WARRANTY, WHETHER EXPRESS OR IMPLIED.

EXCLUSIVE REMEDY

The Waite Group, Inc. will replace any defective disk without charge if the defective disk is returned to The Waite Group, Inc. within 90 days from date of purchase.

This is Purchaser's sole and exclusive remedy for any breach of warranty or claim for contract, tort, or damages.

LIMITATION OF LIABILITY

THE WAITE GROUP, INC. AND THE AUTHORS OF THE PROGRAMS SHALL NOT IN ANY CASE BE LIABLE FOR SPECIAL, INCIDENTAL, CONSEQUENTIAL, INDIRECT, OR OTHER SIMILAR DAMAGES ARISING FROM ANY BREACH OF THESE WARRANTIES EVEN IF THE WAITE GROUP, INC. OR ITS AGENT HAS BEEN ADVISED OF THE POSSIBILITY OF SUCH DAMAGES.

THE LIABILITY FOR DAMAGES OF THE WAITE GROUP, INC. AND THE AUTHORS OF THE PROGRAMS UNDER THIS AGREEMENT SHALL IN NO EVENT EXCEED THE PURCHASE PRICE PAID.

COMPLETE AGREEMENT

This Agreement constitutes the complete agreement between The Waite Group, Inc. and the authors of the programs, and you, the purchaser.

Some states do not allow the exclusion or limitation of implied warranties or liability for incidental or consequential damages, so the above exclusions or limitations may not apply to you. This limited warranty gives you specific legal rights; you may have others, which vary from state to state.

GRASP Multimedia Order Form

I want to be a multimedia wizard. Since I've bought Multimedia Creations, please send me GRASP MULTIMEDIA for only $249.00 plus shipping and handling. That's a savings of $300.00, nearly 55% off the retail price! I am enclosing my check or Visa/Master card number.

To order by phone, call 800-944-0191 or 503-488-2322
or return this form to Paul Mace Software, Inc.

Name

Company

Address
Street Address Only, No P.O. Box

City   State   ZIP   —

Telephone

Quantity and Type

Name	Quantity	Price	
GRASP MULTIMEDIA	☐	x $249.00 =	

Shipping — Add $8 USA, $12 Canada , or $30 Foreign for shipping and handling. Standard shipping is UPS Ground. Allow 2 to 3 weeks for delivery. Purchase orders are subject to credit approval.

Shipping

Total Due

Disk size, required: (Please check one) ☐ 5.25-inch   ☐ 3.5-inch

---

Method of Payment

Checks or money orders, payable to Paul Mace Software Inc. To pay by credit card, complete the following:

☐ Visa   ☐ Mastercard   Card Number

Cardholder's Name _____ Exp. Date

Cardholder's Signature _____

Phone Number _____

Please fill out this card if you wish to know of future updates to *Multimedia Creations*, or to receive our catalog.

Company Name: _____

Division _____ Mail Stop: _____

Last Name: _____ First Name: _____ Middle Initial: _____

Street Address: _____

City: _____ State: _____ Zip: _____

Daytime telephone: (_____) _____

Date product was acquired: Month _____ Day _____ Year _____ Your Occupation: _____

Overall, how would you rate *Multimedia Creations*?

☐ Excellent ☐ Very Good ☐ Good
☐ Fair ☐ Below Average ☐ Poor

What did you like MOST about this product? _____

_____

What did you like LEAST about this product? _____

_____

Please describe any problems you may have encountered with installing or using the software: _____

_____

How do you use this book (tutorial, reference, problem-solver…)?

_____

How did you find the pace of this book? _____

What is the primary use for your computer?

_____

What is your level of computer expertise?

☐ New ☐ Dabbler ☐ Hacker
☐ Power User ☐ Programmer ☐ Experienced professional

Is there any program or subject you would like to see The Waite Group cover in a similar approach?

_____

Please describe your computer hardware:

Computer _____ Hard disk _____
5.25" disk drives _____ 3.5" disk drives _____
Video card _____ Monitor _____
Printer _____ Peripherals _____

Where did you buy this book?
☐ Bookstore (name: _____)
☐ Discount store (name: _____)
☐ Computer store (name: _____)
☐ Catalog (name: _____)
☐ Direct from WGP   ☐ Other _____

What price did you pay for this book? _____

What influenced your purchase of this book?
☐ Recommendation ☐ Advertisement
☐ Magazine review ☐ Store display
☐ Mailing ☐ Book's format
☐ Reputation of The Waite Group ☐ Topic

How many computer books do you buy each year? _____

How many other Waite Group books do you own? _____

What is your favorite Waite Group book?

_____

Additional comments? _____

_____

_____

_____

☐ Check here for a free Waite Group Press™ catalog

Send to Waite Group Press™, 200 Tamal Plaza, Corte Madera, CA 94925   *Multimedia Creations*

BUSINESS REPLY MAIL

FIRST CLASS MAIL   PERMIT NO. 9   CORTE MADERA, CA

POSTAGE WILL BE PAID BY ADDRESSEE

Waite Group Press, Inc.

Attention: *Multimedia Creations*

200 Tamal Plaza, Suite 101

Corte Madera, CA 94925

FOLD HERE